D1798764

CAREERS OF UNIVERSITY GRADUATES

VIEWS AND EXPERIENCES IN COMPARATIVE PERSPECTIVES

HIGHER EDUCATION DYNAMICS

VOLUME 17

SCOPE OF THE SERIES

Higher Education Dynamics is a bookseries intending to study adaptation processes and their outcomes in higher education at all relevant levels. In addition it wants to examine the way interactions between these levels affect adaptation processes.It aims at applying general social science concepts and theories as well as testing theories in the field of higher education research. It wants to do so in a manner that is of relevance to all those professionally involved in higher education, be it as ministers, policy-makers, politicians, institutional leaders or administrators, higher education researchers, members of the academic staff of universities and colleges, or students. It will include both mature and developing systems of higher education, covering public as well as private institutions.

The titles published in the series are listed at the end of this volume.

Careers of University Graduates

Views and Experiences in Comparative Perspectives

Edited by

Ulrich Teichler

International Centre for Higher Education Research Kassel, Germany

A C.I.P. Catalogue record for this book is available from the Library of Congress.

ISBN-13 978-1-4020-5925-4 (HB)
ISBN-13 978-1-4020-5926-1 (e-book)

Published by Springer,
P.O.Box 17, 3300 AA Dordrecht, The Netherlands.

www.springer.com

Printed on acid-free paper

TABLE OF CONTENTS

ULRICH TEICHLER

GRADUATE EMPLOYMENT AND WORK: VARIOUS ISSUES IN A COMPARATIVE PERSPECTIVE

1. THE CONCEPTUAL FRAMEWORK

When researchers from various countries decided in the late 1990s to jointly prepare a research design for a major comparative study on employment and work of higher education graduates, the findings of which are presented in this volume, and when they analysed previous public debates and research in this domain (see the summaries undertaken in the framework of this project presented in Figure 1), they saw this as an opportunity to reach out beyond the concepts and findings of previous research in two respects:

– They did not consider a large team of researchers from different countries and disciplines as a danger for a coherent research approach with a strong conceptual and methodological top-down project management, but rather as an opportunity *to integrate a variety of concepts, themes and major issues* into a single research design.
– Unlike many studies that addressed a large number of countries and tended to focus on common issues in such a way that the specific conditions of the individual countries came into play only superficially, this research project was seen as an excellent opportunity to examine if views on the relationships between higher education and the world of work *in economically advanced societies* could really be based on a *common ground or*, on the contrary, if *specific characteristics* of national higher education systems, various views of the role of higher education in preparing for work, culturally shaped notions of professions, as well as the specific economic and social conditions of graduate employment and work in the individual countries prevailed.

The relationships between higher education and the world of work have been among the key public debates on higher education over the last four decades. These debates tended to put emphasis on selected issues when this thematic area was high on the agenda. Hence the main issues changed quickly over time. For example, the contribution of higher education expansion to economic growth, the dangers of "over-education" and a "mismatch" between demand and supply, the diversity of higher education and employment opportunities, the rise in graduate unemployment and precarious employment, the growing role of "key qualifications", and the trend towards a globalisation of the graduate labour markets belong to these sequences of changing priorities. But researchers note that the relevance of certain issues does not fade away when they are no longer in the limelight. Rather, both the changing public debates and the growing research activities make us increasingly aware of the complexity of the relationships between higher education and the world of work.

U. Teichler (ed.), Careers of University Graduates, 1–14

Therefore, a project can be viewed as a worthwhile undertaking which leaves the safe harbour of established disciplinary paradigms and research approaches or the framework of debates representing the *Zeitgeist*, i.e. the dominant concerns during a certain period of time. Admittedly, even a research project that aims to take up many aspects that have been addressed in the public debate and in research on higher education and the world of work in recent decades will have to make conceptual choices, and the conceptual and thematic range is bound to be influenced by limits of resources and the major research methods that have been chosen.

Figure 1. Summaries of the Debates and Research on Higher Education and Graduate Employment and Work

Paul, J.-J., Teichler, U. and van der Velden, R. (eds) (2000). "Higher Education and Graduate Employment" (special issue). *European Journal of Education*, 35(2).

Schomburg, H. and Teichler, U. (2006). "Developments, Prior Research and the Concepts of this Study Higher Education and Graduate Employment in Europe." In: Schomburg, H. and Teichler, U. (2006) *Higher Education and Graduate Employment in Europe. Results of Graduate Surveys from 12 Countries*. Dordrecht: Kluwer, pp. 11-28.

Teichler, U. (1999). "Research on the Relationships between Higher Education and the World of Work: Past Achievements, Problems and New Challenges." *Higher Education*, 38(2). 169-90.

Teichler, U. (1999). "Higher Education Policy and the World of Work: Changing Conditions and Challenges." *Higher Education Policy*, 12(4). 285-312.

International comparison was a key perspective in the public debates as well as in research on the relationships between higher education and the world of work in the last few decades. On the one hand, a widespread belief was influential in this debate that the contribution of knowledge to economic growth, the *homo oeconomicus*, the logic of an achievement society, higher education expansion and diversification, the growing importance of key qualifications are basically common phenomena of all modern societies. Countries are often viewed as cooperating or being in competition in the search for the most advanced solution. On the other hand, we are aware of substantial differences between countries concerning established characteristics of higher education, the labour market and the social fabrics and we note that these differences are often so stable that we tend to perceive a persistence of national and cultural characteristics. Moreover, debates about the most desirable option of the future state of higher education, the labour market and the social fabric rarely lead to a consensus about the future optimum, but are characterised by a diversity of political choices. Debates are continuously shaped by a mix of universalistic, idiosyncratic and political assumptions. Admittedly, even this project, which includes 12 countries, does not cover the full range of economically advanced countries. It gave priority to 10 countries of Western Europe, on the practical ground that the core funding for the project was made available by the European Commission. But the willingness and the successful fundraising of researchers from other countries led to the inclusion of the Czech Republic as one of the Central and Eastern European countries in the process of economic and social transition and of Japan as the economically advanced country that was most suitable to challenge our conventional wisdom as far as common characteristics of economically advanced societies are concerned. Thus, the 12 countries could be viewed as a good testing ground for the role played by common features and national characteristics.

2. THE DESIGN OF THE CHEERS STUDY

This volume is based on the findings of a comparative study jointly undertaken by researchers from 13 universities and research institutes in 11 European countries and Japan (see the overview in Figure 2). The CHEERS Project (Careers after Higher Education – a European Research Study) was launched by the author of this chapter in the late 1990s. The European Union funded the project in the framework of its Targeted Socio-Economic Research Programme (TSER) for nine participating countries (Austria, Finland, France, Germany Italy, the Netherlands, Norway, Spain and the United Kingdom), and national foundations and state agencies provided additional funds for the inclusion of the Czech Republic, Sweden and Japan.

In 1999 and early 2000, a highly standardised questionnaire was sent to some 100,000 persons who had graduated about four years earlier from bachelor, master or similar programmes. The 16-page questionnaire with about 80 questions and about 600 variables addressed the socio-biographic background, schooling and the course of study up to graduation, the transition to employment and career start, the current employment situation, the work assignment and the substantive links between study and work, the competences and job requirements, the study orientations and job satisfaction as well as regional and international mobility. In addition, interviews were undertaken with employers' representatives and some graduates.

The return rate of the questionnaires was about 40 per cent. In the end, the comparative analysis was based on the responses of about 36,000 graduates. The surveys were carried out by the researchers of the respective countries, and data processing was undertaken in a decentralised way, while the overall coordination and analysis were ensured by Harald Schomburg (International Centre for Higher Education Research Kassel).

An overview of the findings was presented in Schomburg and Teichler 2006 (see Figure 1). Figure 3 presents a list of major publications among the more than 200 monographs and articles published up to 2004 on the CHEERS Project. This volume presents in-depth analyses of the major themes addressed in the Project written by key members of this project.

Figure 2. The Design of the CHEERS Study at a Glance

Data base	A representative survey of about 40,000 graduates in 11 European countries and Japan:
	☐ Higher education graduates of the academic year 1995
	☐ Conducted about three to four years after graduation
	☐ Field phase 1999-2000
	☐ At least 3-year-study programmes
	☐ Only first degree (e.g. Bachelor, Diplom, Laurea)
	☐ About 3,000-3,500 graduates in each country
	☐ Common research instrument: master questionnaire in English
	    ■ Highly standardised
	    ■ Few open questions
	    ■ National adaptations of some questions (e.g. regarding the educational system)
	    ■ Use of national and international classification (ISCED97, NACE, ISCO88(COM), NUTS
	☐ Broad scope of questions
	    ■ 16 pages
	    ■ 80 questions
	    ■ 600 variables
	☐ Mailed questionnaire
	    ■ Three mailings (questionnaire-reminder-reminder+questionnaire)
	Interview surveys with graduates and employers (about 400 interviews)

Coordinators	Ulrich Teichler and Harald Schomburg, Centre for Research on Higher Education and Work, University Kassel, Germany
Partners	13 research institutions in 12 countries
Countries	Austria, Czech Republic, Finland, France, Germany, Italy, Japan, Netherlands, Norway, Sweden, Spain, United Kingdom
Funds	Predominantly funded by the European Commission (Targeted Socio-Economic Research Programme – TSER), national funding in the Czech Republic, Japan and Sweden
Website	http://www.uni-kassel.de/cheers.htm

Figure 3. Major Publications on the CHEERS Project

Aguilera, J. et al. (eds) (2003). *Educación superior y empleo: la situación de los jóvenes titulados en Europa. La encuesta CHEERS.* Granada: Universidad de Granada 2003.

Aracil, A. G. (2003). *Labour Market Analysis for European Higher Education Graduates.* Ph.D. thesis, Departament d'Anàlisi Económica, Universitat de València, Valencia, Spain.

Brennan, J. et al. (2001). *The Employment of UK Graduates: Comparisons with Europe and Japan.* London: Open University (HEFCE Report 01/38).

Guggenberger, H., Kellermann P., and Sagmeister, G. (2001). *Wissenschaftliches Studium und akademische Beschäftigung. Vier Jahre nach Studienabschluss – Ein Überblick.* Forschungsbericht. Klagenfurt.

Javier, V. G. (ed) (2003). *Métodos de análisis de la inserción laboral de los universitarios.* Consejo de Coordinación Universitaria (Madrid); Universidad Leon, Secretariado de Publicaciones y Medios Audiavisuales, Leon.

Kôtôkyôiku to shokugyô ni kansuru kokusai hikaku chôsa – yôroppa-gawa hôkoku (ooshûiinkai heno hôkoku) kara no bassui (International Comparative Study on Higher Education and Employment: Excerpts from the Report by the European Side to the European Commission). Tokyo: Nihon Rôdô Kenkyû kikô 2003 (Shriô shirizu, no. 135).

Mohr, J. et al. (2000). "Studieren zum Erfolg. Die Berufschancen der Studenten." *DER SPIEGEL*, 46 (http://www.spiegel.de/spiegel/ 0,1518,102098,00.html).

Mora, José-Gines (ed) (2007) "The Labour Market of European Higher Education Graduates: Some Analytical Approaches" (special issue). *European Journal of Education* 42(1).

Murdoch, J. (2002). The Effect of the Reputation and the Teaching Quality of Higher Education Departments on Graduate Employment – A Comparison across 7 European Countries and Japan. Ph.D. thesis, IREDU, Université de Bourgogne, Dijon, France.

Sáenz de Miera, A. (ed) (2002). *En torno al trabajo universitario. Reflexiones y datos.* Madrid (Ministerio de Educación, Cultura y Deporte; Cuadernos del Consejo de Universidades).

Schomburg, H. et al. (eds) (2001). *Erfolgreich von der Uni in den Job.* Regensburg, Düsseldorf und Berlin: Fit for Business.

Yoshimoto, K., Inenaga, Y., and Nakajima, H. (eds) (2004). *Ôshu no kôtôkôiku to rôdôshijo* (Country Reports on Higher Education and Labor Market in Europe and Japan). Hiroshima: Research Institute for Higher Education, Hiroshima University (Reviews in Higher Education, no. 77).

Yoshimoto, K. (ed) (2001). *University and Work in Europe and Japan – A Survey Report on Higher Education and Work among Twelve Countries.* Tokyo: Japan Institute of Labour (report no. 143) (in Japanese).

A list of over 200 publications and conference contributions is available at http:\www.uni-kassel.de/wz1/cheers.htm

3. THE LABOUR MARKET PERSPECTIVES

A substantial share of the public debates and of the research on the relationships between higher education and the world of work has certain common assumptions and views. We could name these the dominant *labour market* or *employment* perspectives of the relationships between higher education and employment. They have three characteristics in common:

- They focus on the contribution of higher education to individual and collective *economic and social success* in terms of economic growth as well as high remuneration, non-monetary rewards and status.
- They are based on the belief that the relationships between higher education and the world of work are predominantly based on a reinforcement of the norms of the individual as *homo oeconomicus* (in the economic version) or status seeker (in the sociological version). The desirable competences of individuals for the economy are provided, because the employment system provides the respective rewards, and the logic of the differential positions and rewards in a meritocratically based achievement society takes care that learners are stimulated to do their best to become well-qualified members of society.
- They are primarily interested in *quantitative-structural data*, notably levels of educational attainment, types of higher education institutions and degrees, employment status, economic sectors and occupational groups as well as positions and income levels.

The common characteristics of these perspectives have to take care that a considerable continuity of issues are addressed both in the public debate and in research on the relationships between higher education and employment. There is continuity in the analytical questions about the extent to which a balance is struck between demand for highly qualified labour and the provision of highly qualified graduates, as well as about the extent to which a high level of educational attainments is rewarded by a high level of monetary and non-monetary returns and a high status. In some respects, the subsequent changing debates and research approaches can be viewed as ways of identifying the imperfections and the endemic deviations from the ideal-type assumptions of higher education preparing and selecting for high-level occupations in the framework of a more or less perfect match between demand and supply.

Over the years, we note the emergence of various new dominant themes as far as these imperfections and endemic questioning of the traditional assumptions are concerned. First, both policy debates and research from this perspective tend to be interested, and clearly were predominantly interested in the *dynamic balance between demand and supply* when the debate and research on the relationships between higher education and the world of work gained momentum around the 1960s. Does the expansion of higher education – overall or with respect to certain sectors – match the changes of graduate employment, or can signs of substantial shortages or oversupply in the highly educated labour force be observed? Does the expansion of higher education stimulate or retard the economic growth and modernisation of society? It was obvious that planning gaps could not be avoided: Shortages and oversupplies of graduates can be redressed only after some period, and it was also questionable whether market adaptations took place rapidly.

Second, it soon became obvious that these debates and research approaches could be based too much on the view that certain categories of higher education were clearly articulated around certain categories of the employment system. They could be too strongly based on the assumption that an ideal articulation between higher education and the employment system would be achieved if, for example, all engineering graduates were active in the occupational category "engineers", and if all engineers were training in the category "engineering". A certain degree of *openness*, *vagueness* and "*flexibility*" became increasingly seen as desirable to take care of the broad variety of occupations, newly emerging job roles and innovative tasks across established occupational categories, innovations in the employment systems triggered off by changes in higher education, equipping students with the abilities to handle indeterminate work tasks as well as equipping graduates with abilities to cope if the ideal match could not be achieved on the labour market.

Third, greater attention was paid to *endemic signs of a less close match* between education and employment than the concepts of a market-regulated adaptation of demand and supply and of an achievement society based on educational meritocracy would suggest: is an open education system in a society that rewards high-level education bound to lead to overheated competition for educational success and for continuous "over-education?" Do successful careers upon graduation from certain universities only to a limited degree indicate differences of educational quality and predominantly artificial "credentialism" or "degreeocracy"? Is access to the best career largely determined by smart search processes on the part of the individuals or their higher education institutions instead of by respective competences? Altogether, are moderate economic rewards for educational attainment and a moderate educational meritocracy the normal state of affairs?

Fourth, attention was increasingly paid to *unemployment, precarious employment as well as employment in low-level occupations and positions* of higher education graduates. Both, a general rise in unemployment and unstable employment in the majority of economically advanced countries as well as an endemic loss of privileges of a share of the higher education graduates contributed to the growing attention paid to the extent and the causes of their employment problems.

Finally, *the dynamics of the transition process from higher education to employment* became one of the key issues of the debate and analysis of the links between higher education and employment. This reflected the fact that graduates' job searches and graduate recruitment became more and more a costly, time-consuming and protracted process. Lack of information, uncertainties about occupational motivations on the part of the graduates and ambivalences of recruitment criteria on the part of the employers contributed to extended periods of decision-making and to extended trial-and-error periods.

A large-scale comparative study on graduate employment and work must provide answers to the major questions which derive from the mainstream public debates. The CHEERS study is designed in such a way that it provides findings that are indicative for the key questions typically raised in the framework of the "labour market" or the "employment" approach, such as: Do we note substantial imbalances between demand and supply? How close are the links between educational and professional success? How frequent are serious employment problems of graduates and what types of graduates are most seriously affected by them? How smooth or protracted is the transition from higher education to employment, and to what extent do specific features of search and recruitment affect graduates' employment opportunities?

4. THE KNOWLEDGE AND WORK PERSPECTIVES

Higher education has a qualifying function for the world of work and for all life spheres of graduates. It is responsible for knowledge generation, transmission and preservation. Students are taught and are provided with an environment that is conducive to enhancing their competences on their own. Therefore, the public debates and research on the relationships between higher education and the world of work have a second major area of emphasis. We also note a variety of perspectives which we could call the *qualification perspectives*, i.e. the way "qualification" is used in many languages: as individuals' acquired abilities that are potentially relevant for professional practice. Or we could call them the *knowledge and work perspectives* which address the substantive links between what is learned in higher education and the work tasks.

Analyses in the domain of labour market and employment approaches, often undertaken by economists and sociologists, focus on the knowledge dimension. But they address it indirectly by assuming, for example, that a person trained in engineering is most suitable to be employed in the occupational category engineers or that employers pay high salaries to those whose competences are in high demand. Analyses in the domain of knowledge and work approaches, which are predominantly based on education, psychology or sociology, however, aim to address issues of acquisition and use of knowledge directly. They focus on students' competences upon graduation and how they have acquired these and the relationships to the job requirements. The issue of the appropriate balance between demand and supply is raised again, but not in terms of quantitative-structural categories of education and jobs for the learners and the professionals as a whole, but rather for individual dimensions of competences and work tasks. Observations, tests, or ratings by experts, employers, students and graduates are the most frequent modes of inquiry.

The major themes addressed in the public debates and research projects on the knowledge and work of graduates resemble in many respects those addressed in debates and research activities on employment.

First, there is the question of how well the study programmes lay the foundation or prepare graduates directly so that their *competences match the job requirements*. And discrepancies are interpreted as calls for curricular reforms.

Second, there is a long tradition in the debates and analysis of education and job requirements of weighing the strengths of the *training of specialists against* those of *a broad range of knowledge*. Views vary with respect to the need for specialised knowledge for successful job performance, the extent to which one can put trust in a broad transfer of knowledge, and the extent to which specialised knowledge should be acquired during the course of study or initial job training after graduation. Labour market imperfections have begun to play a stronger role since the 1970s in the debates about the need for specialists and generalists. As discrepancies between supply and demand cannot be avoided, graduates who are not highly trained as specialists could be more easily absorbed by the employment system and could be in a better position to adapt to unanticipated work tasks.

Third, the debate on the acquisition and use of knowledge of higher education graduates differs substantially from that of those from other types of schools and vocational training. Higher education graduates from are expected to perform well in the framework of established job requirements and professional practices, but they are also trained to constantly reflect and *challenge the established links between knowledge and work tasks*. Higher education trains for critical thinking, reflection, innovation, coping with indeterminate work tasks and for pro-active change of occupations on the basis of new knowledge. Views vary considerably in the public debates and the research hypotheses regarding the extent to which higher education must be "responsive" to the perceived demands or must be pro-active in training students to challenge the perceived demands.

Fourth, there has been a growing conviction in the last few decades that higher education should play a stronger role in fostering *competences beyond systematic cognitive knowledge*. Universities are generally seen as having the core function of transmitting theories, methods and a systematic body of knowledge related to certain disciplines or professional areas. Terms such as "extra-functional qualifications", "orientation towards practice", "key qualifications", "personality", "employability" etc. became popular at different historical stages of these debates and in different countries during the last few decades. This signals that higher education should also foster competences that are relevant for successful professional practice which are based to a lesser extent on cognitive and systematic learning. Though no generally agreed conceptual basis emerged to classify these job requirements and competences, most analyses emphasise five additional dimensions of work-relevant competences:

- abilities to transmit systematic knowledge to work tasks and apply systematic knowledge on the job (e.g. "problem-solving" abilities),
- competences that are relevant for reflection, innovation and creativity,
- successful working styles (e.g. "working under time pressure"),
- socio-communicative skills (e.g. "teamwork", "leadership"),
- motives and values conducive to successful professional work.

Fifth, claims are frequently made that the qualifying function of higher education ought to be changed in the light of the more rapid emergence of new knowledge, more rapid obsolescence of knowledge, rapid changes of the graduate labour market's distinct job requirements at various career stages. A growing need is seen for "continuing professional education", "recurrent education" and – the most popular term since the 1990s – *lifelong learning*. According to these concepts, graduates should to a lesser degree be equipped up to the time of graduation with competences that are immediately useful for professional practice and to higher degree with a general foundation of knowledge. Students should "learn how to learn" in the course of their studies.

A large-scale comparative study on graduate employment and work cannot limit itself to addressing issues of knowledge and work tasks only indirectly, as was customary in traditional labour market studies on graduate employment, because available research has shown that this would lead to distortions. For example, prior research has shown that many graduates who were employed in occupational categories that traditionally were not filled by graduates observed a close link between the knowledge they acquired during the course of study and their work tasks. On the other hand, large-scale and highly standardised questionnaires cannot cover the complexity of all the relevant dimensions of competences and work tasks and all the best modes of measurements. Therefore, two priority areas were selected in the CHEERS Study while other areas were addressed less thoroughly or not at all. These two priority areas were graduates' overall assessments of the links between knowledge and work tasks as well as between acquired competences and job requirements beyond systematic academic knowledge.

5. THE VALUES AND OPTIONS PERSPECTIVES

As already pointed out, a substantial share of the research on the relationships between higher education and the world of work analyses graduates' professional success in terms of high remuneration and/or high occupational rank. It is taken for granted that a modern, economically advanced society is largely based on a basic consensus about the most desirable careers and that the individual can be viewed as a *homo oeconomicus* or a status seeker who will strive for the highest career, if he or she has the potential to do so.

There are good reasons, though, to assume that students' and graduates' motives and activities cannot only be viewed as primarily driven by a desire to maximise income and status. Six, partly interrelated, areas of values could be quoted in this respect.

First, professionals hold in high esteem a *pride in good professional work* and in the use of their competences. *Intrinsic motivation* is often seen as a more important drive for good professional practice than extrinsic motivation striving for rewards such as income and status.

Second, *autonomous work* in terms of disposition to decide about the goals, the process, the timing etc. of one's work assignments is held in high esteem by a substantial proportion and notably is part of the professional pride of highly qualified persons.

Third, we note that some *values* which are closely *associated with the innovative function of systematic knowledge* are held in high esteem by highly qualified persons: opportunities to undertake research, curiosity, interest in further learning, improving and revolutionising society.

Fourth, research on job satisfaction has revealed a wide range of *work conditions and employment conditions* which are held in high esteem. Good contacts with colleagues, time for regular leisure activities and other assets of certain job roles could explain the occupational choice and the daily behaviour of the work force.

Fifth, values related to the *socio-communicative environment outside the world of work* have often been pointed at in recent years as highly influential for work-related decisions. The choice of certain regions as place of work or place of residence and career sacrifices for the sake of partnerships, families and children are examples of this.

Sixth, *gender differences* of occupational conditions, values and behaviour have been one of the major themes of debate and research in this framework in recent decades. Debates and analysis do not only address the extent to which occupational values and behaviour of men and women vary, but also try to establish whether the different values and activities must be viewed as adaptations to unequal opportunities or can be viewed as genuinely distinct values and options.

Views vary as far as changes of these values over time are concerned. On the one hand, a growing weight of intrinsic motives is observed as a shift toward "*post-industrial values*": the more a certain wealth of society due to the dynamic of the industrial societies could be taken for granted, the more persons turn to improvements of life and society beyond the previously material rewards strived for. Similarly, the *values characteristic of the highly qualified professions* seem to *spread in the process of educational expansion*. On the other hand, monetary and non-monetary labour market rewards as well as status motives are viewed as getting momentum *when employment problems grow*. Similarly, there is the notion that there is a revival of the *homo oeconomicus* when the *Zeitgeist* is shaped by *neo-liberal economic values*.

Prior analyses have shown that some value dimensions could conflict with those of the *homo oeconomicus* and status seekers might be interpreted as appreciation of non-monetary economic rewards or one dimension of a broad spectrum of status dimension. Moreover, prior analyses have shown that there was a high positive correlation between income and status and work conditions such as autonomous work, opportunity to make use of one's competences, opportunities for lifelong learning, etc. which were held in high esteem by professionals.

Yet graduates' values and motives obviously cannot be seen as being so closely embedded in the dominant notions of what a successful career looks like that they do not need to be made a major explicit theme of analysis in studies on the relationships between higher education and the world of work. The researchers involved in this study were convinced that it would be biased from the outset if the variety of graduates' values and orientations and their links with features of their actual careers were not one of the key areas of analysis.

6. UNIVERSAL DYNAMICS AND NATIONAL SPECIFITIES

When the relationships between higher education and the world of work were high on the agenda in the public debates on higher education, labour perspectives tended to play a major role and were based on general, i.e. *not country-specific assumptions on modern economies and societies*. They seemed to believe in universal mechanisms of societies or at least in common mega-trends of modern societies. It did not matter whether one addressed the contribution of educational expansion to economic growth, the endemic over-education in educational meritocracies, the shrinking of gainful work as a consequence of automatisation and computerisation, the relevance of key qualifications for productive work of highly educated persons, or the impact of globalisation on graduate employment and work – all these debates and analyses addressed common features and trends or were based on the assumption that countries were seeking and were in competition for the best possible solutions according to common criteria.

Such general or universal approaches, of course, do not negate differences between countries. But these *country differences could be viewed as indicating the relative position of the individual country according to common criteria.* For example, one could analyse the relationships between the level of domestic income growth and the ratio of graduates in the labour force or the links between annual economic growth and graduate unemployment. They do not assume, for example, that the labour market of the country X needs more specialists and the labour market of the country Y needs more generalists because views prevail among employers, politicians and academics in country X that higher education programmes should train specialists and views prevail in country Y which are more in favour of broad knowledge.

But, obviously, there are also features of the higher education system, of notions of employment, work and professions as well as of a desirable social fabric in each country which are clearly distinct from other countries and which are a relatively stable frame of reference for choices of, for example, study programmes, rationales of curricula, recruitment practices or the design of occupational roles within the respective country. Any effort to rank these features on a scale of modernity or economic rationality is based on cultural imperialism.

It is impossible even for a large team composed of researchers from all the countries under scrutiny to take into account and examine the wealth of concepts that exist in each country about the characteristics of its higher education system and of specific notions of employment and work as well as other relevant characteristics of their society. It was clear from the outset that the project was not in a position to cover the abundance of claimed specifics. In seeking for a feasible approach, two choices were made.

First, it was agreed that special attention should be paid to those characteristics which in previous public debates and research activities were seen as major challenges to the more or less universal assumptions about graduate employment and work. Obviously, there are four areas in the relationships between higher education and the world of work where national characteristics are important factors in affecting potentially general mechanisms:

– In many European countries, the typical *notions of educational meritocracy* never seem to have affected the values and activities of the majority of the population. At most, modest intergenerational mobility is taken for granted, and more emphasis is placed on social justice between different social groups than on social justice through individual opportunity for social mobility. In contrast, Japan is often seen as the country where the values of educational meritocracy are most strongly rooted and where success in pre-career education is considered crucial for careers. The U.S. are often depicted as a country where the opportunity for individual mobility is also the key criterion of social justice, but instead of a strong emphasis on pre-career education success, as observed in Japan, the view is widespread in the U.S. that individuals have a lifelong opportunity for success.

- We note striking differences between countries as far as *general or specific approaches of education and training* are concerned. Where a generalist's view prevails, for example in the Anglo-Saxon countries and in Japan, specialised training is viewed as "narrow" both in terms of restraining professional flexibility and personality development. Where a specialist's view dominates, notably in France and to a certain extent in Germany, the acquisition of specific knowledge is considered as a process of exemplary in-depth learning which ensures transfer to other areas of expertise, and is viewed as compatible with a broad culture.
- There is also a substantial variety of concepts of employment and work-related identity. In France and Germany, these are generally expected to be a major force for individual identity. This tradition, for example, has reinforced a high level of professional pride in skilled workers in Germany. In the U.S., we note a stronger emphasis on the status and remuneration level; if professional pride is referred to, a clear distinction is made – as in the United Kingdom – between (high-level) "professions" and other "vocational" areas. In Japan, an affiliation to one's employing organisation tends to be viewed as a more important source of work-related identity than to a certain occupation.
- Finally, the views differ substantially as regards the roles of strategic political action in shaping the relationships between higher education and employment. In the U.S., faith in the self-regulatory forces is most widespread as far as educational preparation for employment and work in a market-driven economy is concerned. In European countries, different degrees of macro-planning and steering of education are considered essential to strike a balance between economic and other social and cultural rationales. At the same time, stronger measures are taken to align a predominantly market-driven economy with social cohesion based on a moderate degree of social inequality. The term "welfare society" was frequently used to define the latter notions.

Second, the members of the research team agreed to adopt an inductive approach. Whenever graduates from certain countries differed strikingly in their responses to the questions raised in the questionnaire, the researchers of these countries were asked to examine whether these responses reflected certain characteristics of the higher education system, or the professional values and the social fabric.

7. THE APPROACH OF THIS PUBLICATION

As already pointed out above, the two coordinators of the projects provided an overall overview of the findings of the CHEERS project in one volume (Schomburg and Teichler 2006, see Figure 1). In this second volume various members of the international team undertook an in-depth-analysis on individual thematic areas of the survey.

Brenda Johnston and Brenda Little (The Open University, London, United Kingdom), members of the British team, analysed the sociobiographic background of the graduates up to the entry to higher education. Jake Murdoch and Jean-Jacques Paul (Institut de Recherche sur l'Economie de l'Education, Faculté des Sciences Mirande, Université de Bourgogne, France), members of the French team, identified the extent to which content and process of higher education shape the competences upon graduation and the subsequent employment. Jim Allen and Rolf van der Velden (Research Centre for Education and the Labour Market (ROA), Maastricht University, The Netherlands) of the Dutch team observed the dynamics of transition to employment. Trine Stavik and Clara Åse Arnesen (Norwegian Institute for Studies in Research and Higher Education (NIFU) Oslo, Norway), members of the Norwegian team, identified the career change within the first few years after graduation. José García-Montalvo, José-Ginés Mora and Adela Garcia-Aracil (Department of Economics, University of Valencia, Spain) looked at the employment situation a few years after graduation, i.e. at the time the survey was conducted. Questions of the relationships between the competences acquired at the time of graduation and the job requirements a few years later were addressed from different perspectives in two chapters: by Paul Kellermann (Institute of Sociology, University of Klagenfurt, Austria) of the Austrian team on the one hand, and by Osmo Kivinen and Joumi Nurmi (Research Unit for the Sociology of Education, University of Turku, Finland), members of the Finnish team, on the other hand. Jake Murdoch and Jean-Jacques Paul also analyzed the professional success of graduates in terms of knowledge used on the job and links between educational attainments and position. Gunhild Sagmeister (Institute of Sociology, University of Klagenfurt, Austria) of the Austrian team pointed out the role of early-career education. Torgerdur Einarsdottir (Faculty of Social Science, University of Iceland, Reykjavík, Iceland) of the Swedish team identified the extent to which careers of women and men vary in the first few years after graduation. Roberto Moscati and Michele Rostan (Istituto di Ricerca (IARD), Milano, Italy), members of the Italian team, pointed out the role which regional economic conditions of each country play for graduate employment and work. Volker Jahr and Ulrich Teichler (International Centre for Higher Education Research Kassel, University of Kassel, Germany), members of the German team, address the links between international experience during the course of study and international mobility and work tasks after graduation. Egbert de Weert (Center for Higher Education Policy Studies (CHEPS), University of Twente, Enschede, The Netherlands) of the Dutch team analyses the employers' views (based on interviews) on graduation, employment and work. Harald Schomburg (International Centre for Higher Education Research Kassel, University of Kassel, Germany) of the German team, points out how work orientation and job satisfaction is linked to actual employment and work. Finally, Ulrich Teichler aims to establish the extent which the project has confirmed what has been know beforehand and where the project has provided new insights.

BRENDA JOHNSTON AND BRENDA LITTLE

SOCIO-BIOGRAPHICAL BACKGROUND AND EDUCATIONAL PATH

1. INTRODUCTION

This chapter describes and analyses the relationships between socio-biographical background, routes into higher education, choice of field of study and type of institution or programme, as well as the study path up to graduation. Two areas are of particular interest: (1) issues of social equity and access to higher education and the relationships between gender and higher educational outcomes; and (2) how these relationships vary by country.

The analysis draws on OECD, Eurostat and EURYDICE and national offices educational statistics and the information provided by the graduates surveyed. Most information refers to the early and mid-1990s because the graduates surveyed in the CHEERS study graduated in the academic year 1994/95, i.e. they started their studies between the late 1980s and early 1990s.

2. EDUCATIONAL AND HIGHER EDUCATION BACKGROUND

2.1. Educational Background

The underlying trend is one of rising educational attainment levels, although the picture varies greatly across the countries surveyed. The proportion of the population completing upper secondary education was over 80 per cent in Sweden, Norway, Austria, Germany, Finland, France, the United Kingdom and the Czech Republic in 1995, but in Spain and Italy it was under 50 per cent (OECD 1997, p. 39). In most Western European countries, students are divided into different "tracks" of secondary education, typically academic and vocational. The most "prestigious and demanding" of these usually lead to higher education (Teichler 1988, p. 5).

The proportion of the population completing tertiary education has also been increasing. In Norway and Sweden over 25 per cent of the population aged between 25 and 64 had obtained a tertiary level qualification by 1995, whereas in Austria, Italy, Spain, France and the Czech Republic the figure was under 20 per cent (OECD 1997, p. 38). If we look at the proportion of the population aged between 25 and 34 in 1995 who had completed tertiary education, it was greater in most countries than for the previous group, as one would expect, given the recent expansion of higher education. In Spain and France, where this expansion was most pronounced, the percentage difference between the two groups was especially noticeable at 11 per cent and 6 per cent respectively, whereas for most countries in the study it was between 1 per cent and 3 per cent.

U. Teichler (ed.), Careers of University Graduates, 15–40

2.2. *Selection and Access to Higher Education*

Access routes to higher education and selection systems prior to higher education varied substantially between countries. As Teichler (1988, p. 5) points out, "a typology of access to higher education has to take into account the [system of] selectivity for admission [to higher education] and the [likely] consequences for subsequent educational and career stages as well". He suggests four models for the typology of access.

- Selection takes place *during secondary education.* By the time of admission, for those who have the necessary secondary entry qualifications, entry to higher education mainly consists in selecting a field. The prestige of universities is more or less the same. In Germany, Austria and the Netherlands this admission system still prevails.
- Selection takes place in two stages: *within secondary education and again at entry to higher education* where different higher education institutions and/or fields of study enjoy different degrees of prestige. The United Kingdom is an example of this approach.
- Selection takes place more or less *entirely at the admission* stage. This is the case when most secondary school leavers are entitled to apply for higher education and where the quality of the institutions is very uneven and where the institution attended has a critical influence on future careers. In these systems competition at the point of entry to higher education is fierce. This is the case in Japan and Finland and for the Grandes Ècoles in France.
- Entry to higher education is open to most secondary school leavers and, though there is a meritocratic selection at the entry point, *most students can enter the type* of institutions they want. This can tie up with the belief that lifelong competition should keep opportunities open beyond early higher education. In Norway, Spain and Italy this type of low-key selection is the norm. In Spain, all students who complete secondary education may attend university as a constitutional right, but they may find themselves unable to study in the field of their choice because of limited places and entrance examinations in some subjects (López-Valcárcel and Quintana 1998).

As from the 1960s, attempts were made to widen access to higher education in several ways. One was to make movement between the different "tracks" of secondary education possible so that those who had not completed academic secondary education could enter higher education. In Sweden in the 1980s, for example, opportunities were created for people to collect gradually through individual courses the credentials they needed as prerequisites for entry to higher education in the 25:4 (at least 25 years of age with four years' work experience) scheme. In the Netherlands, opportunities to transfer between different tracks and levels of the different types of secondary and vocational education were opened up. In the United Kingdom and the Netherlands, "open" university courses were offered to people who had no formal entry qualifications. Also, in the United Kingdom, special admissions schemes for older students helped to make access easier for older students (OECD 1997, p. 162; Svanfeldt 1994, p. 246; Teichler 1988, p. 6-7).

Also, many European countries made efforts to establish more accessible and more regionally dispersed higher education institutions for people who had hitherto been disadvantaged. Thus, in Norway, for example, state colleges were created. In the Nordic and other countries, universities were founded in remote regions. An additional type of higher education with a vocational emphasis was offered in various countries, starting with the polytechnics in the United Kingdom, the IUTs in France and the *Fachhochschulen* in Germany. Among subsequent such developments were the HBOs in the Netherlands, the largest higher education sector of this kind.

Thus, two distinct sectors emerged in some countries. The new sector consisted largely of more "vocationally oriented", "less academically demanding" and more "regionally dispersed" institutions. They tended to require lower entry qualifications and sometimes offered shorter cycle courses. These new institutions tended to be more open to those from regionally and socially disadvantaged groups than traditional institutions, thus making higher education more accessible. However, this type of development can be seen as institutionalised mechanisms whereby disadvantaged groups were educated in seclusion from more privileged groups (Teichler 1988, p. 7). This development of two strong sectors did not occur in all countries. In Austria, Spain, Italy and Finland universities continued to dominate the higher education scene (Meek et al. 1996).

It is important to note that the traditional academic route to higher education remains the "king's road". As many as one third of all students in higher education may take alternative routes, but of these, under 10 per cent overall and 5 per cent in some countries enter prestigious institutions and courses in each country (Teichler 1988, p. 7).

3. GRADUATES' SOCIO-BIOGRAPHICAL BACKGROUND

3.1. Educational Level of Graduates' Parents

In line with notions of cultural and academic capital, access to higher education appears somewhat more open for better educated groups. In 1995, in countries of the European Union as a whole, 55 per cent of those whose parents had higher education entered higher education, compared to 17 per cent of those whose parents had only primary or lower secondary education (see Table 1). In Spain, France and Italy, more than 60 per cent of young people whose parents had higher education participated in higher education, compared to about 20 per cent of those whose parents had only completed primary or lower secondary education. One should bear in mind that all types of tertiary education are included in "higher education" in EU statistics.

Table 1. Participation Rates for 19-24 Year Olds in Higher Education, by Educational Level of Parents and Country (percentage)*

	Country						Total
Educational level of parents	IT	ES	FR	NL	FI	SE	
Primary or lower secondary education	17	22	22	16	8	15	17
Higher education	61	63	68	43	37	55	55

* Data is not available in this Eurostat table for many countries in our survey.

Source: Eurostat, Labour Force Survey, 1995; Finland and Sweden National surveys, Key Data p. 174

In our survey, 36 per cent of graduates had parents (at least one) with higher education. According to OECD figures, the percentage of the population which has completed tertiary education in the 45-54 age group (approximately the age range in which we expect to find many of our graduates' parents), we would only expect an overall parental higher education rate of 18 per cent (see Table 2). If we take the older age group that OECD lists, i.e. people between the ages of 55 and 64, the percentage is even lower (OECD p. 40). Clearly, access to higher education is far more open to children of highly educated parents.

In our survey, the countries with the most highly educated profile for parents, i.e. where 40 per cent or more of graduates have at least one parent with higher education, are Norway, the Netherlands, the Czech Republic and the United Kingdom. Countries with the least educated profile for parents, i.e. with 70 per cent or more graduates where neither parent has higher education, are Spain, Austria and Finland.

Table 2. Percentage of Respondents with Parents Having Completed Tertiary Education, by Country

	Country										
	IT	ES	FR	AT	DE	NL	UK	FI	SE	NO	CZ	EUR
Population aged 45-54 completing tertiary education	8	11	17	7	24	21	21	20	29	27	11	18
Graduates' parents having completed higher education	30	23	38	26	36	42	40	28	m	51	40	35

Note: For the data from the CHEERS survey, this table takes the highest educational level, whether that of mother or father, for each graduate.
m = missing data

Sources: OECD Database, OECD 1997, p. 40, CHEERS survey data

Overall in our survey and in each individual country, entrants who are 31 years or more are slightly more likely to have parents without higher education. Overall and in each individual country, entrants who are aged 19 or under are slightly more likely to have parents with higher education. This is as expected, given the recent expansion of higher education. Those in the older age brackets are less likely to have parents who had the opportunity of entering higher education themselves, especially in countries such as Spain where expansion in higher education began relatively late.

3.2. Gender Balance

In the past, females were generally less well-represented than males in both secondary and tertiary education. By 1995, these differences had largely disappeared or been reversed. As can be seen in Table 3, women were in the majority in 1995 amongst tertiary education students in Spain, France, Finland, Norway and Sweden, but remained in the minority in Germany, the Netherlands and the Czech Republic. More or less the same picture was true for men and women graduating in 1995.

Table 3. Net Enrolment in Public and Private Tertiary Education for Persons aged between 17 and 34 in 1995, by Gender and Country (percentage based on head counts)

	Country											
	IT	ES	FR	AT	DE	NL	UK	FI	SE	NO	CZ	EUR	JP
Men	m	10.8	12.2	m	10.2	11.2	9.2	13.2	8.7	11.8	6.7	10.4	m
Women	m	12.7	15.1	m	8.4	10.3	9.3	14.9	9.8	13.7	6.4	11.2	m

m = missing data
Source: OECD Database, OECD 1997, p. 171

4. ENTRY TO HIGHER EDUCATION

The transition from upper secondary to tertiary education occurs at a different age in the countries analysed (OECD 1997, p.153). It depends on the typical age for completing upper secondary education as well as traditions about and opportunities for deferral of entry to higher education (employment, military service, other educational activities, etc.).

In some countries, students tended to enter higher education directly from school. In the Czech Republic, Spain, Italy and Japan 70 per cent or more of the respondents in our sample entered higher education before the age of 20. The majority in France, Austria, the United Kingdom and the Netherlands also entered at this age. The average proportion overall was 49 per cent. Countries where one quarter or less entered higher education at this age were Germany, Sweden, Norway and Finland (see Table 4).

Many countries have a high proportion of students entering higher education between the ages of 20 and 25. In our survey, the average percentage was 42 per cent, as can be seen in Table 4. Finally, over 20 per cent of new entrants were over 25 years in Norway and the United Kingdom.

As presented in Table 4, a slightly higher proportion of the women surveyed than the men entered higher education at age 19 or under, as was the case for those aged 31 or more. Men started later in some countries because of military service, more frequent choice of vocational education (e.g. in Germany) or more frequently extended preparation for admission to higher education (notably in Japan). Some women entered higher education at a later stage because of childcare and other responsibilities, especially in the Nordic countries (and UK).

Table 4. Respondents' Age at Entry to Higher Education, by Country and Gender (percentage)

	Country												Total
	IT	ES	FR	AT	DE	NL	UK	FI	SE	NO	CZ	JP	
Male													
19 or under	68	73	53	52	7	45	51	25	13	24	77	64	47
20-25	28	23	43	42	83	48	28	65	73	62	18	35	46
26-30	2	3	2	3	8	3	6	4	7	9	1	0	4
31 or more	2	2	2	2	2	4	14	6	6	6	4	0	4
Female													
19 or under	75	76	62	64	27	55	57	24	17	16	80	83	51
20-25	23	20	34	29	64	37	22	59	63	58	16	16	38
26-30	1	2	1	3	6	3	5	5	8	10	2	0	4
31 or more	1	2	3	4	3	5	16	11	12	16	2	0	7
Total													
19 or under	71	74	58	58	15	50	54	25	15	19	78	70	49
20-25	26	21	38	36	75	42	25	62	68	60	17	29	42
26-30	2	3	2	3	7	3	6	5	8	9	2	0	4
31 or more	1	2	2	3	2	5	15	9	9	12	3	0	5
Total*	100	100	100	100	100	100	100	100	100	100	100	100	100

Question B1: Please, provide information about all higher education courses you have ever taken (including part-time, post graduate, and courses not completed).
Notes: The age at entry was calculated by subtracting the year of birth of the graduate from the entry year to higher education.
Percentages may not add up to 100 exactly because of rounding.
* Count by Country: IT (2965); ES (2614); FR (21950); AT (2241); DE (3476); NL (2954); UK (3233); FI (2608); SE (2560); NO (3182); CZ (3090); JP (3361); Total (35234).

Source: CHEERS survey data

There were substantial variations between countries in the lapse of time between obtaining entry qualifications and entering higher education, depending on traditions about deferral and mechanisms for transfer. In the United Kingdom, the Netherlands, Spain, France and Japan 40 per cent or more of graduates in our sample had started higher education within three months of obtaining their entry qualifications, whilst this was true for 15 per cent or less in Austria, Germany, Finland and the Czech Republic. In contrast, 15 per cent or more had deferred their entry in higher education by more than four years in the Netherlands, the United Kingdom, Finland, Sweden, Norway and the Czech Republic (see Table 5).

Table 5. Lapse of Time Between Acquiring Entry Qualifications and Entering Higher Education, by Country (percentage)

	Country													Total
	IT	ES	FR	AT	DE	NL	UK	FI	SE	NO	CZ	EUR	JP	
0-3 months	33	40	42	15	15	54	47	6	29	34	0	28	70	32
4-9 months	42	37	20	45	22	8	12	22	6	2	0	19	0	17
10-24 months	13	8	6	24	27	12	16	27	18	20	69	23	21	22
25-48 months	6	7	24	8	22	9	10	26	29	24	16	17	8	16
49 months or more	6	8	9	8	14	18	16	20	18	21	15	14	2	13
Total*	100	100	100	100	100	100	100	100	100	100	100	100	100	100

* Count by Country: IT (2918); ES (2560); FR (2730); AT (2139); DE (3426); NL (2418); UK (2518); FI (2461); SE (2339); NO (3105); CZ (3089); EUR (29703); JP (3269); Total (32972).

Source: CHEERS survey data

Asked about the activities they had undertaken between obtaining their higher education qualification and enrolling in higher education, 31 per cent of the graduates surveyed stated that they had been employed for some period. 14 per cent had been engaged in other education and training activities. 11 per cent had interrupted their educational career for military and other services, and 3 per cent had spent this period in child and family care. There were clear differences by country, as can be seen in Table 6.

Table 6. Respondents' Activities Between Obtaining Entry Qualification and Enrolment in Higher Education, by Country (percentage)

	Country												Total
	IT	ES	FR	AT	DE	NL	UK	FI	SE	NO	CZ	JP	
Employment/ self-employment	15	6	13	36	39	38	16	77	m	57	m	23	31
Education/training/ apprenticeship	5	5	4	5	22	11	9	19	m	25	m	33	14
Military or civilian service	3	1	1	21	38	3	0	24	m	17	m	0	11
Child rearing, family care	2	1	2	2	2	1	2	5	m	9	m	0	3
Not employed, seeking employment	4	0	1	19	15	2	3	11	m	5	m	0	6
Other	10	3	2	27	24	21	6	18	m	12	m	1	12
No answer	68	86	81	19	7	38	77	11	m	17	m	50	46
Total*	106	103	104	128	147	115	113	165	m	142	m	107	122

Question A5: How many months did you spend on the following activities between obtaining the entry qualification and your first enrolment in higher education?

m = missing data

* Count by Country: IT (3102); ES (3024); FR (3051); AT (2312); DE (3506); NL (3087); UK (3460); FI (2675); SE (m); NO (3329); CZ (m); JP (3421); Total (30967).

Source: CHEERS survey data

5. RELATIONSHIPS BETWEEN SOCIO-BIOGRAPHICAL FACTORS AND ENTRY QUALIFICATION

In the countries surveyed, more pupils followed vocational than academic upper secondary education, although more men than women chose the former (European Commission 1997, p. 64). As most of those who obtained vocational qualifications did not enter higher education (often they were not qualified to do so according to the entry requirements), most students in higher education came from academic secondary education. As Table 7 shows, only 22 per cent of the graduates surveyed did not have academic secondary education. This was the case for more than 30 per cent in Austria, Italy, the Czech Republic and the Netherlands. In some countries, other types of secondary education prepared for entry to some sectors of higher education (notably *Fachoberschulen* in Germany and *hoger allgemeen voortgezet onderwijs* in the Netherlands; see Goedegebuure et al. 1993). Again, the proportion of women entering higher education via academic secondary education (81%) was higher than that of men (76%).

Table 7. Percentage of Respondents with Academic Secondary Education, by Country and Gender

	Country												Total
	IT	ES	FR	AT	DE	NL	UK	FI	SE	NO	CZ	JP	
Male	66	90	90	67	73	48	77	97	71	76	59	94	76
Female	72	94	91	73	86	53	83	98	78	72	72	96	81
Total*	69	92	91	70	78	51	81	97	75	74	65	95	78

* Count by Country: IT (3091); ES (3009); FR (3032); AT (2305); DE (3500); NL (3069); UK (3322); FI (2654); SE (2623); NO (3312); CZ (3092); JP (3400); Total (36411).

Source: CHEERS survey data

In all the countries surveyed, a greater proportion of respondents with academic secondary qualifications had parents with higher education than graduates with other (e.g. vocational) types of entry qualifications. Amongst those whose parents had higher education, 85 per cent had followed academic secondary education (varying between 61 per cent and 99 per cent by country), whilst of those whose parents had no higher education, only 72 per cent had followed academic secondary education (ranging by country from 45% to 97%).

In all the countries surveyed, a higher proportion of graduates in the younger age groups had academic secondary entry qualifications than in the older age-groups where greater proportions had other types of qualifications. 85 per cent of those entering higher education at age 19 or under had academic secondary qualifications, while of those above 30, only 47 per cent had academic secondary qualifications (see Table 8). Often, vocational qualifications were acquired after additional years of learning, or those with a vocational qualification had initially entered working life and decided after some years to enrol in higher education.

Table 8. Percentage of Respondents with Academic Secondary Education, by Age of Entry to Higher Education and Country

Age	IT	ES	FR	AT	DE	NL	UK	FI	SE	NO	CZ	JP	Total
							Country						
19 or under	72	97	94	87	92	60	96	99	93	93	68	96	85
20-25	65	84	88	48	78	44	73	99	77	79	59	92	76
26-30	57	61	71	44	62	39	60	93	57	51	58	47	59
31 or more	31	48	76	29	44	24	47	84	46	34	33	81	47
Total	69	92	91	70	78	51	81	97	75	74	65	95	78

Source: CHEERS survey data

6. CHOICE OF INSTITUTION AND PROGRAMME

6.1. Institutional and Programme Patterns

Higher education can be classified according to three different aspects. First, there are different types of institutions, varying according to objectives, research and teaching functions, possibly entry requirements, the nature of courses offered and regional location. Second, there are different levels of programmes or degrees. The length of the programmes may vary in terms of years of study required, and there are advanced programmes subsequent to initial programmes. Third, there are also informal differences of reputation between institutions of the same type. This seems to be most pronounced in Japan and the United Kingdom amongst the countries surveyed. As informal differences are less easily discernible, the following analysis, except for Japan, focuses on enrolment in various types of higher education institutions and levels of programmes (OECD 1991, Wijnards van Resandt 1991, Jablonska-Skinder and Teichler 1992, OECD 1997, Meek et al. 1996).

Higher education in the countries surveyed has different patterns. One also has to take into consideration that the graduate survey did not include all types of institutions and all levels; rather it focused on graduates who were awarded a first or second degree that required at least 3 years and at most 6 years of study at institutions considered to be "higher education" institutions in the respective countries, Thus, we excluded graduates from other tertiary education institutions, from programmes requiring less than three years of study, from advanced academic programmes (leading to a doctoral degree) and from continuing education programmes. The different patterns within the segment of the higher education systems analysed will be described briefly.

Italy: More than 90 per cent of the students enrol in regular university programmes requiring 4-5 years of study up to the *laurea*. Shorter programmes were mostly established during the 1990s (Moscati and Rostan 2000, p. 1). Only graduates from the *laurea* programmes are included in our analysis.

Spain: Students can graduate after three years of successful study at a university or an *escuela universitaria* or after a regular university programme of mostly five or more years. Three year programmes tend to be newer and more regionally dispersed (Mora, Garcia-Montalvo and Garcia-Aracil 2000, p. 229). Our study includes 31 per cent of graduates from short programmes and 69 per cent from long programmes.

France: We find two-year programmes at various types of higher education institutions (extended during the 1990s to three-year programmes in some cases) as well as the DEUG 2-year certificate at universities, a three-year degree at universities (*licence*) in humanities and natural sciences, often taken as an exit point for teacher training, as well as 4-5 year programmes at universities (leading to a *maîtrise* or professional titles). Moreover, three-year programmes at the *Grandes Écoles* are subsequent to 2 years of initial study at other institutions (Kaiser and Neave 1993); thus, their degrees are considered as equivalent to five-year programmes. Our study includes graduates from 3-5 year programmes of universities as well as those from *Grandes Écoles* programmes.

Austria: University programmes require at least four years of study. Institutions in charge of teacher training for primary schools, social work etc. were not viewed as higher education institutions at the time the respondents of this survey were enrolled. Moreover, *Fachhochschule* programmes did not begin before 1993. Therefore, our survey only includes university graduates in programmes requiring at least four years of study.

Germany: Universities mostly offer programmes requiring 4-5 years of study. *Fachhochschulen*, the vocationally oriented second institutional type, provide 4-year programmes, including phases of practical experience. There are similar institutions for public administration (*Verwaltungsfachhochschulen*) which offer 3-year programmes. Comprehensive universities offer two levels of degrees: the first is similar to that of *Fachhochschulen* and the second is the same as in all other universities (Teichler 1996). Our study includes graduates with *Fachhochschule* qualifications (37%) and university degrees (63%).

Netherlands: The regular university programmes usually require four years, while the HBO (*hoger beroeps onderwijs*) institutions, usually called *hogescholen*, provide 4-year programmes, including phases of practical experience (Huisman 1996). Graduates from both the HBO sector (63%) and the universities (37%) are included in this study.

United Kingdom: Up until 1991, those who wanted to study could choose between enrolling in universities, polytechnics and other colleges, all offering bachelor degrees of mostly 3 years' and in other cases 4 years' (or infrequently even 5 years') duration. Upon graduation, some would embark on 1-2 year graduate or professional programmes. In 1992, polytechnics were upgraded to universities (Fulton 1996). In this study, bachelor graduates (94%) are included from "old universities", "new universities" (former polytechnics), colleges and the Open University, as well as a small number of master's graduates (6%).

Finland: Universities offer programmes requiring four years of study or more (Kivinen, Nurmi and Salminitty 2000, p. 165). As the introduction of a second type of higher education (*ammattikorkeakoulu*) and of bachelor degrees started only on a small and experimental basis in the early 1990s, our survey only includes graduates from university programmes requiring at least four years of study.

Sweden: University first-degree programmes vary in length by field of study between 3 and 5 years (6 years in medicine). They are offered by universities or university colleges. The higher education system in Sweden is understood as comprehensive (Bauer 1996) and universities can also offer short and vocationally oriented programmes. Also, the 3-year university programmes prepare for doctoral studies. Thus, the graduates of the 3-6 year initial university programmes surveyed (shorter programmes were not included) were not subdivided according to institutional type or length of study in the subsequent analysis.

Norway: Short programmes (2 to less than 4 years) are predominantly offered by regional or other colleges (Arnesen 1999, p. 221). Long programmes (4 or more years), possibly initial programmes or advanced programmes subsequent to the short programmes, are mostly offered at universities, but also at regional colleges. Our study includes graduates of short programmes requiring at least 3 years of study (65%) and of long programmes (35%).

Czech Republic: The regular university programmes require at least four years of study. In the early 1990s, some three-year bachelor programmes were introduced (Kucha, Hendrichová and Holda 1998, p. 4). Our study includes graduates from these bachelor programmes at universities (9%) and graduates from the regular university programmes.

Japan: The majority of graduates from higher education institutions acquire a university bachelor degree after four years of study (6 years in medicine). Some go on to 2-year master programmes. There are also junior and technical colleges with 2-year post-secondary programmes, as well as other tertiary education institutions offering mostly 3-year vocational programmes (Arimoto and de Weert 1993, p. 166). Our study only includes graduates of first-degree (bachelor) university programmes, whereby a distinction is made according to the reputation of the institutions between the most prestigious institutions (national, public and prestigious private universities), middle-level private, and finally low-level private universities.

In the subsequent analysis, we include seven countries (France, Germany, the Netherlands, the United Kingdom, Sweden, Norway and Japan) in the analysis of different types of higher education institutions and five countries (Spain, France, the United Kingdom, Norway and the Czech Republic) in the comparison between short and long programmes.

In five of these seven countries, the majority of respondents surveyed had graduated from universities. In Norway and the Netherlands, however, the number of graduates from other institutions of higher education was larger than that of those from universities. Long programmes dominate in Spain, France and the Czech Republic and short ones in the United Kingdom (see Table 9).

In many countries surveyed, students in long and traditional university programmes or the otherwise most prestigious sectors were likely to gain access to higher education via academic secondary education, while other secondary education credentials were more likely to lead to shorter programmes, other institutional types or otherwise less prestigious sectors of higher education:

Table 9. Country and Type of Higher Education Institution Attended, by Gender (percentage)

Country and type of higher education institution	Gender		
	Male	Female	Total
France			
University	80	90	86
Engineering school (grande école)	13	4	8
Business school (grande école)	7	6	6
Total	100	100	100
Count	1498	1553	3051
Germany			
University	50	57	53
Comprehensive university	16	16	16
College of art and music	0	1	0
Fachhochschule	26	17	22
College of public administration	7	10	8
Total	100	100	100
Count	2048	1439	3487
Netherlands			
University	36	37	37
HBO	63	63	63
Total	100	100	100
Count	1509	1544	3053
United Kingdom			
Old university	44	42	43
New university	42	39	41
College	8	15	12
Open university	4	3	4
Total	100	100	100
Count	1435	2008	3443
Sweden			
University	87	77	82
College	13	23	19
Total	100	100	100
Count	1116	1513	2629
Norway			
University	43	24	32
University college	5	3	4
State college	51	74	64
Total	100	100	100
Count	1371	1957	3328
Japan			
National public and prestigious private university	51	48	50
Middle-level private university	32	40	35
Low-level private university	17	12	15
Total	100	100	100
Count	2310	1110	3420

Source: CHEERS survey data

In Germany, the Netherlands and Norway, some non-academic types of secondary education offer open access to other higher education institutions, but not to universities. Hence, entry qualifications differ more substantially according to institutional and programme types than in the other countries surveyed. In Germany, only 9 per cent of the respondents from universities had non-academic secondary education, as compared to 56 per cent of those from *Fachhochschulen* (see Table 10). The respective figures for the Netherlands were 15 per cent, as compared to 69 per cent (HBO) and for Norway, it was 10 per cent, as compared to 35 per cent (state colleges).

Table 10. Percentage of Female Graduates, Graduates with Non-Academic Secondary Education, Over 25 Year Old Students at Time of First Enrolment and Graduates with Parents with Higher Education, by Country and Type of Higher Education Institution Attended

Country and type of higher education institution attended	Female	Non academic secondary education	Over 25 years at first enrolment	Parents with higher education
Italy				
University	53	31	3	30
Spain				
University	57	8	4	23
France				
University	61	9	4	35
Grande école	37	9	1	55
Austria				
University	48	31	6	26
Germany				
University	46	9	7	42
Fachhochschule	32	56	15	24
College of public administration	56	37	15	21
Netherlands				
University	54	15	6	52
HBO	57	69	8	35
United Kingdom				
Old University	58	9	12	49
New University	58	26	26	34
Colleges	73	18	25	47
Open University	52	43	96	20
Finland				
University	61	3	14	28
Sweden				
University	53	24	16	m
College	71	30	24	m

to be continued

Table 10. Continued

Country and type of higher education institution attended	Female	Non academic secondary education	Over 25 years at first enrolment	Parents with higher education
Norway				
University	50	10	10	64
University college	45	16	7	56
State college	68	35	28	42
Czech Republic				
University	58	30	4	41
Japan				
National, public and prestigious private university	46	4	1	m
Middle-level private university	54	3	0	m
Low-level private university	34	10	0	m

Question B1: Please, provide information about all higher education courses you have ever taken (include part-time, post graduate, and courses not completed).
m = missing data

Source: CHEERS survey data

In the United Kingdom, similarly, 9 per cent of the respondents with a degree awarded at an "old university" had non-academic secondary education, as compared to 26 per cent from "new universities".

In Spain, 71 per cent of the respondents with an academic secondary education qualification, as compared to 48 per cent of those with other entry qualifications graduated from a long university programme.

Table 11. Type of Entry Qualifications, by Country and Type of Degree (percentage)

Country	Type of degree	Type of entry qualification: Academic secondary	Other secondary (e.g. vocational)	Total
Spain	Short	29	52	31
	Long	71	48	69
France	Short	42	42	42
	Long	58	58	58
Germany	Short	24	85	37
	Long	76	15	63
Netherlands	Short	38	88	63
	Long	62	12	37
Norway	Short	57	86	65
	Long	43	14	35
Czech Republic	Short	9	10	9
	Long	91	90	91

Source: CHEERS survey data

In contrast, only small differences (or none at all) in entry qualifications with respect to different institutions and lengths of programmes could be observed in France, Sweden and the Czech Republic.

In almost all the countries for which data were available, the proportion of students who had parents with higher education was highest in the most prestigious sector of higher education. The selection pattern according to parental background noted in Section 1.4 in relation to secondary education, obviously continues to the stage of higher education (Euriat and Thélot 1995, Teichler 1988).

- This holds true for university students as compared to students from other types of institutions. In Germany, 42 per cent of the respondents who graduated from universities had parents with a higher education qualification, as compared to 24 per cent of those from *Fachhochschulen*. The respective figures for the Netherlands were 52 per cent, as compared to 35 per cent and in Norway 64 per cent, as compared to 42 per cent (state college).
- Similarly, the quota of students with parents with higher education was high at the French Grandes Écoles (55% vs. 35%), at "old universities" in the United Kingdom (49% vs. 34% at polytechnics) and in long programmes in Spain (27% as compared to 16%).
- Again, the Czech Republic was the exception. Students in short programmes did not differ significantly from those in long programmes as far as their parents' educational background was concerned.

Studies on educational differences by gender often point out that, while women have caught up or even surpassed men with respect to secondary education and while overall enrolment in higher education has become more or less equal by gender in industrialised societies, the advantages of men are associated with the kind of higher education chosen. Table 9 and Table 10 suggest that this holds true with respect to type of higher education institution or type and length of programmes attended in Spain, France, Sweden and Norway, but not consistently across all countries. The data are obviously confounded by the distribution according to field of study discussed below, which plays a major role in selection at this stage. Altogether, gender selection in higher education according to institutional type or type and length of programme seemed to be smaller than according to field of study.

In almost all countries surveyed, a higher proportion of mature students (over 25 at enrolment) could be found, as one might expect, outside the more prestigious sector. As can be seen in Table 9, there was a relatively high proportion of mature students at German *Fachhochschulen*, Dutch HBO, new universities in the UK, and in Norwegian state colleges. There was also a relatively high proportion of mature students in short programmes in Norway, as well as in Spain, Sweden and the Czech Republic. In France, the picture was more complex, with university long programmes having relatively many mature students, while in Japan the – anyway small – quota of mature entry students did not differ significantly according to institutional prestige.

The proportion of respondents starting study at universities immediately after acquiring the higher education entry qualifications was not consistently higher than those starting immediately at other types of institution. However, the average age at entry at other institutions of higher education was relatively high in Germany, the

Netherlands and Sweden because a substantial proportion of students at these institutions acquired their entry qualification in their 1920s.

In sum, we observe some variation of higher education programmes in all the countries surveyed. In Italy, Austria and Finland, however, exceptions to the rule of a unitary system were so rare in the early 1990s that our survey comprises only graduates from long university programmes. In Japan, only graduates from bachelors' programmes were surveyed for pragmatic reasons. In the remaining eight countries, the differences were clear and were based on institutional type and type and length of programme, or both.

As a rule, the alternatives to the most prestigious sector, i.e. the other colleges or the short programmes (in France, the universities as compared to the Grandes Écoles) are more likely to be open to the less advantaged groups. In fact, our study shows that graduates who did not acquire their entry qualification through the academic secondary education track, whose parents had no higher education qualification, who began their study at a mature age and who were women were more strongly represented in the less prestigious sector of higher education. This recalls the eternal debate as to whether "alternatives to universities" are a "cooling-out device" for the less privileged or an opportunity they would not have had without such an alternative (OECD 1991). Our data suggest that this traditional pattern of inequality is no longer so clear. Apart from the case of mature students, there are several countries where the expected relationship is not confirmed, and in some other cases, the differences in the expected direction are relatively small. What is needed is to examine the diversity as shown in the findings reported above.

7. FIELD OF STUDY

7.1. *Country and Gender*

The field of study chosen at entry to higher education largely predetermines the occupational area and the economic sector where graduates find employment. Of course, some students change field of study, and a substantial proportion never graduates. But one of the subsequent chapters shows that about two-thirds of graduates from most groups of field of study end up in one or two economic sectors that are closely related to the respective field some four years after graduation. Therefore, a strong emphasis is placed in this study on the analysis of differences of graduate employment and work by field of study.

Analysis according to field of study is complicated, because there is no single generally agreed upon grouping of fields of study. In this section, we will use both the Eurostat classification and the group according to 20 fields of study used in the UNESCO ISCED classification. For some of the analysis, we will use the Eurostat division into eight different subject fields and for more detailed analyses, we will use the ISCED division (see Figure 1).

Figure 1. Definition of Subject Groups According to EUROSTAT and ISCED

Eurostat	ISCED
Humanities	Arts, humanities
Social sciences	Social and behavioural sciences, journalism and information, business and administration
Law	Law
Natural sciences	Life sciences, physical science
Mathematics	Mathematics and statistics, computing
Engineering	Engineering and engineering trades, manufacturing and processing, architecture and building, transport services
Medical science	Including veterinary medicine and health professions
Other	Personal development, teacher training and education science, agriculture, forestry and fishery, social services, personal services, environmental protection, security services, combined general studies

There were considerable differences in the number of graduates from the various subject areas across all the countries in 1995. In the European Union as a whole, and using the Eurostat subject divisions, almost a quarter of the graduates completed social science courses (including business administration, mass communication and documentation). The "other" category of subject fields, which includes teacher education and training, accounted for the next largest group of 19 per cent, as can be seen in Table 12. "Medical sciences" (including nursing) and "engineering and architecture" came next with 15 per cent of graduates each (European Commission 1998, p. 102 and 174).

Countries varied considerably in the number of graduates from particular fields of study. For example, the social sciences were popular in Japan, the Netherlands and Norway. In Italy and Sweden, it was the "other" category (comprising education and teacher training). Engineering and architecture had large shares of graduates in Finland, Germany and the Czech Republic. Finally, medical studies were exceptionally frequent in Finland. As Teichler (2000) points out, differences are sometimes extreme. 62 per cent of graduates in Finland, but only 21 per cent in Norway were science and engineering graduates. He cited the synthesis report of the OECD project *Transition from Higher Education to Employment* as saying that "the higher education systems of industrial countries differ strikingly in their quantitative emphasis on the sciences or on the humanities and social sciences". Teichler (2000, p. 147) adds that it would be "interesting to examine how far differences in the subject composition of graduates reflect corresponding differences in the occupation and economic structure between the European countries or indicate different links between subjects and occupational areas".

Table 13 shows that, according to Eurostat data, women are most strongly represented amongst students of all the countries addressed in this study in humanities, education and medical studies and men in engineering and mathematics. Men and women are more or less equally represented in the social sciences, law and natural sciences. There are some differences in the gender distribution which, however, do not call into question the general pattern. The Czech Republic is the only exception: men dominate in the humanities as well as in "other" fields (including education).

Table 12. Graduates from Tertiary Education, by Country and Field of Study (percentage)

	Field of Study									
Country	Hum.	Soc.	Law	Nat.	Math.	Med.	Eng.	Other	Total	Count
IT	9	15	9	4	2	15	8	38	100	183
ES	10	24	14	5	4	11	13	19	100	178
FR	m	m	m	m	m	m	m	m	m	m
AT	13	21	9	5	4	11	13	22	100	19
DE	8	21	3	6	4	17	23	17	100	338
NL	8	37	5	3	2	12	12	20	100	81
UK	16	27	4	7	5	15	13	12	100	470
FI	6	9	2	3	6	30	23	22	100	28
SE	6	21	3	3	5	18	18	26	100	35
NO	22	34	4	2	1	9	9	19	100	51
CZ	28	21	5	3	2	10	23	8	100	20
EUR	11	24	6	6	4	15	15	19	100	1428
JP	16	41	**	3	***	5	20	16	100	493
Total	12	28	5	5	3	12	16	18	100	1921

* Only first university degree, ** Included in social sciences, *** Included in natural sciences.
m = missing data

Source: Eurostat, UOE, Key Data 1997, p. 174; National Statistics

Table 13. Female Students, by Country and Field of Study (percentage)

	Field of Study								Total
Country	Hum.	Soc.	Law	Nat.	Math.	Med.	Eng.	Other	
IT	79	50	57	52	43	53	23	71	53
ES	64	56	58	50	32	69	24	70	53
FR	m	m	m	m	m	m	m	m	m
AT	62	48	43	40	22	59	17	63	46
DE	61	42	43	33	23	63	15	66	43
NL	62	47	48	32	10	70	13	57	47
UK	60	50	51	45	24	77	14	68	51
FI	70	56	50	51	18	84	15	70	53
SE	64	57	52	47	27	75	20	74	55
NO	64	50	52	40	31	79	19	63	55
CZ	37	61	69	35	15	70	21	46	43
EUR	66	50	54	44	28	68	19	67	50

m = missing data

Source: Adapted from Eurostat, UOE. Key Data 1997, p. 171-72

Table 14 shows the distribution of graduates who responded to the CHEERS questionnaire by field of study and gender. We should bear in mind, on the one hand, that the Eurostat statistics include graduates from higher education institutions requiring less than three years of study, as well as graduates from institutions that are not considered to belong to higher education in their countries, but rather are viewed as "other" tertiary education or even as non-tertiary vocational education. In addition, no data are provided in the Eurostat statistics on graduates in France. On the other hand, the respondents may not be totally representative as a consequence of sampling problems or uneven return rates. Moreover, the CHEERS survey included almost the same number of graduates per country and thus, as compared to general statistics of graduates in all the countries studied, gives a higher weight to graduates from small countries. But a comparison between Table 13 and Table 14 shows that the proportion of graduates of each group of fields of study in the CHEERS study differ at most by 3 per cent from that based on official statistics.

Table 14. Female Graduates in the CHEERS Survey, by Country and Field of Study (percentage)

	Field of Study								Total
Country	Hum.	Soc.	Law	Nat.	Math.	Med.	Eng.	Other	
IT	82	50	56	57	46	52	24	59	53
ES	70	59	59	58	33	69	26	67	57
FR	67	59	58	41	23	72	24	35	51
AT	71	48	41	39	16	58	12	61	45
DE	66	42	45	34	33	47	14	66	41
NL	66	49	56	41	14	75	14	66	51
UK	71	61	53	52	43	83	25	67	59
FI	73	61	49	57	36	66	19	73	56
SE	74	57	53	71	42	69	24	78	58
NO	55	50	50	43	15	84	24	82	59
CZ	58	49	42	33	0	59	17	59	44
JP	70	21	21	24	13	48	13	50	32

Source: CHEERS survey data

7.2. Parents' Education

Prior studies suggest that some fields tend to have large proportions of students with higher education-trained parents, while in others we often find first-generation students. Amongst the graduates surveyed, the differences by field of study were by no means extreme across countries, as can be seen in Table 15. On the one hand, 42-44 per cent of graduates in arts, law, physical science and health had parents with higher education, as compared to 36 per cent of all graduates surveyed. In contrast, the proportion was 30 per cent or less in manufacturing and processing, teacher training and social services. In all individual countries, the respective differences by field of study were higher; the relatively small difference across countries is due to the fact that the fields with high proportions of students whose parents have higher education vary between countries. The largest difference can be found in Germany, where only 23 per cent of the graduates of social services had parents with higher education, as compared to 60 per cent of graduates in medicine.

In some fields of study, the relative share of graduates with parents who had higher education varied substantially between countries. For example, business and administration attracted a relatively low percentage of students who had parents with higher education in the United Kingdom and Germany, but a high percentage in Finland and France. Similarly, while the social and behavioural sciences had relatively few students whose parents had higher education in Italy, France, Austria and Finland, this was a field which was chosen fairly often by those whose parents had higher education in Spain, Germany and Norway.

Table 15. Percentage of Graduates with Parents Who Have Higher Education, by Country and Field of Study

	Country									
	IT	ES	FR	AT	DE	UK	FI	NO	Total	Count
Teacher training and education science	16	14	LN	17	35	39	17	38	29	2197
Arts	LN	24	35	LN	45	44	39	60	44	690
Humanities	29	21	34	31	38	47	27	63	36	2653
Social and behavioural science	18	29	29	19	42	40	20	57	31	2379
Journalism and information	m	18	53	24	38	30	22	LN	32	352
Business and administration	27	19	49	21	29	31	36	53	31	3559
Law	44	27	43	36	46	43	44	68	43	2149
Life science	25	35	37	24	42	57	27	63	39	746
Physical science	36	LN	46	38	46	42	25	65	44	1080
Mathematics and statistics	21	LN	41	29	48	29	LN	LN	33	449
Computing	29	28	39	13	33	32	32	62	34	795
Engineering and engineering trades	31	33	42	23	31	40	30	54	37	2810
Manufacturing and processing	LN	16	40	15	49	31	34	m	27	355
Architecture and building	27	31	LN	30	29	42	33	59	39	1020
Agriculture, forestry and fishery	31	28	m	21	34	LN	33	56	31	447
Veterinary	38	LN	m	32	43	LN	LN	LN	38	179
Health	39	28	LN	37	60	49	34	44	42	2505
Social services	m	16	m	m	23	LN	m	42	30	693
Country average	30	24	39	26	37	41	28	51	36	25798

This table uses the ISCED subject classification.
Subject fields with low numbers across all countries have been eliminated. LN (low numbers) < 20.
m = missing data

Source: CHEERS survey data

7.3. *Entry to Higher Education*

In the traditional fields of study, an above-average proportion of students comes from academic secondary education. Amongst the graduates surveyed in this study, the proportion was highest in the natural sciences (92%), law (89%) and the humanities (87%). Medical sciences (80%) were close to the average, because in various countries they included para-professional health students, a high proportion of whom had obtained vocational entry qualifications, as well as social sciences (77%). Finally, engineering and other fields (70% each) had the lowest share of graduates who qualified for entry to higher education via academic secondary education.

In some fields of study, a relatively high proportion of graduates from the various countries surveyed had begun their studies when they were over 25. This holds true for social services (26%), combined general studies (24%), teacher training and education (19%), and health studies (19%).

Many enrolled in higher education some time after having acquired the entry qualification. In contrast, the proportion of those who began their studies at a relatively advanced age was low in most areas of engineering and natural sciences.

8. THE PERIOD OF STUDY

Students have various options in the way they structure their period of study. In some countries, they can study in such a way that they are likely to complete their study and graduate at the end of the period officially required, or they may extend their study period. The length of study can be related to the number of weekly hours they spend on study. For example, they could study – officially registered that way or de facto – as part-time students, thereby accepting an overall longer period of study than full-time students. Furthermore, they could change their field of study or interrupt their study period. In those cases, the overall period of study is likely to be extended as well.

Altogether, the European graduates surveyed spent about 20 months during the overall study period predominantly on other activities, doing self-study or doing recreational activities, almost 14 months on average on paid work, of which six months were related to study or possible future work, and more than two months on internships. Child rearing and family care, search for employment and military or civilian service comprised around one month each on average. Patterns varied substantially by country, as can be seen in Table 16. Finnish students spent almost three times as many months on paid work during their overall study period as French students. Japanese respondents hardly mentioned any of these activities.

Dutch and German respondents mentioned the longest periods for internships. This is because many HBO programmes in the Netherlands and many *Fachhoch-schule* programmes in Germany require a six-month or longer mandatory period of internship.

Altogether, 35 per cent of the graduates believed that the work experience they acquired during the course of study was closely related to their studies. 30 per cent participated in internships, and 33 per cent t reported that they took jobs during their course of study which were related to their future employment.

Table 16. Duration of Activities During Period of Reference Study, by Country (arithmetic mean of months)*

	Country													Total**
	IT	ES	FR	AT	DE	NL	UK	FI	SE	NO	CZ	EUR	JP	
Employment/work not related to study or possible future work	8.9	6.3	6.8	9.5	6.0	8.6	8.8	8.5	6.0	7.9	7.2	7.6	.1	6.9
Employment/Work related to study or possible future work	5.3	4.5	2.6	9.5	6.1	5.4	3.3	14.1	4.0	6.5	7.0	6.0	.0	5.5
Work placement/ Internship (as part of your degree course)	.7	2.1	2.4	1.7	4.0	6.0	2.4	1.7	1.7	3.1	.0	2.4	.0	2.2
Child rearing/family care	2.4	1.2	.6	1.8	.8	1.0	1.6	1.5	1.4	3.0	1.2	1.5	.0	1.3
Military or civilian service	1.7	.6	.7	.7	.3	.4	.0	1.0	.5	.7	.0	.6	.0	.5
Not employed, seeking employment	.6	1.5	.7	3.0	.4	.3	1.3	.3	.4	.3	.0	.8	.0	.7
Other	2.2	1.7	.7	1.7	.7	1.3	.6	.6	.8	1.1	.0	1.0	.1	.9
Sum of activities arithm. mean	21.8	17.9	14.5	27.9	18.5	23.1	18.0	27.7	14.8	22.6	15.5	20.0	.3	18.1

Question B4: How many months between first enrolment in higher education and graduation in 1994 or 1995 did you spend predominantly on:
* Including those naming no activity of that kind.
** Count by Country: IT (3102); ES (3024); FR (3051); AT (2312); DE (3506); NL (3087); UK (3460); FI (2675); SE (2634); NO (3329); CZ (3092); EUR (33273); JP (3421); Total (36694).
Source: CHEERS survey data

During term-time, the respondents spent on average 32 hours per week on study, self-study, attending courses etc. The weekly study load varied substantially by country from slightly more than 40 hours in Italy, Spain and Sweden to about 30 hours in Austria, Finland, the Netherlands and the United Kingdom and finally 27 hours on average in Japan (see Table 17).

The weekly study time differed slightly by field of study, because different national norms prevailed. By and large, however, students in science and engineering fields seemed to spend on average about 4-5 hours more on study per week than those in the humanities and social sciences.

In addition, students spent on average about four hours per week on extra-curricular activities and about five hours on employment and work which were partly related to their studies. Two findings are most striking in this context. First, Japanese students spent more than twice as much time as European students on work during term-time in order to earn money. It is quite customary in Japan that parents pay the tuition fees and basic living costs, while students spend substantial time on "arubaito" (occasional jobs) in order to have money for a more comfortable life. On the other hand, as already reported above, Japanese respondents hardly spent any extended period during their course of study on non-study activities. Second, it worth noting that Swedish students spent little time on extra-curricular activities and employment during term-time.

Table 17. Study and Other Activities During Term-time in Reference Study, by Country (arithmetic mean of hours)*

	Country												Total*
	IT	ES	FR	AT	DE	NL	UK	FI	SE	NO	EUR	JP	
Major subjects: attending lectures	17.7	23.5	21.6	11.6	21.7	15.7	15.7	11.5	19.8	18.2	16.3	21.4	16.7
Major subjects: other study activities (inc. self-study etc.)	23.2	16.4	11.9	17.2	12.3	13.1	14.6	12.5	18.6	15.9	14.0	5.2	13.2
Other subjects	.0	2.4	.8	1.7	1.1	3.5	1.5	5.4	3.7	.2	1.7	m	1.7
Extra-curricular activities (e.g. societies, drama, sports, student union)	6.6	4.2	4.2	5.8	5.4	4.9	5.2	2.4	1.1	4.1	4.0	6.9	4.3
Employment/work (excluding work placements/internships)	4.8	4.5	4.4	7.5	5.6	7.0	5.8	5.7	2.0	4.8	4.7	12.1	5.4
Other	.6	.9	1.2	1.6	.7	.7	1.2	.9	m	.9	1.0	m	1.0
Sum of activities	54.4	52.3	45.1	46.7	47.4	46.2	45.2	41.8	46.0	45.4	47.2	46.2	47.1

Question B6: How many hours per week during your study (that you graduated from in 1994 or 1995) did you spend on average on each of the following activities? Please estimate.
* Including those not naming any activity of that kind
m = missing data
* Count by Country: IT (3022); ES (2999); FR (2981); AT (2245); DE (3469); NL (3001); UK (3372); FI (2461); SE (2584); NO (3225); EUR (29359); JP (3372); Total (32731).

Source: CHEERS survey data

The data on other programmes and other degrees awarded are somewhat confusing. In some cases, taking a prior degree was a matter of procedure to obtain a university degree (notably from a *licence* to a *maîtrise* in France), while in other cases, the award of two degrees could mean studying almost twice as long. Altogether, the data suggest that in some countries up to 10 per cent took other degrees than necessary stages of degrees, and that in some 10 per cent or more opted for a major change of their field of study before being awarded a degree in the former one.

The overall duration of the study period was 5 years on average for all respondents. Naturally, it varied according to the required length, national customs of prolongation and other factors. For graduates from long university programmes in Europe, the average period of study was 7.2 years in Italy; 7.0 years in Spain; 6.0 years in Norway; 5.8 years in Germany; around five and a half years in Spain,

France, the Netherlands and the Czech Republic; 5.1 years in Finland; and 4.7 years in Sweden.

Students of the 3-4 year German *Fachhochschule* programmes reported on average a study period of 4.3 years and those of the 4-year Dutch HBO reported 4.2 years on average. The Czech short-cycle graduates took a relatively long time on average (4.9 years). The students from mostly three-year programmes in other countries studied on average 4.3 years in Sweden, 4.2 years in France, 3.7 years in Spain and 3.3 years in Norway.

The United Kingdom and Japan are known as those countries included in the survey where students as a rule graduate within the required period of study. Bachelor graduates in the United Kingdom studied on average 3.5 years and those with a master's degree on average two years more. Japanese graduates are mostly required to study 4 years and reported an average duration of 4.1 years.

The differences between countries in the prolongation beyond the required period of study cannot be explained by differences in the weekly hours of study or by major activities outside the lecture periods which are not directly linked to study. One has to assume that other factors which contribute to extensions of the study period are in play in various countries.

9. CONCLUSION

The pattern of higher education provision in the countries surveyed differs by type of institution (including nature of programmes offered and regional location); by levels of programmes; and by informal differences of institutional reputation. In describing and analysing the relationships between socio-biographical background and educational paths we have drawn particular attention to issues of social equity and access to higher education, and the relationships between gender and higher educational outcomes. Basically, what we were interested in was "which" students went "where" to study "what".

We have seen that access to higher education continues to be more open to children of highly educated parents, but there are variations by country. For example, in Norway, the Netherlands, the Czech Republic and the UK, 40 per cent or more of the graduates had at least one parent with higher education, whereas in Spain, Austria and Finland, 70 per cent or more of graduates had parents with no higher education. And in terms of higher education entry qualifications, we find that a greater proportion of respondents with academic secondary qualifications had parents *with* higher education than those with other (vocational) types of entry qualification. Also, in many of the countries surveyed, students on long and traditional programmes (or otherwise more prestigious parts of higher education) were likely to gain access to higher education via academic secondary education. Thus, we find that in almost all the countries surveyed, the proportion of students who had parents with higher education was highest in the most prestigious sector of higher education.

In terms of "what" our respondents studied, we found great differences in students' parental background by field of study in individual countries. In Germany, only 23 per cent of social services graduates had parents with higher education, compared to 60 per cent of those in medicine. In some fields of study, there was also variation between countries in the relative share of graduates whose parents had higher education. So, for example business and administration had a relatively low percentage of students who had parents with higher education in the UK and Germany, but a high percentage in Finland and France.

Gender selection in higher education according to institutional type and length of programme seemed to be less pronounced than selection according to field of study. Women were most strongly represented in the humanities, education and medical studies, and men in engineering and mathematics.

In all the countries surveyed, older age-group students tended to have entry qualifications other than academic secondary qualifications. Whereas 85 per cent of those entering higher education at age 19 or under had academic secondary qualifications, only 47 per cent of those aged over 30 years had these entry qualifications. Further, in almost all countries, a higher proportion of mature students was found outside the more prestigious sector of higher education. In some fields of study (social services, combined general studies, teacher training and education, and health studies) a relatively high proportion of students had started their studies as mature students (aged older than 25).

Thus, we see that there are clear trends for different groups of graduates, which may well have an impact on subsequent patterns of employment. Those from better educated backgrounds are more likely to attend more academic and traditional institutions; to study different subjects from those who come from less educated backgrounds; and to do longer degrees. Men tend to be more likely than women to pursue certain subjects and to do longer degrees in most countries. Older students are more likely to be female; more likely to have vocational entry qualifications than younger students; more likely to go to less traditional and less academic institutions and to do shorter degrees. Subject choice is a key factor in this complex picture and relates to parental background, gender, age and entry qualifications.

10. REFERENCES

Arimoto, A. and de Weert, E. (1993). "Higher Education Policy in Japan." In Goedegebuure, L. et al. (eds) *Higher Education Policy: An International and Comparative Perspective*. Oxford: Pergamon, pp. 162-87.

Arnesen, C. A. (2000). "Higher Education and Graduate Employment in Norway." *European Journal of Education* 35(2), 221-28.

Bauer, M. (1996). "From Equality Through Equivalence to Quality Through Diversification: Changes in Swedish Higher Education Policy in the 1990s." In Meek, V. L. et al. (eds) *The Mockers and Mocked: Comparative Perspectives on Differentiation, Convergence and Diversity in Higher Education*. Oxford: IAU Press/Pergamon, pp. 155-62.

European Commission (1997). *Key Data on Education in the European Union 97*. Luxembourg: Office for Official Publications of the European Communities.

Euriat, M. and Thélot, C. (1995). "Le Recrutement Social De L'élite Scolaire En France." *Revue Francaise de Sociologie* 36, 403-38.

Fulton, O. (1996). "Differentiation and Diversity in a Newly Unitary System: The Case of the U.K." In Meek, L. V. et al. (eds). *The Mockers and Mocked: Comparative Perspectives on*

Differentiation, Convergence and Diversity in Higher Education. Oxford: IAU Press/Pergamon, pp. 163-87.

Goedegebuure, L. et al. (1993). "Higher Education Policy in the Netherlands." In Goedegebuure, L. et al. (eds) *Higher Education Policy: An International and Comparative Perspective*. Oxford: Pergamon, pp. 188-213.

Huisman, J. (1996). "Diversity in The Netherlands." In Meek, V. L. et al. (eds) *The Mockers and Mocked: Comparative Perspectives on Differentiation, Convergence and Diversity in Higher Education*. Oxford: IAU Press/Pergamon, pp. 138-54.

Jablonska-Skinder, H. and Teichler, U. (1992). *Handbook of Higher Education Diplomas in Europe*. Muenchen: K.G. Saur.

Kaiser, F. and Neave, G. (1993). "Higher Education Policy in France." In Goedegebuure, L. et al. (eds) *Higher Education Policy: An International and Comparative Perspective*. Oxford: Pergamon, pp. 104-31.

Kivinen, O., J. Nurmi, and R. Salminiitty (2000). "Higher Education and Graduate Employment in Finland." *European Journal of Education* 35(2), 165-77.

Kucha, P., J. Hendrichova, and D. Holda (1998). *Structure and Development of the Higher Education in the Czech Republic*. Prague.

Lopez-Valcárcel, B. G. and Quintana, D. D. (1998). "Economic and Cultural Impediments to University Education in Spain." *Economics of Education Review* 17(1), 93-102.

Meek, V.L. et al. (eds) (1996). *The Mockers and Mocked: Comparative Perspectives on Differentiation, Convergences and Diversity in Higher Education*. Oxford: IAU Press/Pergamon.

Mora, J.-G. J. Garcia-Montalvo, and A. Garcia-Aracil (2000). "Higher Education and Graduate Employment in Spain." *European Journal of Education* 35(2), 227-37.

Moscati, R. and Rostan, M. (2000). "Higher Education and Graduate Employment in Italy." *European Journal of Education* 35(2), 202-09.

OECD (1992). *Alternatives to Universities*. Paris: OECD.

OECD (1997). *Education at a Glance: OECD Indicators*. Paris: OECD.

Teichler, U. (1988). "European Practice in Ensuring Equality of Opportunity to Higher Education." *Journal of Higher Education Studies* 3(2), 2-11.

Teichler, U. (1996). "Diversity in Higher Education in Germany: The Two-Type Structure." In Meek, V.L. et al. (eds). *The Mockers and Mocked: Comparative Perspectives on Differentiation, Convergence and Diversity in Higher Education*. Oxford: IAU Press/Pergamon, pp. 117-37.

Teichler, U. (2000) "Graduate Employment and Work in Selected European Countries." *European Journal of Education* 35(2), 141-56.

Wijnards van Resandt, A. (ed) (1991). *A Guide to Higher Education Systems and Qualifications in the European Communities*. Luxembourg: Office for Official Publications of the European Communities.

JAKE MURDOCH AND JEAN-JACQUES PAUL

STUDY CONTENT AND PROCESS, COMPETENCES UPON GRADUATION AND EMPLOYMENT

1. INTRODUCTION

In studying the relationships between higher education and graduate employment and work, we were not solely interested in variations of employment and work according to countries, fields of study, type or level of degree, or any kind of quality ranking of institutions, as it was the case in most of the studies undertaken hitherto. We also wanted to find out what had been emphasised less frequently in the past (see Kogan and Brennan 1993; Brennan, Kogan and Teichler 1995), i.e. how higher education institutions shaped the study processes and if the substance of study was relevant for the students' competences upon graduation and their subsequent employment and work. We did not want to be confined to the question that is often raised "Does College Matter?". We also asked "Does the Programme Matter?" (Schomburg and Teichler 1993).

Ample research has been undertaken on the impacts of college, notably in the US (see the overview in Pascarella and Terenzini 1991), but also in other countries. However, no instrument that was generally accepted by the experts in this field emerged to measure the competence-relevant environment of higher education institutions or their departments. In an internationally comparative study, it is even more difficult to agree on the best possible measures because we do not only observe different educational environments in different national higher education systems, but we also have to take into account divergent views between countries as regards the most important dimensions to be chosen for analysing an educational environment in higher education. Hence, we decided pragmatically to choose measures of teaching and learning modes in higher education which had been developed and frequently used in studies on internationally mobile students and had been fruitful in this context to compare educational environments internationally (Opper, Teichler and Carlson 1990; Maiworm, Steube and Teichler 1991). In addition, we developed within the CHEERS research team an instrument, i.e. a question comprising a long list of items for measuring the study provisions and study conditions, taking into various prior studies (notably Teichler et al. 1987), with a list of major descriptors of the study conditions and provisions. As some of the themes that were newly addressed in the latter question should be rated in comparison to those already addressed in the former question, some items were employed in the latter which are similar or identical to some in the former question.

This chapter first deals with the modes of teaching and learning emphasised by the higher education institutions, or more precisely within the course programmes the respondents graduated from, as well as the quality of the study provisions and conditions, as they were perceived by the graduates retrospectively. In this framework, we

U. Teichler (ed.), Careers of University Graduates, 41–54

examined in what way the countries analysed, the fields of study and the types of degree programmes differed according to major dimensions of teaching and learning modes as well as provisions and study conditions. Second, we tried to establish the impacts of the modes of teaching and learning and of the study provisions and study conditions on the competences acquired up to graduation according to the graduates' retrospective assessment and on the income about four years after graduation, i.e. at the moment the survey was conducted in eleven European countries and Japan.

2. MAJOR DIMENSIONS OF TEACHING AND LEARNING MODES

The graduates had been asked to rate retrospectively which modes of teaching and learning were emphasised at the institution they had graduated from and in the course of study in which they had been enrolled. They had been provided with a list of 12 items and had been asked to rate them on a five-point scale from 1 = "to a high extent" to 5 = "not at all". The graduates of all the countries surveyed believed that theories, concepts and paradigms were most strongly emphasised, followed by independent learning, writing a thesis, and facts and instrumental knowledge. On average, they placed the following items close to the middle of the five-point scale: regular class attendance, teacher as the main source of information and understanding, freedom to choose courses and areas of specialisation, project- and problem-based learning, and detailed regular assessment of academic progress. Finally, they believed that out-of-class communication and direct acquisition of knowledge were emphasised least on average.

According to country, their average ratings were most homogeneous concerning the emphasis on the teacher as the main source of information and understanding, and on theories, concepts and paradigms. In contrast, the most striking differences in the national environments of teaching and learning concerned facts and instrumental knowledge (least emphasised in the Czech Republic, Italy and Spain) and in the assessment modes (most emphasis on writing a thesis in Italy and least in Spain, most emphasis on detailed regular assessment in Sweden and least in Austria and Italy).

In using a factor analysis, we established four indices of teaching and learning modes (see Table 1), where each one corresponded to the weighted sum of the scores of its variables :

- "Practical learning" based on the items, direct acquisition of work experience, attitudes and social communicative skills, project and problem-based learning, facts and instrumental knowledge, as well as detailed regular assessment of academic progress;
- "Free choice" using the items' freedom to choose courses and areas of specialisation, and writing a thesis;

- "Teaching", drawing from the items teacher as the main source of information and understanding as well as regular class attendance;
- "Theory" corresponds to the item theories, concepts and paradigms.

The findings will be discussed below after having presented the measures of the educational environment, i.e. the study conditions and study provisions.

Table 1. Emphasis Placed in the Course of Study on Modes of Teaching and Learning as Rated Retrospectively by Graduates, by Country (arithmetic mean)*

	Country													Total*
	IT	ES	FR	AT	DE	NL	UK	FI	SE	NO	CZ	EUR	JP	
Theories concepts or paradigms	2.1	1.8	2.2	2.0	2.2	2.3	2.0	1.7	1.9	1.8	1.7	2.0	2.1	2.0
Independent learning	2.1	3.2	2.5	2.4	2.4	2.2	2.1	2.2	2.2	2.1	2.5	2.4	2.9	2.4
Writing a thesis	1.0	4.0	2.5	2.8	2.7	2.2	1.9	2.3	2.5	2.7	2.8	2.5	2.2	2.5
Facts and instrumental knowledge	3.5	3.5	2.7	1.9	2.1	2.5	2.1	2.7	2.0	2.3	3.4	2.6	2.5	2.6
Out-of-class communication between students and staff	3.9	3.6	3.2	4.2	3.8	3.7	3.2	4.0	3.7	3.5	4.0	3.7	3.5	3.7
Regular class attendance	2.5	2.5	3.3	3.0	2.8	2.7	2.2	3.1	2.9	2.9	2.9	2.8	2.4	2.8
Teacher as the main source of information and understanding	2.9	2.6	2.9	2.9	3.0	2.8	2.9	2.9	3.0	2.8	2.8	2.9	3.2	2.9
Freedom to choose courses and areas of specialisation	2.8	3.2	2.9	2.7	3.0	3.0	2.6	2.6	3.2	3.3	3.0	2.9	2.4	2.9
Attitudes and socio-communicative skills	3.5	3.7	3.2	3.7	3.7	2.7	2.8	3.4	3.1	2.8	3.1	3.2	3.3	3.2
Project and problem-based learning	3.8	3.5	3.2	3.5	3.4	3.3	2.6	3.3	3.0	2.7	4.2	3.3	2.9	3.3
Detailed regular assessment of academic progress	4.1	3.7	3.6	4.2	3.4	3.4	2.5	3.8	1.8	3.5	3.1	3.4	3.0	3.3
Direct acquisition of work experience	4.3	4.3	4.0	4.2	3.9	3.0	3.7	3.6	3.4	3.2	4.0	3.8	4.0	3.8
Index variables														
Practical learning	3.8	3.7	3.3	3.5	3.3	3.0	2.7	3.3	2.7	2.9	3.6	3.3	3.1	3.2
Free choice	1.9	3.6	2.7	2.8	2.8	2.6	2.2	2.5	2.8	3.0	2.9	2.7	2.3	2.7
Structured teaching	2.7	2.6	3.1	3.0	2.9	2.8	2.6	3.0	3.0	2.9	2.9	2.8	2.8	2.8
Theory	2.1	1.8	2.2	2.0	2.2	2.3	2.0	1.7	1.9	1.8	1.7	2.0	2.1	2.0

Question B8: If you look back to the course of study you graduated from in 1994 or 1995: to what extent were the following modes of teaching and learning emphasised by your higher education institution and its teachers? *Scale from 1 = "To a very high extent" to 5 = "Not at all".

* Count by Country: IT (3102); ES (3009); FR (3017); AT (2291); DE (3497); NL (3047); UK (3418); FI (2657); SE (2621); NO (3311); CZ (3090); EUR (33059); JP (3407); Total (36466).

Source: CHEERS survey data

3. MAJOR DIMENSIONS OF STUDY PROVISIONS AND STUDY CONDITIONS

Graduates were also asked to rate retrospectively the conditions and provisions they had experienced in the study programme they had graduated from about four years prior to the time they were surveyed. They were provided with a list of 18 items and were asked to rate these on a five-point scale from 1 = "very good" to 5 = "not at all".

As Table 2 shows, most graduates from the 12 countries considered retrospectively the contacts with fellow students as good. They also appreciated the course content of the major, the library equipment and holdings, and the variety of courses offered. In various respects, they viewed the quality of teaching, the supply of teaching material, assistance for the final examination, the design of the degree programme, the testing and grading system, the opportunities to choose courses and areas of specialisation, the academic advice offered in general, and finally the quality of the teaching equipment (e.g. computers) as neither good nor bad on average. The ratings were less favourable for the practical emphasis of teaching and learning, the opportunities of out-of-class communication with the teaching staff, the research emphasis of teaching and learning, the chance for students to have an impact on university policies, the provision of work placements and other forms of work experience, and finally the chances to participate in research projects.

Most of these items varied to a similar extent according to country. The greatest variation was noted with respect to the provision of placements and other work experience which, according to the graduates, were least well provided by course programmes in Italy and Spain.

With the help of a factor analysis, six indices were created for the study provisions and study conditions:

- "Content and design" relied on variety of courses offered, opportunity to choose courses and areas of specialisation, design of degree programme, as well as course content of major.
- The second index, "quality of teaching and advice", used the items academic advice offered in general, assistance/advice for the final examination, as well as teaching quality.
- The third index, "equipment", was based on equipment and holdings of libraries, supply of teaching material, as well as quality of technical equipment.
- The fourth index, "research", was based on chances to participate in research projects, as well as research emphasis on teaching and learning.
- "Practical experience" was the fifth index which was created, using provision of work placements and other work experiences, as well as practical emphasis of teaching and learning.
- The last index, "communication", was elaborated on the basis of contacts with fellow students, chance of students to have an impact on university policies, as well as opportunities for out-of-class contacts with teaching staff.

Table 2. Quality of Study Provisions and Study Conditions in the Course of Study as Perceived Retrospectively by Graduates, by Country (arithmetic mean)*

	Country													Total
	IT	ES	FR	AT	DE	NL	UK	FI	SE	NO	CZ	EUR	JP	
Contacts with fellow students	2.3	2.1	2.3	2.0	2.0	2.1	2.1	2.0	1.8	1.7	2.0	2.0	2.6	2.1
Course content of major	2.7	2.8	2.4	2.6	2.7	2.4	2.1	2.4	2.3	2.7	2.5	2.5	2.4	2.5
Equipment and library holdings	3.1	2.7	2.8	2.5	2.8	2.4	2.5	2.2	2.3	2.2	3.0	2.6	2.3	2.6
Variety of courses offered	2.7	2.9	2.4	2.4	2.7	2.3	2.3	2.7	3.4	2.8	2.9	2.7	2.8	2.7
Quality of teaching	2.8	3.1	2.7	2.7	2.7	2.7	2.3	2.8	2.8	2.8	2.5	2.7	3.4	2.8
Supply of teaching material	3.3	2.9	3.2	3.0	3.0	2.6	2.8	2.5	2.4	2.4	3.0	2.8	2.8	2.8
Design of degree programme	3.3	3.4	2.6	3.0	2.9	2.9	2.4	2.7	2.7	2.8	2.8	2.9	2.8	2.9
Testing/grading system	3.3	3.3	2.9	2.9	3.0	2.8	2.5	3.3	2.6	2.6	2.6	2.9	2.9	2.9
Opportunity to choose courses and areas of specialisation	2.9	3.5	2.9	2.7	3.0	2.8	2.5	2.9	3.3	3.2	2.9	3.0	2.7	2.9
Assistance/advice for your final examination	3.0	3.7	3.4	3.4	3.0	2.9	2.6	2.8	2.8	2.7	2.3	2.9	2.4	2.9
Quality of technical equipment (e.g. PC, measuring instruments, etc.)	3.8	3.5	3.2	3.3	3.1	2.7	2.8	2.6	3.0	2.9	3.2	3.1	2.9	3.1
Academic advice offered in general	3.7	3.5	3.2	3.4	3.2	3.3	2.5	3.0	3.4	2.9	2.4	3.1	2.6	3.1
Practical emphasis of teaching and learning	4.0	3.8	3.3	3.5	3.5	2.7	2.6	3.3	3.2	3.0	3.4	3.3	3.1	3.3
Opportunities for out-of-class contacts with teaching staff	3.9	3.3	2.8	4.0	3.7	3.1	3.2	3.4	3.2	3.3	3.8	3.4	3.3	3.4
Chance for students to have an impact on university policies	3.9	3.6	3.9	3.6	3.6	2.9	3.5	3.1	3.0	3.5	3.5	3.5	3.6	3.5
Research emphasis of teaching and learning	3.9	4.2	3.3	3.4	3.6	3.2	3.1	2.9	3.5	3.5	4.0	3.5	3.1	3.5
Provision of work placements and other work experience	4.6	4.2	3.9	3.7	3.3	2.6	3.7	3.4	3.2	3.3	3.9	3.6	3.4	3.6
Chances to participate in research projects	4.1	4.2	3.5	3.7	3.8	3.1	3.5	3.5	3.8	3.9	3.9	3.7	3.7	3.7
Index variables														
Content and design	2.9	3.1	2.6	2.7	2.8	2.6	2.3	2.7	2.9	2.9	2.8	2.8	2.7	2.7
Quality of teaching and advice	3.2	3.4	3.1	3.2	3.0	3.0	2.5	2.8	3.0	2.8	2.4	2.9	2.8	2.9
Equipment	3.4	3.0	3.1	2.9	2.9	2.6	2.7	2.5	2.6	2.5	3.1	2.8	2.7	2.8
Communication	3.4	3.0	3.0	3.2	3.1	2.7	2.9	2.8	2.7	2.8	3.1	3.0	3.2	3.0
Practical experience	4.3	4.0	3.6	3.6	3.4	2.7	3.1	3.4	3.2	3.2	3.6	3.5	3.3	3.4
Research	4.0	4.2	3.4	3.6	3.7	3.1	3.3	3.2	3.6	3.7	4.0	3.6	3.4	3.6

Question B9: How do you rate the study provision and study conditions you experienced in the course of study you graduated from in 1994 or 1995? * Scale from 1 = "Very good" to 5 = "Very bad".
Count by Country: IT (3071); ES (2997); FR (3026); AT (2291); DE (3491); NL (3049); UK (3429); FI (2661); SE (2624); NO (3307); CZ (3079); EUR (33025); JP (3408); Total (36434).

Source: CHEERS survey data

4. EDUCATIONAL ENVIRONMENTS IN THE VARIOUS COUNTRIES

As compared to average ratings of the graduates across the 12 countries, the teaching and learning modes at British higher education institutions seemed to put an above-average emphasis on free choice and on practical learning. Japanese graduates also observed ample opportunities for choice, and Finnish graduates stressed practical learning. Italian universities were described by their graduates as allowing for free choice, but as giving little attention to practical learning. Norwegian graduates also rated the emphasis on practical learning as relatively low. Finally, programmes in Spain were perceived as offering little choice and little practical learning (see Table 1 above).

As regards study provisions and conditions, Table 2 suggests that the Western European countries (the Netherlands and the United Kingdom) and the Nordic countries (Finland, Sweden and Norway) stressed practical dimensions, such as practical experience, communication and good equipment above average. The average ratings by graduates from these countries, however, were not consistently similar. Notably, practical experience was rated most positively with respect to British higher education institutions, as we already have noted above.

Italy clearly seemed to have an opposite mode of functioning in those respects. Practical experience (4.3 as compared to 3.4 amongst all graduates), communication (3.4 as compared to 3.0) and equipment (3.4 as compared to 2.8) were rated very poorly by former students. Again, practical experience was rated as relatively poor in Spanish higher education institutions.

A second theme cutting across the dimensions addressed in both sets of questions (see Table 1 and Table 2) dealt with student freedom in the organisation of their studies. This dimension was based the indices free choice, as well as content and design. The higher education institutions in the United Kingdom were rated as quite good according to both dimensions. Italian universities were rated most positively and Japanese universities as well above average with respect to free choice, as already mentioned, but not above average regarding programme content and design.

Finally, the research emphasis within the study provisions and conditions was viewed as strongest by former students from the Netherlands and Finland. There seemed to be little emphasis placed on research-linked education in Spain, Italy and the Czech Republic.

Altogether, according to all the 10 dimensions presented at the bottom of Tables 1 and 2, German higher education institutions were consistently viewed as close to the average of the 12 countries. In contrast, those in Italy and Spain were seen most frequently as clearly distinct, both with respect to little practical emphasis and little research-oriented education, but otherwise varying in their difference to the average of the 12 countries.

5. DIFFERENCES OF THE EDUCATIONAL ENVIRONMENT ACCORDING TO TYPE OF DEGREE AND FIELD OF STUDY

As already discussed in the previous section, the CHEERS survey did not only include university graduates from long university programmes, but also those from bachelor-level programmes of universities and from 3-4 year programmes of other higher education institutions. We compared graduates from long university programmes (4 to 6 years) to those from other higher education institutions, i.e., HBO in the Netherlands, *Fachhochschulen* in Germany and regional or other colleges in Norway, as well as to three-year bachelor degree graduates in countries with only a university sector (Spain, France, the United Kingdom and the Czech Republic).

A simple comparison showed that the differences between these the two types of degree programmes were small with regard to most of the dimensions of the educational environment surveyed. However, we found some differences in practical and research emphasis. The data almost exclusively confirmed differences according to the two dimensions which were viewed as indicative for the two types.

On the one hand, the graduates perceived a stronger research link in teaching at the universities than at other higher education institutions in those countries where structural differentiation was based primarily on types of institutions, i.e. in Germany, the Netherlands and Norway. In addition, graduates noted more choice and freedom in long programmes in France and Germany.

On the other, a relatively strong emphasis on practical learning and experience was also reported for programmes provided by *Fachhochschulen* in Germany, HBO in the Netherlands, and in regional and other colleges in Norway. In contrast, a similar difference could not be found for France and the United Kingdom. In the case of France, the stronger emphasis on practical learning and experience in the long programmes could be explained by the large number of graduates of engineering and business schools amongst those enrolled in long degrees. In the United Kingdom, the stronger role of practical learning and experiences was quoted by graduates enrolled for four and more years, because they provided mostly information on post-graduate programmes, many of which were specialised and professionally oriented.

Although programmes in some fields of study are shaped by specific national traditions and conditions, it is worth analysing the extent to which specific educational environments exist in the various groups of field of study across the countries surveyed. Law obviously is a field which is quite specific across all the countries. Altogether, law is lowest in many countries as regards practical emphasis, student freedom to choose, the quality of teaching and the research emphasis (see Table 3 and Table 4). This is quite pronounced in countries as diverse as, for example Italy, Germany or Norway, and it is also true, though to a lesser extent, for Japan. According to the graduates, the educational environment in law was in a critical state.

Medicine stood out, as far as a practical emphasis and a structured curriculum with little choice were concerned. Indeed, medical students must cover all aspects of medicine initially, are trained for practical application and only have a choice with respect to their speciality at a late stage. Thus, the description of the educational environment by the graduates was fairly similar in all the countries surveyed.

Engineering was also described as having a practical emphasis. In contrast to medicine, however, graduates did not have quite the same freedom of choice. This was emphasised by the respondents of most countries included in the survey. The only exceptions here were France, the United Kingdom and Norway.

Table 3. Emphasis Placed in the Course of Study on Modes of Teaching and Learning as Rated Retrospectively by Graduates, by Field of Study (arithmetic mean)*

	Field of study								Total
	Edu.	Hum.	SoSc.	Law	Nat.	Math.	Eng.	Med.	
Independent learning	2.4	2.2	2.5	2.3	2.4	2.4	2.5	2.4	2.4
Theories, concepts or paradigms	2.0	2.1	1.9	1.9	1.9	1.8	2.0	2.0	2.0
Writing a thesis	2.6	2.2	2.4	2.9	2.3	2.4	2.2	2.9	2.4
Facts and instrumental knowledge	2.5	2.7	2.7	2.8	2.4	2.6	2.5	2.2	2.6
Regular class attendance	2.3	2.7	2.9	3.2	2.8	3.0	2.9	2.4	2.8
Teacher as the main source of information and understanding	2.7	2.9	2.9	3.2	2.9	2.9	2.9	2.9	2.9
Freedom to choose courses and areas of specialisation	3.2	2.6	2.7	2.9	2.7	2.8	2.8	3.9	2.9
Attitudes and socio-communicative skills	2.6	3.1	3.1	3.7	3.6	3.6	3.6	2.9	3.2
Project and problem-based learning	3.2	3.4	3.2	3.7	3.3	2.9	3.1	3.3	3.3
Detailed regular assessment of academic progress	3.1	3.3	3.4	3.8	3.4	3.4	3.3	3.2	3.3
Direct acquisition of work experience	3.2	4.1	3.8	4.4	4.1	4.0	3.8	3.0	3.8
Out-of-class communication between students and staff	3.7	3.5	3.7	4.0	3.5	3.6	3.7	3.8	3.7
Count	3690	4630	10685	2805	2410	1421	7178	3460	36280

Question B8: If you look back to the course of study you graduated from in 1994 or 1995: to what extent were the following modes of teaching and learning emphasised by your higher education institution and its teachers? * Scale from 1 = "To a very high extent" to 5 = "Not at all".

Source: CHEERS survey data

Table 4. Quality of Study Provisions and Study Conditions in the Course of Study as Perceived Retrospectively by Graduates, by Field of Study (arithmetic mean)*

	Field of study								Total
	Edu.	Hum.	SoSc.	Law	Nat.	Math.	Eng.	Med.	
Contacts with fellow students	2.0	2.3	2.2	2.3	2.0	2.0	2.0	1.9	2.1
Course content of major	2.5	2.4	2.5	2.6	2.4	2.4	2.5	2.6	2.5
Equipment and library holdings	2.5	2.5	2.6	2.5	2.6	2.6	2.6	2.5	2.6
Variety of courses offered	3.0	2.7	2.6	2.7	2.6	2.6	2.6	2.9	2.7
Supply of teaching material	2.8	2.9	2.9	3.0	2.9	2.7	2.7	2.8	2.8
Quality of teaching	2.7	2.6	2.8	2.9	2.7	2.7	2.8	2.8	2.8
Assistance/advice for your final examination	2.8	2.9	2.9	3.3	2.9	2.9	2.7	3.0	2.9
Design of degree programme	3.0	2.9	2.8	3.0	2.8	2.8	2.8	2.9	2.9
Testing/grading system	2.9	2.9	2.9	3.2	2.8	2.8	2.8	2.9	2.9
Opportunity to choose courses and areas of specialisation	3.2	2.7	2.8	3.1	2.8	2.9	2.7	3.8	2.9
Academic advice offered in general	3.0	3.1	3.1	3.4	3.0	3.0	2.9	3.2	3.1
Quality of technical equipment (e.g. PC, measuring instruments, etc.)	3.1	3.3	3.1	3.6	2.9	2.7	2.8	3.2	3.1
Practical emphasis of teaching and learning	3.0	3.4	3.4	3.8	3.3	3.3	3.2	2.9	3.3
Opportunities for out-of-class contacts with teaching staff	3.3	3.2	3.4	3.7	3.2	3.1	3.4	3.5	3.4
Chance for students to have an impact on university policies	3.4	3.6	3.5	3.6	3.6	3.5	3.4	3.5	3.5
Research emphasis of teaching and learning	3.6	3.4	3.6	3.9	2.9	3.4	3.4	3.4	3.5
Provision of work placements and other work experience	3.2	4.0	3.6	4.2	3.7	3.6	3.5	3.2	3.6
Count	3685	4622	10686	2798	2407	1417	7165	3463	36243

Question B9: How do you rate the study provision and study conditions you experienced in the course of study you graduated from in 1994 or 1995? * Scale of answers from 1 = "Very good" to 5 = "Very bad".

Source: CHEERS survey data

Education graduates perceived their studies as characterised by the importance given to structured teaching in their programme. Hence, teaching was viewed as teacher-oriented and regularity of class attendance was ensured. This held true for most countries, notably Spain, Austria, the Netherlands and Sweden. A strong practical emphasis was noted for the United Kingdom and the Netherlands.

According to the graduates' retrospective view, those in humanities were given many opportunities to design their programme of studies. Free choice was frequently referred to, except in the Czech Republic.

Finally, the natural sciences were described similarly in one respect by graduates from all countries: a strong research-orientation of education. In contrast, the modes of teaching and learning and the study provisions and conditions seemed to differ most between countries in the social sciences and in mathematics.

In examining the individual countries, we noted that teaching and learning, as well the study conditions and provisions, were extraordinarily diverse according to fields in some countries, whilst the differences, according to the graduates, were much smaller in other countries. Both Sweden and Norway seemed quite heterogeneous in this respect, whilst a common higher education culture could be observed in Spain, Italy, France and Japan.

6. IMPACTS

Educational environments in higher education have developed or are deliberately shaped in order to develop or reinforce certain competences. Also, some teaching and learning modes, as well as study conditions and provisions, could be considered as more suitable to prepare for certain careers than for others. The expectation of a link between the educational environment and respective competences and careers was most obvious in the public debate when some programmes or institutions were viewed as practice-oriented and others as research-oriented. Therefore we tried to examine how far certain dimensions emphasised in the educational environment in the course programmes, as perceived by the graduates, really led to the development of certain competences and how far they shaped subsequent careers.

The competences analysed comprised, as will be discussed in detail two sections below, language and computer skills, leadership, skills linked to the management of complex tasks and the responsiveness to unexpected events (concentration, organisation and planning, analytic skills, adaptation, etc.). Knowledge skills (theory, general knowledge, etc.), as well as behavioural and manual skills (loyalty, fitness, etc.) were also addressed. Amongst the indicators of the graduates' careers, we selected graduates' annual gross income about four years after graduation.

Regressions analyses were undertaken in order to assess the links between the educational environment, the competences acquired upon graduation, and the income about four years after graduation. Altogether, 156 regression analyses were needed to establish the impact of the various dimensions of the educational environment experienced by the graduates in their course programme on each dimension of competences and on the income in each of the 12 countries surveyed. In reporting the most important results, we only referred to findings with a regression coefficient of the standardised variables that was higher than .10.

The graduates' recollection of the educational environment and their self-rating of the competences acquired upon graduation suggested that a practical emphasis (notably the "Practical learning" index) in the course programme developed competences of leadership and of management skills (e.g. organisation and planning, adaptation and analytic skills). This was notably the case in Spain, France, the Netherlands, the United Kingdom, Sweden and Norway. In addition, we noted that an emphasis on practical experience was often reported by former students who rated their competences in information technology as high. This was true for Italy, Spain, France, Germany, the Netherlands and Finland.

Second, graduates who noted an emphasis on the quality of teaching tended to rate their general knowledge highly. This was true of most countries (France, Germany, the Netherlands, the United Kingdom, Finland, Sweden, Norway and Japan).

Third, those graduates who had been enrolled in course programmes which, according to their recollection, emphasised theoretical learning, considered themselves to be highly competent in theories. This was the case in all the countries surveyed.

Fourth, we saw that course programmes which encouraged communication amongst students and between students and teachers were more likely to lead to adaptation competences and the ability to cooperate with other people. This was observed by most graduates in Italy, Spain, Germany, the Netherlands, the Czech Republic and Japan.

Finally, graduates of some countries who had substantial free choice in their course of study considered themselves as highly competent upon graduation in IT and analytic and general knowledge skills. This was predominantly the case in Austria, Germany, the United Kingdom and Sweden.

We could also identify a link between the learning and environment in higher education institutions and income about four years after graduation in three respects. First, those having experienced a strong emphasis on the acquisition of practical experiences had a relatively high income about four years after graduation. It is interesting to note that a closer link could be established between practical experience associated with the courses and income, while, as stated above, competences upon graduation seemed to vary more strongly according to the practical learning at the higher education institutions.

Second, the quality of the course programme seemed to be relevant for the careers of graduates. As stated above, the "content and design" index was based on the variety of courses offered, the opportunities of choice and specialisation, as well as a good design and good substance, i.e. on variety, clarity and demanding level. Graduates who had experienced such an emphasis had a relatively high income about four years after graduation, notably in Austria, Germany, Finland, Sweden, Norway and the Czech Republic. In addition, good equipment in higher education was also associated with a higher income in France, the United Kingdom and the Czech Republic.

Finally, graduates who had experienced a strongly research-oriented study programme were likely to earn relatively good salaries in Germany, Sweden, Norway and Japan. In Germany and Norway, this could reflect different career opportunities of graduates from the different types of higher education institutions.

7. CONCLUSION

Most graduate surveys focus on the employment dimension, i.e. the formal elements of the world of work: employment status, employment conditions, economic sectors, occupation or position, and income. Also, many graduate surveys only comprise structural information on higher education, e.g. types of programmes and institutions, fields of study or possibly the reputation of an institution. The CHEERS survey is unique in also addressing the content dimensions of higher education and the world of work in an internationally comparative large scale survey.

According to the graduates' retrospective views, the higher education environments varied considerably between countries. Italian and Spanish higher education institutions were often described by their graduates as having little concern for practice and as having a low research emphasis in their study provisions. Moreover, the educational environment at Italian universities was criticised as poor in various respects, while graduates only seemed to appreciate the broad range of choice. Programmes in the Nordic countries as well as in the Netherlands and the United Kingdom, in contrast, were seen as being educationally targeted in the various degrees of emphasis on practical experience, good equipment and opportunities for communication.

The national characteristics of educational environments were reflected in more or less all major fields of study. However, most disciplines were also characterised by a specific educational environment in all or most countries. Medical and engineering programmes tended to be strongly practice-oriented, the former leaving little room for choice. In contrast, students in humanities enjoyed most opportunities of choice. Programmes in education were quite elaborate as far the processes of teaching and learning were concerned. Teaching in the natural science was most strongly research-oriented. Finally, the programmes in law were rated most negatively by their former students in many respects. In contrast, programmes in social sciences and mathematics varied more strongly according to national educational environments. Moreover, we observed that environments varied substantially according to discipline in some countries, e.g. Sweden and Norway, whereas they had more in common in other countries.

By and large, the graduates perceived a consistency between the educational provisions and the competences successfully fostered in many respects. An emphasis on communication in teaching and learning was likely to improve communication skills, whereas a theoretical emphasis was likely to foster the development of theoretical competences, etc. The study, however, showed that this was not true for all the dimensions of competences and not for all countries surveyed.

As regards graduates' income, the findings suggest that a research emphasis, the provision of practical experience and a demanding, well structured programme with choices were likely to be helpful. In contrast, there were fewer indications that the processes of education and the communication patterns were relevant for the graduates' income about four years after graduation. Again, we have to take into consideration variations by country and field of study.

8. REFERENCES

Brennan, J., Kogan, M. and U. Teichler (1995). "Higher Education and Work: A Conceptual Framework." In Brennan, J., Kogan, M. and U. Teichler (eds). *Higher Education and Work*. London and Bristol, PA: Jessica Kingsley Publishers, pp. 1-24.

Kogan, M. and J. Brennan (1993). "Higher Education and the World of Work: An Overview." *Higher Education in Europe*, 18(2), 2-23.

Maiworm, F., Steube, W. and U. Teichler (1991). *Learning in Europe: The ERASMUS Experience*. London: Jessica Kingsley Publishers.

Opper, S., Teichler, U. and J. Carlson (1990). *Impacts of Study Abroad Programmes on Students and Graduates*. London: Jessica Kingsley Publishers.

Pascarella, E.T. and P.T. Terenzini (1991). *How College Affects Students*. San Francisco, CA: Jossey-Bass.

Schomburg, H. and U. Teichler (1993). "Does the Programme Matter? Approach and Major Findings of the Kassel Graduate Survey." *Higher Education in Europe* 18(2), 37-58.

Teichler, U. et al. (1987). *Hochschule – Studium – Berufsvorstellungen*. Bad Honnef: K.H. Bock.

JIM ALLEN AND ROLF VAN DER VELDEN

TRANSITIONS FROM HIGHER EDUCATION TO WORK

1. INTRODUCTION

The transition period ("rite de passage") has traditionally been defined as an intermediate status between full-time schooling and full-time employment (Hannan and Werquin 1999). This traditional view has been abandoned as it became clear that the transition itself became more complex and precarious (OECD 2000). Since the eighties it has become more difficult for young people to integrate the labour market, as is reflected by longer periods of unemployment, job shifts and job mismatches. Moreover, the borderline between education, vocational training and work has become less clear, with mixed statuses (e.g. combining education and work as in the dual system), diversified pathways and more and more people crossing the line more than once in their working life.

Although the precariousness of the transition period expressed itself most clearly among those with low levels of education, the employment prospects of those with higher education also deteriorated as a result of the mass expansion of higher education in all Western societies (Teichler 1999). Concern was expressed about the effect of over-education on the returns to education (Halaby 1994). Moreover, concern has been expressed as to the long-term effects of transition problems. Does youth unemployment lead to social exclusion or is it a temporary phenomenon in the individual career? Does under-utilisation of skills lead to skills obsolescence?

Although many countries express the same concern about these issues, the problems are not universal, nor are the solutions. Some countries like the Netherlands, Germany and Japan seem to experience rather smooth transitions, whilst others like France and Spain face serious and lasting problems (Shavitt and Müller 1998; OECD 2000; Ryan 2001).

This chapter gives an overview of the transition from higher education to work in the 12 countries studied in the CHEERS project. In the first section we will concentrate on key indicators of the transition period: these include indicators of job search and job search behaviour of the graduates on the one hand and the selection criteria of the employers on the other. In the following section we will explore the relationships between the different indicators of the transition process. Finally, we will explore the effects of having a smooth or a difficult transition on later labour market outcomes.

U. Teichler (ed.), Careers of University Graduates, 55–78

2. KEY INDICATORS OF THE TRANSITION PERIOD

2.1. *Job Search*

Graduating from tertiary education does not automatically imply a transition to work. In France, Japan, and Spain more than 10 per cent of the graduates initially embarked on some form of further education after graduation (see Table 1). In some countries a substantial proportion entered the labour market prior to graduation. This was the case for 15 per cent of graduates in Finland and 14 per cent of graduates in the Czech Republic. These anomalies notwithstanding, the vast majority followed the regular pattern of entering the labour market after graduation. About three-quarters of all graduates looked for work after graduation. This percentage varied quite considerably between countries, from 88 per cent in the United Kingdom to only 54 per cent in the Czech Republic. In the latter country, 22 per cent obtained a job without searching. This was also the case with a substantial proportion of graduates in Austria (14%) and Germany (16%).

Table 1. Job Search Since Graduation, by Country (percentage)

Job search since graduation	Country													Total
	IT	ES	FR	AT	DE	NL	UK	FI	SE	NO	CZ	EUR	JP	
Yes	73	72	78	68	70	73	88	69	85	80	54	74	80	74
No, self-employed	2	2	0	1	1	2	0	2	1	1	3	1	0	1
No, job before graduation	6	6	1	6	3	5	4	15	3	4	14	6	1	5
No, study	9	12	19	9	7	6	3	2	5	5	4	7	12	8
No, job without search	7	6	0	14	16	13	3	12	6	7	22	10	4	9
No, other	2	1	2	3	3	2	1	1	1	3	3	2	2	2
Total*	100	100	100	100	100	100	100	100	100	100	100	100	100	100

Question C1: Did you look for a job since graduation in 1994 or 1995?
* Count by Country: IT (3048); ES (2977); FR (3028); AT (2278); DE (3334); NL (3065); UK (3433); FI (2656); SE (2630); NO (3303); CZ (3093); EUR (32844); JP (3402); Total (36246).

Source: CHEERS survey data

In discussions concerning the transition from school to work, a central role was assigned to the time it takes to obtain one's first job. This provides a first indication of the relative smoothness of the transition. There are different ways in which search duration can be measured. First of all, it needs to be decided what kinds of jobs are to be included under the definition of first job. The figures presented here refer to any job not considered by the respondent to be a casual job. Secondly, the search duration may depend on what point in time one considers to be the starting point of the search period. As will become apparent in the following section, there are great differences between the 12 countries in the percentage of graduates who start looking for work prior to graduation. Job search prior to graduation is fundamentally different from that after graduation for the simple reason that in the former case it is undertaken while study is the respondents' primary activity. In the latter case, a large proportion of the graduates are unemployed during the search period, or at least they are not actively participating in the labour market or in formal education. In this chapter, we put emphasis on the job search period between graduation and the first job, since it is during this period that failure to find work quickly is most likely to give rise to high material and psychological costs for the graduates. A third factor to be taken into account is how to deal with graduates who obtain work without searching. They can either be left out of the analyses, or counted as having a zero search period. In this chapter, the latter strategy is applied, since graduates who find a job without searching enjoy the smoothest of possible transitions. Finally, those who were initially self-employed or engaged in study after graduation and those who continued to work in a job they already had prior to graduation were not included in the figures, since they did not have a (potential) search period immediately after graduation.

Table 2 shows the duration of the search after graduation for the first "regular" job. Spain and Italy had the highest percentages with a search period after graduation of more than six months. Respectively 41 per cent and 34 per cent of the graduates took more than six months to find a job (many of them more than a year). This percentage was also quite high in France (27%). At the other extreme, a very small proportion of graduates in the Czech Republic (2%), Japan (5%) and Norway (6%) required more than six months after graduation to obtain their first job. It should be noted that in the latter countries, as discussed, they often looked for a job for a few months prior to, or around the time of graduation.

Table 2. Length of Search Period After Graduation for First Job, by Country (percentage)

	Country													Total
Search duration	IT	ES	FR	AT	DE	NL	UK	FI	SE	NO	CZ	EUR	JP	
0 months	19	21	23	40	48	39	32	46	46	52	60	40	86	45
1 to 3 months	28	22	31	27	26	38	41	31	32	34	33	31	5	28
4 to 6 months	19	16	19	16	14	12	14	11	11	9	5	13	5	12
more than 6 months	34	41	27	17	12	11	13	12	11	5	2	16	5	15
Total*	100	100	100	100	100	100	100	100	100	100	100	100	100	100

Question C7: For how many months did you look for your first job after graduation in 1994 or 1995? In the table only the duration of a search period *after graduation* is taken into account. Graduates who started to look for a job before graduation and who reported a search duration which was shorter than the time span from the beginning of the search to the time of graduation are considered here as having a search duration of zero months.

* Count by Country: IT (1861); ES (1835); FR (1048); AT (1465); DE (2509); NL (2172); UK (1993); FI (1505); SE (1490); NO (1952); CZ (2065); EUR (19898); JP (2620); Total (22518).

Source: CHEERS survey data

In Table 3 we examine if a "long" search period after graduation (more than 6 months) is more prevalent in some fields than in others. Despite the large general differences between the countries, there were some fairly systematic differences between fields of study, which applied across most of the countries. Many graduates in the arts and humanities and social sciences seemed to take a long time to obtain their first job in most countries. A long search period after graduation was relatively rare for graduates in engineering, health, natural sciences and business studies, although there were some exceptions. In particular, health graduates in Spain had the highest percentage, with a long search period after graduation. Law graduates showed a mixed picture. In some countries (France, Austria, the United Kingdom and Sweden), a relatively high percentage had a long search period after graduation. By contrast, this percentage was relatively low in Germany and Finland.

Table 3. Search Period After Graduation of More than 6 Months, by Field of Study (percentage)

	Country													Total*
Field of study	IT	ES	FR	AT	DE	NL	UK	FI	SE	NO	CZ	EUR	JP	
Arts and humanities	45	52	33	18	19	14	16	11	9	3	m	20	7	18
Social sciences	48	40	34	21	20	18	14	17	10	9	m	25	6	20
Business	31	42	16	15	10	5	11	14	17	3	m	16	5	15
Law	33	47	39	23	4	16	19	9	15	12	m	24	4	20
Natural sciences	41	37	23	10	14	10	11	14	13	15	m	19	3	18
Engineering	22	31	25	17	12	10	14	10	7	7	m	14	2	13
Health	25	41	25	16	6	10	5	8	4	1	m	8	3	8

Question C7: For how many months did you seek your first job after graduation in 1994 or 1995?
m = missing data
* Count by Country: IT (1861); ES (1835); FR (1048); AT (1465); DE (2509); NL (2172); UK (1993); FI (1505); SE (1490); NO (1952); CZ (m); EUR (19898); JP (2620); Total (22518).

Source: CHEERS survey data

As indicated in the previous section, the timing of the job search differed significantly by country (see Table 4). In Japan, almost all graduates started to look for work at least 3 months prior to graduation (most for more than six months prior to graduation). At the other extreme, a relatively high percentage of graduates in Italy, France and Spain waited until graduation or even later to start looking for work. The other countries were in an intermediate position.

Table 4. Start of Job Search, by Country (percentage)

							Country							Total
Start of job search	IT	ES	FR	AT	DE	NL	UK	FI	SE	NO	CZ	EUR	JP	
>3 months before graduation	11	17	8	19	29	21	35	26	25	24	29	23	96	31
1-3 months before graduation	5	6	9	12	19	21	13	18	28	39	19	18	1	17
At time of graduation	42	35	18	39	34	37	24	40	33	23	27	32	2	29
1-3 months after graduation	25	21	16	13	10	10	12	6	6	7	14	12	0	11
>3 months after graduation	17	21	48	16	7	11	15	10	8	7	12	14	1	13
Total*	100	100	100	100	100	100	100	100	100	100	100	100	100	100

Question C2: When did you start looking for a job?
* Count by Country: IT (2144); ES (2021); FR (1043); AT (1378); DE (2233); NL (2222); UK (2702); FI (1735); SE (2132); NO (2549); CZ (1669); EUR (21829); JP (2467); Total (24295).

Source: CHEERS survey data

Table 5 shows the differences in percentage of graduates who started to look for work before graduation by field of study. Although it varied quite strongly in many countries, there was no prevailing pattern across the 12 countries. Health and engineering graduates often started early in many countries, although in several countries they were among the least likely to do so. The proportion of law graduates who started to look for work prior to graduation was relatively low, particularly in Austria and Germany. In France, graduates in business studies showed a much stronger propensity to start searching prior to graduation than all other categories of graduates. In Italy, Spain, Austria and Japan, the differences between fields of study were quite small.

Table 5. Start of Job Search Before Graduation, by Field of Study and Country (percentage)

							Country							Total
Field of study	IT	ES	FR	AT	DE	NL	UK	FI	SE	NO	CZ	EUR	JP	
Arts and humanities	20	17	15	32	30	33	41	46	49	73	m	39	97	45
Social sciences	15	29	16	39	39	46	40	28	46	56	m	34	96	46
Business	20	32	28	38	51	45	53	49	50	70	m	43	97	49
Law	16	19	15	7	13	36	54	39	39	30	m	24	98	36
Natural sciences	10	27	15	37	46	41	47	37	41	59	m	36	100	39
Engineering	15	27	17	30	56	44	58	54	59	66	m	47	98	52
Health	10	18	0	34	61	50	79	46	75	61	m	50	98	51

Question C2: When did you start looking for a job?
m = missing data
* Count by Country: IT (2144); ES (2021); FR (1043); AT (1378); DE (2233); NL (2222); UK (2702); FI (1735); SE (2132); NO (2549); CZ (m); EUR (21829); JP (2467); Total (24295).

Source: CHEERS survey data

The search methods differed greatly by country (see Table 6). The "conventional" method of applying for an advertised vacancy was frequently used in all countries, although noticeably less in Italy than in the other countries. With the notable exception of German and Japanese graduates, contacting employers without waiting for a vacancy also proved to be a popular method. Placing an advertisement only seemed to be popular among German graduates. Not really a search method, but certainly a possible way of finding a job was to be approached by an employer. This only applied to a minority of graduates in all countries, although about a quarter of the Czech graduates and a fifth of the Italian, Dutch, Finnish and Norwegian graduates indicated that they had been approached by an employer. Public employment agencies were commonly used in almost all countries, although the percentage of graduates who used this particular channel was low in Japan, the United Kingdom and Norway. Commercial agencies seemed to be popular in the Netherlands, and to some extent in Spain and the United Kingdom.

Table 6. Methods Used in Searching for First Job After Graduation, by Country (percentage)

	Country													Total
Search method	IT	ES	FR	AT	DE	NL	UK	FI	SE	NO	CZ	EUR	JP	
Reply to advertisement	48	61	75	64	74	84	69	73	78	84	62	71	73	71
Contacted employers	70	43	79	65	60	69	40	62	61	41	63	57	13	52
Public employment agency	40	52	63	32	40	42	26	43	48	23	38	39	13	36
Personal connections	54	49	39	36	26	37	27	20	25	15	38	32	21	31
Careers placement office	10	40	14	13	7	12	37	26	3	3	19	17	63	22
Contacts during study	11	12	21	24	28	31	17	28	20	21	20	21	3	19
Approached by employer	19	8	10	4	12	19	9	21	18	19	26	15	14	15
Commercial employment agency	14	33	16	13	4	54	27	4	m	6	22	20	13	19
Teaching staff	13	8	6	11	8	12	9	9	5	6	10	9	23	10
Placed advertisement	10	10	24	13	11	1	1	11	1	1	7	7	1	6
Self-employment	9	4	2	6	6	2	2	4	m	1	3	4	0	3
Other	8	39	12	7	10	5	7	4	5	4	4	9	10	9
Total	306	359	361	288	286	368	271	305	264	224	312	301	247	293
Count	2143	2106	1122	1487	2284	2238	2889	1791	2181	2627	1672	22539	2671	25210

Question C4: How did you try to find your first job after graduation?

Source: CHEERS survey data

The high percentage of Japanese graduates who started to search for work prior to graduation was reflected in the search methods. The most popular was the career placement office at their institution. This method was also quite commonly used in Spain and the United Kingdom, but very little in most other countries. Japanese graduates also made more use of the assistance of teaching staff at their school than graduates in other countries, although this method was much less popular than the careers placement office. Interestingly, Japanese graduates were least likely to make use of other contacts established during their course of study. This method was most often used in Germany, the United Kingdom and Finland. A relatively high percentage of graduates in Italy and Spain made use of other personal contacts (family, friends, etc.) This percentage was relatively low in Germany. In this country, a relatively high proportion of graduates attempted to set up their own business as a way of finding their initial employment after graduation.

The use of a given method says little in itself about successful means of finding work. Therefore graduates were asked to state which method was the most successful for them. As Table 7 suggests the pattern changed. Application for an advertised vacancy and self-search were the most successful methods, as Table 7 shows, leading to success in the case of almost one third and almost one fifth of all the graduates respectively. Private contacts were decisive for one seventh. In contrast, search with the help of a public employment agency was crucial for only about one tenth of the graduates. Applying for an advertised vacancy was the most successful method of job search in seven of the countries surveyed, notably in Norway, Sweden and the United Kingdom. Searching on one's own initiative was the most successful method in Austria, the Czech Republic and France, while private contacts were very important in Italy and Spain.

Table 7. Most Important Method for Finding First Job After Graduation, by Country (percentage)

	Country													Total
Search method	IT	ES	FR	AT	DE	NL	UK	FI	SE	NO	CZ	EUR	JP	
Reply to advertisement	11	20	17	25	33	24	40	31	40	55	18	31	31	31
Contacted employers	20	14	29	33	25	15	12	25	24	13	31	20	3	19
Personal connections	31	28	19	16	11	8	12	7	7	6	20	14	13	14
Contacts during study	4	4	7	10	10	11	7	11	5	10	7	8	1	7
Approached by employer	8	3	3	2	4	7	3	8	12	7	6	6	6	6
Commercial employment agency	1	4	1	1	0	21	11	1	0	1	2	5	5	5
Careers placement office	2	4	3	2	1	1	6	2	0	1	5	2	21	5
Public employment agency	0	5	11	2	3	4	2	6	5	2	4	4	2	4
Teaching staff	3	1	1	2	3	3	1	4	1	2	2	2	9	3
Placed advertisement	1	2	1	1	1	0	0	1	0	0	1	1	0	1
Self-employment	4	2	1	1	2	1	1	1	0	1	1	1	0	1
Other	14	13	8	4	8	4	4	3	6	2	2	6	8	6
Total	100	100	100	100	100	100	100	100	100	100	100	100	100	100
Count	1841	1837	1023	1275	2164	2180	2718	1715	1941	2552	1620	20865	2546	23411

Question C5: Which method was the most important for finding your first job after graduation in 1994 or 1995? Please fill in the item number from question C4.

Source: CHEERS survey data

In order to see the relative effectiveness of the methods employed, for each method the proportion of graduates who indicated that it was most important for obtaining their first job was calculated, expressed as a percentage of the number of graduates who used it. These percentages are shown in Table 8.

Table 8. Efficiency Rate of Methods Used in Searching for First Job After Graduation, by Country (percentage of graduates who used a specific search method)

	Country													Total
Search method	IT	ES	FR	AT	DE	NL	UK	FI	SE	NO	CZ	EUR	JP	
Personal connections	62	58	47	42	3	23	42	34	28	38	55	42	63	44
Reply to advertisement	23	32	22	36	44	29	55	41	49	64	28	42	42	42
Approached by employer	31	27	32	35	27	34	32	35	53	35	23	34	37	34
Contacts during study	36	33	31	37	33	28	37	37	21	49	33	34	39	35
Contacted employers	28	31	36	48	1	21	29	40	39	32	49	31	23	31
Self-employment	41	44	59	23	14	39	35	30	m	26	20	31	73	31
Commercial employment agency	8	12	6	8	7	39	41	17	m	12	10	25	34	26
Teaching staff	24	16	11	14	40	26	12	40	25	29	25	24	37	27
Careers placement office	16	11	18	14	8	11	15	10	8	28	26	14	33	20
Placed advertisement	10	14	4	10	23	0	0	13	m	6	17	12	29	12
Public employment agency	1	9	17	6	7	10	8	14	10	9	11	9	18	10
Other	67	37	65	64	73	64	63	64	63	53	58	54	82	58
Count	1841	1837	1023	1275	2164	2180	2718	1715	1941	2552	1620	20865	2546	23411

Questions C4 and C5: see Tables 6 and 7.
m = missing data

Source: CHEERS survey data

In general, the most efficient methods were applications for advertised vacancies, direct contact with employers and use of contacts either established during the course of study or outside. Being approached by an employer and self-employment were also generally efficient, although less so than one could imagine. In about two-thirds of the cases when an employer approached graduates, this did not result in a job. It is not clear from the data whether this was decision on the part of the employer or of the graduates. Similarly, many attempts to set up one's own business failed. Public employment agencies showed a low efficiency rate in most countries, which may indicate that for many graduates they were not so much a search channel as a requirement for entitlement to unemployment benefits. Commercial employment agencies frequently found jobs for graduates in the Netherlands and the United Kingdom while, for a relatively high number of Japanese graduates, it was the careers placement offices at their school or the teaching staff that found them a job. These methods had a much lower success rate in most of the countries, which may indicate that they may play a different role in different countries. In Japan and some other countries, the educational institutions and/or their staff may see it as part of their task to mediate between graduates and employers, whereas in other countries these activities may be restricted to those graduates who have trouble in finding work through other means. This also seemed to be the case for placing an advertisement which, judging by the low success rates in most countries, was a last resort when all else failed.

In the previous section, we saw that great differences between countries existed in the search period after graduation. It is interesting to see how active the graduates were during this search period and the number of employers contacted. Table 9 shows the mean number of employers contacted by graduates prior to obtaining their first job. Because these figures may be influenced by the length of the job search after graduation, they are broken down accordingly.[1]

Table 9. Number of Employers Contacted Before First Job, by Length of Search Period After Graduation and Country (mean)

	Country													Total
Search duration	IT	ES	FR	AT	DE	NL	UK	FI	SE	NO	CZ	EUR	JP	
1 to 3 months	12	31	33	15	20	8	21	8	9	12	6	15	11	15
4 to 6 months	19	45	75	28	28	19	33	16	17	35	12	30	16	30
More than 6 months	23	59	140	44	57	31	70	19	27	50	12	52	23	51
Total	18	48	75	25	26	13	32	11	14	15	6	24	20	24
Count	1477	1451	874	994	1845	1694	1798	1164	1137	1680	1336	15449	2417	17866

Question C6: How many employers did you contact before you took up your first job after graduation in 1994 or 1995?

Source: CHEERS survey data

In general, the number of employers contacted increased with the length of job search after graduation. There was without exception a positive relation between the length of search after graduation and the number of employers contacted. However, in Italy, Spain, Finland, the Czech Republic and Japan, this increase tapered off as the length of search after graduation grew, which may suggest that in those countries a high search intensity was effective to help graduates to obtain work quickly. In the other countries the number of employers contacted continued to rise quite sharply, even for those who had searched for quite a long time. This was especially noticeable for French graduates: those with a search period of six months or more after graduation had contacted an average of 139 employers before obtaining their first job.

[1] Graduates with zero search duration after graduation were not included in the table. Many had had a substantial search period *prior to graduation,* during which time they had contacted a large number of employers. Important for our purposes is the development of the search intensity over the time *after* graduation.

2.2. *Employers' Selection Criteria*

Graduates were asked to rate the importance of various selection criteria for employers in their initial job after graduation. Table 10 presents the percentage of graduates who indicated that a given criterion was "important" or "very important" for the employer who recruited them. In general, "personality" and "field of study" were most often quoted by graduates as being (very) important. The importance of these two criteria differed however from country to country. "Personality" was least important in the Czech Republic, Italy and Spain and most important in the Netherlands. Japan had a relatively low percentage of graduates who mentioned "field of study" as an important criterion. This percentage was also quite low in the United Kingdom, and very high in Finland. "Main subject or specialisation" was also an important criterion in most countries, although there were great variations. This percentage was especially high in Finland and France, whereas Japan and the Czech Republic showed relatively low scores.

Table 10. Importance of Recruitment Criteria According to the Graduates' Perception, by Country ("important" percentage, answers 1 and 2)

	Country													Total
Recruitment criterion	IT	ES	FR	AT	DE	NL	UK	FI	SE	NO	CZ	EUR	JP	
Personality	58	61	74	80	78	83	81	75	81	m	57	73	80	74
Field of study	70	68	69	77	77	68	54	85	78	m	78	72	37	68
Main subject/ specialisation	38	62	66	46	51	36	45	73	57	m	28	49	32	47
Work experience during studies	21	20	52	49	55	50	41	54	29	m	31	40	16	38
Computer skills	35	42	40	47	44	36	40	37	19	m	57	40	17	37
References	21	29	26	29	27	28	45	32	49	m	29	32	27	32
Exam results	37	24	8	17	42	11	39	34	24	m	25	28	28	28
Work experience before studies	10	29	18	16	29	17	30	22	23	m	15	22	5	20
Reputation of institution	19	16	19	17	16	15	23	24	23	m	26	20	41	22
Experience abroad	11	11	21	16	13	13	10	17	17	m	15	14	8	13
Foreign language skills	25	26	28	31	24	20	9	40	23	m	42	26	13	24
Count	1791	1983	1030	1664	2602	2527	2832	1997	2040	m	2281	20784	2475	23273

Question C8: How important, according to your perception, were the following aspects for your employer in recruiting you for your initial employment after graduation? Scale of answers from 1 = very important to 5 = not at all important.

m = missing data

Source: CHEERS survey data

"Work experience during study" also varied greatly by country. About half the graduates in Germany, France, Finland, the Netherlands and Austria thought that this criterion was (very) important. By contrast, in Italy, Spain and Japan less than a quarter thought so. A third study-related criterion which varied greatly in its importance was exam results. The percentage of graduates who felt that this was an important criterion was relatively high in Germany and the United Kingdom, but very low in France and the Netherlands. "Reputation of the educational institution" only seemed to be important as a selection criterion in Japan, where it was slightly more important than "field of study". "Computer skills" seemed relatively important as a selection criterion in the Czech Republic and relatively unimportant in Sweden and Japan. "References" were relatively important in the United Kingdom and Sweden. "Foreign language proficiency" was quite often quoted as an important criterion in Finland and the Czech Republic, and was not at all important in the United Kingdom and Japan. The low score in the latter two countries reflects their strong focus on their own language. "Work experience before study" and "experience abroad" were generally rather unimportant as selection criteria in the majority of cases.

In looking at the configuration of the criteria, we noted that the combination of specific knowledge (field of study and additionally the area of specialisation) and personality were at the top of the list in all European countries, whilst, in Japan, personality stood out and the reputation of the higher education institution came next. Other major criteria were computer skills in the Czech Republic as well as work experience during one's studies in Germany, Finland, the Netherlands and Austria.

Table 11 shows the variation between country in the importance of three distinctive selection criteria. The first is field of study, the second the reputation of the educational institution, and the third the personality of the graduate.

Table 11. Importance of Selected Recruitment Criteria, by Field of Study (percentage of "important", answers 1 and 2)

	Country												Total
Field of study	IT	ES	FR	AT	DE	NL	UK	FI	SE	NO	CZ	EUR	JP
Recruitment criterion													
Arts and humanities	52	66	57	71	69	69	44	88	80	m	m	67	33	62
Social sciences	40	66	51	58	74	60	35	78	73	m	m	58	21	50
Business	76	66	80	76	74	64	53	76	72	m	m	71	23	66
Law	76	62	78	86	83	63	67	92	76	m	m	76	23	67
Natural sciences	69	78	73	76	73	77	57	88	82	m	m	72	51	71
Engineering	83	76	77	75	78	68	71	86	78	m	m	77	66	76
Health	90	61	47	94	92	74	82	94	85	m	m	80	74	80

to be continued

Table 11. Continued

	Country													Total
Field of study	IT	ES	FR	AT	DE	NL	UK	FI	SE	NO	CZ	EUR	JP	
Reputation of institution														
Arts and humanities	11	10	9	8	8	14	19	21	17	m	m	15	40	18
Social sciences	8	16	8	9	11	11	19	15	19	m	m	14	47	21
Business	25	15	28	24	18	17	15	28	21	m	m	21	33	22
Law	22	10	13	24	3	14	33	20	17	m	m	18	41	22
Natural sciences	14	17	25	16	15	18	22	16	18	m	m	19	40	20
Engineering	28	25	25	27	25	18	30	40	36	m	m	28	44	30
Health	16	15	16	10	10	12	42	17	22	m	m	22	34	22
Personality														
Arts and humanities	56	57	73	75	65	83	83	78	80	m	m	74	84	76
Social sciences	60	68	73	85	89	83	87	81	79	m	m	78	84	79
Business	63	74	79	95	76	88	84	83	93	m	m	82	85	82
Law	62	60	77	78	55	91	78	86	51	m	m	70	82	72
Natural sciences	51	61	65	75	76	78	80	64	74	m	m	70	72	70
Engineering	54	64	78	81	83	77	80	70	82	m	m	75	67	74
Health	56	50	100	67	88	86	81	55	76	m	m	64	76	64

Question C8: How important, according to your perception, were the following aspects for your employer in recruiting you for your initial employment after graduation? Scale of answers from 1 = very important to 5 = not at all important.
m = missing data
Count by Country: IT (1791); ES (1983); FR (1030); AT (1664); DE (2602); NL (2527); UK (2832); FI (1997); SE (2040); NO (m); CZ (m); EUR (20784); JP (2475); Total (23273).

Source: CHEERS survey data

"Field of study" was generally an important selection criterion for graduates in health, law and engineering, and not for graduates in social sciences and arts and humanities. There were, however, notable exceptions. It was relatively unimportant for health graduates in Spain and France and law graduates in Japan.

"Reputation of institution" was generally very important in engineering and business, although in the United Kingdom and Japan business graduates were least likely to quote it. In general, graduates in social sciences, arts and humanities, and health were fairly unlikely to quote it as an important criterion. One exception was the United Kingdom where health and law graduates were most likely to find it an important criterion.

Social science and business graduates were likely to mention "personality" as an important selection criterion. Few graduates in arts and humanities and the natural sciences regarded this criterion as important.

3. RELATIONSHIPS BETWEEN TRANSITION CHARACTERISTICS

In this section we shall try to determine how different aspects of the transition are related. Do graduates who started to look for work before graduation search differently from those who started around or after graduation? To what extent do the timing and the intensity of the job search affect the duration of the search? Do graduates who took a long time to find their first job encounter different selection criteria from those experienced by graduates who found their first job quickly?

Two key indicators are the start of the job search and the number of employers contacted. Graduates may try to improve their chances of a successful transition by starting early in their search, or by approaching a large number of employers. It is of interest to see to what extent the use of one of these strategies also implied the use of the other. The two strategies may be complementary, may substitute each other, or may even be unrelated. In Table 12 the mean number of employers contacted per month of job search (subsequently called "search intensity") is presented separately for those who started searching before, around and after graduation.

Table 12. Number of Employers Contacted per Month, at Time of Starting the Job Search and by Country (mean)

	Country													Total
Start of job search	IT	ES	FR	AT	DE	NL	UK	FI	SE	NO	CZ	EUR	JP	
Prior to graduation	3.7	7.5	10.9	6.6	5.7	3.8	12.2	3.9	5.8	4.7	2.5	5.8	4.4	5.4
Around graduation	4.4	8.3	16.2	5.0	5.9	3.5	7.1	3.2	4.5	4.8	3.5	5.3	1.7	5.3
After graduation	3.5	7.5	12.8	6.1	5.3	2.7	8.7	3.7	2.8	4.6	3.5	6.2	3.9	6.2
Total	3.9	7.8	13.0	5.8	5.7	3.5	9.7	3.6	4.8	4.7	3.0	5.8	4.4	5.6
Count	1472	1459	853	994	1838	1692	1804	1145	1134	1683	1336	15413	2230	17643

Questions C2, C6 and C7: see Tables 2, 4 and 9.

Source: CHEERS survey data

In most countries there was little difference in search intensity between those who started to seek before, around and after graduation. This suggests that the two strategies were not closely related. Those who started searching early were not necessarily likely to contact a large number of employers. There were some exceptions, which however did not conform to any general pattern.

In France, search intensity was highest among those who started searching around graduation and lowest among those who started prior to graduation. This may indicate that the two strategies were to some extent substitutes for each other. Those who did not start to look for work until around the time of graduation may attempt to compensate for this by approaching more employers. However, this fails to account for the fact that the large proportion of French graduates who waited until after graduation searched less intensively than those who started around the time of graduation.

The opposite pattern was observed in the United Kingdom. The highest level of search intensity was found among graduates who started to look for work prior to graduation, and lowest among those who started to look at the time of graduation. This seems to indicate that timing and intensity may be to some extent complementary, since an early start was often accompanied by a high number of job applications. A clearer pattern of complementarity was found in Sweden, and to some extent also in the Netherlands, where search intensity was negatively related the start of the job search.

Table 13 shows the relationships between the duration of the job search after graduation and the most successful method in obtaining the first jobs. Since graduates were free to use any or all of the methods, a long search period only indicates that the method in question was disproportionately successful for graduates who failed to find work quickly. This could mean that the method itself was not very effective, or that it was a last resort for graduates who had trouble in finding work by other means.

Graduates who successfully contacted employers without knowing about a vacancy generally had a relatively short search period after graduation. The same applied to those who obtained their first job through the careers placement office at their institution, through contacts established during the course of their studies, as a result of being approached by an employer, or, as in Spain, Germany, the Czech Republic and Japan, through the teaching staff at their institution.

Interestingly, those who obtained their first job by enlisting the help of social contacts who were not related to their studies had a relatively long search period after graduation on average. This suggests that this form of "social capital" may be more of a remedy than a choice used to ensure a smooth transition. Graduates whose first job was obtained by enlisting the help of public employment agencies had a relatively long search period on average. This did not apply to those who obtained work through a commercial agency: in several countries, the search of these graduates was quite short. The most commonly used method that of replying to an advertisement, occupied intermediate position in most countries.

Table 13. Search Duration After Graduation, by the Most Important Search Method and Country (mean)

	Country												Total
Search method	IT	ES	FR	AT	DE	NL	UK	FI	SE	NO	CZ	JP	
Careers placement office	4.1	7.7	4.7	3.4	3.4	2.4	2.4	5.1	m	0.5	1.4	0.7	2.0
Teaching staff	7.2	5.3	7.8	3.0	2.2	4.0	2.0	6.0	2.5	2.7	1.3	0.4	2.6
Placed advertisement	9.4	11.0	2.6	3.9	2.5	1.0	m	2.7	m	m	1.5	1.3	3.0
Contacts during studies	6.6	8.7	2.6	4.2	2.3	3.2	2.3	3.4	1.5	1.2	0.9	1.8	3.1
Reply to advertisement	7.8	8.4	7.7	5.0	4.2	3.3	3.4	3.2	3.6	1.6	1.5	1.0	3.4

to be continued

Table 13. Continued

Search method	IT	ES	FR	AT	DE	NL	Country UK	FI	SE	NO	CZ	JP	Total
Contacted employers	7.2	7.3	5.7	4.8	3.4	2.6	2.9	3.2	3.3	1.9	1.3	0.4	3.9
Approached by employer	6.4	6.6	4.0	3.5	4.0	2.9	4.7	4.1	4.1	1.5	1.2	0.5	3.4
Commercial employment agency	6.4	11.6	5.3	7.3	2.4	3.2	2.9	1.9	m	2.9	1.3	0.2	3.4
Public employment agency	20.0	10.4	7.9	6.6	5.3	4.3	4.6	6.2	4.1	4.7	2.1	4.4	5.8
Personal connections	8.0	10.8	7.9	7.6	6.5	4.5	3.8	5.8	2.7	4.1	1.9	1.4	5.9
Self-employment	10.6	13.1	7.6	10.7	5.1	9.1	8.8	2.7	m	2.3	3.0	0.9	6.7
Other	11.0	14.7	7.4	4.5	5.8	6.7	3.0	4.3	5.5	3.7	0.6	3.2	7.8
Total	8.1	10.0	6.6	5.3	3.8	3.4	3.3	3.8	3.6	1.9	1.5	1.1	4.1
Count	1633	1630	896	1060	1919	1781	1882	1178	1193	1712	1398	2471	18753

Questions C5 and C7: see Tables 2 and 7.

Source: CHEERS survey data

A number of multivariate (ordinary least squares regression) analyses were conducted in each country to determine the relationship, if any, between search behaviour and the time taken to obtain work. The dependent variable in each case was the natural logarithm of the search period in months after graduation.

Two indicators were used: the moment when graduates started looking for work (before, around or after graduation), and the search intensity in terms of the number of employers contacted per month of job search. As was the case for the search period, the latter variable was also included in logarithmic rather than linear form.

In order to properly assess the effects of search behaviour, it is important to take into account the characteristics of graduates at the time of graduation. The relation between search behaviour and search period may be a spurious one because both are influenced by graduate characteristics. In the analyses, we included as control variables field of study (with arts and humanities as reference category) and type of studies (at universities or other institutions), grades upon entry to higher education, age, gender, work experience obtained during study, work placement during studies, duration of studies, and hours per week spent during the course on studies and on extracurricular activities. For each country two analyses were conducted. First, a model was estimated which contained only the graduate characteristics, and subsequently a model was estimated in which the indicators of search behaviour were added. In this way we could not only determine whether search behaviour had an effect, but also whether this effect in any way altered or accounted for the relation between graduate characteristics and search duration.

Table 14. Determinants of Search Duration, by Country

		Country											
		IT	ES	FR	AT	DE	NL	UK	FI	SE	NO	CZ	JP
1	Field of education (humanities = reference cat.)												
	Social sciences				+/0				+/+	+/+	+/+		
	Business		–/0		+/0		–/–	–/0	+/+	+/+	0/+	+/0	
	Law								+/+	+/0	+/+		–/0
	Natural sciences		–/0				–/0				+/+	+/0	
	Engineering	–/–	–/0				–/0			0/+	+/+	+/0	–/0
	Health	–/–			0/–	–/–	–/–	–/–		–/0			–/0
2	Type of education (university type = ref. cat.)												
	Non-university	m	m		m	–/0		+/0	m	m	–/–	m	m
3	Grades (ref. cat. = low grade)												m
	High		–/0	–/–		–/0		–/–					m
	Medium							0/–					m
4	Age					+/0							
5	Gender (ref. cat. = male)												
	Female		0/+	0/+		+/0						+/0	
6	Experience during study	–/–	–/–	–/–	–/0	–/–	–/–			0/–	–/0	–/0	
7	Work placement		–/0									m	
8	Study duration									m		m	m
	Up to 1 year too long			0/+		+/0				m		m	m
	More than 1 year too long					+/+				m	+/0	m	m
9	Study intensity (hours per week)				0/+							m	
10	Extracurricular activity (hours per week)							–/0			0/–	m	
11	Start of job search (ref. cat. = around graduation)												
	Prior to graduation	–	–	–	–	–	–	–	–	–	–	–	–
	After graduation												
12	Search intensity	–	–		–		–	–	–	–	–	–	–

+ significant positive effect; – significant negative effect; m = variable not included; +/– signs before slash: significant effect before the search variables are included, and after the slash after they were included; 0 and blanks: no significant effects.

Source: CHEERS survey data

Table 14, which gives an overview of the significant outcomes of these analyses, shows that field and type of education are related to search duration in many countries, although the pattern of effects is not generally consistent across countries. Exceptions were graduates in the social sciences, who searched for a long time in several countries, and health graduates, who often seemed to have a shorter search period. High grades on entry to higher education were associated with a shorter search period in several countries. Women sought longer than men in some countries. In many countries, work experience acquired during the course of study reduced the search period. This may to some extent be due to increased market value through acquired experience, but also to the contacts that experienced graduates had established with employers.

Looking at the search behaviour, it was apparent that an early start to the job search greatly reduced the duration of the search after graduation in all countries. But it did not seem to make any difference whether graduates started to seek around the time of graduation or thereafter. A high search intensity, in terms of employers contacted per month of job search after graduation, reduced search duration in most countries. These results show that graduates had some influence over the time taken to obtain their first job. By starting earlier and by seeking more intensively, they increased their chances of finding work quickly.

Table 15 (see next chapter) shows the relationships between the duration of job search after graduation and the perceived importance of various selection criteria for obtaining the first job after graduation. There is obviously no question of a causal relation here.

In general, most criteria were more important for those with a short search duration after graduation than for those who sought for a longer period. This seems to suggest that after failing to find work quickly, graduates "lowered their sights" and applied for vacancies for which the requirements were less stringent. The differences varied considerably between countries and between criteria. The difference in employer requirements was most pronounced in France and Germany, and least in the Netherlands, the United Kingdom and Sweden. The difference between short and long duration was generally great for the field of education and main subject or specialisation criteria. By contrast, employers of graduates who found work quickly hardly differed from those of graduates who took longer to find a job in terms of the importance they attached to the experience prior to study, experience abroad, foreign language proficiency, computer skills, references and personality.

4. JOB SEARCH AND LABOUR MARKET OUTCOMES

In this section, we shall examine how far the smoothness of transition affected the graduates' later labour market outcomes. Notably, the duration of the job search after graduation was taken into consideration. In a number of multivariate analyses, we tried to establish the effects of (the natural logarithm of) search duration on the probability of finding a job for which one's own level of education was a minimum requirement, the probability of having a temporary job and on the (natural logarithm of) the hourly wage in the current main job. The former two analyses comprised logistic regression analyses, the latter ordinary least squares regression. As in the analyses of the previous section, we verified the effects of graduates' characteristics at the time of graduation.

Table 15. Importance of Recruitment Criteria, by Search Duration and Country (percentage)

Recruitment criterion	Country													Total*
Duration	IT	ES	FR	AT	DE	NL	UK	FI	SE	NO	CZ	EUR	JP	
Field of study														
Short	75	70	73	79	79	68	50	87	78	m	78	73	37	68
Long	62	58	59	71	62	66	47	72	77	m	66	63	27	61
Main subject/ specialisation														
Short	41	63	69	48	53	35	43	73	58	m	27	48	32	46
Long	30	52	58	39	37	36	39	58	57	m	18	44	25	43
Exam results														
Short	38	26	7	16	43	12	39	35	24	m	24	28	29	28
Long	36	20	7	15	37	6	30	24	17	m	19	23	20	23
Experience during studies														
Short	22	20	58	50	57	51	38	53	29	m	30	41	16	38
Long	19	20	41	44	43	47	29	48	23	m	25	30	24	30
Experience prior to studies														
Short	10	29	18	15	31	16	29	22	20	m	14	21	5	19
Long	9	24	14	14	23	20	27	20	24	m	14	19	11	18
Reputation of institution														
Short	22	19	24	19	18	15	21	23	24	m	27	21	42	24
Long	14	9	9	12	9	9	15	21	21	m	13	12	29	13
Experience abroad														
Short	12	14	25	15	14	14	10	17	19	m	14	15	8	14
Long	10	8	10	19	10	10	9	16	17	m	17	11	4	11
Foreign language proficiency														
Short	26	30	33	31	25	20	10	40	23	m	42	28	13	26
Long	23	21	15	33	25	19	8	43	22	m	42	23	15	23
Computer skills														
Short	37	45	44	47	44	35	43	38	18	m	57	42	16	39
Long	33	42	36	45	49	33	42	41	26	m	48	39	23	38
Recommendations/ references														
Short	21	32	25	28	27	27	44	33	46	m	29	31	28	30
Long	23	29	24	30	25	34	43	28	48	m	40	29	27	29
Personality														
Short	58	66	76	80	79	84	81	77	80	m	56	74	81	75
Long	57	62	68	83	78	80	77	73	75	m	71	68	80	69

Questions C7 and C8: see Tables 2 and 10.
m = missing data
* Count by Country: IT (1635); ES (1696); FR (890); AT (1389); DE (2332); NL (2120); UK (1915); FI (1436); SE (1131); NO (m); CZ (2034); EUR (1673); JP (4233); Total (218940).

Source: CHEERS survey data

Table 16 shows that the probability of holding a job which is at (at least) one's own level differed strongly by field of study in most countries, as well as by type of degree programme, age and gender, as will be discussed in another chapter. In some countries, significant positive effects were also observed for the grades and work experience aspects, which were seen to be important selection criteria for many first employers (see Table 10). Moreover, a long search reduced the probability of finding a job at one's own educational level in most countries. This also accounted for some of the effects of graduate characteristics, particularly age and study duration.

Table 16. Effects on Probability of Finding a Job at or above Owns Level of Educational Attainment, by Country

		Country										
		IT	ES	FR	AT	DE	NL	UK	FI	SE	NO	JP
1	Field of education (humanities = reference cat.)											
	Social sciences					+/+						–/–
	Business	+/+										
	Law	+/+			+/+	+/+	+/+					
	Natural sciences	+/+		+/+			+/+					
	Engineering	+/+	+/+						–/–			
	Health	+/+	+/+		+/+	+/+	+/+		+/+			+/+
2	Type of education (university type = ref. cat.)											
	Non-university	m	m	+/+	m		+/+		m	m		m
3	Grades (ref. cat. = low grade)											
	High		+/+	+/0								m
	Medium											m
4	Age		–/0			–/0			–/0	–/–		
5	Gender (ref. cat. = male)											
	Female					–/–	0/–		–/–			–/–
6	Experience during study		+/+			+/0						
7	Work placement							+/+				
8	Study duration											
	Up to 1 year too long									m		m
	More than 1 year too long		–/–						–/0	m	–/0	m
9	Study intensity (hours per week)			–/–								
10	Extracurricular activity (hours per week)											
11	Search duration (log)	–	–	–		–	–	–	–	–	–	

+ significant positive effect; – significant negative effect; m = variable not included; +/– signs before slash: significant effect before the search variables were included, and after the slash after they were included; 0 and blanks: no significant effects.

Source: CHEERS survey data.

The analysis of factors contributing to obtaining a temporary job presented in Table 17 also provides findings which are discussed in another chapter. In addition to the influence of field of study, type of degree programme and gender, we noted that the search duration significantly increased the probability of holding a temporary job in less than half the countries. However, this hardly accounted for any effects of graduate characteristics.

Table 17. Effects on Probability of a Temporary Job, by Country

		Country										
		IT	ES	FR	AT	DE	NL	UK	FI	SE	NO	JP
1	Field of education (humanities = reference cat.)											
	Social sciences		–/–		–/–						0/–	
	Business	–/–			–/–	–/–	–/–		–/–	–/–	–/–	
	Law		–/0				–/–				–/–	
	Natural sciences			–/–								
	Engineering	–/–	–/–		–/–	–/–		–/–	–/–	–/–	–/–	
	Health				+/+	+/+	0/+		+/+			
2	Type of education (university type = ref. cat.)											
	Non-university	m	m	–/–	m	–/–	–/–		m	m	–/–	m
3	Grades (ref. cat. = low grade)											
	High			–/0								m
	Medium											m
4	Age											
5	Gender (ref. cat. = male)	+/+	+/+			+/+			+/+		+/+	+/+
	Female											
6	Experience during study								+/+			
7	Work placement											
8	Study duration									m		m
	Up to 1 year too long									m		m
	More than 1 year too long											
9	Study intensity (hours per week)											
10	Extracurricular activity (hours per week)											
11	Search duration (log)	+		+			+		+		+	

+ significant positive effect; – significant negative effect; m = variable not included; +/– signs before slash: significant effect before the search variables were included, and after the slash after they were included; 0 and blanks: no significant effects.

Source: CHEERS survey data

Finally, Table 18 shows the effects of graduate characteristics and search duration on the graduates' income, calculated in terms of hourly wages. In addition to the effects described in another chapter we noted that a long search duration after graduation led to lower wages in most countries. This hardly accounted for any of the effects of field of study and other characteristics.

Table 18. Effects on Hourly Wages, by Country

		Country										
		IT	ES	FR	AT	DE	NL	UK	FI	SE	NO	JP
1	Field of education (humanities = reference cat.)											
	Social sciences								–/–			
	Business	+/+			+/+		+/+			+/+	+/+	
	Law					–/–	+/+			+/+		
	Natural sciences			+/+			+/0			+/+	0/+	
	Engineering	+/+	+/+							+/+	+/+	
	Health					0/–		+/0		+/+		+/+
2	Type of education (university type = ref. cat.)											
	Non-university	m	m		m	–/–	–/–		m	m	–/–	m
3	Grades (ref. cat. = low grade)											
	High		+/+					+/0				m
	Medium											m
4	Age		+/+				+/+				+/+	
5	Gender (ref. cat. = male)		–/–	0/–		–/–	–/–	–/–	–/–	–/–	–/–	–/–
	Female		+/+				+/0			+/0		
6	Experience during study								–/–			
7	Work placement											
8	Study duration					+/+	–/–			m		m
	Up to 1 year too long		–/–			0/+				m		m
	More than 1 year too long											
9	Study intensity (hours per week)											
10	Extracurricular activity (hours per week)											
11	Search duration (log)	–		–			–	–	–		–	–

+ significant positive effect; – significant negative effect; m = variable not included; +/– signs before slash: significant effect before the search variables were included, and after the slash after they were included; 0 and blanks: no significant effects.

Source: CHEERS survey data

Taken together, the results of the analyses in this section show that a long search after graduation was linked to a lower quality of work which graduates could expect about four years after graduation. In all the countries, graduates who had a long search period after graduation had, on average, either fewer chances of finding a job which was at least at an appropriate level, a higher chance of having a temporary job, or a lower wage than comparable graduates who obtained work more quickly. With the partial exception of the job level, the effects of a longer search on future job quality were largely independent of the effects of graduate characteristics.

5. CONCLUSION

What do the findings presented in this chapter tell us about the transition from higher education to work in the participating countries? On the one hand, there is evidence that the transition has become more complex for some tertiary graduates, just as it has for school-leavers at lower levels of education. A considerable proportion of graduates delayed the transition, moving on to further education rather than entering the labour market immediately. Others were already in employment prior to graduation. On the other, such "anomalies" notwithstanding, a clear majority of graduates in all of the countries showed a very simple – almost "traditional" – pattern of transition: leaving higher education and then immediately offering their services in the labour market.

With respect to the question of whether the transition from higher education to work has become highly precarious, the findings are mixed. A relatively large group of job-seeking graduates in several countries – notably Spain, Italy and France – failed to find work within six months after graduation. As Chapter 5 makes clear, the employment situation of graduates in these countries about four years after graduation still lags beyond that in the other countries in some respects. Further-more, as is apparent from the analyses in Chapter 3, the situation at the time the survey was conducted, i.e. about four years after graduation, is partly – though not entirely – influenced by the smoothness of the transition. However, even in these countries, a clear majority of graduates did find work quickly, many virtually immediately upon graduating. The conclusion seems justified that while the transition is somewhat precarious for a minority of graduates, most graduates enjoy a rather smooth and successful transition.

Apart from the time taken to find work, there are some clear qualitative differences between the countries involved in the pattern of the transition process. For example, each country showed its own quite a distinctive pattern of search methods. German graduates often placed their own advertisements, commercial employment agencies were mainly popular in the Netherlands, Japanese graduates engaged the services of the career placement office and teaching staff at their own school, and graduates in Italy and Spain made the most use of personal contacts. A similar story can be told for the selection criteria applied by the graduates' initial employers. "Main subject or specialisation" was especially important in Finland and France, "work experience during study" in Germany, France, Finland, the Netherlands and Austria, "exam results" in Germany the United Kingdom and "reputation of the educational institution" in Japan.

Despite these and other differences, in most respects the pattern of transition was surprisingly similar across the participating countries. This is particularly the case for the European countries: in almost all respects, these countries resembled each other much more than they resembled Japan. In as far as there were real systematic differences between the European countries, it would appear that the southern European countries (Spain, Italy, and to some extent France) also have a somewhat distinctive pattern, which may in part be related to their somewhat poorer labour market prospects.

6. REFERENCES

Halaby, C.N. (1994). "Over-education and Skill Mismatch." *Sociology of Education* 67, 47-59.

Hannan, D.F. and Werquin, P. (1999). *Education and Labour Market Change: The Dynamics of Education to Work Transitions in Europe*. Paper presented at the European Socio-Economic Research Conference, Brussels 28-30 April 1999.

OECD (2000). *From Initial Education to Working Life*. Making Transitions Work. Paris: OECD.

Ryan, P. (2001). "The School-to-Work Transition: A Cross-National Perspective." *Journal of Economic Literature*, 39, 34-92.

Shavitt, Y. and Müller, W. (1998). *From School to Work. A Comparative Study of Educational Qualifications and Occupational Destinations*. Oxford: Clarendon Press.

Teichler, U. (1999). "Research on the Relationships between Higher Education and the World of Work: Past Achievements, Problems and New Challenges." *Higher Education* 38, 169-90.

TRINE STAVIK AND CLARA ÅSE ARNESEN

EARLY CAREER

1. INTRODUCTION

What characterises a "successful" transition from higher education to the world of work? Should an immediate and smooth transition to stable and regular employment be viewed as the norm? Available data show a substantial variation by country (Teichler 2000) as well as in the effects of this transition and the conditions of first employment on subsequent career (De Vreyer et al. 2000)

The diversity of factors in play are, for example, reflected by Van der Velden and Wolbers (2001): "In countries with a less strict employment protection legislation, school-leavers find a (stable) labour market position more easily than in countries with high strictness of employment protection legislation". Müller and Shavit (1998) underline the significance of the social organisation of education in the various countries in explaining the occupational attainment process and subsequent career. According to Reyneri (1999), job seekers in Italy, Spain and Portugal with high or medium level education often wait for a job whilst living with their parents. Educated youth do not accept unskilled jobs because of the perceived risk of their being stuck there – a vicious circle which is most pronounced in Southern European countries (Mjøset, 2001). Studies also show that the risk of future unemployment is closely related to previous unemployment in most countries (Layte et al. 2000). There are different assumptions or conclusions as to whether this is due to selection effects (heterogeneity) or state/history dependence. The heterogeneity/selection analysis explains long-term unemployment by assuming that the long-term unemployed are persons with special personal attributes (e.g. age, gender, social background, social skills, place of residence, education, mental/physical health, etc) and lower job probabilities. State dependence may be caused by changes in preferences, skills and other personal attributes (e.g. self-esteem and motivation) as a consequence of unemployment, which may influence the risk of future unemployment and job probabilities.

To be sure, this study does not intend to identify an iron law on the relationships between transition and graduates' career, because in analysing the transition of those who graduated in the mid-1990s, we must take into account the major changes in the 1990s with respect to values and life styles, family patterns, educational environment and the labour market. In looking at the literature on the changes in the youth labour market (Furlong and Cartmel 1997), we noted a rapid expansion of a flexible or peripheral sector of the workforce (Gallie et al. 1998). Part-time and temporary work could be seen as a strategy used by firms to gain numeric flexibility (Nätti 1993; Atkinson 1987). These new forms of employment provided students with opportunities of work during and after their studies which were probably unheard of a couple of decades ago (Lucas 1997). But new entrants to employment faced more problems on the route to adulthood than previous generations (Smith 1999) and higher education graduates, although rather privileged, were also affected (Wolbers 2000). This route

U. Teichler (ed.), Careers of University Graduates, 79–94

became less linear and lead to more "uncommon" career paths in the first years after graduation. Spells of unemployment could be followed by periods of employment and further studies. For some graduates, the first job was the start of a career which matched their educational background, for others it was the first step in a job search process. In explaining these phenomena, some experts saw the new transition process as a protracted process of search and experimentation (OECD 1999). Others saw the post-industrial society as moving towards risks and individualism (Beck 1992; Giddens 1991) or a "postfordististic life course" (Esping-Andersen 1993, 1995), whilst others noted a deterioration of the labour market in general.

The aim of this chapter is first to describe graduates' major activities in 11 European countries and Japan during the first three to four years after graduation. Second, we analyse how differences in labour force status and type of job contract are related to individual factors (e.g. age, gender, field of study) or to country differences. Third, we examine whether the labour market situation 12 months after graduation is a good predictor of the labour market position about four years after graduation.

A detailed analysis of the first four years after graduation was possible because graduates in the CHEERS survey were asked to record the incidence and timing of change in their major activity (employment, unemployment, not in the labour force, etc.) in the period after graduation. One must take into account, however, that the quality of such retrospective data could suffer from certain weaknesses. Some respondents did not provide information for all the stages (e.g. for the first months after graduation, for certain months in between, or for the whole period), and, even if the information does look complete, respondents may have forgotten certain events – notably short or unpleasant activities (Gallie et al. 1998). Moreover, our analysis does not take into account all the dimensions of employment (e.g. part-time employment is not included). Yet we believe that the major trends of the early career can be illustrated.

2. CHANGES IN THE LABOUR FORCE STATUS IN THE EARLY CAREER

Figure 1 shows the labour force status for all graduates during the first four years after graduation. We see that, the proportion of graduates who were employed in all 12 countries increased from less than a quarter in the first month after graduation to about 80 per cent about four years after graduation. The percentage of those reporting unemployment (i.e. not employed *and* seeking employment) was stable during the period at 3 per cent or less. The proportion outside the labour force (neither employed nor unemployed) was lowest during the first month after graduation (5%), reached a peak after one year (16%) and decreased slowly thereafter. This is quite astonishing, as we would expect these percentages to be highest at the beginning of the period. However, this could be explained by the large number of graduates who failed to report their labour force status the first months after graduation.

Permanent employment dominated from the outset and its share grew. The proportion of all graduates in temporary jobs increased during the first year and there after remained stable at about 15 per cent. One must bear in mind, though, that some respondents did not specify their type of contract.

Figure 1. Labour Force Status and Type of Contract of All Graduates About Four Years After Graduation (percentage)

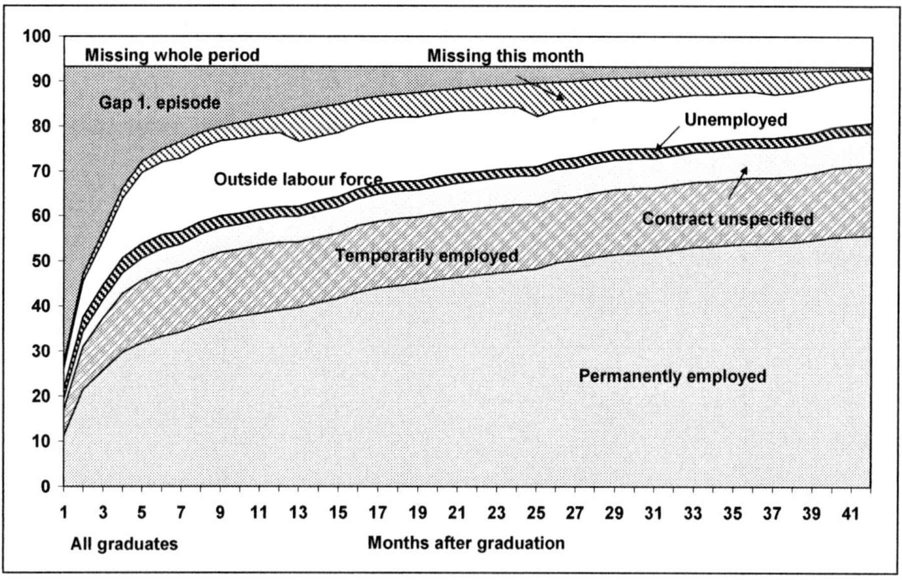

Question C10: Please inform us about your current major activity. Open question; the date of the beginning and end of an activity were asked; for jobs, the type of contract (permanent, temporary) and the working time (full-time, part-time) .
Gap 1. episode: graduates did not provide information regarding their activities between the time of graduation and the first episode.
Source: CHEERS survey data

In comparing the early career of women (Figure 2) with that of all graduates (Figure 1), we see surprising similarities between women and men. There was no significant difference in the first year after graduation. Also, the share of unemployed women was only marginally higher than that of men over the whole period observed (up to 3%). After 3½ years, about 80 per cent of women as compared to about 90 per cent of men were employed. The most striking difference concerned temporary contracts: about one sixth of women – or slightly more – from one year after graduation onwards, compared to about one eighth of men.

As this was the phase of life when many people settled down and had a partner and children, one could have expected a greater disparity in the early careers of men and women, since it was more common for women to stay at home while the children were small. About a quarter of the women surveyed had children at the end of the period analysed (see Einarsdottir in this volume). As regards employment, we noted that about 10 per cent more women than men were not in the labour force (see above) and that about 10 per cent more women than men were employed part-time (see Einarsdottir in this volume).

Figure 2. Labour Force Status and Type of Contract of All Female Graduates About Four Years After Graduation (percentage)

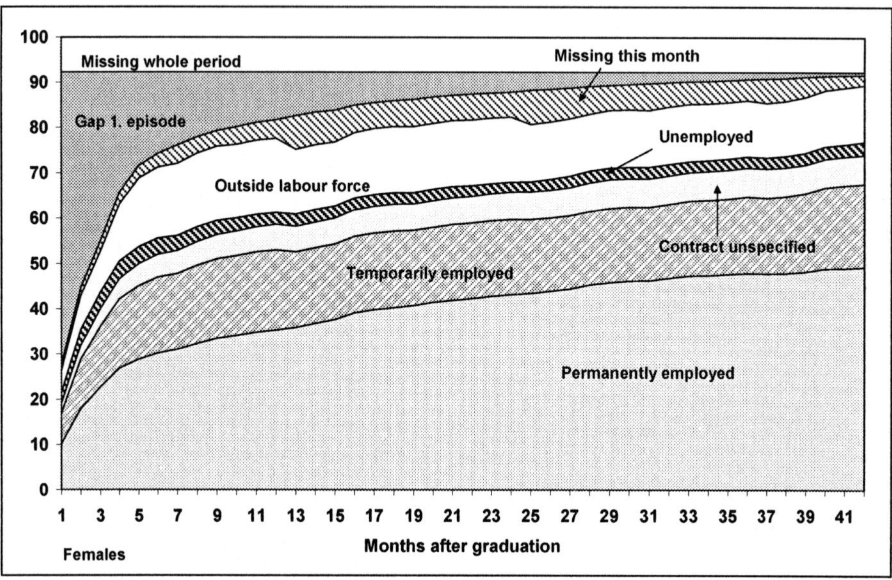

For explanations see footnote to Figure 1.

Source: CHEERS survey data

Differences in labour force status according to field of study could be explained by varying employment problems or prospects. Second, the tendency to undertake further studies may vary by field. The proportion of those who were employed was highest amongst engineers, with about one quarter in the first month and up to about 90 per cent after 3½ years (see Figure 3). The lowest share was observed amongst graduates in natural science during the whole period (from 13% initially to almost 75%). But the high quota of natural scientists who were not in the labour force (rising from less than 10 per cent initially to more than one third 12 months after their studies and thereafter levelling off to less than a quarter) was due to the fact that many non-employed graduates in these fields were in full-time advanced academic study or professional training (18 % at the time of the survey).

Figure 3. Labour Force Status and Type of Contract of Engineering Graduates About Four Years After Graduation (percentage)

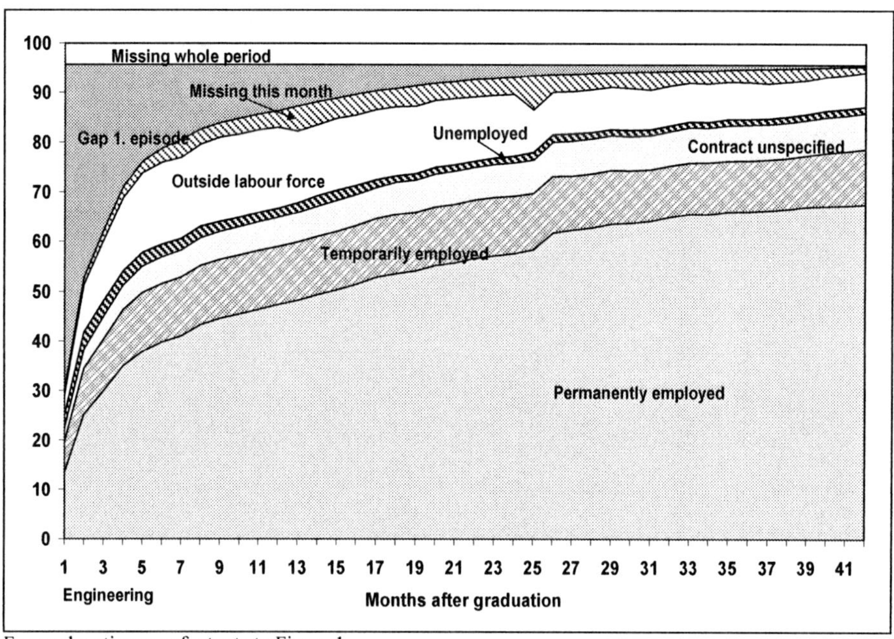

For explanations see footnote to Figure 1.

Source: CHEERS survey data

Graduates in humanities and law reported a similar pattern more often than those in the natural sciences, but the major activities of those outside the labour force were more diverse. Graduates in the other fields of study fell in between these groups.

In most fields, the share of unemployed graduates increased for about six months, then decreased up to about two years after graduation and remained fairly stable for the remaining period observed. The levels varied by field of study between about 5 per cent for graduates in humanities six months after graduation to less than 2 per cent for those in medicine and education. Two years after graduation and thereafter, unemployment varied between 1 per cent and 3 per cent for the different fields of study.

As already suggested in the available literature (see Teichler 2000), the speed of transition from higher education to employment varied substantially by country. For example, Finland (see Figure 4) belonged to those countries where almost 70 per cent of the graduates were employed after six months. In contrast, this level was only reached after more than three years in France (see Figure 5).

Figure 4. Labour Force Status and Type of Contract About Four Years After Graduation – Finland (percentage)

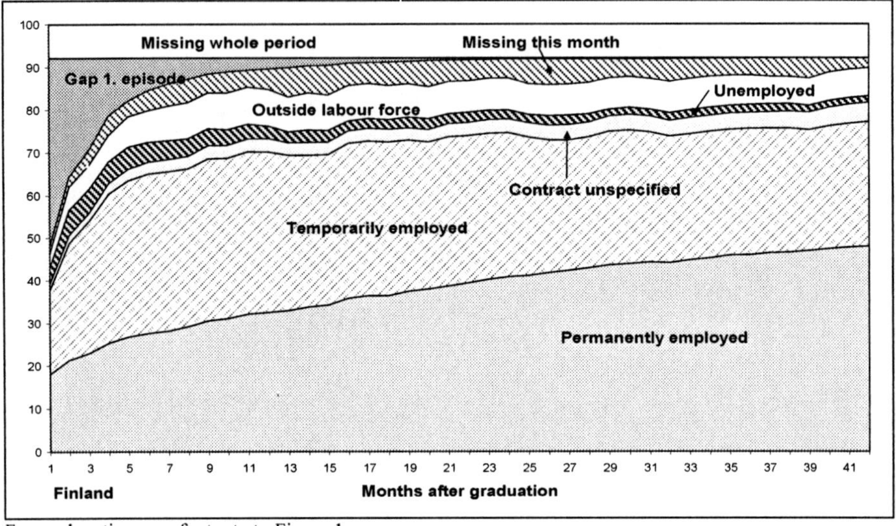

For explanations see footnote to Figure 1.

Source: CHEERS survey data

Figure 5. Labour Force Status and Type of Contract About Four Years After Graduation – France (percentage)

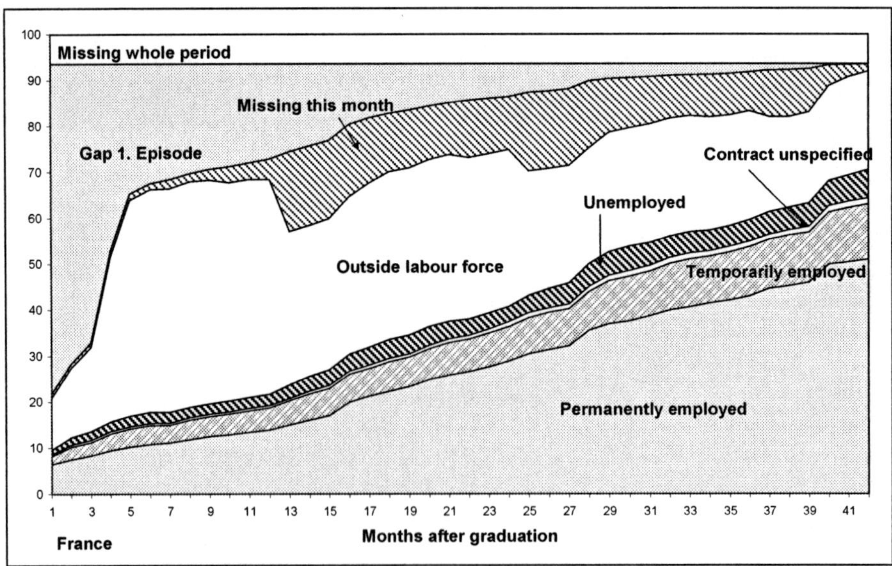

For explanations see footnote to Figure 1.

Source: CHEERS survey data

Rapid transition prevailed in Japan, Norway, Sweden and the Netherlands. Low levels of early transition to employment were found in France, Italy and Spain, but the alternatives varied: while many of the who were not employed were outside the labour force in France, many Spanish graduates who were not employed considered themselves as unemployed. A high number of graduates in temporary employment during the whole period was found more especially in Finland and Spain, whilst the figure was relatively low in Japan, Sweden and France.

3. FACTORS EXPLAINING THE LABOUR FORCE STATUS

So far, we have described the labour force status separately by gender, field of study and country. In order to obtain a more refined picture of the impact of each of these variables, we carried out multivariate analyses. In addition to information about the graduates' age and type of degree (bachelor, master level etc.), gender, country and field of study were included as explanatory variables. Descriptive statistics of the dependent and independent variables included in the analyses are presented in the appendix. We studied the labour force status one year and about four years after graduation and by type of job contract about four years after graduation (using multinomial logistic regression, which means that the dependent variable consisted of more than two categories).

Table 1 presents the results of the analysis of the labour force status 12 months after graduation. There are three sets of regression coefficients: one for unemployment, one for not in the labour force and one for no answer. The coefficients are not easily interpreted, and we will restrict our comments to the sign of the coefficients. A positive coefficient in the unemployment set indicates that the probability of being unemployed increased when the variable studied increased by one unit and the other variables were held constant. We found that women were more likely than men to be unemployed 12 months after graduation. Our analysis also shows that the probability of being unemployed as well as being outside the labour force differed between fields of study and country. For example, graduates in humanities, natural science and law faced a higher risk of being unemployed or outside the labour force than otherwise identical graduates from other fields of study.

The analysis also indicates that labour force status one year after graduation varied more between countries than between fields of study. In addition, the data indicated that age and type of degrees (short/long) were not important in predicting the risk of being unemployed one year after graduation. However, older graduates as well as those graduating in a long degree programme were less likely to be outside the labour force at that time.

Table 1. Descriptive Statistics of Dependent and Independent Variables (percentage or arithmetic mean[1])

	Country												Total*
	IT	SP	FR	AT	DE	NL	UK	FI	SE	NO	CZ	JP	
Gender (females)	53	57	50	45	41	50	58	56	57	59	44	32	50
Age (in 1999)	31	29	28	32	32	30	30	33	33	32	28	27	30
Field of study													
Education	2	10	0	14	7	15	6	15	18	14	19	6	10
Humanities	17	10	19	8	11	10	26	17	8	6	8	18	13
Social science	27	33	36	26	30	35	26	26	33	17	28	36	30
Law	15	11	12	12	7	5	4	4	4	6	5	10	8
Natural science	8	3	17	4	8	2	10	6	3	5	6	4	7
Mathematics	3	5	9	6	5	36	7	4	3	3	–	1	4
Engineering	17	18	8	18	25	21	12	21	20	25	29	21	20
Medical science	11	11	0	13	7	9	8	8	11	26	6	4	10
Total	100	100	100	100	100	100	100	100	100	100	100	100	100
Type of degree (long)	100	69	58	100	63	37	6	100	100	35	91	0	60
Unemployment rate[2]	7	13	7	3	6	2	3	7	4	2	2	3	5
Labour force status 12 months after graduation													
Employed	47	29	19	60	67	73	60	73	60	79	69	77	60
Unemployed	2	11	2	1	1	2	2	3	1	1	1	1	2
Outside labour force	15	21	47	16	12	12	16	9	8	12	16	14	17
No answer[3]	37	39	32	23	20	13	22	15	31	8	15	8	22
Total	100	100	100	100	100	100	100	100	100	100	100	100	100
Labour force status about four years after graduation													
Employed	75	54	65	83	83	87	80	82	71	86	85	88	79
Unemployed	2	8	6	2	2	1	2	2	1	0	2	2	2
Outside labour force	12	12	21	9	9	5	8	7	10	10	13	5	10
No answer[3]	11	26	8	6	6	7	10	10	19	4	1	5	9
Total	100	100	100	100	100	100	100	100	100	100	100	100	100
Temporary contract 12 months after graduation	10	16	5	18	17	17	14	38	14	18	9	8	15
Temporary contract about four years after graduation	17	25	12	21	16	17	14	29	9	13	12	7	16

1) Percentage of all graduates in the national sample, not percentage of employed graduates.
2) Unemployment rate in 1998 for people with tertiary education aged 25-64 (OECD 2000:215-217).
3) Including cases on which we lack information about their career, i.e. the group of cases that we have excluded from the multivariate analyses.
* Count by Country: IT (3102); ES (3022); FR (3051); AT (2312); DE (3506); NL (3087); UK (3449); FI (2675); SE (2634); NO (3329); CZ (3092); JP (3421); Total (36692).

Source: CHEERS survey data

Table 2. Factors Predicting Labour Force Status 12 Months After Graduation (multinominal logistic regression)

	Unemployed/ Employed		Not in labour force/Employed		No answer/ Employed	
	B	SE	B	SE	B	SE
Intercept	−5.96 ***	1.29	7.52 ***	0.48	1.84 ***	0,51
Gender (1 = female)	0.5 ***	0.08	−0.08 **	0.03	−0.14 ***	0,03
Age 99 (years)	0.11	0.07	−0.40 ***	0.03	−0.12 ***	0,03
Age 99^2	0.00	0.00	0.00 ***	0.00	0.00 ***	0,00
Field of study (ref.: Humanities)						
Education	−0.57 ***	0.17	−0.43 ***	0.07	−0.30 ***	0.07
Social science	−0.59 ***	0.12	−0.66 ***	0.05	−0.56 ***	0.05
Law	−0.13	0.15	0.07	0.07	−0.40 ***	0.07
Natural science	0.06	0.16	0.65 ***	0.06	−0.14 **	0.07
Mathematics	−1.11 ***	0.23	−0.54 ***	0.09	−0.66 ***	0.09
Engineering	−0.48 ***	0.13	−0.27 ***	0.06	−0.58 ***	0.06
Medical science	−0.78 ***	0.16	−0.43 ***	0.07	−0.36 ***	0.07
Type of degree (1 = long)	−0.16	0.11	−0.45 ***	0.05	0.12 **	0.05
Country (ref.: Austria)						
Italy	0.96 ***	0.30	0.08	0.08	0.57 ***	0.07
Spain	3.58 ***	0.27	0.52 ***	0.08	0.37 ***	0.08
France	2.39 ***	0.29	1.32 ***	0.08	1.12 ***	0.08
Germany	−0.04	0.33	−0.53 ***	0.08	−0.22 ***	0.07
Netherlands	0.99 ***	0.29	−1.00 ***	0.09	−1.18 ***	0.09
United Kingdom	0.63 **	0.31	−1.05 ***	0.09	−0.60 ***	0.09
Finland	1.24 ***	0.28	−0.72 ***	0.09	−1.17 ***	0.09
Sweden	−0.07	0.37	−0.59 ***	0.10	0.19 **	0.07
Norway	0.28	0.31	−0.88 ***	0.09	−1.53 ***	0.10
Czech Republic	−0.84 **	0.40	−0.71 ***	0.08	−0.71 ***	0.08
Japan	0.19	0.33	−1.46 ***	0.10	−1.52 ***	0.11
N	33777					
− 2 log likelihook	17934.006					

** $p < 0.01$, ** $p < 0.05$, * $p < 0.10$.
Graduates with missing labour force status for the whole four-year period are not included in the analysis. The "no-answer" group consists of persons who did not provide information about their status 12 months after graduation.

Source: CHEERS survey data

In analysing the labour force status 3½ years after graduation (see Table 2) we wanted to see whether differences between males and females or graduates from different field of studies levelled out with time, or whether they also applied several years after graduation. The subsequent analysis initially included the same list of possible factors as the previous one (Model 1) and thereafter additionally the labour force status 12 months after graduation (Model 2).

The analysis of Model 1 suggests that the significance of several factors was different about four years after graduation from that one year after graduation. The risk of being unemployed increased over time for women. Graduates with a long type of degree about four years after graduation were less likely to be unemployed than otherwise identical graduates graduating from a short type of degree. Compared to those in humanities, those in social sciences, mathematics, engineering and medical sciences were still less likely to be unemployed. Graduates in natural sciences were the only ones with a higher risk of being unemployed than those in humanities. As regards country, graduates from Spain and France still had a significantly higher risk and graduates from the Netherlands, the United Kingdom, Sweden and Norway were now much less likely to be unemployed than the Austrian graduates. Finally, the data suggest that this risk decreased over time for Finnish graduates compared to the Austrian graduates.

In model 2, we noted that graduates who had been unemployed, but also those who had been temporarily employed or outside the labour force one year after graduation, had a much greater risk of being unemployed about four years after graduation. It is also interesting to note that introducing labour force status one year after graduation in the model had a relatively small impact on the size of the other coefficients in the model, thus indicating stable differences between countries and fields of study. However, there were some exceptions. Graduates in social sciences no longer had a significantly lower risk of being unemployed than otherwise equal graduates in humanities, and graduates from Finland were now much less likely to be unemployed than Austrian graduates.

In Model 3 and 4 we included the 1998 national unemployment rate (ranging from 2-13 per cent, see OECD 2000, pp. 215-17) to verify country differences in economic activity. We also introduced geographical groupings of countries. While Model 3 included the same list of potential factors as Model 1, Model 4, like Model 2, also included the labour force status one year after graduation.

Without describing the findings in detail, we noted, first, that the national unemployment rate had a direct effect in predicting the risk of being unemployed. Second, some of the country groupings turned out to be influential. Both findings suggest that a thorough analysis of the early career paths requires the inclusion of the economic, social and cultural conditions within the various countries addressed.

In Table 3, we analysed the factors that predicted the probability of being in temporary employment or being permanently employed according to the same model as used in Table 2. In analysing Model 1 we noted that women, when the other factors in the model were verified, had a higher risk than men of being in a temporary job than in a permanent job about four years after graduation. Compared to graduates in humanities, those in natural sciences and medical sciences had a significantly higher probability and graduates in education, social sciences, law, mathematics and engineering a significantly lower probability of being in a temporary job about four years after graduation. Having a long type of degree also increased the risk of being in a temporary job about four years after graduation. As regards country, we observed that graduates from Spain and Finland had a higher probability and graduates from most other countries had a lower probability of being in a temporary job about four years after graduation than the Austrian graduates.

Table 3. Factors Predicting Unemployment About Four Years After Graduation (multinomial logistic regression)

	Model 1		Model 2		Model 3		Model 4	
	B	SE	B	SE	B	SE	B	SE
Intercept	–6.01 ***	1.12	–7.67 ***	1.14	–5.10 ***	0.96	–7.51 ***	1.01
Gender (1 = female)	0.45 ***	0.08	0.37 ***	0.08	0.28 **	0.11	0.30 ***	0.11
Age 99 (years)	0.14 **	0.06	0.17 ***	0.06	0.03	0.05	0.11 **	0.06
Age 99^2	0.00 *	0.00	0.00 **	0.00	0.00	0.00	0.00	0.00
Field of study (ref.: Humanities)								
Education	–0.15	0.15	–0.10	0.16	–0.12	0.15	–0.07	0.15
Social science	–0.32 ***	0.11	–0.15	0.11	–0.29 ***	0.11	–0.11	0.11
Law	–0.04	0.15	–0.02	0.15	–0.05	0.14	–0.01	0.15
Natural science	0.35 ***	0.13	0.24 *	0.14	0.42 ***	0.13	0.31 **	0.14
Mathematics	–0.99 ***	0.24	–0.77 ***	0.24	–0.91 ***	0.24	–0.71 ***	0.24
Engineering	–0.72 ***	0.14	–0.65 ***	0.15	–0.74 ***	0.14	–0.64 ***	0.14
Medical science	–0.85 ***	0.17	–0.88 ***	0.18	–0.91 ***	0.17	–0.90 ***	0.18
Type of degree (1 = long)	–0.55 ***	0.10	–0.53 ***	0.10	–0.45 ***	0.08	–0.41 ***	0.09
Country (ref.: Austria)								
Italy	0.03	0.21	–0.06	0.22				
Spain	1.98 ***	0.18	1.20 ***	0.19				
France	1.23 ***	0.19	0.81 ***	0.20				
Germany	–0.04	0.21	0.04	0.21				
Netherlands	–0.74 ***	0.24	–0.72 ***	0.25				
United Kingdom	–0.60 **	0.23	–0.59 **	0.24				
Finland	–0.24	0.23	–0.46 **	0.23				
Sweden	–1.07 ***	0.33	–1.01 ***	0.33				
Norway	–1.95 ***	0.34	–1.81 ***	0.34				
Czech Rep.	–0.29	0.23	0.02	0.23				
Japan	0.36	0.23	–0.05	0.24				
Country (ref.: At/De/Nl/Uk)								
It/Es/Fr					0.29 *	0.16	0.26	0.16
Fi/Se/No					–0.70 ***	0.15	–0.74 ***	0.15
Cz/Jp					0.21 *	0.13	0.42 ***	0.13
Female*It/Es/Fr					0.25 *	0.15	0.08	0.15
Unemployment rate					0.20 ***	0.01	0.13 ***	0.02
Status 12 months after graduation(ref. perm. job/self-empl.)								
– Unemployed	3.23 ***	0.13			3.25 ***	0.13		
– Temp. employed	1.00 ***	0.13			1.02 ***	0.13		
– Outside labour force	1.68 ***	0.12			1.76 ***	0.12		
– No answer	1.11 ***	0.13			1.15 ***	0.13		
N	33777		33777		33777		33777	
–2 log likelihood	12198.745		17842.374		12431.869		17924.231	

*** $p < 0.01$, ** $p < 0.05$, * $p < 0.10$.

Compared to employment as a reference group. Graduates with missing labour force status for the whole four-year period are excluded from the analysis.

Source: CHEERS survey data

Model 2, which includes information about labour market status one year after graduation, indicates that graduates who either were temporarily employed, unemployed or outside the labour force one year after graduation had a higher risk of being in a temporary job about four years after graduation. In addition, Model 2 largely confirms the findings of Model 1. The effects decreased somewhat for graduates from most fields of study. Those in natural sciences no longer had a higher risk of being temporarily employed than graduates in humanities. We also noticed great stability in the country coefficients.

Table 4. Factors Predicting Temporary Employment 42 Months After Graduation (multinomial logistic regression)

	Model 1		Model 2		Model 3		Model 4	
	B	SE	B	SE	B	SE	B	SE
Intercept	−0.34	0.50	−2.67 ***	0.52	−0.87 *	0.45	−3.47 ***	0.49
Gender (female = 1)	0.37 ***	0.03	0.36 ***	0.04	0.36 ***	0.04	0.35 ***	0.04
Age 99 (years)	−0.04	0.03	−0.01	0.03	−0.05 **	0.03	0.01	0.03
Age 99^2	0.00	0.00	0.00	0.00	0.00	0.00	0.00	0.00
Field of study (ref.: Humanities)								
Education	−0.14 **	0.06	−0.17 **	0.07	−0.08	0.06	−0.10	0.07
Social science	−0.65 ***	0.05	−0.49 ***	0.06	−0.65 ***	0.05	−0.47 ***	0.05
Law	−0.72 ***	0.07	−0.66 ***	0.08	−0.71 ***	0.07	−0.64 ***	0.08
Natural science	0.22 ***	0.07	0.03	0.07	0.19 ***	0.06	0.00	0.07
Mathematics	−0.90 ***	0.09	−0.77 ***	0.10	−0.90 ***	0.09	−0.77 ***	0.10
Engineering	−0.77 ***	0.06	−0.64 ***	0.06	−0.75 ***	0.06	−0.58 ***	0.06
Medical science	0.45 ***	0.06	0.34 ***	0.06	0.48 ***	0.06	0.39 ***	0.06
Type of degree (1 = long)	0.41 ***	0.05	0.21 ***	0.05	0.43 ***	0.04	0.24 ***	0.04
Country (ref.: Austria)								
Italy	−0.14 *	0.08	−0.08	0.08				
Spain	1.19 ***	0.08	0.84 ***	0.09				
France	−0.45 ***	0.09	−0.66 ***	0.09				
Germany	−0.08	0.07	−0.12	0.08				
Netherlands	−0.06	0.08	0.02	0.09				
United Kingdom	−0.26 ***	0.09	−0.29 ***	0.10				
Finland	0.58 ***	0.07	0.18 **	0.08				
Sweden	−0.75 ***	0.09	−0.82 ***	0.10				
Norway	−0.38 ***	0.08	−0.37 ***	0.09				
Czech Rep.	−0.69 ***	0.08	−0.24 ***	0.09				
Japan	−0.78 ***	0.10	−0.41 ***	0.11				
Country (ref.: (ref.: At/De/Nl/Uk)								
It/Es/Fr					−0.71***	0.07	−0.58 ***	0.08
Fi/Se/No					−0.10 **	0.04	−0.26 ***	0.05
Cz/Jp					−0.42 ***	0.05	−0.06	0.06
Female*It/Es/Fr					0.09	0.07	0.06	0.08
Unemployment rate					0.18 ***	0.01	0.13 ***	0.01

to be continued

Table 4. Continued

	Model 1		Model 2		Model 3		Model 4	
	B	SE	B	SE	B	SE	B	SE
Intercept	−0.34	0.50	−2.67 ***	0.52	−0.87 *	0.45	−3.47 ***	0.49
Gender (female = 1)	0.37 ***	0.03	0.36 ***	0.04	0.36 ***	0.04	0.35 ***	0.04
Age 99 (years)	−0.04	0.03	−0.01	0.03	−0.05 **	0.03	0.01	0.03
Age 99^2	0.00	0.00	0.00	0.00	0.00	0.00	0.00	0.00
Status 12 months after graduation (ref.: perm. job/self-empl.)								
– Unemployed			2.20 ***	0.10			2.26 ***	0.10
– Temp. job			3.05 ***	0.05			3.07 ***	0.05
– Outside labour force			2.03 ***	0.06			1.99 ***	0.06
– No answer			1.93 ***	0.05			1.87 ***	0.05
N	33777		33777		33777		33777	
–2 LL	17996.456		26525.500		182444.524		26579.646	

*** $p < 0.01$, ** $p < 0.05$, * $p < 0.10$.
Compared to permanent employment as reference group. Graduates with missing labour force status for the whole 42-months period are excluded from the analysis.

Source: CHEERS survey data

The analysis of the results of Model 3 and Model 4 hardly differ from those of the analysis of Model 1 and Model 2. When introducing labour market position one year after graduation, we noted that graduates from the Czech Republic and Japan no longer had significant lower risks of being temporarily employed than being permanently employed about four years after graduation than graduates from Austria.

4. CONCLUSION

The main topic of chapter was the career development over the first 3½ years after graduation. We analysed the development in the labour force status and different types of job contracts in this period. One of our main questions was whether the distribution of unemployment and temporary employment was related to individual factors such as age and gender, field of study and country. We also analysed the extent to which the graduates' labour market position, in terms of labour force status and type of contract in early career, was a good indicator of their situation later in their career.

The figures as well as the multivariate analyses showed that the labour force status and type of job contract in the period studied were affected by gender, field of study and country.

An overall impression was that there was a sharp increase in the proportion of those employed about four years after graduation. Amongst all graduates surveyed, it rose from about 20 per cent one month after graduation to about 50 per cent six months after graduation. This was followed by a moderate steady increase to 80 per cent about four years after graduation. The proportion of those who were temporarily employed (included in the figures stated above) increased over the first year to about 15 per cent and remained more or less constant thereafter. The percentage of those considering themselves as unemployed (not unemployment rate) was surprisingly low and stable during the period surveyed at a level of at most 3 per cent. Finally, the proportion of those outside the labour force (predominantly in education and training or in child rearing and family care) was most of the period between 10 per cent and 15 per cent for most of the period .

Women started off their careers very similarly to men over at least the first year. The proportion of unemployed was only marginally higher over the whole period analysed. However, about four years after graduation, about 10 per cent less women than men were employed, of whom some 5 per cent more were in temporary employment and about 10 per cent more were in part-time employment – at a time, when about one quarter of the female graduates were mothers.

Graduates from different fields of study experienced a different labour market situation. For instance, those in natural sciences were least employed and had the highest proportion outside the labour force. Most of those who were not employed were in advanced study or professional training. Graduates in humanities and law had the second lowest employment quota with more mixed alternatives for those who were not employed. In contrast, graduates in engineering, had the highest percentage of those who were employed during the whole period. The percentage of unemployed differed somewhat between the various fields of study at different points in time. Finally, the proportion of those who were temporarily employed was highest amongst the graduates in medical sciences.

Fewer graduates with a long type of degree (masters degree or longer) than those with a short or non-university degree were outside the labour force, but more were re employed part-time. The proportion of those who were unemployed did not vary substantially be type of degree.

We noted a different timing of the typical period of transition from higher education to employment between countries. The transition took place relatively early and the employment rates were relatively high for all or most of the period in Japan, as well as in Norway, Sweden and the Netherlands. On the other hand, the transition was relatively protracted and the rate of employment relatively low during most of the period analysed in Spain, France and Italy.

Finally, our analyses showed that the labour market position, in terms of unemployment and type of contract, one year after graduation, was an important indicator of labour market position about four years after graduation. Thus, our main conclusion could be that obtaining a permanent job early in the career "protected" against unemployment and temporary jobs later in the career, and that early unemployment *caused* subsequent unemployment. But, in these analyses we only took into account a very restricted number of potential selection factors (age, gender, field and duration of study, etc.); so we are unable to answer the question whether the documented state dependence is spurious, owing to unknown characteristics of the graduates (Andress 1989). This means that we have to stress, as Hammer (1997) did in her study of state dependence in youth unemployment, that we have no statistical evidence to support either the hypothesis of selection or that of (true) state dependence.

The findings also confirm previous research about the importance of the labour market development immediately after graduation amongst higher education graduates. Van der Linden and Van der Velden (1998:123), for example, in a study of university graduates in the Netherlands, concluded that "both youth unemployment and educational mismatch have a negative effect on future careers, future matches and, in the case of unemployment, on future earnings".

Our results concerning temporary employment are also interesting, but we must be careful in labelling temporary jobs as "secondary jobs", because they could often be the normal first step for a successful career. For example, initial employment in the public sector in various European countries is based on short-term contracts. This, again, suggests that further detailed analysis would be commendable.

5. REFERENCES

Andress, H. J. (1989). "Recurrent Unemployment – The West German Experience: An Exploratory Analysis Using Count Data Models with Panel Data." *European Sociological Review* (3), 275-97.

Atkinson, J. (1987). "Flexibility or Fragmentation." *Labour and Society* 12(1), 87-105.

Beck, U. (1997). *The Risk Society*. London: Sage Publishers.

De Vreyer, Ph. et al. (2000). "The Permanent Effects of Labour Market Entry in Times of High Unemployment." In Gallie, D. and Paugam, S. (eds) *Welfare Regimes and the Experience of Unemployment in Europe*. Oxford: Oxford University Press, pp. 134-52.

Esping-Andersen, G. (1993). "Post-industrial Class Structures: An Analytical Framework." In Esping-Andersen, G. (ed) *Changing Classes*. London: Sage, pp. 7-31.

Esping-Andersen, G. (1995). "Equality and Work in the Post-Industrial Life-Cycle." In Miliband, D. (ed) *Reinventing the Left*. Cambridge: Polity Press, pp. 167-85.

Furlong, A. and Cartmel, F. (1997). *Young People and Social Change*. Buckingham: Open University Press.

Gallie, D. et al. (eds) (1998). *Restructuring the Employment Relationship*. Oxford: Clarendon Press.

Giddens, A. (1991). *Modernity and Self-Identity*. Cambridge: Polity Press.

Hammer, T. (1997). "History Dependence in Youth Unemployment." *European Sociological Review*, 13(1), 17-33.

Layte, R. et al. (2000). "Unemployment and Cumulative Disadvantage in the Labour Market." In Gallie, D. and Paugham, S. (eds) *Welfare Regimes and the Experience of Unemployment in Europe*. Oxford: Oxford University Press, pp. 153-74.

Lucas, R. (1997). "Youth, Gender and Part-Time Work: Students in the Labour Process." *Work, Employment and Society* 11, 595-613.

Mjøset. L. (2001). "Employment, Unemployment, and Ageing in the Western European Welfare States." In Petit, P.and Soete, L. (eds) *Technology, and the Future of European Employment*. Cheltenham: Edward Elgar, pp. 451-506.

Müller, W. and Shavit, Y. (1998). "The Institutional Embeddedness of the Stratification Process." In Shavit, Y. and Müller, W. (eds) *From school to Work: A Comparative Study of Educational Qualifications and Occupational Destinations*. Oxford: Clarendon Press, pp. 1-48.

Nätti, J. (1993). "Atypical Employment in the Nordic Countries: Towards Marginalisation or Normalisation?" In Boje, T.P. and Olsson Hort, S.E. (eds) *Scandinavia in Europe*. Oslo: Scandinavian University Press, pp. 171-213.

OECD (1999). *Preparing Youth for the 21st Century*. Paris: OECD.

Reyneri, E. (1999). "Unemployment Patterns in the European Countries: A Comparative View." [http://www.lex.unict.it/dml-online]

Smith, M. (1999). *Young people, Atypical Work and the School to Work Transition*. Paper presented at the Workshop of the European research network Transitions in Youth (TiY), Oslo, September 2-5 1999.

Teichler, U. (2000). "Graduate Employment and Work in Selected European Countries." *European Journal of Education*. 35(2), 141-56.

Van der Velden, R.K.W. and Wolbers, M.H.J. (2001). *The Integration of Young People into the Labour Market within the European Union: The Role of Institutional Settings*. Paper presented at the European Research Conference on "Labour Market Change, Unemployment and Citizenship in Europe", Helsinki, Finland, 20-25 April 2001.

Van der Linden, A.S.R and van der Velden, R.K.W. (1998). "The Effects of Unemployment and Mismathes on Future Job Match and Earnings." In Lange. T. (ed) *Understanding the School-to-Work Transition: An International Perspective*. New York: Nova Science Publishers, pp. 109-124.

Wolbers, M. (2000). "The Effects of Level of Education on Mobility Between Employment and Unemployment in the Netherlands." *European Sociological Review* 16, 185-200.

JOSÉ GARCÍA-MONTALVO, JOSÉ-GINÉS MORA AND ADELA GARCIA-ARACIL

THE EMPLOYMENT SITUATION ABOUT FOUR YEARS AFTER GRADUATION

1. THE ECONOMIC, LABOUR MARKET AND EDUCATIONAL CONTEXT

The aim of this chapter is to describe the labour market situation of higher education graduates in 11 European countries and Japan about four years after graduation, i.e. at the time when they filled in the questionnaire. Before that, we shall describe the economic and labour market situation and the patterns of educational expenditures and enrolment of the countries included in this study.

As an indicator of the countries' relative level of development, we included in Table 1 the GDP per capita (row 1), measured in dollars converted through the purchasing power parity (PPP), though, as it is well known this is just a proxy for the actual level of development. Thus, Norway and Japan are the richest countries of the sample, with over $24,000 PPP, followed by Germany, the Netherlands and Austria (between $22,000 and $23,000). Other countries, i.e. France, Italy, the United Kingdom, Sweden and Finland are at approximately $20,000, while Spain and the Czech Republic are the poorest in the sample (below the $16,000 level).

The labour market indicators chosen here are the labour market participation rate (row 2) and the unemployment rate (row 3). Sweden and Norway show the highest participation rates with over 84per cent. At the other extreme, we find Spain (67.9%) and Italy (63.5%). With respect to unemployment in 1997, the Netherlands have the lowest level at 2.3 per cent, i.e. only a frictional unemployment. In contrast, we find Spain with 15.8 per cent. France and Finland also show rates of over 10 per cent and Germany close to 10 per cent .

As regards educational expenditure, we note that the Nordic countries outperform the rest of the countries in the sample. The share of public and private education of the GDP (row 4) in Sweden reaches 8.5 per cent, followed by Finland (6.9%), Austria (6.7%) and Norway (6.6%). In contrast, a level below 5 per cent for this indicator is found in Italy and Japan. Looking at total expenditures in tertiary education (row 5), we find, again, that the highest level is in the Nordic countries: only Sweden, Norway and Finland spend more than 2 per cent of the GDP on tertiary education, while Italy and the Czech Republic report the least expenditure. However, in calculating the ratio of expenditure per student over GDP per capita (row 6), we note a somewhat different ranking order. Again, the expenditures are highest in Sweden, followed by Austria, Germany and Netherlands, while Spain comes at the bottom of the list.

U. Teichler (ed.), Careers of University Graduates, 95–114

Table 1. Statistics of Economic Development, Unemployment, Educational Expenditures and Enrolment, by Country, 1997 (arithmetic mean and percentage)

	IT	ES	FR	AT	DE	NL	UK	FI	SE	NO	CZ	JP
1. GDP per capita (thousand dollars PPP)	21.3	16	21.3	23.1	22.1	22.1	20.5	20.8	20.4	26.9	13.1	24.6
2. Participation rate in the labour market [1]	63.5	67.9	77.2	70.5	75	73	79.8	78.4	84.1	84.4	79.3	78.3
3. Unemployment rate, population aged between 25 and 64	9.5	15.8	10.7	4.1	9.9	2.3	5.1	11.1	7.4	3.1	5.3	3.3
4. Expenditure in education[2]	4.9	5.8	6.4	6.7	5.9	5.1	4.6	6.9	8.5	6.6	5.5	4.8
5. Expenditure in tertiary education as percentage of GDP[3]	0.9	1.3	1.2	1.7	1.2	1.5	1.3	2	2.4	2.1	0.9	m
6. Expenditure per student in tertiary education as percentage of GDP per capita[4]	n.a.	32	34	43	43	45	40	35	64	38	41	41
7. Net rate of entrants in tertiary education type A[5]	n.a.	9	m	8	14	m	27	12	m	6	13	33
8. Net rate of entrants in tertiary education type B[6]	42	41	m	28	28	52	48	58	59	56	22	36

m = missing data

1. Of population aged between 25 and 64.
2. Public and private, including subsidies to families, as percentage of GDP. JP: not including subsidies. UK and NO only public expenditure.
3. Including subsidies to families.
4. AT and NO: not including subsidies. UK: only public education.
5. DE and JP: gross rate.
6. JP: gross rate.

Source: OECD (2000). Education at a Glance: OECD Educational Indicators 2000. Paris: OECD

The final two rows provide information on enrolment in higher education. Row 8 addresses new entrant students in bachelor programmes or longer university-type programmes, i.e. the type of students who were addressed in this graduate survey, while row 7 provides information on new entrant students in other tertiary education programmes requiring at least two years of study. According to row 8, the Nordic countries have the highest rates, while the Czech Republic, Austria and Germany have lowest rates of new entrants.

2. LABOUR FORCE PARTICIPATION AND UNEMPLOYMENT RATES

88 per cent of the graduates surveyed in the CHEERS study participated in the labour force (employed, self-employed or unemployed) about four years after graduation. As Figure 1 shows, the rate was 90 per cent and above in the Netherlands, Finland, Austria, Japan and the United Kingdom. In general, it was higher in all the countries analysed than that of the whole population (see Figure 1).

Figure 1. Labour Force Participation of Graduates Four Years After Graduation, by Country (percentage of respondents)

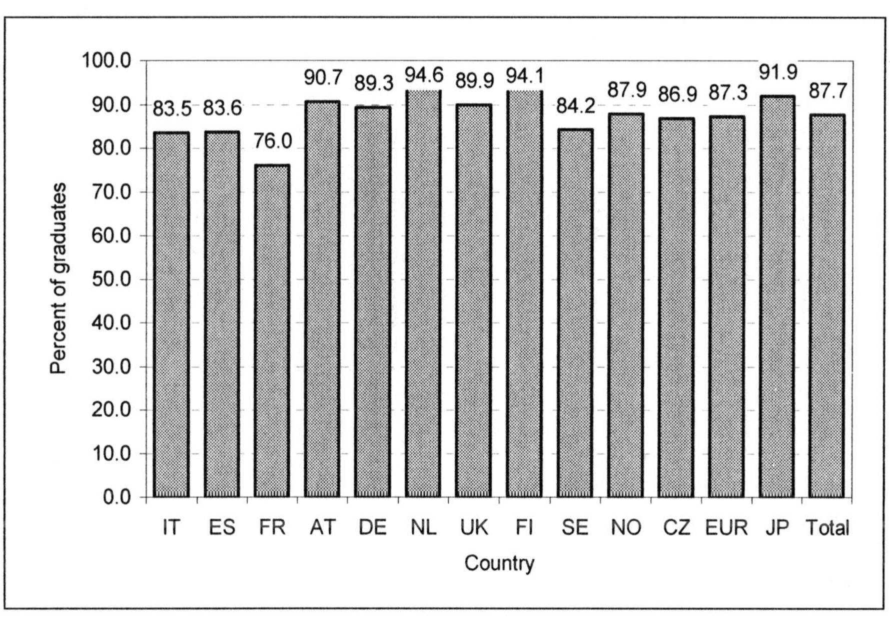

Question C10: Please inform us about your current major activity.
Labour force participation is defined here as the major activity status "employed", "self-employed" or "unemployed". Not included in the labour force are graduates with a major activity as "professional training", "study", "family" and "other activities".

Source: CHEERS survey data

Figure 2 shows that the unemployment rate for those graduates who participated in the labour force (i.e. not the proportion of all graduates responding) about four years after graduation was highest in Spain (12.5%) and France (9.6%); in both countries, unemployment among the respondents did not differ substantially from the overall national employment rates. In all other countries, the percentages of these graduates were between 0.9 per cent and 5.7 per cent. The rates of Finnish and German graduates were lowest compared to the national unemployment rates in the overall labour force.

Figure 2. Unemployment of Graduates Four Years After Graduation, by Country (percentage of graduates who participated in the labour force)

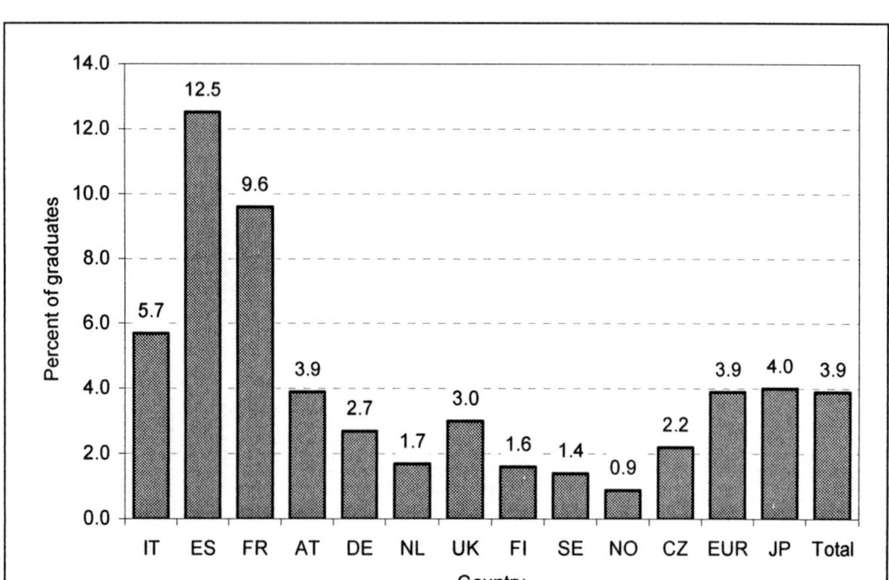

Question C10: Please inform us about your current major activity.
Unemployment: Proportion of unemployed graduates amongst graduates who participated in the labour force (see footnote of Figure 1).
Source: CHEERS survey data

Of the female graduates surveyed, 84 per cent as compared to 91 per cent of male graduates participated in the labour force about four years after graduation. The unemployment rates were 5 per cent and 3 per cent respectively. Altogether, the participation rate in the labour force of the women surveyed was more than 7 per cent lower and that of those employed (including self-employment) almost 10 per cent lower than that of the men surveyed.

Table 2 shows that, in contrast to the dominant pattern, the labour market participation rate about four years after graduation of the women surveyed in France was not lower than that of men; at the other extreme, 17 per cent fewer women than men participated in the labour force in the Czech Republic. There were also exceptions: women in the United Kingdom and Finland were less often unemployed than male graduates about four years after graduation. On the other hand, this unemployment rate in Italy and Sweden was three times as high as that of men.

Table 2. Labour Force Participation and Unemployment of Graduates Four Years After Graduation, by Country and Gender (percentage and ratio)

	Labour force participation		Unemployment rate		Relative labour force participation	Relative unemployment rate
	Male	Female	Male	Female	(female/male)	(female/male)
Italy	86.6	80.7	2.7	8.6	0.9	3.2
Spain	87.3	80.8	9.2	15.3	0.9	1.7
France	75.9	76.1	6.3	12.7	1.0	2.0
Austria	94.1	86.5	2.6	5.6	0.9	2.2
Germany	93.2	83.8	2.1	3.8	0.9	1.8
Netherlands	97.4	91.8	1.3	2.1	0.9	1.6
United Kingdom	92.7	88.0	4.0	2.4	0.9	0.6
Finland	97.1	91.7	1.6	1.5	0.9	0.9
Sweden	89.3	80.5	0.7	2.0	0.9	2.9
Norway	92.5	84.6	0.9	0.9	0.9	1.0
Czech Republic	94.3	77.4	1.7	2.9	0.8	1.7
Europe	91.0	83.8	2.9	5.0	0.9	1.7
Japan	94.3	86.8	3.7	4.7	0.9	1.3
Total	91.4	84.0	3.0	5.0	0.9	1.7

Question C10: Please inform us about your current major activity.

Source: CHEERS survey data

Figure 3 and Figure 4 show that the graduates surveyed differed according to field of study to a similar extent as according to country as far as these employment indicators were concerned. The labour force participation rate was the lowest and the unemployment rate was the highest for graduates in natural sciences; one must bear in mind, though, that a high proportion was predominantly engaged in advanced academic or professional training about four years after graduation. In contrast, a high labour force participation was reported by graduates in engineering, mathematics and social sciences, whereas the unemployment rate of the latter was about twice as high as that of those from the two other fields.

Figure 3. Labour Force Participation of Graduates Four Years After Graduation, by Field of Study (percentage of respondents)

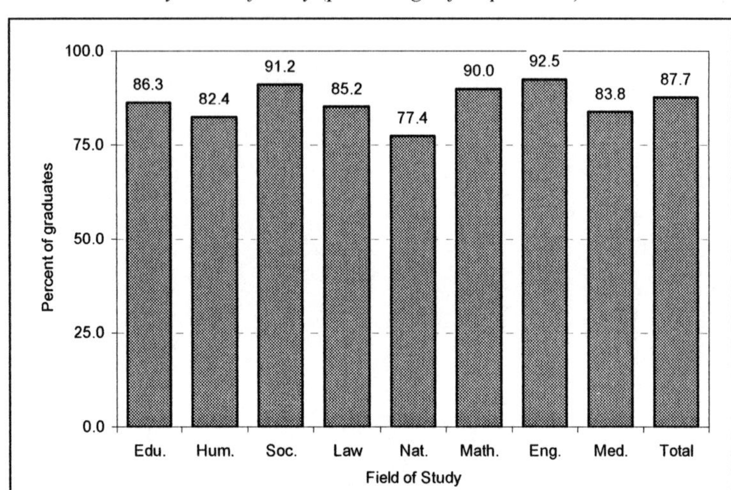

Question C10: Please inform us about your current major activity. Labour force participation is defined here as the major activity status "employed", "self-employed" or "unemployed". Not included in the labour force are graduates with a major activity as "professional training", "study", "family" and "other activities".

Source: CHEERS survey data

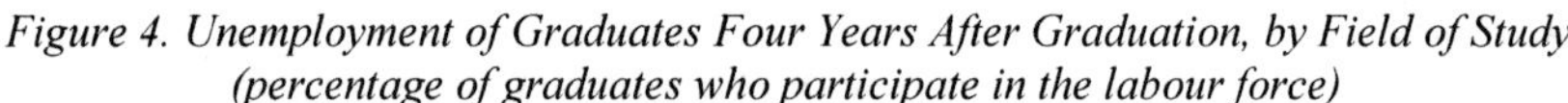

Figure 4. Unemployment of Graduates Four Years After Graduation, by Field of Study (percentage of graduates who participate in the labour force)

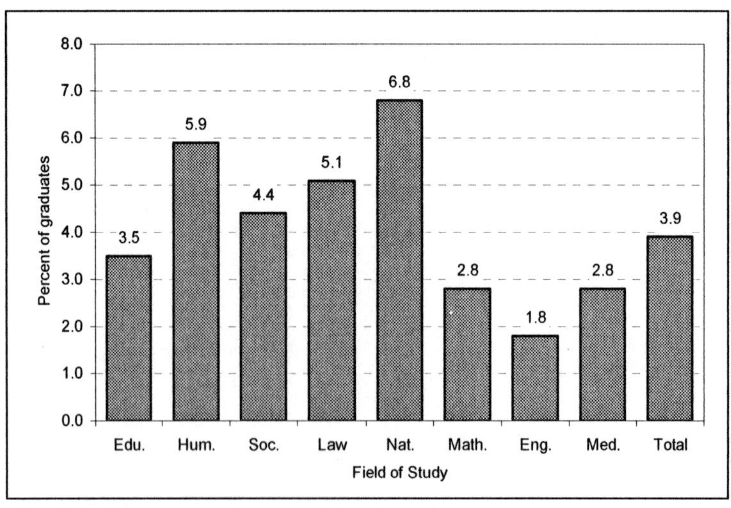

Question C10: Please inform us about your current major activity. Unemployment: Proportion of unemployed graduates of those graduates who participate in the labour force (see footnote of Figure 1).

Source: CHEERS survey data

3. ECONOMIC SECTOR AND OCCUPATIONAL GROUP

In addressing the economic sector where the graduates surveyed were professionally active about four years after graduation (see Table 3), we noted that the highest proportion worked in the education sector (18.0%), followed by mining and manufacturing (14.7%), the health sector (10.4%) and public administration (8.6%). These four sectors account for about half the graduates.

One should bear in mind that in all these sectors, except for engineering, a degree from a higher education institution was or tended to be seen as a mandatory entry requirement for a professional career. Large numbers of graduates in Finland (34.9%) and in Sweden (22.9%) were active in the education sector. The highest proportion of graduates in mining and manufacturing was observed in Japan (19.6%) and Germany (17.3%). Norway had the highest proportion of graduates employed in public administration (10.2%) and also headed the ranking in the health sector (26.0%).

Table 3. Economic Sector of Graduates Four Years After Graduation, by Country (percentage of employed graduates)

Economic sector	Country													Total
	IT	ES	FR	AT	DE	NL	UK	FI	SE	NO	CZ	EUR	JP	
Agriculture, hunting, forestry, fishing	.3	.2	.7	.1	.5	.5	.6	.0	.3	.2	2.8	.6	.6	.6
Mining & manufacturing	17.8	13.0	16.8	12.8	17.3	11.4	11.6	16.9	14.3	10.8	15.5	14.2	19.6	14.7
Electricity, gas and water supply	.2	.9	.9	1.3	.8	.4	1.1	1.0	.8	1.0	2.1	.9	2.2	1.1
Construction	.8	4.3	1.0	1.8	1.6	2.0	3.5	1.0	1.1	2.0	7.2	2.4	5.3	2.7
Trade	7.4	6.8	8.8	5.4	2.6	6.2	7.7	2.8	5.2	2.0	6.9	5.5	11.4	6.1
Transport, storage and communication	3.6	4.0	5.7	2.1	3.3	3.9	5.4	6.0	2.9	1.9	3.8	3.8	3.5	3.8
Financial intermediation	4.9	8.7	5.9	7.2	4.9	7.4	5.4	3.2	3.3	1.4	6.9	5.3	7.8	5.5
Computer and related activities	3.5	4.1	10.4	4.4	5.6	7.8	5.0	2.1	5.1	3.1	4.9	5.0	2.9	4.8
Research & development	2.5	2.1	1.4	2.1	2.9	1.9	1.4	4.0	4.2	1.9	1.5	2.3	4.6	2.6
Legal activities	8.6	.0	2.8	3.5	2.7	1.5	3.1	.7	1.0	1.2	4.8	2.7	1.9	2.7
Arch. & eng. consultants	6.6	.0	.8	2.6	4.0	4.7	.9	1.3	2.8	4.7	.6	2.8	1.4	2.6
Other business activities	10.8	13.1	6.3	7.6	7.3	11.9	7.4	4.9	7.5	2.1	2.3	7.3	.7	6.7
Public administration	8.5	5.2	7.9	6.1	13.1	7.5	8.4	5.9	9.1	10.2	6.6	8.2	12.0	8.6
Education	11.4	17.8	20.4	19.4	17.9	14.1	18.3	34.9	22.9	14.4	17.5	18.8	10.3	18.0
Health	7.8	14.5	2.3	13.1	8.2	9.3	10.3	7.7	10.2	26.0	7.5	10.9	5.3	10.4
Social work	1.8	.0	2.4	3.2	3.1	5.0	1.4	2.0	3.2	14.8	.6	3.7	.9	3.4

to be continued

Table 3. Continued

	Country													Total
	IT	ES	FR	AT	DE	NL	UK	FI	SE	NO	CZ	EUR	JP	
Other service activities	3.6	5.2	5.4	7.3	4.3	4.4	7.5	5.7	6.1	2.2	8.5	5.4	8.1	5.6
Other	.0	.0	.0	.0	.0	.0	1.0	.0	.0	.0	.0	.1	1.4	.2
Total*	100	100	100	100	100	100	100	100	100	100	100	100	100	100

Question D5: In which economic sector are you currently working?
* Count by Country: IT (2498); ES (2025); FR (1918); AT (2018); DE (2833); NL (2877); UK (3100); FI (2396); SE (2434); NO (3028); CZ (2575); EUR (27703); JP (2846); Total (30549).
Source: CHEERS survey data

Table 4. Economic Sector of Graduates Four Years After Graduation, by Field of Study (percentage of employed graduates)

Economic sector	Field of study								Total
	Edu.	Hum.	Soc.	Law	Nat.	Math.	Eng.	Med.	
Agriculture, hunting, forestry, fishing	.2	.2	.3	.2	.8	.3	1.8	.1	.6
Mining & manufacturing	3.1	9.7	13.9	4.8	18.6	11.6	33.1	2.9	14.7
Electricity, gas and water supply	.1	.2	1.1	.7	1.3	.6	2.6	.1	1.1
Construction	.4	1.2	2.0	1.0	1.5	.7	7.9	.4	2.7
Trade	2.5	6.5	9.9	4.3	4.2	3.6	4.5	4.5	6.1
Transport, storage and communication	1.3	4.0	4.9	2.4	2.7	5.8	5.4	.4	3.8
Financial intermediation	1.4	2.4	11.7	9.8	1.7	8.5	1.5	.7	5.5
Computer and related activities	1.5	2.4	3.7	1.3	6.5	32.9	6.8	.4	4.8
Research & development	.4	1.7	1.2	.8	11.2	2.8	4.7	1.1	2.5
Legal activities	.6	1.2	1.5	24.4	1.4	.5	.4	.1	2.7
Arch. & eng. consultants	.4	.8	.7	.2	2.5	.9	10.1	.0	2.6
Other business activities	1.4	5.7	12.6	8.5	4.8	5.1	3.9	1.1	6.6
Public administration	3.6	7.4	11.6	27.2	5.9	5.0	4.8	3.3	8.6
Education	64.8	33.7	8.8	5.4	26.9	17.0	7.0	6.1	17.9
Health	2.8	3.7	4.7	2.3	5.0	2.4	2.4	73.2	10.4
Social work	11.2	1.3	5.2	.9	.8	.1	.3	4.0	3.4
Other service activities	4.3	17.6	5.9	5.6	4.1	1.7	2.6	1.2	5.6
Other	.1	.4	.3	.1	.1	.4	.1	.4	.2
Total	100.0	100.0	100.0	100.0	100.0	100.0	100.0	100.0	100.0
Count	(3115)	(3502)	(9153)	(2256)	(1821)	(1237)	(6315)	(3000)	(30400)

Question D5: In which economic sector are you currently working?
Source: CHEERS survey data

Table 4 shows the extent to which graduates are concentrated or dispersed over economic sectors. We note that the highest concentration of medical graduates is in the health sector (73.2%) and that the highest concentration of education graduates is in the education sector (64.8%). Similarly, though not in a single category, we see that about 60 per cent of engineering graduates are in mining and production-dominated industries and that 52 per cent of law graduates are in legal activities and public administration. The concentration is lower for graduates in the humanities (33.7% in education) and mathematics (32.9% in computer and related activities), while social science graduates are widely dispersed across economic sectors.

Most graduates from all groups of field of study about four years after graduation are classified as professionals or as legislators, senior officials and managers. The proportion of those who worked in either of these two categories ranges, as Table 5 shows, from slightly more than 60 per cent in the humanities, social sciences and medical fields to about 80 per cent in mathematics, natural sciences, engineering and education. The proportion of technicians and associated professionals was very high amongst the graduates in medical fields (32.7%) – especially those in nursing and other types of para-medical education. Finally, the highest proportion of those working as clerks or service and sales workers came from the humanities and social sciences.

Table 5. Occupation of Graduates Four Years After Graduation, by Field of Study (percentage of employed graduates)

	Field of study								Total
	Edu.	Hum.	Soc.	Law	Nat.	Math.	Eng.	Med.	
Legislators, senior officials and managers	12.2	7.2	14.3	8.1	7.0	7.9	9.2	3.7	10.0
Professionals	63.1	59.8	47.5	66.0	72.3	71.9	69.7	60.8	60.4
Technicians and associate professionals	19.6	14.7	19.3	11.3	13.6	15.8	16.5	32.7	18.4
Lower occupations	5.1	18.3	19.0	14.7	7.1	4.3	4.7	2.8	11.3
Total	100.0	100.0	100.0	100.0	100.0	100.0	100.0	100.0	100.0
Count	(2564)	(3197)	(8089)	(2049)	(1676)	(1136)	(5764)	(2616)	27091

Question C10: Please inform us about your current major activity: Job title (classified according ISCO88 major groups).

Source: CHEERS survey data

4. FULL-TIME/PART-TIME EMPLOYMENT AND WORKING HOURS

Of all the graduates employed (including self-employment) about four years after graduation, more than 10 per cent were employed part-time. As Figure 5 shows, the share was highest in Italy (18.9%), but also above average in Spain, the Netherlands, Germany, Austria and Norway, whilst it was below the 5 per cent mark in the Czech Republic, Japan and Finland. Often the quota was high in problematic labour market conditions, but part-time employment policies also played a role (notably in Norway and the Netherlands).

Part-time work was most frequent amongst graduates in humanities, education and medical fields (17%-19%), i.e. the fields with the highest proportion of women. It was around average (8%-12%) in fields with a balanced gender composition (natural sciences, social sciences and law), and was lowest in engineering and mathematics, i.e. in male-dominated fields. Obviously, these differences are largely due to the much more frequent part-time employment of women (16% altogether) than of men (6%).

The differences in part-time work were relatively small by occupational group, with managers below average (8%), technicians and associate professionals above average (13%) and professionals as well as others (clerks, office and sales workers etc.) around average. Concerning economic sectors, we noted four – again women-dominated – with very high shares of part-timers:

- social work (27%),
- education (20%),
- health (19%) and other service activities (16%).

In all other economic sectors, part-time work is below average.

Figure 5. Part-time Work of Graduates Four Years After Graduation, by Country (percentage of employed graduates)

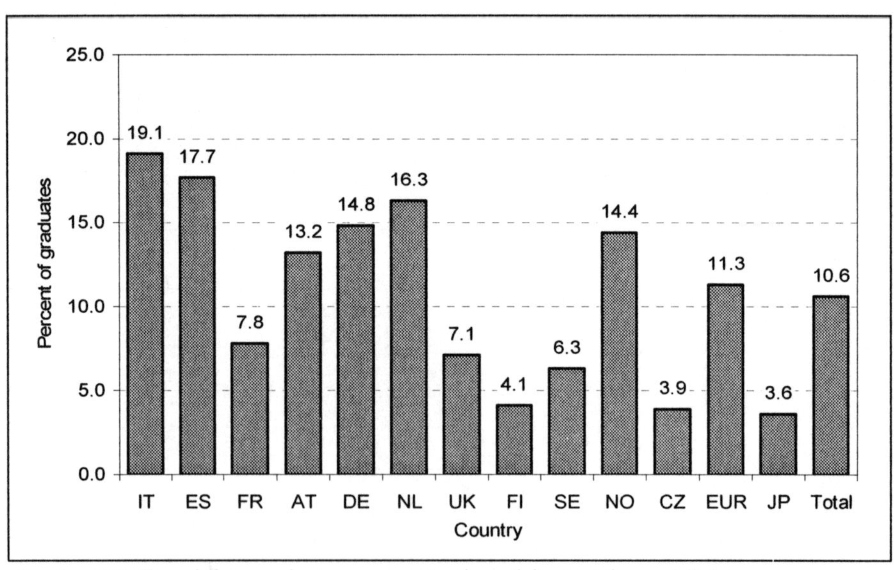

Question C10: Please inform us about your current major activity. Part-time or full-time.
Source: CHEERS survey data

Altogether, we noted similar findings when analysing weekly working hours. The graduates reported that they were professionally active for 44 hours on average (including overtime). By excluding overtime, we note that more than 80 per cent worked at least 35 hours a week.

Again, working less than 35 hours was more frequent amongst women. 6 per cent as compared to 3 per cent of men had less than 20 hour-jobs, and 11 per cent of women, as compared to 3 per cent of men, had a 20-34 hour work load. Jobs of less than 35 hours were most frequent amongst graduates in Spain, Italy (as the data on part-time employment have also shown) and France (see Figure 6).

Figure 6. Weekly Working Hours of Graduates Four Years After Graduation, by Country (percentage of employed graduates)

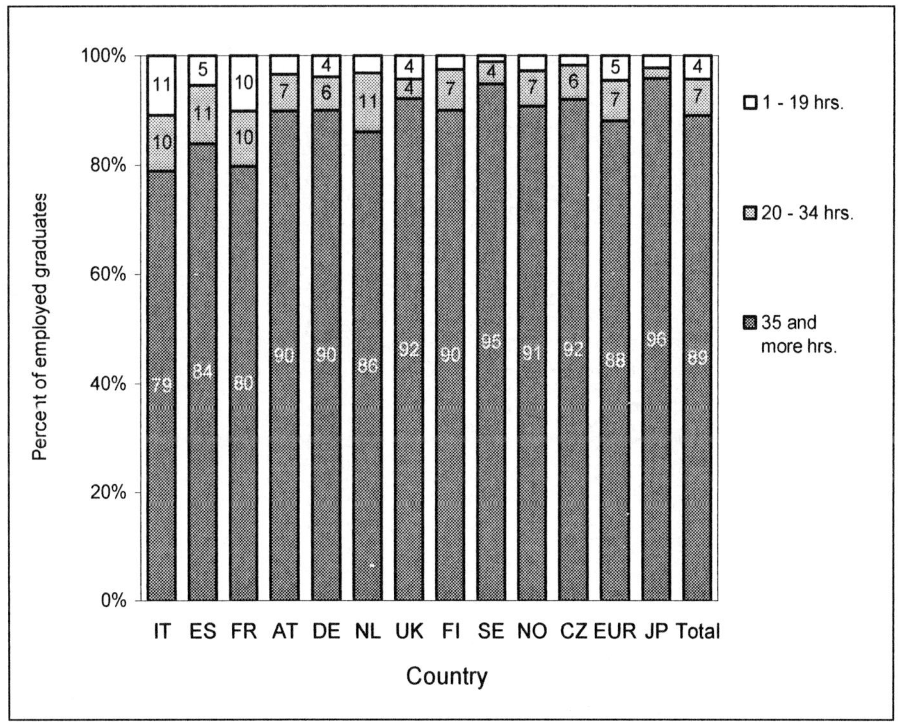

Question D7: How many hours per week are you working on average? a) Contract hours of my major assignment; b) additional working hours of my major assignment (paid and unpaid overtime); c) working hours on other assignments (second occupation, side jobs, etc.); d) total working hours (incl. self-employment). The chart presents the results for the "total working hours".

Source: CHEERS survey data

5. SELF-EMPLOYMENT OR DEPENDENT EMPLOYMENT

Self-employment was chosen by 6 per cent of all the graduates who were working four years after graduation. Men (7%) had a slightly higher propensity to self-employment than women (5%).

The most striking differences can be observed by country. As Figure 7 shows, self-employment was by far most frequent amongst graduates from Italy (18.5%) and second most frequent amongst those from Austria (8.7%). Self-employment was also above average amongst graduates in Spain, Germany and the Czech Republic (7%-8%), whilst it was below average (ranging from 2%-5%) in the remaining countries. The highest proportion was found in countries where graduates faced great problems in transiting to employment and embarking on a professional career.

Figure 7. Self-Employment of Graduates Four Years After Graduation, by Country (percentage)

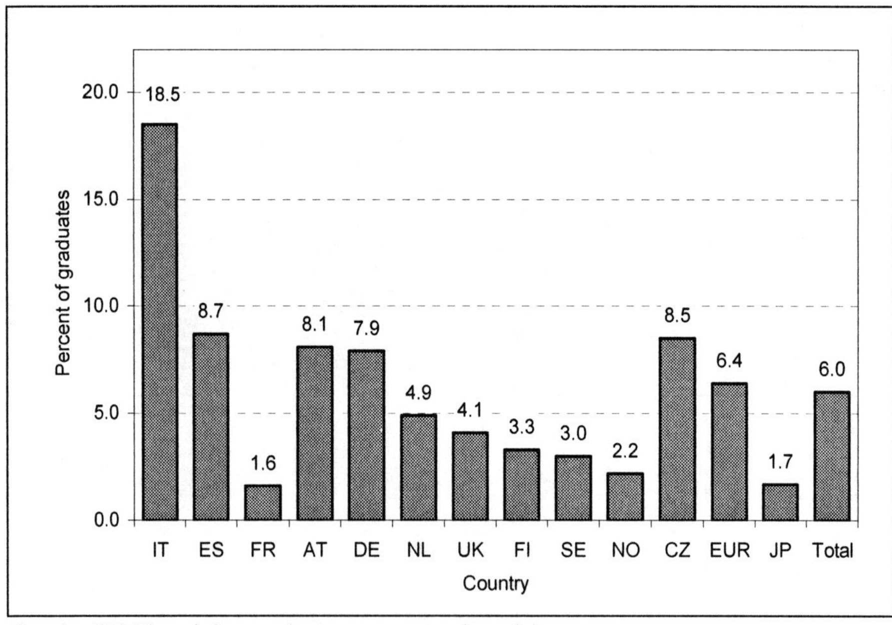

Question C10: Please inform us about your current major activity.

Source: CHEERS survey data

As regards field of study (see Figure 8), we note that the proportion of self-employed graduates was highest for law graduates (12%), which reflects the status of independent legal professionals, and above average for those in the humanities (8.5%). In contrast, relatively low levels of self-employment were observed amongst graduates in education, natural sciences and mathematics (3%-4%).

With respect to the economic sector, legal services scored the highest in self-employed graduates (28%) because many lawyers work independently. Other sectors with high rates of self-employment were architecture and engineering services (21%), other business activities (16%), and agriculture (15%).

Figure 8. Self-Employment of Graduates Four Years After Graduation, by Field of Study (percentage)

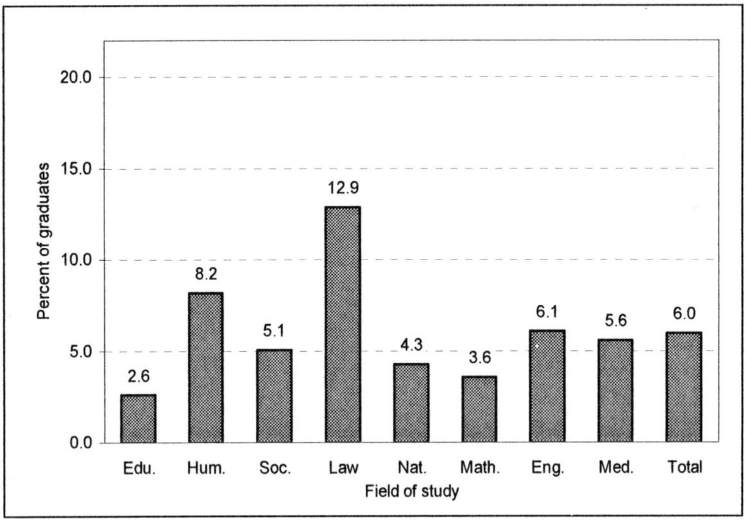

Field of study	Percent of graduates
Edu.	2.6
Hum.	8.2
Soc.	5.1
Law	12.9
Nat.	4.3
Math.	3.6
Eng.	6.1
Med.	5.6
Total	6.0

Question C10: Please inform us about your current major activity.
Source: CHEERS survey data

The latter sector had the highest level of self-employment in general. Many graduates who worked in the agricultural sector in various countries were often owners of small or medium size land resources. The lowest rates of self-employment were found amongst the graduates working in public administration (1%) and the electricity-water-gas sector (2%). The nature of the employer, public administration, and the large size of electricity-gas-water companies explain these low figures.

6. INCOME

A key characteristic of the quality of a job is the income that can be generated from it in the case of self-employment, or the wage, in case of dependent work. Figure 9 shows the gross income of graduates by country measured in Euros corrected by the parity of the purchasing power. We see that the lowest earnings were reported by graduates living in the Czech Republic (only 14,300 Euros) and Spain (17,700 Euros), which also had the lowest levels of income per capita (see Table 1). The highest nominal gross income was reported by graduates from Germany (31,200 Euros) and the United Kingdom (26,400 Euros as compared to slightly less than 24,000 Euros on average among all professionally active graduates surveyed).

Figure 9. Annual Gross Income From Major Job of Graduates Four Years After Graduation, by Country (arithmetic mean; in thousands of Euros standardised by the purchasing power)

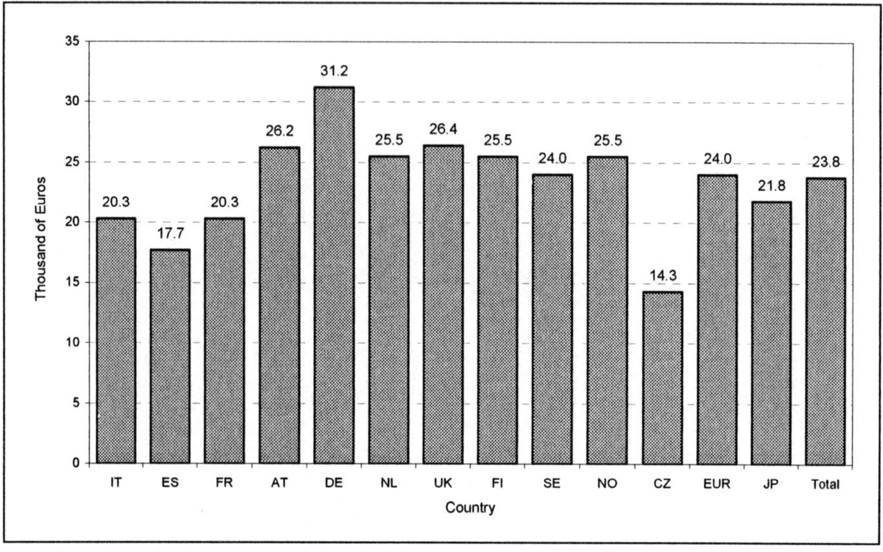

Question D11: What is your approximate annual gross income? a. from your current major job (excluding overtime and extra payments)? b. from overtime and extra payments in your major job? c. from other jobs? The chart presents the results for a) "current major job".

Source: CHEERS survey data

The income varied to a lesser extent by groups of field of study. It was highest on average for mathematics graduates (28,700 Euros) many of whom worked in new technology jobs. In contrast, education graduates had the lowest (19,400 Euros) whereby only part of it was likely to be compensated by high indirect incomes of civil servants. In part, the income differences by fields of study were linked to different percentages of women, who, on average, earned 21 per cent less than male graduates about four years after graduation (including those working part-time).

With respect to the economic sector, Figure 10 shows that the highest incomes were earned by graduates in computer and related activities (28,900 Euros), financial intermediation (28,700 Euros) and mining and manufacturing (27,100 Euros). The lowest level of gross income was found amongst graduates working in education (19,400 Euros) and agriculture, hunting, forestry and fishing (17,600 Euros).

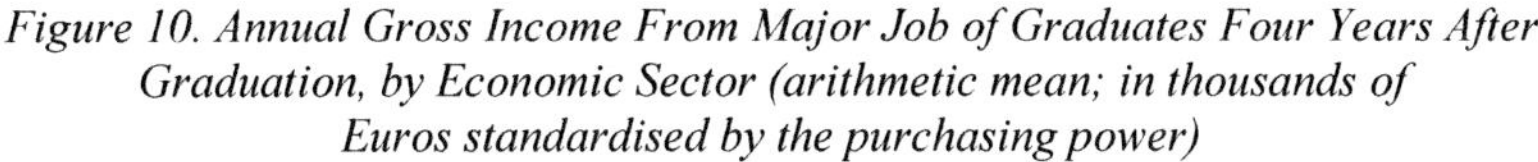

Figure 10. Annual Gross Income From Major Job of Graduates Four Years After Graduation, by Economic Sector (arithmetic mean; in thousands of Euros standardised by the purchasing power)

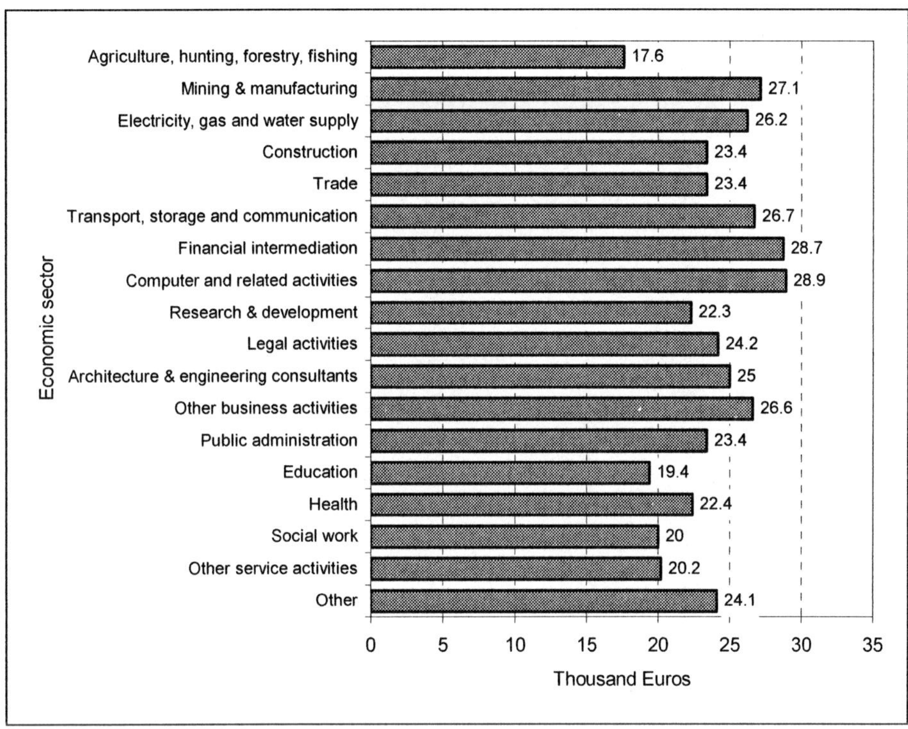

Question D11: What is your approximate annual gross income? a. from your current major job (excluding overtime and extra payments)? b. from overtime and extra payments in your major job? c. from other jobs? The chart presents the results for a) "current major job".

Source: CHEERS survey data

7. PERMANENT OR TEMPORARY CONTRACT

A permanent contract is generally considered as a characteristic of the quality of employment. During the first few years after graduation, however, temporary contracts are frequent and are not consistently a sign of precarious career prospects, as notably the public service in various European countries offers a temporary contract for a few years as an entry stage of a regular career. Over 22 per cent of the professionally active graduates surveyed had a temporary contract about four years after graduation.

Figure 11 shows that the proportion of temporary contracts was by far the highest in Spain where it applied to more than half the active graduates about four years after graduation. This is because it became the general pattern as a consequence of a reform of employment conditions in the mid-1990s.

The second country was Finland where 35.0 per cent of the graduates had a temporary contract. In contrast, Japan was the country where these contracts represented by far the smallest percentage; short-term contracts was still uncommon at the time the graduates surveyed became employed.

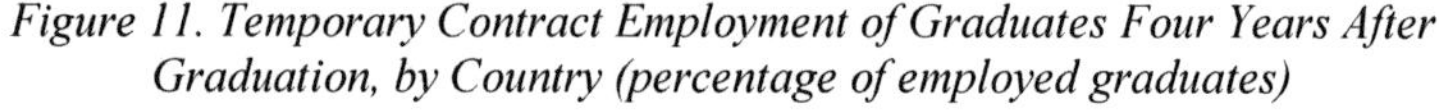

Figure 11. Temporary Contract Employment of Graduates Four Years After Graduation, by Country (percentage of employed graduates)

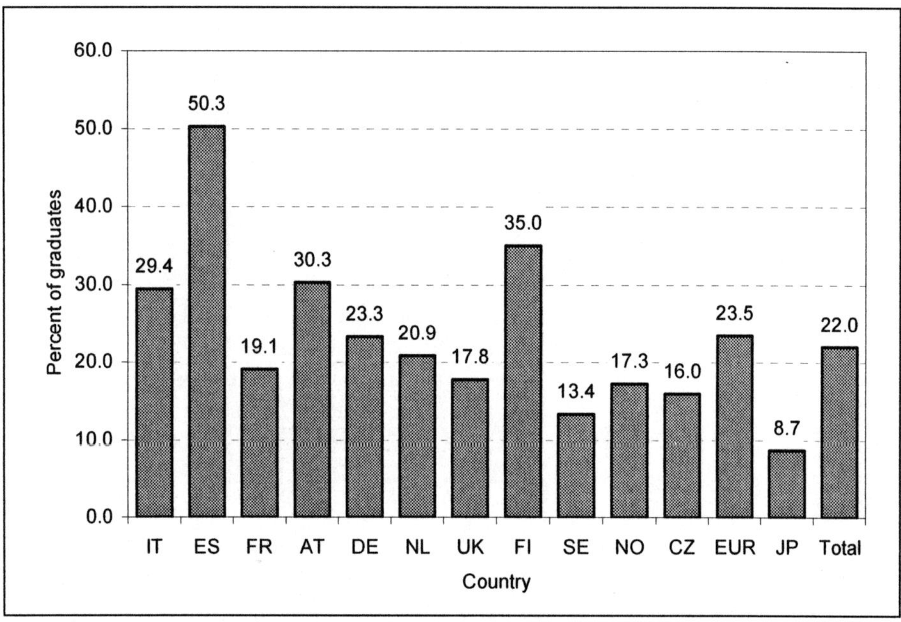

Question C10: Please inform us about your current major activity. Temporary or permanent contract.
Source: CHEERS survey data

Over 30 per cent of graduates in medical sciences, natural sciences and humanities held a temporary contract about four years after graduation while, in contrast, those in engineering and mathematics had the lowest share (below 16%). The high proportion in the former fields of study is largely a career stage phenomenon: many graduates in natural sciences only embarked on a regular position with a permanent contract several years after graduation, notably because many followed advanced academic studies and professional training after graduation, and medical doctors had to undergo various years of professional training and practice before being qualified and professionally settled.

As regards occupational groups, we noted that the proportion of those on temporary contracts amongst professionals was above average (27%). In contrast, most of those who worked as legislators, senior officials and managers seemed to be settled, as the low proportion of permanent contracts (11%) suggests.

The explanations above relating to the causes of large proportions of temporary employment are most visibly confirmed by the distribution by economic sector.

Temporary contracts were most frequent (41.0%) amongst graduates working in the research and development sector – notably in higher education and public research institutions, as other studies have shown. Other sectors with a high level of temporary jobs (see Figure 12) were education (also 40.9%) and the health sector (37.1%). This does not fully explain the higher proportion of temporary contracts amongst the women (27%) than the men surveyed (18%).

Figure 12. Temporary Contract Employment of Graduates Four Years After Graduation, by Economic Sector (percentage of employed graduates)

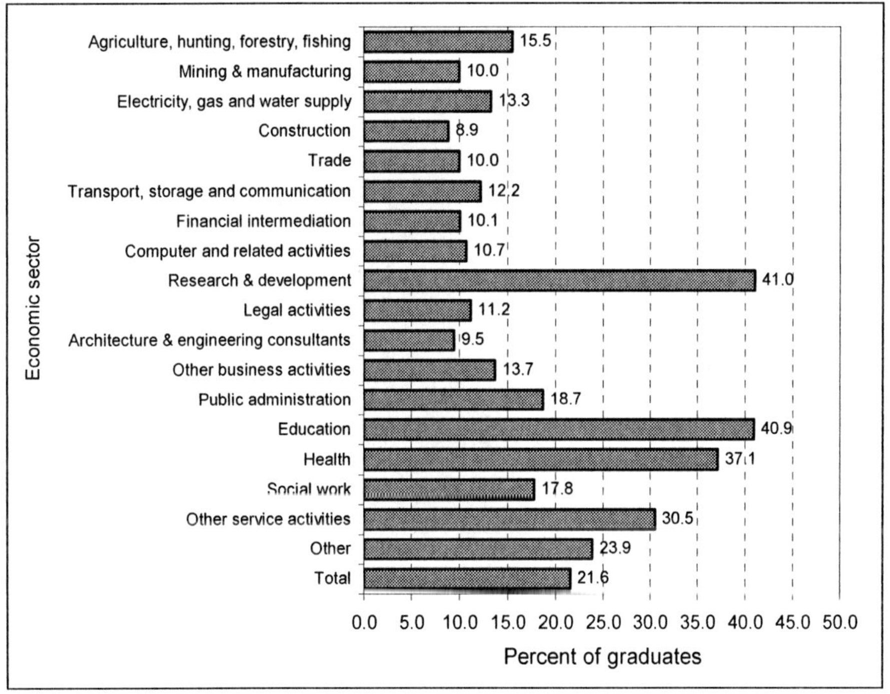

Question C10: Please inform us about your current major activity. Temporary or permanent contract.
Source: CHEERS survey data

8. FIRM SIZE AND GRADUATE EMPLOYMENT

Another important characteristic of graduates' jobs is the size of the firm in which they work. This indicator has two important determinants. On the one hand, the productive structure of a country determines the average size of the firms in each of them and, therefore, influences the results. On the other, being a graduate from a higher education institution may also determine the size of the typical firm that hires her or him. We should note here that public administration is always included as a large "firm" and that this is one of the favourite areas of employment for graduates from higher education institutions .

Graduates tended to work in large firms more frequently than workers in general. But the proportion of graduates who worked in large firms (more than 100 employees) was only 30 per cent in Italy, compared to 68 per cent in Japan and 55 per cent on average in Europe.

As regards fields of study, it comes as a surprise that a very high proportion (66%) of mathematics graduates tended to work in large firms. This could be because a substantial share work in the public sector, which – as mentioned above – tends to be counted as a large size firm, and most of those in the new technology sector tended to be hired by large firms.

9. CONCLUSION

The CHEERS survey addressed the situation of graduates from higher education institutions about four years after graduation at the end of the 1990s. The career stage analysed turned out in most cases to be the moment when initial search and trial and error activities, as well as the initial preparatory training within the firm or the profession, was over and when major steps of career progression had not yet begun. The data show, however, that a substantial number of graduates in Natural Sciences and Medicine is still in a provisional situation four years after graduation because of the frequency of advanced academic education in the Natural Sciences and the long periods of training and provisional professional practice in medical careers.

Most graduates in the 12 countries surveyed were in regular employment four years after graduation. Over 87 per cent of the respondents were professionally active, of whom 6 per cent were self-employed and 4 per cent were unemployed. Thus, the participation rate in the labour force clearly exceeded the average, and the unemployment rate was clearly below the average of the total population at the typical age for employment. 70 per cent were employed as managers and professionals, and about two-thirds of graduates in the majority of groups of field of study worked in one or two economic sectors which were most closely linked to the respective fields. On average, the graduates who were professionally active four years after graduation had an annual gross income of approximately 24,000 Euros.

The situation, however, was not altogether without problems. About 11 per cent were employed as clerks, service and sales officers and in other occupations, i.e. in occupations generally viewed as not appropriate for graduates. Altogether, 11 per cent of those who were professionally active were employed part-time, and (including those who call themselves part-timers) more than 20 per cent held a job in which they worked less than 35 hours a week. Some of the 6 per cent of those who were self-employed were in an unstable, lowly remunerated situation. Last but not least, for a substantial share of the more than 22 per cent of those who were employed on a temporary contract, this indicated a problematic employment situation.

Women were also predominantly in a regular employment situation about four years after graduation. Disparities between men and women, as the chapter dealing specifically with gender issues in this volume shows, were predominantly linked to child-rearing (about one quarter of the women surveyed had children in the household) and to the unequal distribution of women across fields of study. This chapter shows that 7 per cent fewer women than men were professionally active, while 2 per cent more women than men were unemployed about four years after graduation. 10 per cent more of the professionally active women than men were employed part-time. In addition, 15 per cent more women than men reported a weekly workload of less than 35 hours, even though they did not call themselves part-timers. 10 per cent more professionally active women than men were on a temporary contract, and their income was more than 20 per cent less on average than that of men, whereby less than one quarter of the difference seems to be due to less full-time employment and fewer working hours of women.

In analysing the links between field of study, economic sector and occupational group we noted smaller differences by field than by country. On average, across the countries analysed, graduates in engineering and mathematics were more or less consistently, according to the various indicators employed, in the most favourable situation. Graduates in mathematics obviously benefited from the spread of new technologies. In contrast, the highest proportion of graduates in less favoured employment situations were found in the natural sciences and humanities and partly as well in education and health fields.

There were, however, four reasons to relativise the data four years after graduation. First, as has already been stated, many natural scientists and medical doctors were in a provisional employment situation about four years after graduation and were likely to improve their situation at a later stage of their career. Second, the social science category employed in our analysis was heterogeneous: graduates in business studies were also in a very favourable situation on average. Third, the differences between fields and economic sector were less impressive, if the larger indirect income components and the higher job security in the public sectors could be demonstrated. Fourth, the low-income sectors of education, social work and para-professional health occupations and the respective fields of study were frequently chosen by women as the best opportunity of combining employment and the upbringing of children, notably by reducing their weekly work-load on the job.

This study contributes more to the comparison of graduate employment and work across industrialised countries than to the themes discussed hitherto. Obviously, the most striking differences according to country in the speed of transition from higher education to employment and in the employment situation over the first two years, as discussed in previous chapters, have levelled off to some extent about four years after graduation. Still, differences by country in the employment situation about four years after graduation are substantial: The proportion of graduates who were professionally active varied among the 12 countries from more than 90 per cent to about three quarters, and the unemployment rate between 1 per cent and 13 per cent. At one extreme, the proportion of men and women who were professionally active was equal, at the other about 20 per cent fewer women were employed. In two countries, the unemployment rate of women was lower than that of men, while in two other countries, their unemployment rate was three times as high as that of men. Employment in managerial or professional positions varied by country between 95 per cent and

45 per cent. Graduate income differed on average by a ratio of about 1:2 in Western European countries, even if different price levels are taken into consideration. Part-time employment quotas ranged from 4 per cent to 19 per cent and quotas of temporary employment from 9 per cent to 50 per cent .

In various respects of regular employment, but not consistently across all indicators, graduates in the Nordic countries were in the most favourable situation. In addition, they had the highest income in Germany, the most stable employment situation in Japan, the highest chance of being in a managerial and professional position in Austria and a low risk of being unemployed in the Netherlands. In reverse, the employment situation looked consistently worse in Spain and in various respects in Italy, France and the Czech Republic as well.

Obviously, economic wealth, the national unemployment rate as well as the public welfare system are factors that explain some of these differences. But other factors come into play as well. Graduates tended to be relatively privileged in countries with a low ratio of new entrant students. In the Nordic countries, an elaborate welfare system seems to be associated with a large number of employment opportunities in the public sector, with specific opportunities for graduates, notably in fields where women are strongly represented. In Japan, the employers are the guarantors of stable employment. In some countries, notably in the Netherlands and Norway, specific policies of encouraging part-time employment, and possibly thereby reducing unemployment, seemed to affect graduate employment significantly. In Spain, a general policy of granting temporary work contracts was implemented. In Italy, self-employment of graduates seemed to be more acceptable than in other countries. Thus, the study suggests that we must be aware of the diversity of graduate employment across countries and the multitude of factors in play.

PAUL KELLERMANN

ACQUIRED COMPETENCES AND JOB REQUIREMENTS

1. INTRODUCTION

1.1. The Growing Role of Useful Competences

No clear distinction was made between study in general and preparation for a professional activity in the universities of the Middle Ages. Theology and philosophy provided the basis for law and medicine. A clearer distinction was made by Friedrich Schiller and his idealistic colleagues between the "philosophical head", i.e. the thinker for enlightenment, and the "bread scholar", i.e. the striver for money. Nonetheless, studying, learning, researching and teaching at a university continued to be considered ends in themselves. Even the symposium "The Development of a Taxonomy of Educational Objectives" in Chicago/Illinois in 1951 had an idealistic basis. The turning point of conceptions of higher education as preparation for employment could be the OECD conference on "Economic Growth and Investment in Education" in 1961. In the "Sector Working Paper 'Education' " published by the World Bank in 1974, Robert S. McNamarra wrote in the foreword: "While millions of people from among the educated are unemployed, millions of jobs are waiting to be done because people with the right education, training and skills cannot be found." (World Bank, 1974: I). The Sorbonne declaration of May 25, 1998, stressed the universities' role in promoting graduate mobility and employability. The joint declaration of the European Ministers of Education convened in Bologna on the 19th of June 1999 emphasised the "achievement of greater compatibility and comparability of the systems of higher education" in order to increase "the international competitiveness of the European system of higher education". Whether or not these political purposes are met crucially depends on how graduates acquire competences.

1.2. The Meaning of Competence

"Competence" is first of all the term for the ability to act specifically. While in the legal field "competence" means the legitimate right to act on the basis of formal authorisation, in the social domain – and in this analysis – competence, as opposed to incompetence, means the ability, acquired through learning and socialisation, to act successfully. Influenced by variations in dealing with the social and natural environment, personalities differ with regard to knowledge, skills and emotions. With regard to graduates' competence acquisition, the particular world of the universities is of interest: to what extent do higher education studies contribute to the provision and acquisition of competences to act successfully in the world of work? The findings presented here, however, are not based on the observation of actions where

U. Teichler (ed.), Careers of University Graduates, 115–130

competences are used, but rather on the responses to questionnaires asking graduates to rate their acquired competences and to compare them with the competences required by the job.

1.3. Themes and Procedures of Analysis

The following analysis is interested in the practical value of studies and competences which graduates have acquired for professional use and for everyday life because the enrolment quota in higher education has increased substantially in the last few decades and the quality of university education is often criticised. We ask specifically: How satisfied are the graduates with their studies? What do they consider as their strongest acquired competences? What do they view as the most demanding competences required by their jobs? In which areas do their competences acquired at the time of graduation exceed requirements about four years after graduation ("surpluses"), and where do the job requirements substantially exceed the acquired competences ("deficits")?

2. BENEFITS OF STUDY

2.1. Utility of Study for the Profession and Other Spheres of Life

According to the analysis of the data (see Figure 1), 6 out of 10 graduates perceived their studies as quite useful for coping with professional tasks. This compares with only 4 out of 10 recognising benefits of their studies for other spheres of life. This does not mean that the others did not see any benefits: only 4 per cent of the respondents did not see a benefit for their profession and 7 per cent saw no benefits for other spheres than for their professional activities.

By a significant margin, the Czech graduates (84%) saw the greatest professional benefit of their studies, followed by graduates from the three Nordic countries (76%-79%). German, French and Italian respondents (44%-46%) were far more sceptical. The utility of studies for other life spheres was rated highest by Dutch graduates and lowest by French graduates.

The medical graduates (76%) saw most frequently substantial benefits of their studies for their professional activities, whereas those in humanities saw them the least. The views varied to a lesser extent by field of study with respect to the utility of study for other spheres of life (see Figure 2).

Figure 1. Utility of Study, by Country (percentage of employed graduates)

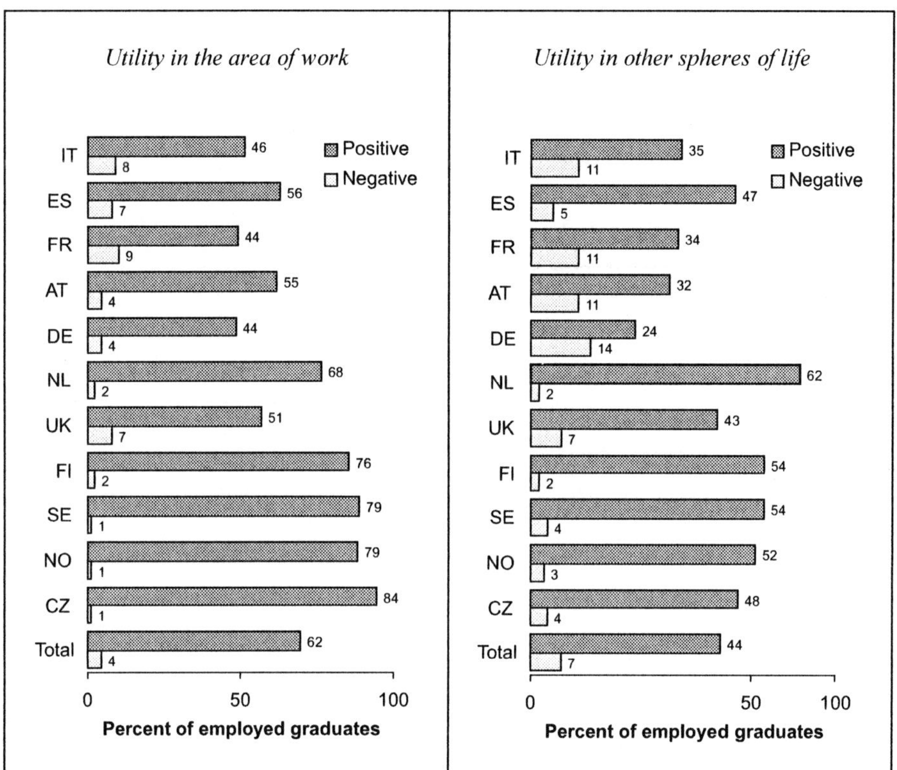

Question E2: To what extent have your studies (you graduated in1994 or 1995) been useful for ...? Scale of answers from 1 = "To a very high extent" to 5 = "Not at all". Positive = scale points 1 and 2; negative = scale point 5.

Source: CHEERS survey data

Compared to graduates from other fields of study in the respective countries, Finnish and Czech medical graduates were deeply convinced of the professional benefits of their studies. Czech (with an amazing rate of 93%), were followed by Swedish, Norwegian and German law graduates. In contrast, Italian, French, Spanish, Austrian and British graduates in the humanities seemed most dissatisfied. These findings seem to reflect the clarity or vagueness of visible links between field of study and occupational area.

As regards benefits for other spheres of life, medical graduates, notably in Germany, but also in Austria, Italy and the Czech Republic held the most negative views. In contrast, graduates in the humanities in Spain, Italy, Austria and Germany as well as in the social sciences in Sweden, Finland, Great Britain and Germany seemed to be most satisfied with the benefits of their studies outside their profession.

Figure 2. Utility of Study, by Field of Study (percentage of employed graduates)

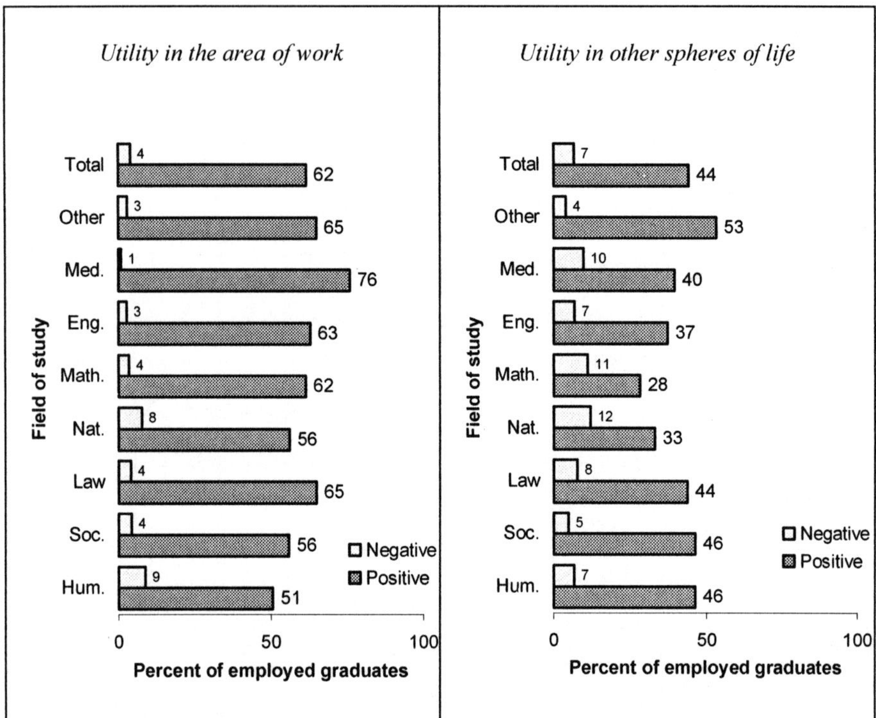

Question E2: To what extent have your studies (you graduated in 1994 or 1995) been useful for ...? Scale of answers from 1 = "To a very high extent" to 5 = "Not at all". Positive = scale points 1 and 2; negative = scale point 5.

Source: CHEERS survey data

2.2. *Professional Relevance of Foreign Language Proficiency*

The professional importance of foreign language communication seemed to be very different in the various countries (see Figure 3). Altogether, about 40 per cent of the European graduates considered foreign language proficiency as important. The Finnish graduates considered it as most important (65%), whilst the British graduates considered it as least important (12%). Obviously, the larger the language area and the more the home language was known internationally, the less foreign language proficiency was considered as professionally relevant.

Figure 3. Importance of Communicating in Foreign Languages, by Country (percentage of employed graduates)

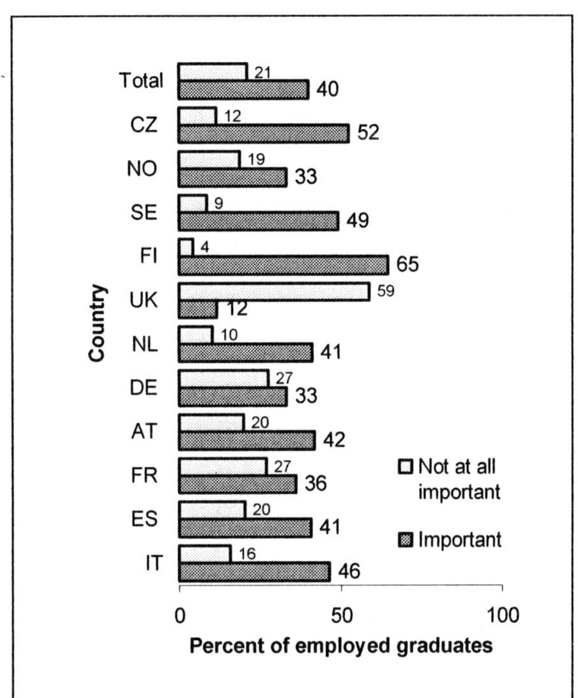

Question E3: How important do you consider the following competences for your current work? d) Communicating in a foreign language. Scale of answers from 1 = "Very important" to 5 = "Not at all important". Important = scale points 1 and 2; "Not at all important = scale point 5.

Source: CHEERS survey data

Across countries, communicating in a foreign language was seen as most relevant by graduates in engineering, natural sciences and humanities – a finding which reflects the need for global communication in the former fields and the language expertise in the humanities. Foreign language proficiency was considered least important by graduates in law, medicine and social sciences – an indication of the predominantly local or national roles of the respective professions. These findings were almost consistent across all countries surveyed.

The responses to the question about foreign language communication competence were very similar to the responses to the question addressed below regarding the job requirement of foreign language proficiency. Thus, it comes as no surprise that the proportion of those who considered foreign language communication as not at all important was almost identical to the percentages of those stating no requirement of foreign language proficiency at all (21%, as compared to 23%, see Table 1).

Table 1. Competences and Requirements Regarding Communicating in Foreign Languages, by Country and Field of Study (percentage of employed graduates from 11 European countries)

	Foreign language proficiency				
	Not at all important	Not at all required	Difference 1 requirement and importance (2 – 1)	Not at all acquired	Difference 2 competence and requirement (4 – 2)
	1	2	3	4	5
Country					
Italy	16	15	–1	4	– 11
Spain	20	30	+10	8	– 22
France	27	29	+2	6	– 23
Austria	20	18	–2	6	– 12
Germany	27	24	–3	9	– 15
Netherlands	10	19	+9	4	– 15
United Kingdom	59	61	+2	49	– 12
Finland	4	4	0	0	– 4
Sweden	9	10	+1	2	– 8
Norway	19	19	0	19	0
Czech Republic	12	12	0	4	– 8
Field of study					
Humanities	21	21	0	10	– 11
Social sciences	25	26	+1	9	– 17
Law	27	28	+1	11	–17
Natural sciences	20	19	–1	10	– 9
Mathematics, computing	24	24	0	10	– 14
Medicine	20	24	+4	17	– 7
Engineering	16	15	–1	7	– 8
Other	20	25	+5	13	– 12
Total	21	23	+2	11	– 12

Question E3: How important do you consider the competence "Communicating in foreign languages" for your current work?
Question E1: Please, state if you had the "foreign language proficiency" competence at the time of graduation in 1994 or 1995 and to what extent it is required in your current work.

Source: CHEERS survey data

The proportion of respondents who had not acquired any foreign language proficiency upon graduation was only 11 per cent. Thus, 12 per cent of the graduates had some foreign language proficiency but did not use it on the job. The proportion of those who did not have any foreign language proficiency, as one might expect, was by far the highest amongst British graduates (49%); Norway had the second highest quota (19%). The respective quota was between 2 per cent and 9 per cent in the remaining European countries.

3. COMPARISON OF ACQUIRED COMPETENCES AND JOB REQUIREMENTS

3.1. Overview

Table 2 provides an overview of the competences graduates had acquired upon graduation and of those required by the job about four years after graduation. The graduates were presented a list of 36 items and were asked to rate both competences (retrospectively) and job requirements. Table 2 shows the affirmative responses (scale points 1 and 2 on a five-point-scale from 1 = "To a very high extent" to 5 = "Not at all acquired/required") and the most negative response (scale point 5).

Broad general knowledge, which could be considered as typical for all graduates, was viewed as highly required and also as highly acquired by about 60 per cent of the respondents. Other competences turned out be both more frequently required and acquired: for example learning abilities (87%/74%), working independently (72%/86%) and power of concentration (72%/77%). Also planning, co-ordinating and organising (38%/78%), problem-solving ability (58%/86%), working under pressure (55%/83%) as well as taking responsibility, decisions (48%/83%) were quoted by more than three quarters of the graduates as very necessary.

Table 2. Acquired Competences at the Time of Graduation and Job Requirements Four Years After Graduation (percentage of employed graduates from 11 European countries)

	Competences			
	acquired		required	
Competences	Positive (1 + 2)	Negative (5)	Positive (1 + 2)	Negative (5)
Broad general knowledge	60	1	58	3
Cross-disciplinary thinking/knowledge	46	1	60	3
Field-specific theoretical knowledge	68	2	62	5
Field specific knowledge of methods	49	3	62	5
Foreign language proficiency	33	11	34	23
Computer skills	31	13	65	6
Understanding complex ... systems	24	11	48	9
Planning, co-ordinating and organising	38	6	78	2
Applying rules and regulations	33	9	58	5
Economic reasoning	27	15	54	8
Documenting ideas and information	45	5	67	4
Problem-solving ability	58	1	86	1
Analytical competences	59	1	71	2
Learning abilities	83	0	74	1
Reflective thinking, assessing one's own work	55	2	73	1
Creativity	47	4	62	4

to be continued

Table 2. Continued

	Competences			
	acquired		required	
Competences	Positive (1 + 2)	Negative (5)	Positive (1 + 2)	Negative (5)
Working under pressure	55	4	83	1
Accuracy, attention to detail	61	1	79	1
Time management	45	4	80	1
Negotiating	21	14	61	6
Fitness for work	58	4	70	3
Manual skills	36	14	35	20
Working independently	72	1	86	2
Working in a team	61	3	81	2
Initiative	53	2	79	1
Adaptability	64	1	79	1
Assertiveness, decisiveness, persistence	51	2	80	1
Power of concentration	72	1	77	1
Getting personally involved	65	1	77	1
Loyalty, integrity	68	2	76	1
Critical thinking	64	1	70	2
Oral communication skills	57	2	85	1
Written communication skills	68	1	76	2
Tolerance, appreciating of different points of view	63	1	73	1
Leadership	28	11	57	6
Taking responsibility, decisions	48	3	83	1

European sample, n = 29,010 minimum and 32,157 maximum (acquired) resp. 25,456 minimum and 28,035 maximum (required).
Question E1: Please, state if you had the following competences at the time of graduation in 1994 or 1995 and to what extent they are required in your current work.
Scale from 1 = "To a very high extent" to 5 = "Not at all".

Source: CHEERS survey data

In two of the 36 areas addressed, one fifth or more of the graduates did not perceive any requirements at all. These were foreign language proficiency (23%), as already discussed above, and manual skills (20%). But there were several areas where more than 10 per cent of the graduates had no competence at all: economic reasoning (15%), negotiating, manual skills (14% each), computer skills (13%), foreign-language proficiency and leadership (11% each).

3.2. *Deficits and Surpluses of Competencies*

Figure 4 indicates major differences between the level of job requirements and the competences acquired upon graduation. A "deficit" is assumed if the scale point of the respective job requirement stated by an individual respondent exceeds that of the perceived competence by 2 or more, and a "surplus", if the scale point for the acquired competence is at least 2 higher than for the respective job requirement. If the scale points do not vary, or at most by 1, the relationship is called "similar".

According to these definitions, the proportion of those considering the job requirements and the competences acquired as "similar" varied according to the 36 items between 89 and 62 per cent. The highest degrees of similarity were stated for learning abilities and power of concentration (89% each). The least similarities were also those where deficits were most often perceived: negotiating as well as planning, co-ordinating and organising (deficits of 36% and 31%). On the other hand, a surplus of competence was most often perceived for foreign language proficiency (16%), field-specific theoretical knowledge (15%), manual skills (12%) and broad general knowledge (10%).

We suggest defining those competences as "core competences" which were rated at most by 2 per cent each of the respondents as not at all required and as not at all acquired. This held true for 23, i.e. most items addressed in the questionnaire. The ratings of competences acquired and job requirements were similar in very many number cases, i.e. for 16 of these 23 items, notably learning abilities, power of concentration and analytical competences. Surpluses of competences were relatively frequent for three of these items, i.e. field-specific theoretical knowledge, broad general knowledge and cross-disciplinary thinking/knowledge and deficits for five: notably planning, co-ordinating and organising, taking responsibilities, decisions, as well as time management.

4. AGGREGATION OF COMPETENCES

With the help of factor analyses of both the competences acquired upon graduation and required by the job about four years after graduation, and using further theoretical considerations we came to the conclusion that graduate jobs could be characterised by five dimensions of competences:

- general-cognitive,
- systematic-operative,
- professionally knowledgeable,
- social-reflexive, and
- physiologically/manually skilled.

We selected one item each which weighed heavily in the factor analyses of competences acquired and required by the job with the respective factors. These items were used in the subsequent analysis as representing the respective dimensions: "broad general knowledge" representing the general-cognitive dimension, "accuracy, attention to detail" representing the systematic-operative dimension, "field-specific knowledge of methods" representing the professionally knowledgeable dimension, "leadership" representing the social-reflexive dimension and finally "manual skills" representing the physiologically/manually skilled dimension. Table 3 and Table 4 show the distribution of these dimensions of acquired and required competences both by country and by groups of field of study.

The acquired and required competences generally varied more strongly according to country than to field of study. The most striking findings were the consistently very high ratings of acquired competences on the part of Swedish graduates and the often relatively low ratings on the part of French graduates.

Figure 4. Differences in the Rating of Competences Acquired upon Graduation and Job Requirements about Four Years After Graduation (percentage of employed graduates from11 European countries)

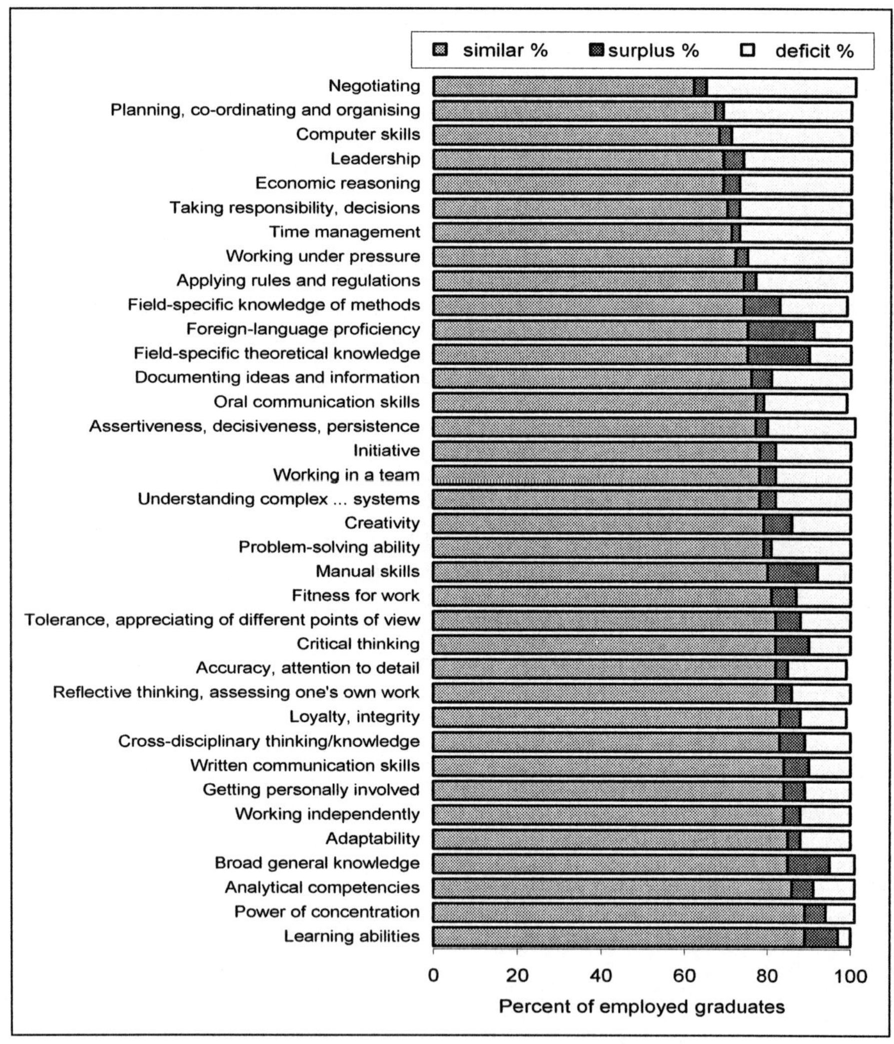

Question E1: Please, state if you had the following competences at the time of graduation in 1994 or 1995 and to what extent they are required in your current work. Scale of answers from 1 = "To a very high extent" to 5 = "Not at all".

Similar: difference of at most 1 scale point; Deficit: requirement at least 2 scale points higher than competence; Surplus: competence at least 2 scale points higher than requirement.

Source: CHEERS survey data

Table 3. Major Dimensions of Competencies Acquired Upon Graduation and Job Requirements about Four Years After Graduation. by Country (percent of employed graduates from 11 European countries)

	General-cognitive Dimension: Broad general knowledge				Systematic-operative Dimension: accuracy, attention to detail				Professionally knowledgeable dimensions: field-specific knowledge of methods				Social-reflexive dimension: leadership				Physiologically/manually skilled dimensions: manual skills			
	acquired		required		acquired		required		acquired		required		acquired		required		acquired		required	
Unit	pos.	neg.	pos.	neg.	pos.	neg.	pos.	neg.	pos.	neg.	pos.	neg.	pos.	neg.	pos.	neg.	pos.	neg.	pos.	neg.
IT	63	0	54	3	57	2	76	1	37	6	62	6	35	7	57	5	32	15	29	25
ES	58	1	43	5	54	2	69	2	40	3	65	5	30	6	42	10	37	11	29	24
FR	47	0	42	5	58	2	67	2	42	3	61	4	22	11	46	8	27	22	17	39
AT	66	1	52	3	64	2	81	1	56	2	53	9	21	24	55	9	29	23	23	31
DE	55	1	48	3	59	1	80	0	54	2	62	5	15	25	56	7	32	15	29	21
NL	63	0	64	1	64	1	86	0	58	2	62	5	29	8	54	6	34	9	27	21
UK	63	0	62	3	69	1	90	0	49	6	60	10	37	6	68	4	26	21	31	25
FI	59	0	69	1	60	1	78	0	52	2	72	5	23	10	54	5	40	10	33	20
SE	70	0	65	1	74	0	85	0	61	1	65	3	40	5	70	2	58	2	57	5
NO	68	1	78	1	67	1	81	0	63	1	65	3	29	9	57	4	45	6	63	3
CZ	53	1	51	2	51	2	72	1	28	6	50	5	27	11	62	4	43	11	45	13

Question E1: Please, state the extent to which you had the following competencies at the time of graduation in 1994 or 1995 and to what extent they are required in your current work. Scale of answers from 1 = "To a very high extent" to 5 = "Not at all".
Source: CHEERS survey data

Table 4. Major Dimensions of Competencies Acquired Upon Graduation and Job Requirements about Four Years After Graduation. by Field of Study (percent of employed graduates from 11 European countries)

	General-cognitive Dimension: Broad general knowledge				Systematic-operative Dimension: accuracy, attention to detail				Professionally knowledgeable dimensions: field-specific knowledge of methods				Social-reflexive dimension: leadership				Physiologically/manually skilled dimensions: manual skills			
	acquired		required		acquired		required		acquired		required		acquired		required		acquired		required	
Unit	pos.	neg.	pos.	neg.	pos.	neg.	pos.	neg.	pos.	neg.	pos.	neg.	pos.	neg.	pos.	neg.	pos.	neg.	pos.	neg.
Hum.	67	0	67	3	68	1	80	1	50	6	57	12	29	13	57	9	32	20	31	25
Soc.	63	0	56	2	57	2	78	1	45	3	53	7	28	10	55	6	27	20	22	28
Law.	64	0	58	2	61	1	83	1	39	7	58	7	30	12	51	7	24	25	19	38
Nat.	54	1	49	4	64	1	77	1	51	3	64	6	23	13	51	6	44	8	42	15
Math.	50	1	42	5	61	1	77	1	56	2	71	3	21	14	52	5	25	22	15	34
Eng.	57	0	51	3	59	1	77	1	43	3	58	3	23	12	59	4	41	8	35	16
Med.	56	1	56	3	66	1	85	1	50	3	76	2	27	11	58	5	50	5	74	4
Other	61	0	65	1	60	1	79	1	56	2	66	5	33	8	60	5	40	9	38	16
Total	60	1	58	3	61	1	79	1	49	3	62	5	28	11	57	6	36	14	35	20

Question E1: Please, state the extent to which you had the following competencies at the time of graduation in 1994 or 1995 and to what extent they are required in your current work. Scale of answers from 1 = "To a very high extent" to 5 = "Not at all".
Source: CHEERS survey data

In order to establish the relative weight of the five dimensions, all positive ratings of the five items representing the ratings were added up and the sum was calculated as 100 per cent. We called this the "competence profile of the graduates of the mid-1990s". Figure 5 gives the profiles of acquired and required competences for selected countries.

The profile of the acquired competences of all European graduates was more strongly shaped by general-cognitive and systematic-operative competences than by other dimensions of competences. This also holds true for the three countries represented in Figure 5, although Austrian graduates stated a relatively high weight of professional knowledge as well. As compared to the acquired competences, the European graduates perceived a substantially higher weight of social-communicative job requirements and a lower weight of general-cognitive job requirements. Of the three countries addressed in Figure 5, it was in Austria that the profile of job requirements differed from that of the competences acquired most strongly. In the profile of job requirements in Austria, the social-reflexive dimension played a much stronger role and the general-cognitive a much weaker role than in the profile of the competences acquired by the Austrian graduates upon graduation.

Figure 5. Profile of Competences Acquired Upon Graduation and of Job Requirements Four Years After Graduation by Selected Countries (percentage of employed graduates from 11 European countries)

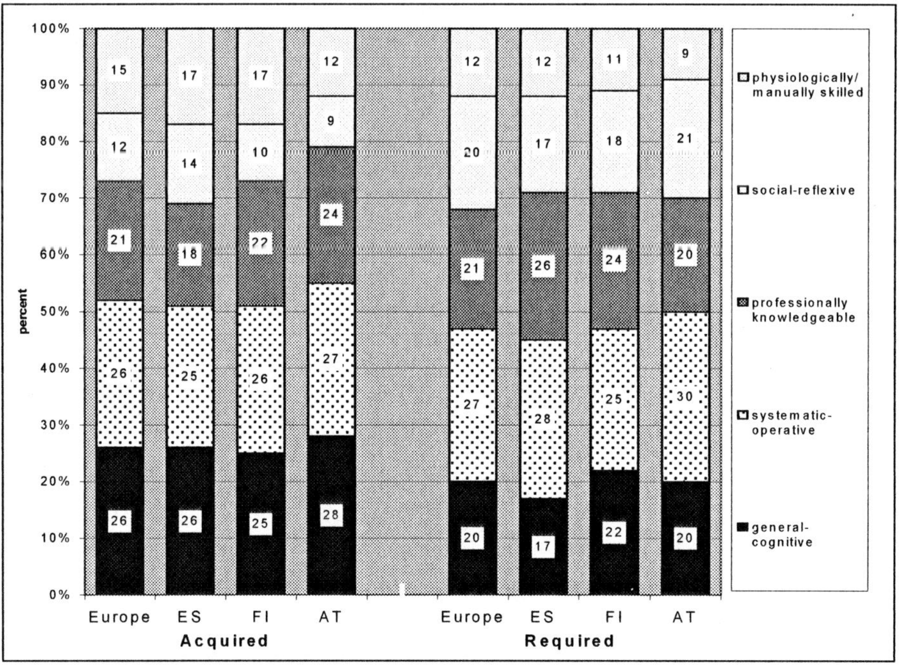

* percentage of all competences rated as 1 and 2 on a scale from 1 = "To a very high extent" to 5 = "Not at all" over the five dimensions addressed in the chart.

Source: CHEERS survey data

5. CONCLUSION

This chapter began with an analysis of the graduates' views on the utility of their studies and their perception of the importance of foreign language proficiency. Subsequently, it addressed the relationships between competences acquired upon graduation and those required by the job four years after graduation.

About 60 per cent of the graduates saw their studies as having been quite useful for professional work and about 40 per cent for other spheres of life. Differences were more striking by country than by field of study. Hence, graduates of the Czech Republic and the Nordic countries were the most convinced of the usefulness of studies for the world of work and those of Germany, Italy and France were the least convinced.

The ability to communicate in foreign languages was considered as important by about 40 per cent of the European graduates. The smaller the language area and the less the language was known internationally, the greater the need was felt for foreign language proficiency. For example, 65 per cent of Finnish graduates as compared to 10 per cent of British graduates considered this ability as important. Altogether, foreign language proficiency was amongst the few dimensions where the competences acquired did not seem to be lower on average than those required on the job.

Altogether the job requirements four years after graduation were perceived as more demanding in most dimensions than the acquired competences. The discrepancy was most striking if percentages were presented of those stating a high level of requirements and of competences acquired. The analysis presented here, in contrast, counted differences between job requirements and acquired competences acquired as one scale-point on a five-point scale as "similar" and those of 2 scale points or more, depending on direction, as "deficits" and "surpluses". On the basis of these definitions, more than three quarters on average of the individual statements of job requirements and competencies acquired are similar, ranging among the 36 items of the questionnaire from 89 per cent to 62 per cent.

Remarkably, a visible surplus of acquired competencies to job requirements could be found only for four aspects addressed: foreign language proficiency, field-specific theoretical knowledge, manual skills and broad general knowledge, whereby the surplus is quite small. In contrast, some deficits show up for the majority of aspects analyzed, among the most striking ones as regards negotiating, planning, co-ordinating and organising as well as computer skills.

The list of 36 aspects can be grouped to five major dimensions of acquired competencies as well as job requirements: the general-cognitive, systematic-operative, the professionally knowledgeable, social-reflexive and physiologically/manually skilled dimensions of competency. The ratings by graduates of items representing these dimensions best vary more substantially by country than by field of study, whereby the Swedish graduates rate their acquired competencies as very high across all the dimensions, while French graduates rate their competencies low across the majority of dimensions.

Finally, a "competency profile of the graduates of the mid-1990s" was established which shows the relative weight of the various dimensions. Accordingly, the European graduates on average consider their general-cognitive and systematic competencies as strongest, while the job requirements suggest a higher weight of socio-communicative competencies and a lower weight of general-cognitive competency. Differences by country are by no means negligible, but by and large confirm the general picture.

OSMO KIVINEN AND JOUNI NURMI

JOB REQUIREMENTS AND COMPETENCES: DO QUALIFICATIONS MATTER?

1. MEASURING COMPETENCES AND JOB REQUIREMENTS

The topic addressed in the previous chapter will be analysed more specifically here. We will examine how deficits or surpluses of competences vary according to occupational areas and links between study and occupation and according to occupational study. The analysis is based on a list of 36 competences, where respondents were asked to state whether they possessed them upon graduation and if they were required on the job at the time the survey was conducted. As shown in the previous chapter, responses were given on a five-point scale from “to a great extent” to “not at all”.

One should bear in mind that the competences and requirements were not measured independently. Rather, graduates were asked to assess their competences upon graduation retrospectively at the time their job requirements were addressed. However, this provided an opportunity to reflect on the differences.

Moreover, we must take into consideration that job “requirements” are not fixed by the employers or the organisation or technology of work, but that, as prior research has indicated, graduates themselves have some impact on shaping their job tasks and that they often do so according to their competences. Thus, the job “requirements” are influenced to some extent by the competences they happen to have.

These considerations do not call into question our analysis, which can be considered a reliable account of the extent to which graduates felt themselves to be prepared already upon graduation for the job tasks a few years later. “Deficit” in this context means that the work tasks a few years after graduation require what was not yet acquired upon graduation, and “surplus” means that more competences were acquired upon graduation than needed a few years later.

Figure 1 shows how competences and job requirements compare according to the various aspects addressed in the questionnaire. Obviously, the graduates are quite differently prepared according to various categories of skills. According to the groups of categories we employ in order to facilitate our analysis, graduates are least prepared at the time of graduation for future socio-communicative and organisational work tasks, whereas they seem to be well prepared in some cognitive and knowledge domains.

U. Teichler (ed.), Careers of University Graduates, 131–142

Figure 1. Differences between Graduates' Competences Acquired Upon Graduation and Required Some Four Years Later (percentage of European graduates employed about four years after graduation)

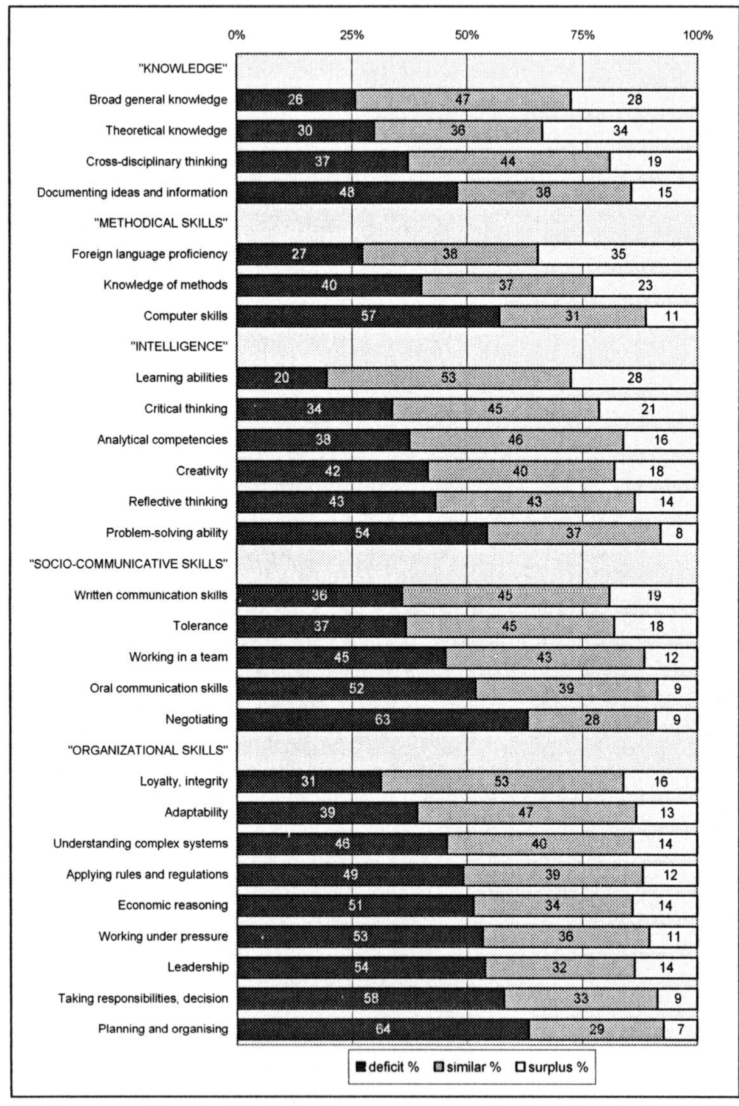

Question E1: Please, state if you had the following competences at the time of graduation in 1994 or 1995 and if they are required in your current work. Scale of answers from 1 = "To a very high extent" to 5 = "Not at all".

deficit% = higher requirements than competences; similar% = requirements correspond competences; surplus% = lower requirements than competences.

Source: CHEERS survey data

We cannot only measure the percentage of graduates noting differences between competences acquired and job requirements we must also measure the degree of differences. The latter will be called deficit ratio and surplus ratio. The deficit ratio, for example, is computed as a ratio of the absolute value of weighted sum of negative differences to the theoretical maximum if all graduates naming a deficit had job requirements "to a great extent" and had "not at all" acquired any competence.

As Figure 2 shows, only 4 per cent out of 57 per cent of graduates stating deficits in computer skills had minimum competences and reported maximum requirements. The deficit ratio of computer skills, thus calculated, was 25.

Figure 2. Differences between Graduates' Computer Skills Acquired Upon Graduation and Job Requirements Some Four Years Later (percentage of European graduates employed about four years after graduation)

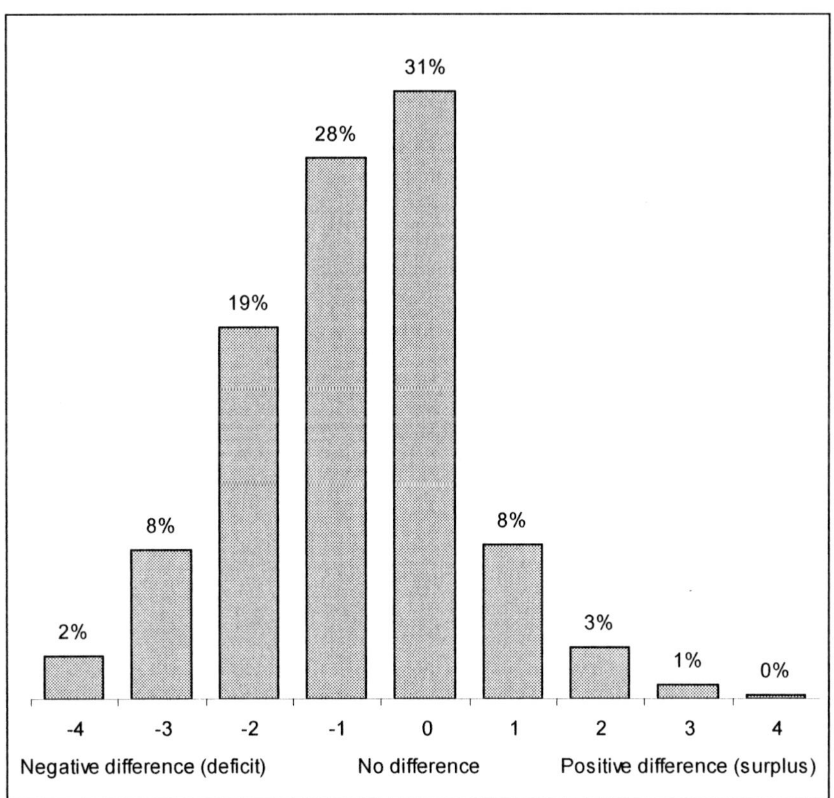

Question E1: Please state the extent to which you had the following competences at the time of graduation in 1994 or 1995 and to what extent they are required in your current work. Scale of answers from 1 = "To a very high extent" to 5 = "Not at all".

Source: CHEERS survey data

2. DEFICITS AND SURPLUSES IN DIFFERENT OCCUPATIONS

In our analysis of the differences of deficits and surpluses of competences according to occupational groups, we classified the respondents surveyed according to ISCO88 which is a hierarchy based on positions within an organisation and supposed level of job requirements. We merged the categories 5 to 9 into a single category of "worker".

We noted that 10 per cent of the European graduates were legislators, senior officials and managers and 63 per cent were professionals. Thus, almost three quarters were in positions that were generally considered as appropriate for graduates from higher education institutions.

20 per cent were employed as technicians and associate professionals. Views differed amongst experts about the extent to which employment in this category could be considered appropriate for graduates from higher education institutions and surveys have shown that the graduates' views were quite different in this respect. Moreover, we must take into consideration that some occupational groups are not treated equally in the various European countries. For example, primary school teachers are counted in some countries as "associate professionals" and in others as "professionals"; also nurses and pre-school teachers are classified differently.

Finally, only 4 per cent of the graduates were employed in the category "clerks" and 2 per cent in the category "workers". The latter category, as already reported, was based on a merger of various categories of ISCO88.

The first step of our analysis came to a surprising result. The technicians and associate professionals were very similar to the managers and professionals in the extent to which they observed deficits and surpluses of competences. On the basis of this finding, we can conclude that "technicians and associate professionals" jobs are often as appropriate as "managers and professionals" jobs.

There was great diversity, however, amongst the technicians and associate professionals. Those with a master level degree reported more frequently surpluses of competences than those with a bachelor degree.

As a next step, we merged managers, professionals and associate professionals into a first category and clerks and workers into a second category. We called the first category "appropriately employed graduates" and the second "inappropriately employed graduates".

The first finding is not surprising: consistently across all categories, the inappropriately employed graduates noted deficits of competences less often and surpluses of competences more often. This shows that the former differed from the latter to a lesser extent in their competences than in the actual job requirements.

Figure 3. Competence Deficits and Surpluses of Appropriately and Inappropriately Employed Graduates (percentage of European graduates about four years after graduation)*

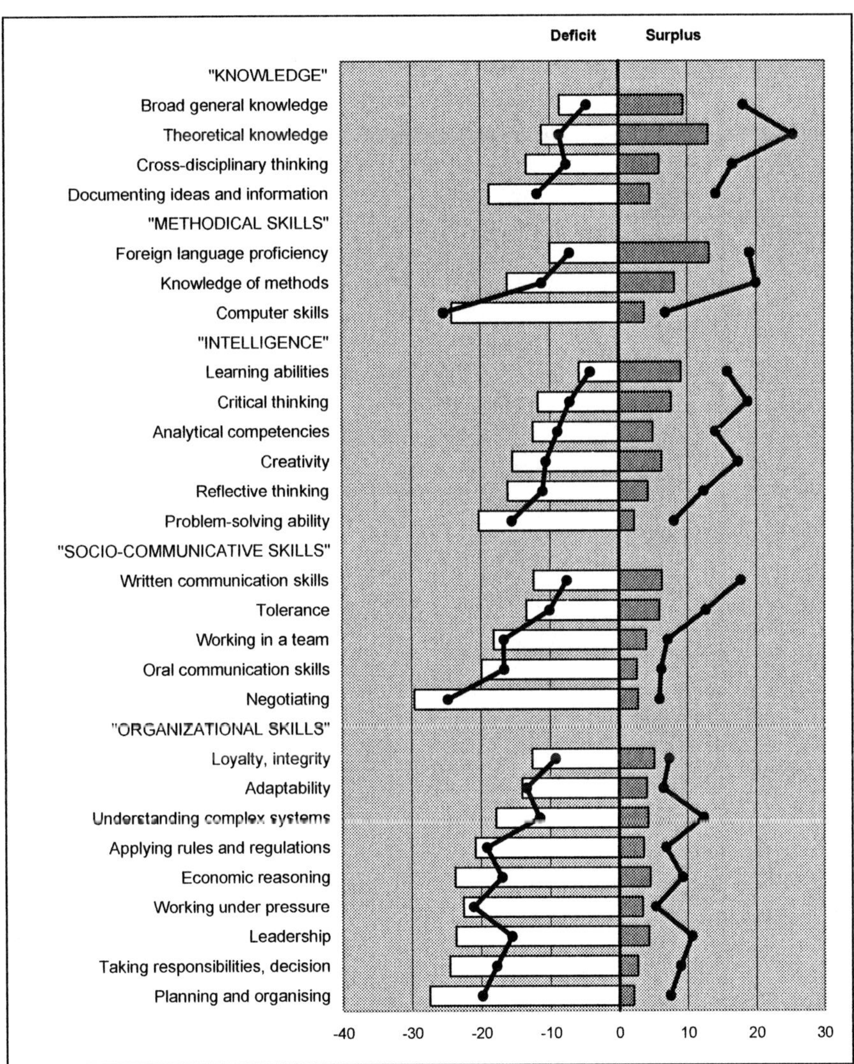

* Bars: Appropriately employed graduates (legislators, senior officials and managers; professionals, technicians and associate professionals); Lines: Inappropriately employed graduates (clerks, workers). Question E1: Please state if you had the following competences at the time of graduation in 1994 or 1995 and if they are required in your current work. Scale of answers from 1 = "To a very high extent" to 5 = "Not at all".

Source: CHEERS survey data

Second, we noted that the differences between the two groups of categories varied according to the areas of competences. For example, they were substantial in respect to understanding complex systems, but marginal regarding computer skills.

Third, we noted that even those who were inappropriately employed reported more deficits than surpluses of competences in some areas. This held true for almost all the socio-communicative and the organisational competences addressed. This finding indicates that "inappropriate jobs" of graduates are quite heterogeneous, whereas many are quite demanding in some respects.

3. THE IMPACT OF THE FIELD OF STUDY

It is generally assumed that certain fields of study serve a more targeted preparation for certain types of jobs than others. In medicine and teacher training, for example, graduation in these respective fields is mandatory as a rule to exercise the profession. Therefore, we examined whether graduates who were employed in an occupational category that corresponded to their field of study felt better prepared for their job, i.e. reported fewer deficits and possibly more surpluses, than graduates whose field of study did not correspond to their occupational category.

We selected seven occupational groups, where we observed an obvious correspondence between occupation and field of study:

- Computing professionals (ISCO88 code 213), whereby we considered computing (ISCED97 code 48) as corresponding and all other fields as not corresponding,
- Architects, engineers and related professionals (214) and engineering, manufacturing and construction (52-58),
- Primary and pre-primary education teaching professionals (233) and teacher training and education science (14),
- Business professionals (241) and business and administration (34),
- Legal professions (242) and law (38),
- Social sciences and related professionals (244) and social and behavioural sciences (31), and finally
- Finance and sales associate professionals and business services agents and trade brokers (341-342) and business and administration (34).

In all these seven groups, the pattern of deficits and surpluses of competences seemed very similar amongst those who had graduated in a corresponding field of study and those who had graduated in a field that did not correspond to the occupational category. The differences in the competence gap between those trained and not trained for a specific occupation were clearly smaller than those between graduates of different occupational groups. This finding certainly comes as a surprise. One could infer that the field of study mattered little for occupational preparation. A more cautious interpretation would be that those who worked in a job that did not correspond to their field of study happened to have acquired competences outside study of the corresponding field which were in many respects similar to the competences of those who entered that occupational category upon graduation from a corresponding field of study.

Figure 4. Competence Deficits and Surpluses of Architects, Engineers and Related Professionals Having Been and Not Having Been Trained in Engineering (percentage of European graduates employed about four years after graduation)*

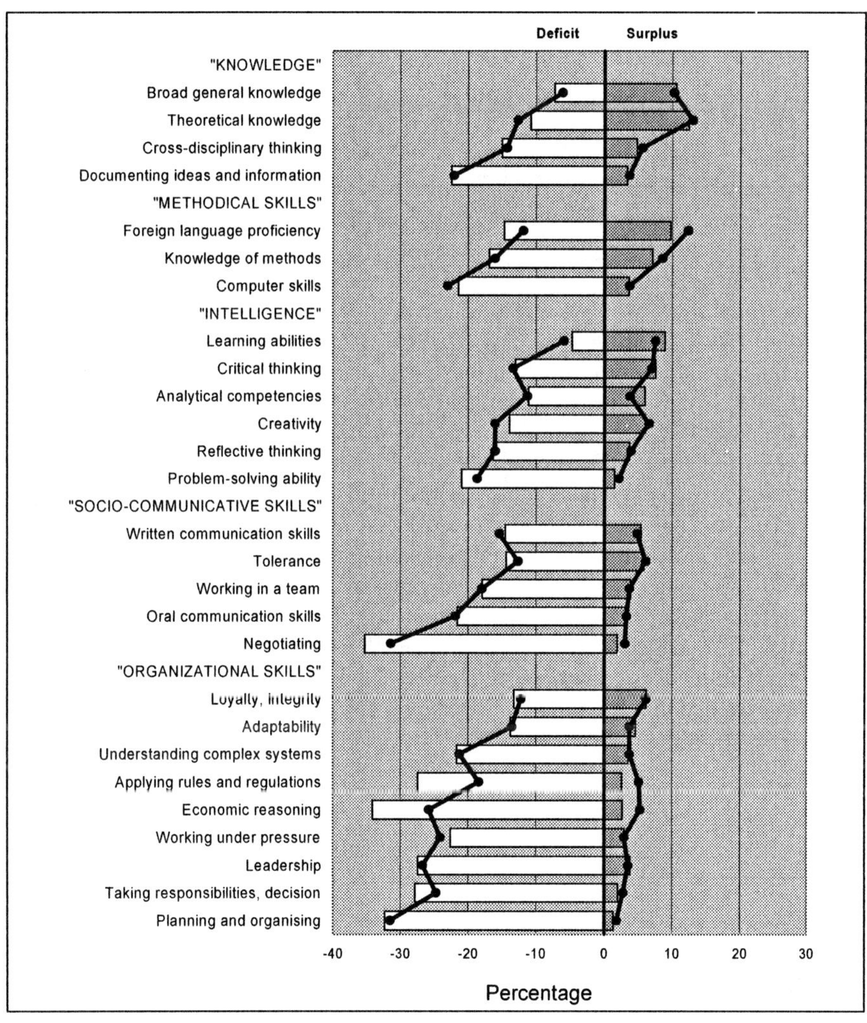

* Bars: Graduates working as engineers and trained in engineering; Lines: Graduates working as engineers and trained in other fields.

Question E1: Please state if you had the following competences at the time of graduation in 1994 or 1995 and if they are required in your current work. Scale of answers from 1 = "To a very high extent" to 5 = "Not at all".

Source: CHEERS survey data

Figure 4 shows the results for the architects, engineers and related professionals. As a comparison with Figure 3 suggests, engineers considered themselves less prepared for most of the organisational job tasks than the average of the graduates. In respect to the issue discussed here, we noted that engineers who had graduated from engineering fields considered themselves equally – well or insufficiently – prepared in most areas of competence addressed as engineers who had graduated from other fields. In two areas, engineers who did not graduate from engineering fields noted smaller deficits: economic reasoning as well as applying rules and regulations.

Figure 5, in comparison to Figure 3, suggests that primary and pre-primary school teachers noted more substantial differences as regards various aspects of intelligence and organisational competences than the average of graduates. In respect to the issue discussed here – the results of the comparison between those trained and those not trained in the field – the findings are much more complex. There are also areas in which those who were not trained for the occupation reported fewer deficits or more surpluses, notably regarding theoretical knowledge and economic reasoning. On the other hand, those trained for these occupations felt better prepared, notably as regards creativity, working in a team and taking responsibility.

In the other five occupational groups, the differences lay somewhere between the two. They were greater than in the case of engineering, but smaller than in the case of primary and pre-primary school teacher training.

Even in specialised areas of knowledge, those graduating from a corresponding field of study were often not better prepared for their work tasks than those who graduated from other fields. Only the computing professionals trained in computer science felt clearly better prepared for the job requirements than computer professionals trained in other fields; similarly, business professionals and associated professions trained in respective fields noted fewer deficits in economic reasoning than those trained in other fields.

Figure 5. Competence Deficits and Surpluses of Primary and Pre-Primary School Teaching Having and Not Having Been Trained in Teacher Training and Pedagogy (percentage of European graduates employed about four years after graduation)*

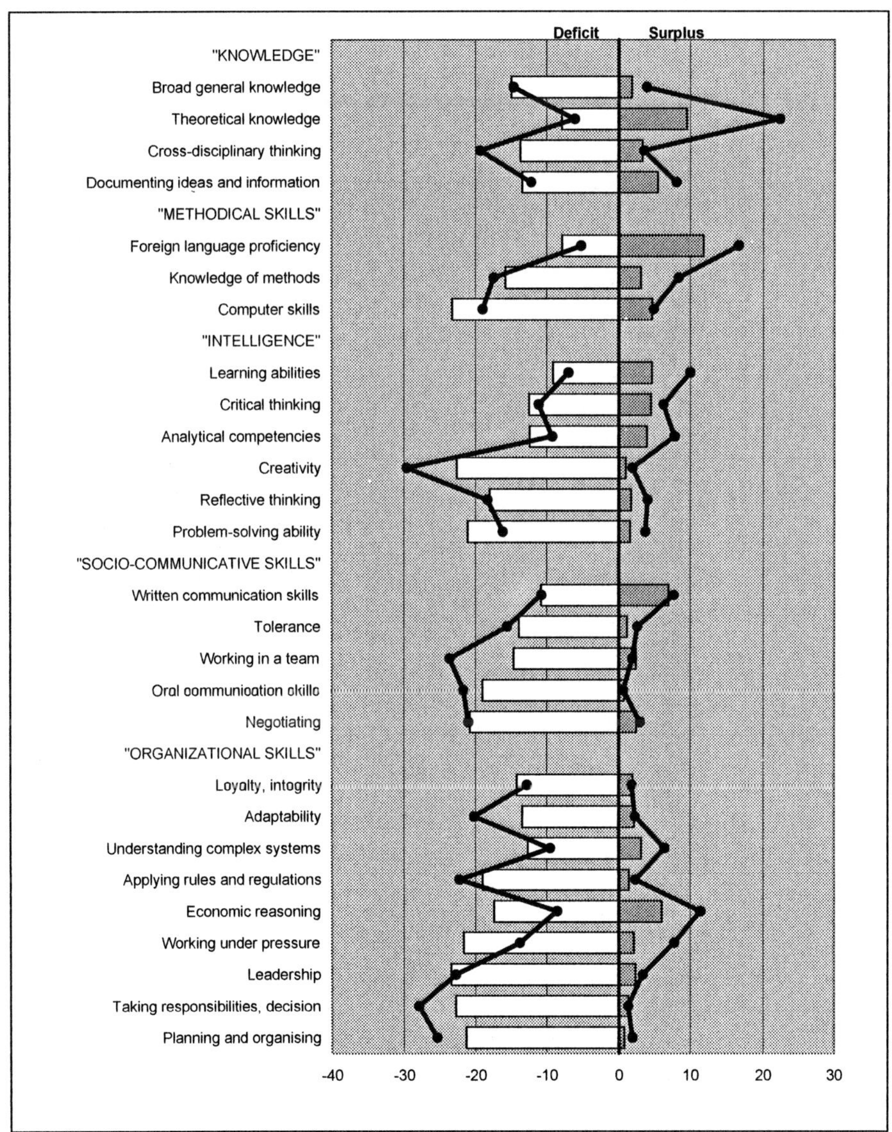

* Bars: Graduates trained in teacher training and pedagogy; Lines: Graduates trained in other fields
Question E1: Please state if you had the following competences at the time of graduation in 1994 or 1995 and if they are required in your current work. Scale of answers from 1 = "To a very high extent" to 5 = "Not at all".

Source: CHEERS survey data

4. PREPARATION FOR SELF-EMPLOYMENT

It is widely assumed that self-employed persons differ from employed persons as far as the socio-communicative and organisational job requirements are concerned. Therefore, we examined whether those who chose self-employment differed from those who became employees as far as their competences upon graduation were concerned, whether they noted different job requirements and whether they considered themselves differently prepared for their job tasks About 8 per cent of the European graduates were self-employed about four years after graduation. About three quarters came from five fields or groups of field of study: law, architecture and building, business and administration, humanities and health. This reflects high numbers of self-employed in the corresponding professions. The highest proportion of those employed among all of those professionally active four years after graduation could be found in

- veterinary science (38%),
- architecture and building (22%),
- law (19%),
- fine arts (18%),
- journalism and information (10%), and
- health (9%).

In all other fields, the proportion of self-employed graduates was below average – including business and administration (6%) and engineering (3%). It is worth noting that graduates who worked in an occupation that was closely related to their field of study tended to be more often self-employed than those who worked in an occupation that was not closely related to their studies (12% as compared to 5%). This is largely because access to some independent professions requires graduation from a certain field of study as an entry qualification.

The self-employed graduates did not differ greatly from those employed by an organisation as far as their perceived competences were concerned. They noted, however, more demanding job requirements and correspondingly, as Figure 6 shows, a higher deficit of competences in various respects. The highest deficit was in economic reasoning. In addition, a somewhat higher deficit was reported with respect to computer skills, problem-solving ability and negotiating. By and large, the findings support the conventional wisdom.

Figure 6. Competence Deficits and Surpluses of Self-Employed as Compared to Other Graduates (percentage of European graduates employed about four years after graduation)*

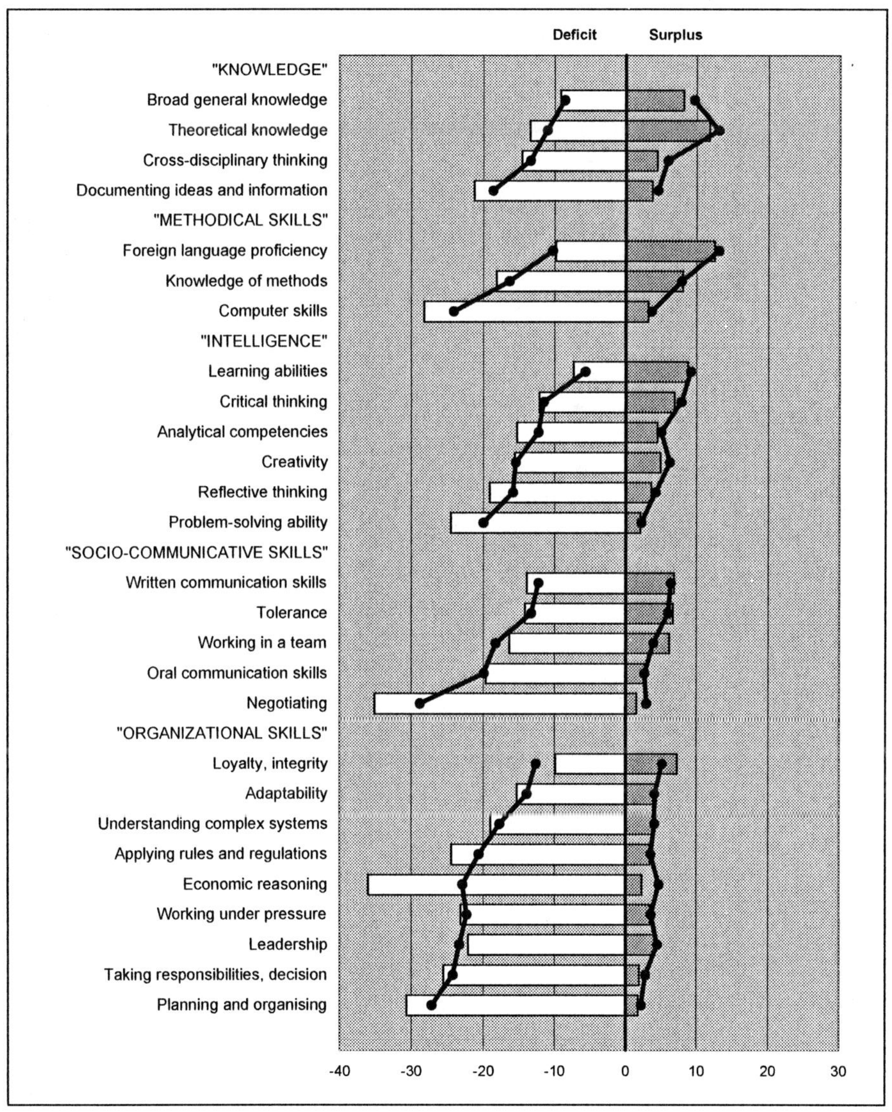

* Bars: self-employed; Lines: others.

Question E1: Please, state if you had the following competences at the time of graduation in 1994 or 1995 and if they are required in your current work. Scale of answers from 1 = "To a very high extent" to 5 = "Not at all".

Source: CHEERS survey data

5. DOES QUALIFICATION MATTER?

We compared the graduates' perceived competences upon graduation with the perceived job requirements about four years after graduation. As already shown in the previous section, there were only a few areas where graduates noted a balance between the competences acquired and the job requirements, i.e. broad general knowledge, foreign language proficiency and learning abilities. Even in these areas, some graduates perceived a deficit while others perceived a surplus. Deficits were most strongly felt in the domain of socio-communicative and organisational competences, notably as far as negotiation and economic reasoning were concerned.

Our analysis shows that those in technicians' and associate professional ranks did not differ significantly from those employed in managerial and professional ranks as far as perceived deficits and surpluses of competences were concerned. Those employed as clerks and workers noted fewer deficits. However, they reported a certain extent of deficits which suggests that some of their jobs were quite demanding in some respects.

There were only a few differences of deficits and surpluses according to occupational categories. The deficits were smaller amongst those having graduated in a field of study usually considered as corresponding to their field of study than amongst those from a non-corresponding field. Finally, the differences of deficits and surpluses of competences amongst the self-employed and amongst other graduates are worth noting in a few areas, but marginal or non-existent in most areas. Altogether, the differences observed according fields of study, occupations, links between fields and occupation and finally occupational status were much smaller than expected.

One could argue that higher education, according to the graduates, provides specific knowledge and a theoretical basis, lacks to some extent in other dimensions of knowledge and intelligence and does not prepare well in most socio-communicative and organisational dimensions of job requirements. This could be seen, on the one hand, as quite natural: the latter could be understood as the typical tasks of learning in the initial years on the job. On the other hand, one could ask whether higher education could be expected and in a position to contribute more substantially to dimensions of competences where major deficits were felt by the graduates: economic reasoning, negotiating, planning and organising, computer skills and taking responsibilities. The fact that the perceived deficits are so similar across occupational areas and fields of study does not lead us to think that the latter concept could work.

JAKE MURDOCH AND JEAN-JACQUES PAUL

LINKS BETWEEN KNOWLEDGE AND WORK AND APPROPRIATE EMPLOYMENT

1. INTRODUCTION

As already discussed in previous chapters, the CHEERS graduate survey addressed the careers of graduates with respect to a broad range of dimensions. It did not only employ "objective" measures, i.e. facts which the respondents could report without major interpretative involvement, e.g. the duration up to first normal employment, the employment status, part-time versus full-time employment, and the gross annual income. The CHEERS questionnaire also asked the graduates to evaluate and interpret their employment and work situation in several respects, where "objective" measures did not suffice.

Collecting a combination of factual information and respondents' rating has become customary in research on employment and work. This holds true, for example, for many projects undertaken by the Research Centre for Education and the Labour Market (ROA) in Maastricht, the Netherlands, which is a leader in this field and which participated in the CHEERS survey (Allen et al. 2001). This can also be observed in previous research projects undertaken by members of the CHEERS team in Austria (Kellermann 1996), Germany (Schomburg and Teichler 1993), Norway (Arnesen 2000) and the United Kingdom (Brennan and McGeever 1988; Brennan et al. 1993).

In the latter domain, graduates were first asked to define their employment and work within the framework of categories which are often used with regard to employees across economic sectors, areas of occupation and position, as well as educational levels. They were asked to state what they considered to be a good job and how far this applied to their job – questions deriving from a tradition of research on "job satisfaction".

Second, the CHEERS survey tried to establish the graduates' views about whether they considered their employment and work as appropriate for a graduate. Research approaches of this kind emerged in 1970s in the wake of the rapid expansion of higher education and the subsequent increase of the quota of graduates from higher education institutions amongst new entrants in the labour force. It became obvious at that time that an analysis of the graduates' whereabouts according to occupational group no longer sufficed to establish whether they were "over-educated" and "under-employed" or whether a job, though not being considered typical for graduates according to the previously common yardstick when the proportion of graduates was relatively small, could be considered "appropriate". It could well be that jobs that were not linked to a high salary and to a privileged position actually were demanding as far as the level of job tasks and job requirements was concerned. Also, it did not seem to suffice anymore to establish whether graduates from certain

U. Teichler (ed.), Careers of University Graduates, 143–158

fields of study ended up in certain professions or sectors of employment in order to establish whether the allocation had worked in linking competences with respective work tasks. It could well be that graduates could make good use of the knowledge acquired in the course of study or could consider their course of study a good preparation for the subsequent work, if the traditional notions of links between fields of study and occupational areas did not suggest that.

A summary of the first generation of research on graduate employment and work that addressed the links between substance of knowledge and work and the appropriateness of employment according to the graduates' perception came to the conclusion that the researchers had chosen such heterogeneous measures that the findings were more revealing as regards the researchers' concepts than regarding the real situation of graduate employment and work (Teichler 1988). So far, no widespread consensus has emerged concerning the most appropriate means of measuring the extent to which study and work both regarding the level of education and employment and the substance of knowledge and work tasks. And surveys employing a broad range of measures did not come to the conclusion that certain individual measures could be viewed as sufficiently covering the issues involved (Teichler and Buttgereit 1992).

We therefore decided to define these relationships in various ways: the extent to which their field of study matched the area of work, the extent to which they used the knowledge acquired in the course of study on the job, what level of course programme and degree was most appropriate for their employment and work as compared to the level of degree they were awarded. Moreover, we asked the graduates to rate the appropriateness of their level of education generally, thereby taking into account all dimensions of their employment and work (status, position, income, work tasks etc.). Finally, they were asked to state if their work situation at the time of the survey met the expectations they had at the time they started their study.

2. FREQUENCY OF MARGINAL USE OF KNOWLEDGE AND INAPPROPRIATE EMPLOYMENT

The first question addressed exclusively the substantive link between study and work. As Table 1 shows, a total of 21 per cent of the graduates saw only little or no use at all of the knowledge and skills they had acquired in their course of study on the job.

In the second question, graduates were asked to define the relationships between their field of study and their area of work with respect both to the level and the substance. With respect to the level of education and employment, 8 per cent of the graduates, as Table 2 indicates, did not see their area of work as requiring higher education study and a degree at all. A further 9 per cent perceived a mismatch between the field of study and the area of work.

In the third question, graduates were asked to state the most appropriate level of education for their employment and work. Again, as shown in Table 3, 8 per cent considered a higher education degree as superfluous .

A further 12 per cent (thus altogether 20%) seemed to see themselves as "over-educated", because they considered that a lower level of higher or tertiary education was more appropriate for their job than the level they had reached. In contrast, 12 per cent believed that a higher level than theirs was most appropriate for their employment and work.

In the fourth question, graduates were encouraged to rate the appropriateness between their level of education and their employment and work by taking all relevant dimensions into account both with respect to the level and the substance of education and work. Table 4 shows that 13 per cent considered their employment and work as predominantly or completely inappropriate.

Altogether we note that, depending on the measure employed, between 8 per cent and 21 per cent of the graduates surveyed perceived a marginal or no link between study and subsequent employment and work. This cannot be viewed as a high rate if compared to that noted on the basis of employment statistics. The findings of our study, indeed, confirmed that a large proportion of graduates ending up in an occupational category that was not clearly typical for graduate employment saw a link between study and employment. The findings, if compared with the results of the surveys of the 1980s, also do not suggest a growth in the number of graduates who considered themselves as wrongly trained or over-educated.

Finally, graduates had been asked to state if their work situation about four years after graduation met the expectations they had at the time of their first enrolment. As Table 6 shows, 7 per cent considered it much worse than expected and 15 per cent somewhat worse than expected. On the whole, these proportions were to be expected on the basis of the responses to the prior four questions.

3. DIFFERENCES BETWEEN COUNTRIES

About half the graduates stated that they made great use of the knowledge and skills they acquired in their course of study in their work tasks (see Table 1). This was the case for almost three quarters of the Norwegian and more than two-thirds of the Finnish graduates. In contrast, as already noted, 21 per cent of whom almost half the Japanese (47%) and more than one third of the French graduates (36%) perceived little or no use.

A more open link between the field of study and the area of employment and work was perceived by about half the graduates (see Table 2). 38 per cent stated that other fields of study could have prepared them for their employment and work area, and 11 per cent believed that the field was not relevant for their area of employment and work, i.e. that various other fields could also be suitable for their employment and work. These views were most frequently held by graduates in Japan (63%), the Netherlands (62%) and France (59%).

Table 1. Use of Knowledge and Skills Acquired in Reference Study as Perceived by Graduates, by Country (percentage and arithmetic mean of graduates employed about four years after graduation)

	Country													Total
	IT	ES	FR	AT	DE	NL	UK	FI	SE	NO	CZ	EUR	JP	
1 To a very high extent	19	21	6	25	14	12	23	35	30	36	23	22	9	21
2	30	27	22	30	29	39	27	34	32	38	31	31	13	29
3	30	27	35	28	34	33	26	19	26	21	30	28	30	28
4	15	19	28	14	20	14	17	10	11	5	13	15	31	16
5 Not at all	6	6	8	3	3	2	8	1	1	0	2	4	16	5
Total*	100	100	100	100	100	100	100	100	100	100	100	100	100	100
Arithmetic mean	2.6	2.6	3.1	2.4	2.7	2.5	2.6	2.1	2.2	1.9	2.4	2.5	3.3	2.5

Question F1: If you take into consideration your current work tasks : To what extent do you use the knowledge and skills acquired in the course of study (you graduated from in 1994 or 1995)?
Scale of responses from 1 = "To a very high extent" to 5 = "Not at all".
* Count by Country: IT (2550); ES (2166); FR (2197); AT (2081); DE (3239); NL (2914); UK (3133); FI (2455); SE (2415); NO (3116); CZ (2628); EU (28893); JP (2927); Total (31821).

Source: CHEERS survey data

Table 2. Relationship between Field of Study and Area of Work as Perceived by Graduates, by Country (percentage of graduates employed about four years after graduation; multiple responses)

	Country													Total
	IT	ES	FR	AT	DE	NL	UK	FI	SE	NO	CZ	EUR	JP	
My field of study is the only possible/by far the best field	51	39	20	47	40	28	37	54	46	51	27	39	23	38
Some other fields could prepare for the area of work as well	31	40	48	26	39	52	35	31	33	43	50	40	25	38
Another field would have been more useful	7	10	12	6	8	9	12	7	7	3	13	9	10	9
The field of study does not matter very much	6	6	11	10	10	10	22	5	3	3	6	9	28	11
Higher education studies are not at all related to my area of work	8	5	15	11	8	3	18	2	0	0	4	7	14	8
Others	1	0	1	1	3	0	3	1	3	1	1	1	0	1
Total*	105	100	107	100	108	102	126	100	192	100	100	105	100	105

Question F2: How would you define the relationship between your field of study and your area of work?
* Count by Country: IT (2534); ES (2157); FR (2192); AT (2076); DE (3210); NL (2915); UK (3076); FI (2442); SE (2634); NO (3109); CZ (2628); EU (26339); JP (2984); Total (29323).

Source: CHEERS survey data

Finally, 17 per cent perceived a mismatch between education and employment, either in terms of another field of study being more useful (9%) or no higher education studies being needed at all (8%) (see Table 3). These two categories were most frequently quoted by those who graduated in the United Kingdom (30%), France (27%) and Japan (24%).

Altogether, 38 per cent of the employed graduates stated that their field of study was the only one possible or by far the best one for their area of work. This was most pronounced, as Table 2 shows, amongst those of the Nordic countries, Italy and Austria.

Two-thirds of the graduates considered their degree as most appropriate for their employment and work. As can be seen in Table 3, the highest proportions of graduates who shared this view are found in the Nordic countries, the Czech Republic and the Netherlands.

12 per cent came to the conclusion, as Table 3 also shows, that their employment and work required a higher level of study. This was most frequently stated by those graduating in France (21%) and the United Kingdom (16%), – i.e. countries where not only the proportions of those surveyed who had graduated from a three-year study programme was high, but also where a relatively high percentage of graduates continued their study beyond a three-year programme.

Table 3. Appropriateness of Level of Course of Study and Degree for Employment and Work, by Country (percentage of graduates employed about four years after graduation)

	Country													Total
	IT	ES	FR	AT	DE	NL	UK	FI	SE	NO	CZ	EUR	JP	
A higher level than the one I graduated from	11	15	21	7	4	11	16	9	12	15	11	12	10	12
The same level	58	55	45	67	68	73	60	78	78	76	74	67	55	66
A lower level of higher/tertiary education	14	11	24	7	19	9	15	9	7	7	5	12	18	12
No higher/tertiary education at all	12	18	7	12	6	7	7	3	2	1	8	7	12	8
Other	4	1	3	6	3	0	2	1	1	1	1	2	5	2
Total*	100	100	100	100	100	100	100	100	100	100	100	100	100	100

Question F3b: What is the most appropriate level of course of study/degree for your employment and work in comparison to that which you graduated from in 1994 or 1995?

* Count by Country: IT (2500); ES (2153); FR (2160); AT (2040); DE (3196); NL (2910); UK (3083); FI (2415); SE (2397); NO (3087); CZ (2629); EU (28569); JP (2962); Total (31530).

Source: CHEERS survey data

The proportion of those stating that a lower level of higher education or tertiary education was sufficient or that no higher education or tertiary education was needed at all was highest in France (31%), Japan (30%) and Spain (29%). In the case of Spain, the item "no higher education at all" was chosen by 18 per cent of the graduates, as compared to 1 per cent-12 per cent in other countries.

In response to the question whether they considered altogether, i.e. taking into account both the substantive and the status dimensions, their employment and work as appropriate to their level of education, about one third stated "completely appropriate". A further third considered the link predominantly appropriate, and about one fifth chose a scale point in the centre between "completely appropriate" and "not all appropriate". Employment and work were rated hardly or not at all appropriate by 13 per cent of employed graduates, as already stated above. Table 4 shows that the most favourable ratings were found amongst Norwegian, Czech and Finnish graduates (this question was not addressed to the Swedish graduates). In contrast, one fifth or more of the graduates in Italy, France and Japan considered their employment and work as predominantly or altogether inappropriate.

Table 4. Appropriateness of Employment and Work and Level of Education as Perceived by Graduates, by Country (percentage and mean of graduates employed about four years after graduation)

	Country													Total
	IT	ES	FR	AT	DE	NL	UK	FI	SE	NO	CZ	EUR	JP	
1 Completely appropriate	19	30	30	28	22	30	40	46	m	55	56	36	12	33
2	29	34	31	37	39	45	28	36	m	32	27	34	31	34
3	30	20	18	22	24	17	14	11	m	10	10	17	37	19
4	16	11	13	8	11	6	11	5	m	3	5	9	14	9
5 Not at all appropriate	6	5	8	4	4	2	7	2	m	1	1	4	6	4
Total*	100	100	100	100	100	100	100	100	m	100	100	100	100	100
Arithmetic mean	2.6	2.3	2.4	2.2	2.4	2.0	2.2	1.8	m	1.6	1.7	2.1	2.7	2.2

Question F3a: If you consider all dimensions of your employment and work (status, position, income, work tasks, etc.: To what extent do your employment and work correspond to your level of education? Scale of responses from 1 = "Completely appropriate" to 5 = "Not at all appropriate".
* Count by Country: IT (2535); ES (2161); FR (2183); AT (2080); DE (3228); NL (2914); UK (3084); FI (2448); SE (m); NO (3115); CZ (2624); EU (26372); JP (2984); Total (29355).

Source: CHEERS survey data

Finally, graduates were asked to state how their current work situation met the expectations they had at the beginning of their studies. We did not consider those who answered "I did not have any expectations". It is interesting to note that a relatively high proportion of graduates (41%) found their current work situation above what they had expected upon enrolment (see Table 5). More than two-thirds of the graduates in Norway (69%) and half the graduates in Finland (49%) shared this view. In addition, more than one third considered their current work as meeting their prior expectations.

In contrast, as already stated, only 22 per cent of the employed graduates thought that their current situation was worse than expected. This was true for about half the graduates in Japan (51%), more than one third in Spain (37%) and almost one third in Italy (30%).

Table 5. Current Work Situation Meeting the Graduates' Expectations at the Time of Enrolment, by Country (percentage and arithmetic means of graduates employed about four years after graduation)

	Country													Total
	IT	ES	FR	AT	DE	NL	UK	FI	SE	NO	CZ	EUR	JP	
1 Much better than expected	6	10	8	12	8	7	8	18	7	25	13	11	8	11
2	26	15	31	33	33	35	29	31	33	44	28	31	15	30
3	38	38	37	41	42	48	39	36	37	24	44	39	26	37
4	15	29	12	9	12	8	17	10	16	5	13	13	33	15
5 Much worse than expected	15	8	11	4	5	2	8	5	6	2	2	6	18	7
Total*	100	100	100	100	100	100	100	100	100	100	100	100	100	100
Arithmetic mean	3.1	3.1	2.9	2.6	2.7	2.6	2.9	2.5	2.8	2.2	2.6	2.7	3.4	2.8

Question F5: Taking all aspects into account, to what extent does your current work situation meet the expectations you had when you started your studies?
Scale of responses from 1 = "Much better than expected" to 5 = "Much worse than expected".
* Count by Country: IT (2327); ES (2065); FR (1882); AT (2059); DE (2941); NL (2575); UK (2739); FI (2439); SE (2134); NO (2923); CZ (2466); EU (26549); JP (2394); Total (28943).

Source: CHEERS survey data

In looking at the responses to the five questions regarding the links between the substance of study and work as well as the level of education and employment and work, we note that Norwegian graduates stated the highest degree of appropriateness. A very high proportion graduated from short-cycle programmes and were employed in associate professional occupations. This, obviously, is not a reason for most of these graduates to cast doubts as regards the appropriateness of work.

Graduates from the other Nordic countries came next in considering their employment and work as corresponding to their level of education, closely followed by the Netherlands and the Czech Republic. Austria and Germany were close to the average of the countries surveyed in these respects.

In contrast, Japanese graduates perceived most frequently an inappropriate employment and work situation, followed by France. Also, the ratings of graduates in the United Kingdom, Italy and Spain tended to be below average.

This rank order of countries is not related to that of the quotas of graduates of the respective age group. Thus, high levels of inappropriate employment cannot be explained by a low selectivity of the higher education system. The rank order of countries according to the frequency, however, is moderately correlated to a rank order of proportions in occupation groups usually considered inappropriate for graduates, i.e. clerks, sales persons, workers and other, where the highest quota was reported in Japan, followed by Spain. This underscores a certain link between objective and subjective criteria of appropriateness of employment. However, French and Italian graduates considered themselves as experiencing inappropriate employment more often than one could expect on the basis of the occupational ranks.

Obviously, another factor comes more strongly into play: graduates in "professional" (including "associate professional") occupations as well as those in the public sector were more likely to consider themselves as being in an appropriate position than graduates in the private sector. It cannot be established whether this is due to a more favourable view of many graduates regarding public-sector employment, whether this primarily reflects a clearer link of career ladders to entry qualifications in the public sector, or whether the private sector is clearly more open than the public sector for employment of graduates below the status bottom line and with less substantive links between education and employment than considered appropriate.

4. DIFFERENCES BETWEEN FIELDS OF STUDY

In response to the question regarding the extent to which study was useful to prepare for the job about four years after graduation, medical graduates perceived the closest substantive link between study and work, followed by graduates in education. In contrast, the link was viewed less closely as on average by graduates in humanities and natural sciences.

The responses are similar to another question as regards how the field of study is linked to the area of work. Again, medical graduates considered most frequently their field of study as the only possible or by far the best field (76%). This proportion was 94 per cent in Sweden, 89 per cent in Italy and Austria and 87 per cent in Germany. It was the lowest in Norway (68%), as can be seen in Table 6.

A relatively close link between the field of study and the area of work was also perceived by graduates in education and law: 54 per cent and 56 per cent respectively thought their field was the only one possible and by far the best. In law, this was most often true in Germany (76%), Sweden (72%) and Italy (71%). In contrast, the links were viewed as lowest by French (35%) and Dutch graduates (42%), where the job prospects of law graduates seemed to be more diversified. About three quarters of the Finnish and Swedish graduates in education considered their field of study as the only possible or by far the best. This was also the case for more than 60 per cent of British and Norwegian education graduates; in these countries, the demand for teachers and the supply of teachers seemed to be more closely matched than in the other countries. In contrast, the respective proportion was only about 40 per cent in Spain, Germany, and Japan and even lower in the Czech Republic.

The proportion of graduates who thought that their field of study was the only one possible or by far the best was lower in other fields of study. We cannot establish if this is due to a high specialisation of fields where similar fields can often prepare as well for work tasks that cut across fields or to a difficult labour market situation. But, again we note exceptions. A close link between field of study and area of work was felt about one and a half times as often by Spanish and Finnish graduates in mathematics as the average of graduates in mathematics, and similarly relatively often by Finnish, Italian and Norwegian graduates in natural sciences.

The two other items signalling a loose substantive link between study and work and partly also a low position, i.e. "The field of study does not matter very much" and "Higher education studies are not at all related to my area of work", were most often quoted by graduates in the humanities (17% and 15% respectively). This was most often the case in the United Kingdom and in Austria, followed by Italy, France and Japan. The situation was somewhat better for graduates in the social sciences (14% and 8% respectively), with most difficulties observed in the United Kingdom (41%) and in Japan (41%).

Table 6. Relationship between Field of Study and Area of Work as Perceived, by Graduates, by Field of Study (percentage of graduates employed about four years after graduation; multiple responses)

	Field of study								Total
	Educ.	Hum.	Soc.	Law	Nat.	Math.	Eng.	Med.	
My field of study is the only possible/by far the best field	54	33	26	56	29	38	32	76	39
Some other fields could prepare for the area of work as well	29	30	46	27	40	48	46	20	38
Another field would have been more useful	6	11	9	6	14	7	10	2	8
The field of study does not matter very much	6	17	14	8	12	6	9	2	10
Higher education studies are not at all related to my area of work	4	15	8	6	11	5	4	1	7
Others	2	2	1	1	1	1	1	1	1
Total	102	109	104	104	107	105	103	101	104
Count	3039	3762	9364	2322	1827	1288	6552	3012	31165

Question F2: How would you define the relationship between your field of study and your area of work?
Source: CHEERS survey data

Asked which level of education was most appropriate, again the medical graduates perceived most frequently a level of employment and work which corresponded to their level of education. As Table 7 shows, 93 per cent considered the same or a higher level of education as most appropriate. The respective ratio was 83 per cent for education, mathematics and engineering, around 75 per cent in law, natural sciences and social sciences, and 63 per cent in the humanities.

Asked to consider all dimensions of employment and work together,

- 81 per cent of medical graduates,
- about three quarters in mathematics (76%) and education (75%),
- slightly more than two-thirds in engineering (70%), law (68%) and natural sciences (67%),
- somewhat fewer in social sciences (62%), and
- again, the lowest proportion of graduates in humanities (55%).

stated that their employment and work was fully or predominantly appropriate for their level of education. Thus, we note that across all the questions and their different emphasis on the substantive and status relationship between higher education on the one hand and employment and work on the other, medical graduates found the closest links. Education was consistently above average, but not always in second place. Finally, graduates in the humanities noted least frequently such a close link.

Table 7. Appropriateness of Level of Course of Study and Degree for Employment and Work, by Field of Study (percentage of graduates employed about four years after graduation)

	Field of study								
	Educ.	Hum.	Soc.	Law	Nat.	Math.	Eng.	Med.	Total
A higher level than the one I graduated from	11	11	10	13	15	14	10	19	12
The same level	72	53	63	66	62	69	72	74	66
A lower level of higher/ tertiary education	8	19	14	12	13	12	11	4	12
No higher/tertiary education at all	7	14	10	7	7	4	6	2	8
Other	2	3	3	3	2	1	2	1	2
Total	100	100	100	100	100	100	100	100	100
Count	3039	3742	9306	2293	1805	1280	6514	2993	30972

Question F3b: What is the most appropriate level of course of study/degree for your employment and work in comparison to that which you graduated from in 1994 or 1995?

Source: CHEERS survey data

The differences according to field of study were consistently smaller than those according to country, but were by no means negligible. In looking at the differences between countries within single fields of study, we already gave examples of variation with respect to the link between field of study and area of work. Similar differences could be observed with respect to the level of educational programme and degree and the level of employment and work. A lower level of educational programme and degree was relatively often considered appropriate by

- German medical graduates,
- Japanese engineering graduates,
- Italian mathematics graduates,
- Spanish, Italian and German education graduates,
- Italian, French and German natural science graduates,
- Spanish, French and Japanese law graduates,
- Italian, Spanish, French and Japanese social science graduates, and
- Italian, Austrian and Japanese humanities graduates.

Naturally, the countries which have already been identified as those where a relatively high proportion of graduates considered employment and work as not completely adequate came up most frequently. The most striking finding in looking at the combination of fields of study and country is the high proportion of Austrian humanities graduates (36%) who believed that no higher education was required for their job. One must bear in mind, though, that colleges for training elementary school teachers, social workers, etc. in Austria are viewed as being outside higher education, while in all other countries they are considered as part of higher education.

5. REASONS FOR ACCEPTING A JOB THAT IS NOT LINKED TO ONE'S STUDIES

Graduates who did not consider their employment and work as corresponding to their level of study and degree were asked to state why they accepted such a position. As Table 8 suggests, most graduates had several reasons.

Table 8. Reasons for Accepting a Job That is not closely Linked to Study, by Country (percentage of graduates employed about four years after graduation; multiple responses)

	Country													Total*
	IT	ES	FR	AT	DE	NL	UK	FI	SE	NO	CZ	EU	JP	
I have not (yet) been able to find a more appropriate job	21	15	16	8	12	7	15	7	10	5	11	11	12	11
In doing this job I have better career prospects	9	8	12	8	11	9	14	7	8	5	19	10	11	10
I prefer an occupation which is not closely connected to my studies	2	1	4	3	3	3	5	11	2	1	6	4	7	4
I was promoted to a position less linked to my studies than my previous position(s)	0	0	1	1	1	1	2	1	2	1	8	2	0	2
I can get a higher income in my current job	4	3	7	6	5	4	12	5	7	4	20	7	7	7
My current job offers me more security	10	8	9	6	8	5	9	8	2	3	20	8	23	9
My current job is more interesting	8	7	12	10	13	12	12	13	12	5	25	12	22	13
My current job provides the opportunity for part-time/flexible schedules etc.	11	6	5	9	9	4	5	6	6	4	9	7	4	6
My current job enables me to work in a locality I prefer	6	7	8	8	11	5	11	8	7	6	22	9	20	10
My current job allows me to take into account family needs	9	4	5	6	7	2	4	5	5	4	17	6	7	6
At the beginning of the career envisaged I have to accept work that does not correspond to my studies	4	5	7	5	5	2	4	8	2	3	12	5	4	5
Other	3	2	6	5	6	7	6	2	6	2	4	5	11	5

Question F4: If you consider your employment and work as hardly appropriate and not linked to your education: why did you accept it? Multiple responses possible.
* Count by Country: IT (2774); ES (2322); FR (2512); AT (2275); DE (3369); NL (2983); UK (3293); FI (2615); SE (2594); NO (3202); CZ (2915); EU (30853); JP (3055); Total (33908).

Source: CHEERS survey data

Five were most frequently quoted:

- "my current job is more interesting" (13% of all employed graduates);
- "I have not yet been able to find a more appropriate job" (11%);
- "In doing this job, I have better career prospects" (10%);
- "My current job enables me to work in a locality I prefer" (10%);
- "My current job offers me more security" (9%).

Only about one third of the graduates being in a job not clearly or even not at all appropriate, i.e. less than 15 percent seem to be in such a job involuntarily. The other about two-thirds who do not consider their job as fully or predominantly adequate accept such a position, because they view their job as attractive in some respects (interesting assignment, promotion prospects, high job security, etc.) or because they took their job in order to accommodate family needs and regional preferences more easily.

Among all the reasons given, those stated by the Spanish, Italian and French graduates most frequently refer to difficulties linked to employment opportunities. In contrast, the Japanese and Czech graduates most frequently state other reasons for excepting such a position.

Finally, across the whole sample, there are clear gender differences in the reasons. Male graduates were more likely to accept a job that was not linked to their studies because it gave them better opportunities for career prospects, higher income, and more interesting work. Female graduates, in contrast, either had less choice in their present situation, or sought part-time jobs for family reasons.

6. THE RELATIONSHIPS BETWEEN CLOSE LINKS AND STATUS LINKS BETWEEN STUDY AND GRADUATE WORK

In debates about the extent to which study and subsequent work are linked, two dimensions tend to be addressed, as discussed in the introduction of this chapter. On the one hand, fields of study could be closely linked to certain areas of work. We call this a "high specificity" of a field of study and the opposite situation, i.e. a loose substantive link, a "low specificity" of a field of study. On the other hand, the status of study and employment could be closely linked. We call "high level occupations" employment and work in occupational areas that could be considered to be appropriate for graduates from higher education institutions; and "low level occupations" those which are not considered as appropriate for graduates.

The analysis undertaken above shows that a distinction of the two dimensions is sound, even if we note that they are not always clearly distinct in the public debate and in the minds of the graduates. Therefore, we created a typology of the inter-relationships between these two dimensions, whereby we take the statement "My field is the best/the only one possible" (see the first lines of Table 2 and Table 6) as the indicator of "high specificity" vs. "low specificity" and the responses "A higher level than the one I graduated from" and "The same level" to the question "What is the most appropriate level of course of study for your job?" (see the first and second lines of Table 3 and 8.7) as the indicator of "high level occupations" vs. "low level occupations".

Certainly, graduates can consider themselves as very privileged if their employment and work are characterised both by a high specificity and a high level. As Figure 1 shows, this applied to medical graduates in all countries and for graduates in law in most countries.

On the other hand, graduates with low specificity and low occupational level were certainly in the worst situation. According to the indicators chosen, this held true for graduates in the humanities and social sciences in all countries surveyed.

Graduates from fields that lead to high positions, but have low specificity can be viewed as being in a relatively good labour market situation - almost as good as the first group quoted above. Even if they do not have the privileges of the highest-level professional status, they come from a field which ensures a broad range of different domains and thus allows them to diversify their career and, in addition, resist the fluctuations in the labour market. This seems to hold true for graduates in engineering in almost all countries and in the natural sciences in most countries.

Graduates from fields with high specificity and leading to low level occupations can probably be considered to be in a difficult labour market situation. Their study might be narrow, thus limiting the graduations' career opportunities. According to Figure 1, this is only the case for graduates from a single or at most two countries each within the majority of fields of study.

Figure 1. Specificity and Level of Occupation, by Field of Study and Country

	High level occupations		Low level occupations	
High specificity	Medicine	*(all countries)*	Mathematics	*(Italy)*
	Law	*(Italy, Germany, Norway, Sweden, Finland, Czech Republic, Netherlands, United Kingdom, Austria)*	Natural sciences	*(Italy)*
	Mathematics	*(Spain, United Kingdom, Finland)*	Education	*(Italy, Austria)*
	Education	*(Netherlands, Sweden, Finland, Norway, United Kingdom)*	Law	*(Spain)*
			Engineering	*(Italy)*
Low specificity	Engineering	*(all countries, except Italy)*	Humanities	*(all countries)*
	Mathematics	*(France, Netherlands, Germany, Sweden, Norway, Japan)*	Social sciences	*(all countries)*
	Natural sciences	*(United Kingdom, Netherlands, Norway, Austria, Finland, Sweden, Czech Republic, Japan)*	Natural sciences	*(Germany, France, Spain)*
	Education	*(Czech Republic)*	Education	*(Spain, Germany)*
			Law	*(France, Japan)*

Source: CHEERS survey data

Two fields of study are most widespread across the four types: education and mathematics. For example, graduates in education noted a high level of specificity and a high occupational level in five countries (the Netherlands, Sweden, Finland, Norway, and the United Kingdom), they seemed to be in a non -specific and highly qualified job in the Czech Republic, in a specific and low-position situation in Italy and Austria, and in a non-specific low-level position in Spain and Germany. Certainly, specific conditions of teacher training, the demand and supply on the market, as well as work characteristics and the status of the teacher within each country play a role.

Across fields of study, Italy was a very peculiar case. Four fields were considered by their graduates as specific but lowly qualified because the "over-qualification" phenomenon seemed to be more frequent on the labour market for graduates in Italy than in almost all the other countries surveyed.

In interpreting the findings reported in this sector, we must bear in mind that the groups of field of study presented are in some cases heterogeneous. Notably, many graduates of some of the social science fields were in high level positions. Also, we noted that a considerable number stated a substantial use on the job of their knowledge and competences acquired in the course of study. Thus, the proportion of graduates perceiving a certain substantive link between higher education and subsequent work was higher than Figure 1 might suggest.

7. CONCLUSION

In analysing the links between study and subsequent employment and work not only according to occupational categories and income, but also with the help of the graduates' perceptions and judgements, we are brought to specify and partly modify the picture. First, the medical graduates noted on average the closest links between study and work about fours years after graduation, even though their average income at that time was not very high. Obviously, many graduates of this field were very confident about four years after graduation that they could expect a promising career.

There were many cases where high income, a high-level position, a perception of being in a high-level occupation and a close link between study and job tasks coincided. We also noted, however, that many graduates considered themselves as being in an appropriate position and having the opportunity to use their knowledge, even if they did not consider their field of study as the best preparation for their area of work: this was often true for graduates in engineering and natural sciences. On the other hand, we noted a perception of a close substantive and status link between study and work, even if the jobs did not yield a very high income: this was true, for example, for most graduates in teacher training who became teachers. Altogether, the findings suggest that many graduates perceiving a clear substantive link between study and work were inclined to rate their position as adequate for their level of education, even if the income was not above average. This was not only true for graduates in education, but also for many others who were employed in the public sector.

Finally, graduates from humanities seemed to be least privileged. This holds true both for "objective" and "subjective" indicators.

Altogether, the differences by country were more impressive than those by field of study as far as the perceived links between study and work were concerned. Across the various measures of substantive and status links, graduates from Norway considered their employment and work most often as appropriate to their level of education and to their knowledge, followed by graduates from other Nordic countries and thereafter graduates of the Netherlands and the Czech Republic. Austria and Germany represented very much the average in this respect. In contrast, Japanese graduates perceived most frequently an inappropriate employment and work, followed by graduates from France. Also, the ratings of the graduates in the United Kingdom, Italy and Spain tended to be below average. Various factors seemed to play a role, among them most strikingly a large segment of public sector seems to reinforce the perception of an appropriate relationship between higher education and the world of work.

8. REFERENCES

Allen, J. et al. (2001). *WO-Monitor 2000. De arbeidsmarktpositie van afgestudeerden van de Nederlandse universiteiten.* Utrecht: VSNU.

Arnesen, C.Å. (2000). "Higher Education and Graduate Employment in Norway." *European Journal of Education* 35, 221-28.

Brennan, J. et al. (1993). *Students Courses and Jobs: the Relationship between Higher Education and the Labour Market.* London: Jessica Kingsley Publishers.

Brennan, J. and P.A. McGeevor (1988). *Graduates at Work: Degree Courses and the Labour Market.* London: Jessica Kingsley Publishers.

Kellermann, P. in cooperation with L. Lassnig (1996). *Hochschulabsolvent/inn/en und Beschäftigung '96* (Forschungsbericht). Klagenfurt.

Schomburg, H. and U. Teichler (1993). "Does the Programme Matter?" *Higher Education in Europe* 18(2), 37-58.

Teichler, U. (1988). "Higher Education and Work in Europe." In Smart, J.C. (ed). *Higher Education: Handbook of Theory and Research,* Vol. IV. New York: Agathon Press, pp. 109-82.

Teichler, U. and M. Buttgereit (eds) (1992). *Hochschulabsolventen im Beruf.* Bad Honnef: K.H. Bock.

GUNHILD SAGMEISTER

EARLY CAREER EDUCATION

1. INTRODUCTION

For higher education graduates, education and training activities do not end when they find employment. Often, their field of study was not, or was only loosely related to their occupational area; in some countries, teacher training programmes only begin after graduation from a higher education programme in one or various of the subject matters graduates will teach. But even if the course of study is specialised and has a professional emphasis and if the graduates find employment in a corresponding area, they are not fully prepared for their job tasks. Types of higher education institutions and programmes, individual higher education institutions, and programmes in the various fields of study differ as regards their requirements for professional learning and practices, or they want to prepare directly for professional practice. We noted various traditions as regards formal qualifications: in some countries and some fields, the degree implied an *effectus civilis*, i.e. the graduates were officially qualified for professional practice; in some countries and fields, graduates were only officially qualified after having participated in professional training periods and passed qualification exams that are provided and supervised by the state, public coordination agencies or professions; and finally, in some countries and occupational areas, training and acceptance of competences are completely left to the individuals and the employers (cf. Jablonska-Skinder and Teichler 1992). Also, employers see a need for initial training and learning in order to cope with the specific requirements of the work place, as well as with company-relevant knowledge. Whatever the conditions, initial training and learning are viewed as indispensable, and often graduates are only considered as fully productive members of the workforce after one year, two, or even more years.

Graduates are also aware that the importance of continuing education has grown in the last few decades (Tuijnman and Schuller 1999). The dynamic increase of new knowledge, which is most pronounced in science and technology, is accompanied by a rapid obsolescence of knowledge. Both new professional skills and lifelong education are required for updating knowledge and career advancement. Lifelong learning has been more strongly advocated recently. Interdisciplinary knowledge is required. Furthermore, changing work environments, e.g. flat hierarchies, a new customer consciousness, new communication systems, more emphasis on economic competition, and quality control, underscore the need to acquire new knowledge. In response, provisions of continuing education have grown and become diversified. Higher education institutions, governmental and professional agencies, other non-profit educational institutions, commercial institutions and in-company training play a major role in this context (OECD 1995). And many graduates participate in continuing education during the first four years after graduation, which are the focus of this study.

U. Teichler (ed.), Careers of University Graduates, 159–178

Finally, re-training provisions are expanding as a consequence of rapid structural changes of the economy which make some professions obsolete and lead to the emergence of new occupational areas, and also because of unemployment and a decreasing stability of employment patterns. Graduates often participate in re-training because they never succeeded in finding employment in occupational areas that were closely related to their field of study or because they soon lost the job they had embarked on.

Last but not least, individuals may learn and make use of educational provisions at any stage of their life for purposes that are not, or only indirectly, linked to their work tasks. Lifelong learning and learning are not confined to a professional function.

Theoretically, it is appropriate to classify education, training and learning during the early career according to the categories presented above. However, the educational provisions often have multiple functions, the institutions play multiple roles (see Teichler 1999), and identical educational provisions can have diverse functions for their participants. In those respects, we noted striking differences by country, as well as by field of study and professional area.

Therefore, we decided to include all major participation activities in early career education and training in our CHEERS survey of graduates in 12 countries about four years after graduation. The subsequent analysis does not include participation in advanced degree programmes or study in another field at the same degree level as previous studies. The following overview is based on information provided by the national teams of the CHEERS project. The aim is to describe major features of continuing education of higher education-trained persons, not to provide a complete account.

In *Italy*, 44 out of 67 professions are regulated by statute. About 20 require a relevant degree. These comprise architects, lawyers, actuaries, biologists, chemists, consultants on industrial property, agronomists, accountants, foresters, town planners, pharmacists, geologists, engineers, surgeons, notaries, dentists, psychologists, psychotherapists, food technicians and veterinary surgeons. Admittance to these professions is by means of public exams, often preceded by a period of internship or apprenticeship. *Spain*: In medicine, graduates have to follow courses if they want to acquire a specialisation (intern courses). These courses are provided by some public hospitals, and graduates are employed for the two to three years that they work and study as intern physicians. Many graduates from other fields, especially business studies, go on to postgraduate studies, which are very expensive.

In *France*, to enter the public service, graduates have to pass a competitive exam and spend at least one year's practical training in a specialised school. For instance, there is a competitive exam to become a teacher. Students prepare themselves for this exam after graduation. When they succeed, they enter a university teacher training institute where they follow practical training and seminars. To become a lawyer, law graduates have to pass a competitive exam and then spend two years as trainees in a cabinet. These training courses are mandatory for the professions, but not part of university studies. Psychologists who wish to become psychotherapists or analysts must follow a therapy (about 3 to 6 years) which they have to pay for themselves.

This training is in addition to a regular job. There is no official exam to become a therapist.

In *Austria*, graduates from a university teacher training programme have to teach for one year at a school to become a teacher. During that period, they are professionally active and attend seminars which are not provided by the university but by an institution that is controlled by the responsible ministry. Law graduates have to follow one year of practice-based training at the court in order be employed at the court, and medical graduates are subsequently trained at select hospitals in order to be qualified for general medical work (two years) or for specific medical areas (five years). These kinds of training are all mandatory for the professions, but not part of the university studies, although in the case of medicine, the schools of medicine are involved.

Graduates from other fields of study, for example psychologists, often take long courses (about 3 to 6 years) in special therapy-training, for which they must pay in addition to, a regular job. They are then entitled to practise. Similar structures can be found for most fields in any kind of advisory professional activity.

The market of providers of continuing education is developing: private institutes, chambers, as well as universities offer more and more special university courses. In addition, Austria has a university in Krems that is specialised in continuing education.

In *Germany*, Graduates from medical fields, law, teacher training and most graduates from *Fachhochschul*-programmes of social work are usually not awarded a university degree, but pass a first (state) examination instead. After a period of mandatory practical work and training, they pass a second examination that entitles them to practise. This second phase of training, except for medical fields, is not linked to higher education institutions.

Higher education institutions provide advanced study programmes called *Aufbaustudien, Zusatzstudien, Ergänzungsstudien* and *Weiterbildende Studien* in various fields. About 1,000 of these programmes were offered in the mid-1990s for graduates or other persons with similar qualifications. Some require full-time, others part-time study, often for one year. Final certificates are awarded. They do not certify that the students have reached an additional stage or level of higher education. The number of participants in these course is often small.

All higher education institutions are involved in one way or another in continuing education. Most programmes are offered outside the mainstream of the organisation. There are a few cases of professors who devote part of their regular teaching load to continuing education. Most continuing education programmes for graduates are provided by employers, continuing education agencies or professional bodies which often recruit academics as teachers. One higher education institution is specialised in continuing education in the domain of public administration (*Verwaltungs – hochschule* Speyer).

The Netherlands: Generally speaking, the situation is not very different from that in Austria and Germany. Courses that prepare for such professions as medical specialists (including general practice), teachers, accountants, lawyers, notaries, architects, engineers in industrial design are mandatory. Some courses last for two to three years, and for some specialists, such as psychotherapists, they last for 6 to 8 years.

These courses are increasingly provided by private organisations. The exception is medical specialists who receive their further training in university hospitals. Most of the teaching staff come from universities but are hired by a private organisation and paid separately.

Management and business programmes both for initial professional training and continuing education have developed considerably in universities and the non-university sector. These studies are not mandatory, but are becoming increasingly important for those who intend to pursue a management career.

In several professions, periodic further training is mandatory in order to keep the registration. Usually a credit system is used: a number of credits have to be collected within a certain period of time. This can be schooling, but can also include other activities such as presenting a paper at a conference, etc. Also, private firms increasingly expect their employees to engage in further training. The duration of courses varies considerably, but they tend to become shorter, e.g. three days or 10 meetings spread over a semester.

United Kingdom: In medicine and related professions, e.g. nursing, physiotherapy, veterinary medicine and dentistry, as well as in engineering, social work and architecture, training after the first degree is mandatory.

Such training is often funded by the employer. The duration of the training periods varies, e.g. in medicine, about three years, but more if medical doctors want to specialise in paediatrics, surgery, cardiology, dermatology, etc. In contrast, a training period of only one year subsequent to the first degree is required in pharmacy.

Licence to practise is controlled by professional bodies. They have a say in the curriculum design of all courses and stipulate the amount of mandatory training subsequent to the award of a degree. Students can enter various professions following their first degree. For example history graduates can pursue a career in accountancy if they can find appropriate employment; they would then need to undertake professional training (which would be mandatory) while working. There are various routes into postgraduate training. There is no close link between the first degree and job route, except in medical fields. Graduates from various fields who intend to become school teachers must attend a postgraduate training programme and work as trainee teachers before being allowed to teach.

Various non-mandatory training programmes are provided by both educational and non-educational bodies. The costs can be covered by the individuals, their employers or through special government schemes.

Finland: There are almost no continuing education courses in Finland. All higher education graduates ought to be qualified to practise their profession after graduation. But there are professions where training courses in early career are customary.

In medicine, graduates (the licentiate of medicine corresponds to the British MB, ChB and the American MD degrees in medicine) are qualified to practise under the supervision and guidance of some other person (both in the private and the public sector). In order to practise medicine independently or to start a private clinic one must follow either a two-year professional postgraduate degree programme (*perusterveydenhuollon lisäkoulutus*, additional training in primary health care) or a 5- to 6-year specialists degree programme in medicine. It is quite common to study for both programmes concurrently because the qualification to become a specialised medical doctor does not comprise the qualification to become a general practitioner.

Both practical training and work programmes are taken in public hospitals or in private clinics. However, universities have a supervisory role and they must approve the posts.

Similarly, law graduates have to undergo a one-year practical training period at a court of appeal, without any linkage to the university, before working as a judge, even though the first degree implies an *effectus civilis* for the position of judge. This qualification is also appreciated in the private sector. Therefore many graduates apply for a judicial trainee activity even if they are not heading for a career in the courts.

To obtain a general teacher qualification, almost one year of study must be devoted to pedagogical courses. These can be included in a master pogramme or taken subsequently. There are also special programmes for teachers who want to qualify as class teachers. These are provided by universities, but the graduates have to pay fees.

In other fields, continuing education programmes vary substantially. There are, for example, four-year part-time licentiate programmes in psychology which are more professionally oriented than most other licentiate programmes.

Sweden: A university degree is generally viewed as the entry qualification to professional practice (*effectus civilis*). Therefore there are hardly any mandatory programmes for professional qualification. There are exceptions, e.g. for physicians, psychotherapists, psychologists and lawyers.

In *Norway*, there is mandatory training (*turnus*) in medicine (1.5 years) to become a doctor, as well as in physiotherapy where it lasts for one year. Law graduates who intend to become lawyers or judges must undergo mandatory professional training. Finally, there are programmes to be taken by those who intend to qualify for various professional areas, e.g. meteorologists or accountants.

Czech Republic: Medical graduates must participate in a three year work-based training programme to qualify. Law graduates need similar work-based training in order to qualify.

2. THE DIVERSITY OF ACTIVITIES

2.1. Participation

In all the countries included in this study, more than half (54%) the graduates *participated* in short courses during the first four years after graduation. 28 per cent participated in long training periods, mostly for the purpose of initial professional training. As can be seen in Table 1, only 33 per cent stated that they had not taken part in major training activities during the first four years after graduation (some enrolled in advanced higher education programmes that are not addressed in this chapter).

Participation in long training periods in order to obtain a professional qualification ranged from over 50 per cent in Italy and about 40 per cent in Austria and Germany to 6 per cent in Norway. Short courses or seminars were attended most frequently by graduates in Spain and Sweden (more than 70 per cent) and least frequently by graduates in France and Japan.

Table 1. Participation in Education and Training Programmes During the First Four Years After Graduation, by Country (percentage of graduates, multiple reply)

	Country													Total
	IT	ES	FR	AT	DE	NL	UK	FI	SE	NO	CZ	EUR	JP	
Long training	52	39	26	41	39	23	26	22	26	6	21	29	24	28
Short courses	37	71	27	68	64	52	66	56	70	66	60	58	19	54
No training	31	19	52	19	22	35	26	34	21	32	35	30	64	33
Total*	119	128	106	128	125	111	118	112	117	105	116	117	107	116

Question H1: Did you follow further education and training that are required to obtain or keep a professional qualification or other longer professional training period since graduation in 1994 or 1995?
Question H2: After obtaining your degree in 1994 or 1995 did you undertake other additional/further education/training (short courses, seminars, workshops, self-study, etc. related to your career or to a possible future career? Do not include professional training programmes stated in response to H1 and what you consider to be completely unrelated to work and career.
* Count by country: IT (2955); ES (3017); FR (3051); AT (2138); DE (3446); NL (2952); UK (3182); FI (2654); SE (2594); NO (3188); CZ (3092); EUR (32270); JP (3367); Total(35636).

Source: CHEERS survey data

Private institutes were mentioned by half the graduates (most often by Austrian, Czech and Dutch graduates and least often by French graduates) as *providers*, followed by in-company training (most often in the United Kingdom and least often in Italy and Spain) and higher education institutions (28%). Higher education institutions played a major role as continuing education providers in Finland (49%) and in Norway (40%) as far as participation in courses was concerned. In contrast, only 5 per cent of graduates from Japanese universities participated in continuing education programmes provided by universities. In addition, one fifth of graduates in Japan and one eighth in Spain followed distance education courses.

The *costs of continuing education courses* were mainly paid by the employers, followed by the graduates themselves and by public funds. The highest share borne by employers in the Netherlands, Norway, the Czech Republic and the United Kingdom, by the graduates in Italy and Spain, and by the public in Italy, Spain and France.

Hence, it is not very surprising to note that graduates in Italy and Spain were those who *attended continuing education courses* outside their paid working hours or during periods of unemployment the most. In the other countries, most courses took place either during working hours (predominantly in Finland, the United Kingdom and France) or at least partly during paid working hours (almost half in Austria and the Czech Republic).

2.2. *Subjects*

From a list of thirteen *topics* addressed in education and training programmes attended (see Table 2), only "new scholarly knowledge of my discipline" was quoted by the majority of graduates (61%). More than a third cited "computer skills" (39%) and "methodological competences" (36%). In France, "computer skills" and "methodological competences" were chosen most frequently, but "oral or written communication/presentation skills" were also mentioned more often than new knowledge. In the United Kingdom, communication and presentation skills were quoted very often, and "relations with customers" and "management competences" were evoked about twice as often as in other countries. "Cross-disciplinary scholarly knowledge" was a relatively frequent topic in Norway and in Austria. Italian graduates mentioned "foreign language proficiency" most frequently but this topic was hardly evoked by British and Dutch graduates.

Table 2. Topics Most Frequently Covered in Graduates' Early Career Education and Training Programmes and Courses, by Country (percentage of graduates; multiple reply)

	Country												Total
	IT	ES	FR	AT	DE	NL	UK	FI	SE	NO	CZ	JP	
New scholarly knowledge	41	63	34	66	70	67	49	42	66	80	71	45	61
Cross-disc. scholarly knowl.	13	28	30	35	32	33	26	20	16	42	27	21	28
Methodological competences	36	22	45	27	32	61	40	34	21	46	41	47	36
Foreign language proficiency	48	24	15	22	13	6	5	20	21	5	35	16	18
Computer skills	19	50	45	34	39	32	44	42	49	33	35	29	39
Managem./leadership comp.	12	11	18	25	22	26	35	24	25	21	27	17	23
Oral/writt. com./presentation	17	12	38	28	26	29	41	34	29	26	35	26	28
Relations with customers	13	7	16	24	24	27	37	19	12	10	27	17	20

Question: Which of the following topics were covered in the course(s)? Multiple reply possible.
* Count by country: IT (1072); ES (2074); FR (786); AT (1554); DE (2173); NL (1503); UK (1836); FI (1447); SE (1824); NO (2062); CZ (1843); JP (691); Total (18793).
Source: CHEERS survey data

2.3. *Goals, Benefits and Needs*

"Updating knowledge" was quoted most frequently as the *purpose* of continuing education. Only British and Spanish graduates cited "enhancing career" slightly more frequently. Retraining already played a role in Spain and Italy.

The most important *outcome* of continuing education according to the graduates of all countries was "help(ed) to get along with the work tasks" and "to enrich the job". In addition, Spanish graduates said more often than others that it provided an opportunity of finding employment.

Asked about *needs,* almost three quarters considered education and training during the first years after graduation as necessary "in order to cope with tasks which could not be envisaged at the time of initial education" (notably those in the Czech Republic, Finland, Austria, Spain and Germany) and "in order to acquire knowledge which can be learned better on the job" (most frequently in the United Kingdom, France, Czech Republic and Germany and least often in Sweden).

Norwegian, Austrian and Finnish graduates emphasised that "initial first study constitutes a good basis for continuous updating of knowledge and skills".

Shortcomings in initial first study were often seen as requiring subsequent training by Italian, Austrian, Spanish and Czech graduates, but relatively seldom by British and Dutch graduates.

2.4. *Modes of Learning*

Reading of professional/scientific journals seemed to be the most common strategy in individual early career learning. More than one third of all graduates did this at least once a week, notably Finnish, Dutch, Austrian and Italian graduates. The low rate in Spain may be due to high rates of unemployment, because professional journals could be less accessible for the unemployed.

Attending relevant professional meetings was also usual. About one quarter of the graduates - of whom almost half were French and Norwegian - attended at least four conferences. In contrast, almost half the graduates in Germany and Spain did not attend a single conference.

Using internet resources to gather relevant information was a weekly activity amongst almost one quarter of the graduates. This was most frequent amongst Finnish and Swedish graduates.

2.5. *Differences by Field of Study*

Initial professional training was characterised in some professional areas by practices that were common across countries. The highest proportion of graduates to participate in long training programmes was those in law and from medical fields. In the respective professional areas, initial professional training was mandatory in all the countries that were surveyed except Finland and Sweden. Many graduates in medical fields and teacher training also participated often in short courses (see below, Table 3).

In contrast, fewer graduates in engineering followed long training programmes; more than half, however, participated in short courses or seminars. The lowest participation rates were found amongst graduates in humanities and natural sciences. Less than half participated in formal education and training during the first four years after graduation, and if they did, it was mostly in a single course.

Graduates in computer science, business studies, engineering and veterinary medicine most frequently chose private institutions as *providers*; except veterinary medicine graduates, in-company training was the second most frequent choice. Higher education institutions were only mentioned by one quarter of the graduates. Universities were the most important providers of further education for physicians.

Different *funding* patterns between fields of study can be largely explained by the funding modes of employers. Private employers tended to provide initial training as part of regular employment; therefore the training of most graduates in business studies, computer science, engineering as well as of many in the natural sciences was funded by employers and was mostly undertaken during paid working hours. In contrast, many graduates in veterinary science and medicine paid for their training.

As regards the topics of education and training (see Table 3), new scholarly knowledge and cross-disciplinary knowledge played prominent roles in health sciences.

Computer skills were frequently mentioned by mathematicians. Methodological competences were underscored by teacher training graduates (included in the category "Others"). Management competences were quoted relatively often by graduates in business studies and engineering. For social science and business studies graduates, communication and presentation competences and relations with customers were frequent topics.

A similar number of men and women participated in initial training and continuing professional education. However, women graduates made greater use of higher education institutions' offers and less of private offers than their male colleagues. Hence, employers paid more often for men, whilst women more often paid for themselves. Most differences in the modes of participation by gender can be explained by the different representation in fields of study and by the fact that women were more often unemployed or out of paid work in order to care for children and family.

Table 3. Topics Most Frequently Covered in Graduates' Early Career Education and Training Programmes and Courses, by Field of Study (percentage of graduates; multiple reply)

	Field of Study									Total
	Hum.	Soc.	Law	Nat.	Math.	Med.	Eng.	Edu.	Other	
New scholarly knowledge	50	47	55	58	54	57	60	85	68	62
Cross-discipl. scholarly knowledge	25	28	21	26	32	21	26	39	31	28
Methodological competences	40	33	29	22	43	41	32	34	47	36
Foreign language proficiency	24	21	20	20	19	13	20	7	14	19
Computer skills	40	40	46	36	38	65	44	16	36	39
Managem./leadership competences	16	23	29	15	20	25	29	14	21	23
Oral or written com./presentation	30	34	33	25	28	26	28	18	27	28
Relations with customers	20	25	27	16	15	14	15	14	20	20
Count	1751	1480	2518	61	968	780	3253	2174	3739	18174

Question H7: Which of the following topics were covered in the course(s)? Multiple reply possible.
Source: CHEERS survey data

3. EARLY CAREER TRAINING PRACTICES IN THE VARIOUS COUNTRIES

As already stated above, professional training practices had much in common in some professional areas across countries. However, national regulations and customs came into play in most fields of study and in most professional areas. Table 4 and Table 5 show the differences in participation and the major topics of education and training attended by the graduates during the first four years after graduation in the various countries surveyed.

Italy showed high rates of law and education/teacher training graduates participating in long training programmes, often provided by private institutes. Foreign language proficiency was often chosen by graduates in humanities, natural sciences and engineering. Many Italian graduates paid for themselves and attended courses outside paid working hours to update their knowledge. Study shortcomings were also frequently mentioned.

Table 4. Graduates' Participation in Short Courses and Long Programmes of Education and Training During the First Four Years After Graduation, by Country and Field of Study (percentage)

	Field of Study								Total
	Hum.	Soc.	Law	Nat.	Math.	Med.	Eng.	Edu.	
ITALY									
Long and short training	17	23	26	26	12	17	19	17	21
Long training only	23	31	57	30	19	20	22	36	30
Short courses only	18	17	4	15	27	27	16	16	17
No education/training	41	29	13	29	42	37	44	32	32
SPAIN									
Long and short training	38	24	37	33	19	24	30	29	28
Long training only	11	10	14	15	13	12	7	6	10
Short courses only	36	45	33	36	40	39	52	46	43
No education/training	15	22	16	16	28	24	10	18	19
FRANCE									
Long and short training	9	2	12	4	8	4	29	6	6
Long training only	41	15	21	17	16	6	14	23	21
Short courses only	14	24	21	17	27	30	43	21	22
No education/training	36	58	46	62	50	60	14	50	52
AUSTRIA									
Long and short training	22	27	52	13	9	10	57	41	31
Long training only	6	8	25	10	5	3	10	14	10
Short courses only	37	47	11	42	54	57	21	29	38
No education/training	36	19	11	35	32	30	11	16	21
GERMANY									
Long and short training	28	22	35	15	13	13	69	38	26
Long training only	21	9	34	18	13	6	5	19	13
Short courses only	27	46	18	31	52	51	23	28	38
No education/training	25	24	12	36	22	30	4	15	23
THE NETHERLANDS									
Long and short training	9	11	17	14	11	12	11	9	11
Long training only	10	11	18	10	4	10	12	11	11
Short courses only	30	45	36	44	60	46	37	42	42
No education/training	52	33	29	32	25	33	39	39	36

to be continued

Table 4. Continued

	Field of Study								Total
	Hum.	Soc.	Law	Nat.	Math.	Med.	Eng.	Edu.	
UNITED KINGDOM									
Long and short training	17	20	48	13	14	19	36	15	20
Long training only	8	9	15	10	9	8	2	4	8
Short courses only	39	39	17	46	46	50	48	49	44
No education/training	37	31	19	32	31	24	14	31	30
FINLAND									
Long and short training	12	12	16	19	8	7	20	16	12
Long training only	14	8	14	9	7	6	20	8	10
Short courses only	36	43	35	39	54	53	34	47	43
No education/training	38	37	35	43	32	34	26	30	35
SWEDEN									
Long and short training	21	18	9	34	19	18	27	10	18
Long training only	24	8	5	16	4	6	7	4	8
Short courses only	37	51	54	51	58	63	49	56	53
No education/training	18	23	33	9	19	13	16	30	21
NORWAY									
Long and short training	1	4	25	0	0	1	12	1	5
Long training only	1	1	5	1	0	1	2	0	1
Short courses only	57	60	48	55	68	63	57	65	60
No education/training	42	35	23	44	33	36	29	34	34
CZECH REPUBLIC									
Long and short training	7	14	20	11	0	11	50	16	16
Long training only	11	4	2	7	0	5	5	5	5
Short courses only	30	51	53	38	0	45	31	42	44
No education/training	52	31	25	43	0	39	14	36	35
JAPAN									
Long and short training	8	7	9	5	12	6	3	7	7
Long training only	19	18	18	13	6	12	12	11	16
Courses only	10	11	15	8	21	15	12	9	12
No continuing education	63	64	58	74	62	67	72	72	66

Source: CHEERS survey data

In *Spain*, graduates in humanities often followed courses and programmes provided by higher education institutions. Computer skills were often part of the training of graduates in social sciences and mathematics, cross-disciplinary knowledge in the case of the humanities and engineering, and methodological competences in the case of humanities. Their main purpose for mathematics and engineering graduates was career enhancement.

In *France*, few natural science and engineering graduates participated in early career education and training. Many law and medical graduates participated in courses provided by higher education institutions. Training in methodological competences and computer skills was frequently followed by mathematics and law graduates, whilst oral and written communication played an important role for graduates in the humanities.

Table 5. Topics Most Frequently Covered in Graduates Early Career Training Programmes and Education Courses, by Country and by Field of Study (percentage of graduates; European countries only; multiple reply)

	Field of Study								Total
	Hum.	Soc.	Law	Nat.	Math.	Med.	Eng.	Edu.	
*ITALY**									
New scholarly knowledge	30	35	39	46	44	46	63	45	41
Methodological competences	39	34	25	44	49	34	35	42	36
Foreign language proficiency	53	50	38	52	41	51	37	48	48
Computer skills	18	24	16	15	26	18	9	13	19
Management/leadership competences	6	17	9	8	15	16	7	6	12
Oral & written commun./presentation	18	22	11	11	15	18	10	10	17
Relations with customers	16	19	9	2	13	11	12	13	13
SPAIN									
New scholarly knowledge	66	50	52	58	69	59	85	71	63
Cross-disciplinary. schol. knowledge	31	22	31	25	19	30	28	32	28
Methodological competences	43	13	9	30	26	15	23	30	22
Foreign language proficiency	32	36	18	28	15	25	13	17	24
Computer skills	45	60	48	44	71	48	27	50	50
Management/leadership competences	5	18	10	4	7	12	5	9	11
Oral & written commun./presentation	15	12	15	10	5	7	13	12	12
FRANCE									
New scholarly knowledge	39	27	37	40	28	32	100	37	33
Cross-disciplinary schol. knowledge	27	26	29	38	31	32	0	39	30
Methodological competences	59	39	44	55	33	41	28	59	45
Foreign language proficiency	18	12	18	16	12	21	14	13	15
Computer skills	46	37	50	44	76	40	0	18	45
Management/leadership competences	8	19	15	22	14	29	14	35	18
Oral & written commun./presentation	50	38	36	35	24	37	28	46	38
Relations with customers	16	25	12	9	8	10	0	18	16
AUSTRIA									
New scholarly knowledge	47	62	63	54	69	56	92	72	66
Cross-disciplinary schol. knowledge	31	31	32	42	24	34	49	34	35
Methodological competences	19	27	14	22	34	28	21	39	27

to be continued

Table 5. Continued

	Field of Study								Total
	Hum.	Soc.	Law	Nat.	Math.	Med.	Eng.	Edu.	
Foreign language proficiency	28	24	28	19	18	31	5	20	22
Computer skills	33	34	41	21	55	41	12	37	34
Management/leadership competences	27	34	17	26	30	31	7	26	25
Oral & written commun./presentation	35	37	24	27	32	30	7	31	28
Relations with customers	19	33	21	15	14	16	21	29	24
GERMANY									
New scholarly knowledge	65	68	75	58	70	65	95	73	70
Cross-disciplinary schol. knowledge.	29	26	17	39	26	29	49	42	32
Methodological competences.	42	25	17	40	42	25	30	48	32
Foreign language proficiency	17	13	9	17	15	19	3	6	13
Computer skills	36	49	31	33	65	49	6	22	39
Management/leadership competences	12	26	15	21	27	31	8	17	22
Oral & written commun./presentation	20	35	12	26	31	29	7	27	26
Relations with customers	16	31	23	17	17	17	19	37	24
THE NETHERLANDS									
New scholarly knowledge	51	66	84	61	74	64	79	67	67
Cross-disciplinary schol. knowledge	29	34	33	50	29	38	30	28	33
Methodological competences	54	55	56	58	66	67	72	63	61
Computer skills	37	32	16	19	47	39	15	30	32
Management/leadership competences	22	32	22	30	27	25	11	25	26
Oral & written commun./presentation	32	33	42	33	24	28	12	27	29
Relations with customers	22	36	30	19	20	21	14	26	27
UNITED KINGDOM									
New scholarly knowledge	45	41	53	43	39	48	76	55	49
Cross-disciplinary schol. knowledge	20	23	29	25	15	32	36	32	26
Methodological competences	40	37	37	43	40	43	32	50	40
Computer skills	53	47	26	48	77	47	9	40	44
Management/leadership competences	30	39	22	36	43	47	27	32	35
Oral & written commun./presention	39	49	47	41	35	38	31	39	41
Relations with customers	40	43	38	35	24	28	31	46	37
*FINLAND**									
New scholarly knowledge	33	32	55	43	50	50	70	36	42
Methodological competences	40	32	13	41	43	28	34	37	34
Foreign language proficiency	24	25	29	15	17	21	9	15	20
Computer skills	41	41	30	51	65	40	29	46	42
Management/leadership competences	14	29	40	14	29	35	19	17	24
Oral & written commun./presentation	37	41	34	29	32	40	15	26	34
Relations with customers	14	28	6	8	15	21	18	15	19

to be continued

Table 5. Continued

	Field of Study								Total
	Hum.	Soc.	Law	Nat.	Math.	Med.	Eng.	Edu.	
*SWEDEN**									
New scholarly knowledge	65	52	53	70	83	67	91	68	70
Methodological competences	15	16	11	33	34	21	21	29	21
Foreign language proficiency	27	23	33	18	16	31	7	16	22
Oral & written commun./presentation	20	36	25	26	30	38	14	18	29
Computer skills	35	55	54	39	73	51	28	52	49
Management/leadership competences	10	23	17	12	25	44	19	17	25
NORWAY									
New scholarly knowledge	59	67	75	74	81	78	86	86	80
Cross-disciplinary schol. knowledge	46	35	33	34	21	34	52	48	42
Methodological competences	40	42	24	49	46	39	41	68	46
Manual skills	42	32	31	30	38	26	51	55	41
Computer skills	39	47	32	47	66	46	20	23	33
Management/leadership competences	16	28	10	11	18	23	19	24	21
Oral & written Commun./presentation	28	28	31	17	26	21	30	31	27
CZECH REPUBLIC									
New scholarly knowledge	61	71	84	66	0	66	94	68	71
Cross-disciplinary schol. knowledge	30	26	22	32	0	19	52	23	27
Methodological competences	44	42	34	51	0	30	33	53	41
Foreign language proficiency	52	40	15	32	0	36	13	36	35
Computer skills	32	41	24	33	0	45	13	30	35
Management/leadership competences	20	39	21	23	0	30	9	20	27
Oral & written commun./presentation	49	42	36	35	0	26	17	39	35
Relations with customers	21	40	32	25	0	21	13	21	27

* Line "Cross-disciplinary scholarly knowledge" is missing in Italy, Finland and Sweden.

Source: CHEERS survey data

In *the Netherlands*, law graduates often followed long training programmes, whilst those in mathematics frequently attended short seminars. Higher education was a relatively frequent provider for graduates in natural sciences, whilst private institutes and in-company training were preferred otherwise. Methodological competences across all fields of study were more often addressed in the Netherlands than in other countries. Enhancing career opportunities seemed to play a major role for graduates in law and natural sciences.

In the *United Kingdom*, medical graduates attended many short courses which were often provided by higher education institutions in addition to long programmes. Lawyers often followed courses provided by private professional institutions. Courses to strengthen oral and written communication competences were often quoted by social scientists and law graduates, and those addressing relations with customers were often quoted by graduates in the social sciences, education/teacher training and humanities. The main purposes were enhancing career for graduates in social sciences, law and engineering, helping to cope with work tasks for graduates from various fields, and to find employment for graduates in law.

In *Finland*, graduates did not attend many training courses during the first years after graduation. These were mainly provided by higher education institutions for graduates in medical fields and natural sciences. Training in computer skills ranked very high in Finland, especially for mathematicians and natural scientists. Presentation and communication skills were often chosen by social scientists and engineers, and management competences by graduates in law.

In *Sweden*, not only medical graduates, but also those in the humanities often participated in long training programmes. New scholarly knowledge and computer skills were frequently addressed across various fields; in addition, engineering graduates often attended seminars that developed management competences and oral and written communication. Swedish graduates seldom considered early career training as necessary to acquire knowledge which could be acquired on the job.

Norway had the highest proportion of graduates who attended only short courses, notably graduates in mathematics. Training – especially for graduates in natural sciences and humanities – was often provided by higher education institutions. Manual skills were frequently chosen by graduates in education and teacher training and by medical graduates. A need for training was often felt across different fields in order to cope with new tasks, but also to acquire knowledge which could be learned better on the job.

In the *Czech Republic*, social science and law graduates often followed short courses, whilst those in the humanities followed very little training during the first years after graduation. Providers of training for social scientists were often private institutes; in-company training units and higher education institutions played some role in the training of the medical graduates. New scholarly knowledge, computer skills and foreign language wee major topics of courses for graduates in social sciences and for the few graduates in humanities who followed training.

4. DIFFERENCES BY PROFESSIONAL SITUATIONS

It is not surprising to find differences in predominant activities since graduation: Those who spent most of their time on a regular job attended further training (59%) more often than other graduates (40%).

Graduates who were not self-employed were more closely involved in initial and continuing short-term professional training, while self-employed graduates participated more frequently in long training programmes. In the first case, this may be due to the fact that self-employed graduates faced more problems in reserving time and funding for continuing education. In the second, it was because of the field. A large proportion of self-employed graduates were active in a professional area where initial professional training was mandatory.

Graduates who were employed part-time about four years after graduation participated more frequently in training programmes than graduates who were employed full-time. In contrast, participation in long programmes was more frequent amongst persons who were permanently employed than amongst those who were temporarily employed. Finally, graduates in managerial positions about four years after graduation had participated both in long and short training programmes less frequently than those who were not in these positions. Two factors come into play. First, those who required long periods of initial training within a professionally or publicly controlled profession were more likely to be employed part-time, to be on a permanent contract and not to have important managerial functions about for years after graduation. Second, those employed full-time, the self-employed and those with managerial functions could have had less time to undertake continuing professional training.

Similar different findings can be reported as regards other conditions of employment and the purposes of learning. Almost all of those who were unemployed about four years after graduation had tried to upgrade their qualifications in computer competences. As already pointed out, many of those who devoted most of their time to child rearing and family care did not participate in continuing professional training. Finally, many of those who were closely involved in initial and continuing professional education were convinced that it had helped them to find employment and to enhance their career.

There were some indications that graduates participated in continuing education in areas in which they noted a gap between their competences at the time of graduation and the requirements on the job. They often participated in continuing education to improve their computer skills and to enhance negotiating or leadership competences and their communication and presentation skills.

5. TOPICS BY PROVIDERS, FUNDING AND PURPOSES

Available information on continuing professional education suggests that some themes are more popular than others with employers and are therefore more often organised and funded by them. Therefore, an analysis was undertaken on how the topics varied according to providers, funds, conditions of attendance, as well as on purpose and perceived impacts (see Table 6).

Table 6 suggests that subjects that are closely linked to working situations are most often offered by private institutes, often directly as in-company training. This is especially true for topics such as management and leadership competences, relations with customers and computer skills. Programmes in these areas are mainly paid by the employers and are mostly or partly attended during paid working hours. Foreign language courses which are provided by private institutes are also chosen, but in this case, the graduates often have to pay and to devote substantially more leisure time.

Similarly, graduates who followed training that was closely linked to their work often believed that it helped to enhance their career. In contrast, those who acquired scientific knowledge considered it useful to update their knowledge and those who were enhancing their computer skills considered it useful to cope with their work tasks.

Table 6. Most Frequently Covered Topics of Continuing Education, by Providers; Funds, Purposes and Outcomes (percentage of graduates, European countries only; multiple reply)

	Topics										Total
	1	2	3	4	5	6	7	8	9	10	
Provided by											
higher education institution	32	32	27	24	22	23	25	40	26	18	28
private institute	51	49	63	55	58	58	55	47	53	54	51
in-company training	42	44	32	47	45	52	42	37	48	53	38
Funded by											
mainly employer	66	69	56	68	66	76	66	57	71	73	63
mainly myself	25	21	37	20	22	15	24	28	17	18	25
mainly public funds	8	8	12	12	11	7	9	14	9	6	9
Attendance											
during working hours	40	43	22	45	44	49	40	33	45	49	40
partly during working hours	33	32	32	27	29	33	33	32	33	31	28
outside working. hours	18	17	32	16	16	12	15	20	14	14	21
was not employed	9	8	15	12	11	6	12	15	8	6	11
Purpose											
to enhance career	30	32	29	32	45	44	33	32	40	39	32
Updating knowledge	69	65	63	63	52	55	64	62	57	59	63
It helped											
to find employment	22	23	25	26	25	23	23	25	25	23	23
to get along with tasks	61	64	55	64	64	66	62	56	65	66	59
to enrich the job	51	53	40	48	55	54	49	50	51	52	46
to raise the status	27	30	20	28	40	39	29	25	35	37	25
to cope with requirements	22	26	36	25	31	35	27	31	33	32	25

1 New scholarly knowledge, 2 Methodological competences, 3 Foreign language proficiency, 4 Computer skills, 5 Competences in business administration, 6 Management und leadership competences, 7 Legal topics, 8 Human ecology, 9 Oral or written communication/presentation, 10 Relations with customers.

Source: CHEERS survey data

6. CONCLUSION

In reviewing the major findings presented above we could state that the participation rate in initial and continuing training during the first few years of the career was high amongst graduates in almost all the countries included in the survey. More than half participated at least in short courses, which were mostly offered by private institutes and paid by employers and which took place during working hours. The main topics were new scholarly knowledge and computer skills. Continuing education activities in order to enhance foreign language proficiency varied more than other topics by country: they played a substantial role for graduates in Italy, but a small role for those in the United Kingdom and the Netherlands.

Second, the study reveals that the differences of continuing education activities by country as well as by fields of study do not only reflect the particular requirements in the various countries and professions. They also are shaped by the characteristics of higher education in the individual countries surveyed.

Third, there are some indications that initial and continuing training did not only address the typical gaps between initial training and actual work tasks. Rather, difficulties in finding a job, time available on the job, as well as obsolescence of knowledge and dynamics of change of knowledge required on the job also played a role (see also Münch 1999).

This survey confirmed that graduates needed both substantial systematic knowledge and "personality", e.g. socio-communicative skills, problem-solving abilities and various other attitudes and skills to cope with their work and their general employment situation. Substantial systematic knowledge was in the forefront of pre-career study programmes, but additional training in the first few years was needed in order to prepare for specific tasks, to update knowledge as a consequence of quickly changing requirements and to train for other jobs if graduates were not successful in finding a job that was closely related to their area of study. Study programmes were expected to better prepare students for the world of work, as far as personality, competences, and "key skills" etc. were concerned. This notwithstanding, it is generally assumed that enhancement in these domains will continue to play a major role in training during the first few years after graduation.

Various graduates underscored the relevance of initial and continuing professional education after graduation with general comments in the questionnaire:

A graduate in computer science stated: "There is a constant requirement for continuing education because of the new technologies. You have to attend seminars or you can acquire the know-how yourself".

A graduate in law remarked: "Continuing education is particularly necessary in the field of expert knowledge, such as new laws etc., Rhetoric would not be bad either".

Another graduate in computer science observed: "… ten years from now, this is like eternity, until then 10 or 15 per cent of your knowledge are still accurate. The basic concerns are still the same. From a pragmatic standpoint you have to say that continuing education is a must in our professional field".

A graduate in psychology stated his views extensively: "*Continuing education* is the magic word for the future. Companies are very challenged. As a society and as a company we will have to create environments in which we enjoy discovering that we have to acquire competencies, skills … in which the employee says learning is fun. Continuing education today does not only mean to send employees to training sessions, but to invent creative ideas in order to motivate employees, to deal with new contents. This can happen via the new media, this can happen via training on the job, job rotation … Knowledge will be transmitted in a more informal way, more related to practice, and more related to experiences. Learning has to be fun, has to be done via one's guts not only one's head. People would prefer this way of learning. The traditional school teaching style where you are taught about a new product for two days will become less and less successful. The university should be self-confident and dare to offer opportunities".

One could add that various employers interviewed in the framework of this study pointed out that they considered continuing education as an integral part of their human resource policy. At the same time, they believed that employers should have a comprehensive perspective of professional training and enhancement and that graduates should take initiatives for continuing education and competence enhancement.

Finally, some of the findings of the graduate surveys and the employers' interviews suggest that initial study programmes should not be expected to prepare graduates for employment and training during the first few years after graduation. They should not be seen primarily as compensating the deficiencies of initial study programmes. One should not expect graduates to be more "employable" in terms of targeted preparation for work tasks, but rather to be prepared to reflect, to be able to solve professional problems and to be able to continue learning on the job (Tippelt and van Cleve 1995). But such a shift would lead to substantial inequalities if funding of continuing professional education were left to the employers and to the private investment of the graduates themselves. Possibly, cooperation all over Europe could help to consider new ways of funding continuing higher education required under these changing circumstances.

7. REFERENCES

Jablonska-Skinder, H. and Teichler, U., in cooperation with Lanzendörfer, M. (1992). *Handbook of Higher Education Diplomas in Europe. A Survey and Study Programmes and of Diplomas, Degrees and Other Certificates Granted by Higher Education Institutions in the European Region.* Munich et al.: K. G. Saur.

Münch, Joachim (1999). Berufliche Weiterbildung in der europäischen Union. Ausgewählte Aspekte und Problemfelder. In: Timmermann, Dieter (ed.) *Berufliche Weiterbildung in europäischer Perspektive.* Berlin.

Organisation for Economic Co-operation and Development (OECD) (1995). *Continuing Professional Education of Highly Qualified Personnel.* Paris.

Teichler, U. (1999). "The University and Lifelong Learning." In Tuijnman, A. and Schuller, T. (eds.) *Lifelong Learning Policy and Research.* London: Portland Press, pp. 173-87.

Tippelt, Rudolf; van Cleve, Bernd (1995). Verfehlte Bildung? Bildungsexpansion und Qualifikationsbedarf. Darmstadt.

Tuijnman, A. and Schuller, T. (1999) (eds.). *Lifelong Learning Policy and Research.* London: Portland Press.

TORGERDUR EINARSDOTTIR

"ON DIFFERENT TRACKS": THE GENDERED LANDSCAPE OF EDUCATIONAL AND OCCUPATIONAL PATHS AMONGST EUROPEAN GRADUATES

1. INTRODUCTION

Which direction are the overall working conditions for young graduates in Europe taking at the turn of the century? There are several distinct approaches to the issue of men and women's occupational opportunities. One addresses the choice and level of education and includes questions about how the level of education affects men and women's access to the labour market and the financial return for education. Men and women's different choice of study field has been an important feature of this issue as one of the factors that contributes to the horizontal segregation of the labour market (Anker 1998).

A second approach deals with the persistent vertical segregation of the labour market, leading to different career paths for men and women and resulting in higher positions for men than for women. Women have made great efforts in recent decades to increase their human capital. Increasing similarities in men and women's education and occupational experience is supposed to improve women's position on the labour market. According to human capital theories, gender differences will be levelled out successively (Becker 1964).

A third approach is based on the issue of family responsibility and the degree to which it interacts with the two aspects mentioned above. Deep transformations are taking place in personal relationships within the private sphere in modern societies. We are facing a dissolution of traditional household patterns and a decline of fertility rates, especially in developed countries. The fertility rates are below replacement in Southern Europe, with Italy and Spain having the lowest rates in the world (Castells 1997).

These aspects are important features of the background for young graduates today, and they will be the guiding questions in this paper. The aim of this chapter is to shed light on the orientation of young graduates in Europe during the first few years after graduation. Are they reproducing or breaking down old patterns of gender structures in areas such as the choice of study field and labour market behaviour? How do educational and occupational patterns interact with child care and family responsibilities? These issues will be addressed in the framework of the transition of European graduates from education to employment. The aim of the study is to help to improve knowledge about the role of gender differences in the interplay between career, family status and child rearing in a hitherto underdeveloped, comparative perspective (Rubery and Fagan 1995; Carrier 1995).

U. Teichler (ed.), Careers of University Graduates, 179–194

2. A BRIEF OVERVIEW OF GENDER DIFFERENCES IN EDUCATION AND EMPLOYMENT

Overall, the situation of the European graduates surveyed in this study seemed to be rather similar before enrolling in higher education, and during the course of study. In several respects, the educational path of men and women graduates did not differ substantially by gender at the outset. The average length of primary and secondary schooling to obtain entry qualification to higher education was identical (12.5 years). However, in a few aspects, women seemed to be advantaged. More women had academic secondary education (81% as compared to 76%), whereas more men had vocational or other secondary education. Women also rated their grades slightly higher than men (36% rated their grades as "high", compared to 33% of men). Women were more internationally mobile before entry to higher education: 8 per cent of the women as compared to 4 per cent of men went abroad before entry to higher education for purposes of education or training, and 7 per cent of the women as compared to 3 per cent of the men went abroad for reasons of employment.

There were, nevertheless, some aspects that predetermined different careers for men and women from the outset. One was the highly gendered choice of field of study. In other respects, gender differences emerged during the process of transition, and in some cases great differences were found within four years after graduation. Thus, about four years after graduation, women were more frequently employed by a public employer than men; they were more often temporarily employed and more often worked part-time. They held lower positions in the occupational hierarchy than men, they shouldered a larger part of domestic responsibilities, and they worked longer hours in the household. These discrepancies meant that, on average, their salaries were 78 per cent of those of men.

3. SOCIO-BIOGRAPHICAL SITUATION

Four years after graduation, about half the graduates lived with a partner: 52 per cent of women and 46 per cent of men. More men than women were single (25% vs. 19%). A quarter of the graduates had children (one or more) in the household: 21 per cent of the men and 26 per cent of the women.

Table 1 shows striking differences according to regions. In Southern European countries (as well as in Japan, which is not shown in Table 1), only a minority of graduates lived with a partner about four after years graduation, and few had children in the household. In Central and Western European countries, the majority lived with a partner, but few had children in the household. In Northern European countries, the majority lived with a partner and almost half had children in the household. These figures confirm the conventional wisdom about country differences in Europe; they reflect different life-styles, as well as different conditions of the welfare system (Castles and Mitchell 1993; Esping-Andersen 1996). Moreover, the age of graduates comes into play. As the average age of graduates about four years after graduation ranged by country from 28 to 33 years, it is not surprising to see that the proportion of those who had children in the household was notably large in countries with a relatively advanced age of graduation (see Figure 1).

Table 1. Rates of Cohabitation and Children in the Household, by Country and Gender (percentage)

	Living with a partner			Children in the household		
Country	Men	Women	Total	Men	Women	Total
IT	32	41	37	11	16	14
ES	25	25	25	11	10	11
FR	53	56	54	12	13	13
AT	64	67	65	31	27	29
DE	64	67	65	23	21	22
NL	61	69	65	14	14	14
UK	43	49	46	17	16	16
FI	m	m	m	42	46	44
SE*	m	m	m	36	44	40
NO	65	74	70	37	56	48
CZ	m	m	m	26	35	30
Total	52	55	53	23	27	25
Count	6014	6947	12982	3591	4630	8232

Question I7: Are there children in your household?
m = data missing
* Swedish graduates were asked whether they had a partner (not whether they lived with a partner).
Source: CHEERS survey data

Child rearing was the prime responsibility of women in all the countries surveyed. Already prior to enrolment in higher education, 4 per cent of women and 0.5 per cent of men had childrearing responsibilities. The respective shares during the course of study were 9 per cent and 2 per cent. As regards the situation after graduation, respondents were asked to state whether child rearing and family care were their major activity. This was predominantly true for 6 per cent of women and 1 per cent of men in the first four years, and for 6 per cent of women and only 0.2 per cent of men at the time the survey was conducted, i.e. about four years after graduation.

In the Czech Republic, most women who had children in the household were predominantly involved in child rearing and family care. In all other countries, the respective proportion was remarkably small. These differences cannot be explained across countries solely by labour market problems or by the conditions of the welfare system.

Figure 1. Graduates with Children and Age of Graduates at Time of Graduation, by Gender and Country (percentage and arithmetic mean)

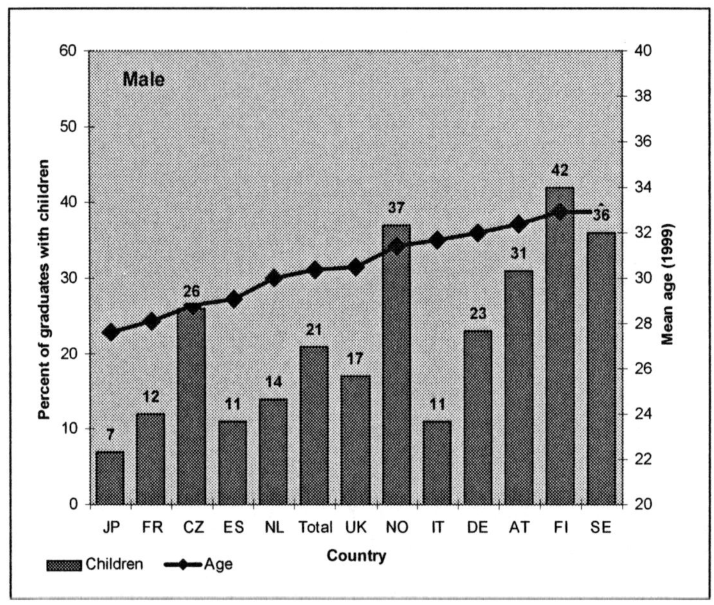

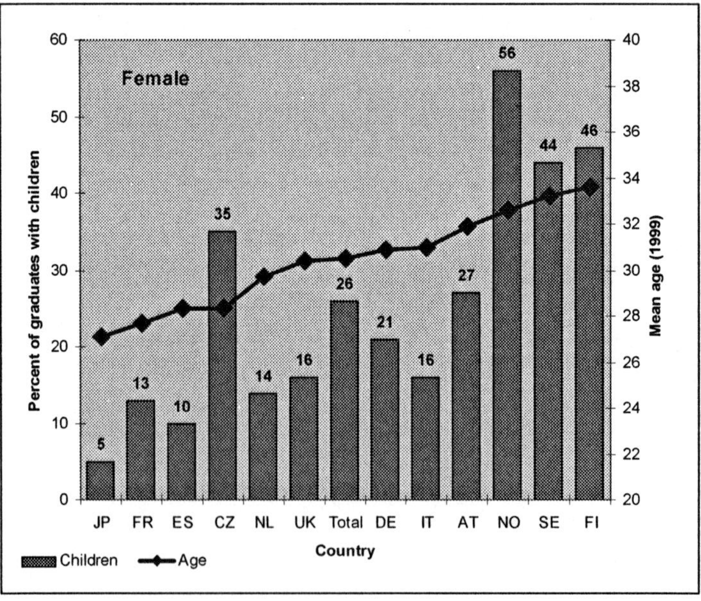

Source: CHEERS survey data

4. FIELD OF STUDY

As has been widely documented, men and women are enrolled in different educational fields from secondary education and vocational training through to higher education. This survey confirms the conventional wisdom. The general picture, with minor cross-country differences, is that women dominate in the humanities and education, as well as in medicine and health studies. Men clearly dominated in all countries in engineering and to a certain degree in science and mathematics as well. This held true irrespective of the various fields amongst the overall number of students.

Table 2. Field of Study, by Country and Gender (percentage)

		Country											Total*
Field of study		IT	ES	FR	AT	DE	NL	UK	FI	SE	NO	CZ	
Education													
	Male	1	6	m	8	3	9	4	7	9	5	11	5
	Female	3	13	m	21	12	20	7	20	25	20	28	15
Humanities													
	Male	7	7	12	4	6	7	20	10	5	6	6	8
	Female	27	12	24	12	18	12	31	22	10	5	10	18
Social sciences													
	Male	28	30	31	24	27	32	24	23	31	16	26	29
	Female	25	36	40	28	35	38	28	29	33	18	31	30
Law													
	Male	14	10	10	13	6	4	5	5	5	7	5	8
	Female	16	11	13	11	7	5	4	4	4	5	4	8
Nature sciences													
	Male	7	3	21	5	9	2	12	6	2	7	7	7
	Female	8	3	14	4	7	1	9	7	4	4	4	6
Mathematics													
	Male	4	8	14	9	6	6	9	5	4	5	0	6
	Female	3	3	4	2	4	1	5	2	2	1	0	2
Engineering													
	Male	28	29	12	27	37	35	23	37	36	45	41	31
	Female	8	9	4	5	9	8	5	8	9	11	14	8
Medical science													
	Male	12	7	m	10	6	5	3	6	8	10	5	6
	Female	11	13	m	17	8	14	12	9	13	37	9	13

m = missing data
Note: 28 per cent of the male graduates in Italy graduated in engineering compared to 8 per cent of the female graduates.
* Count by Country: IT (3102); ES (2988); FR (3022); AT (2265); DE (3469); NL (3021); UK (2989); FI (2663); SE (2622); NO (3329); CZ (3070); Total (32541).

Source: CHEERS survey data

In social sciences, law and natural sciences, the total number of men and women was almost equal amongst all graduates. However, there were striking differences by country, as can be seen in Table 2.

5. EMPLOYMENT SECTOR

The survey provided a broad range of information on the employment situation of women and men about four years after graduation. It confirmed, amongst other things, the differences by gender according to type of employer. Substantially more men than women were employed by a private employer (58% vs. 38%). Conversely, a much larger number of women was employed by a public employer (46% vs. 28%). Finally, women were slightly over-represented in non-profit organisations (7% vs. 5%) and slightly under-represented in self-employment (5% vs. 7%).

Table 3. Public and Private Employment, by Country and Gender (percentage of employed graduates)

	Country											Total
	IT	ES	FR	AT	DE	NL	UK	FI	SE	NO	CZ	
Public sector												
Male	18	26	29	28	29	26	28	43	36	39	23	28
Female	27	33	39	39	48	29	43	65	61	77	40	46
Total	23	30	34	33	37	27	36	55	50	61	30	36
Private sector												
Male	56	61	63	51	55	54	63	48	58	53	54	58
Female	50	54	47	36	31	29	44	25	34	17	36	37
Total	53	57	55	45	45	42	52	36	44	32	47	48

Question D5: Please state the kind of your current employer/institution.
Source: CHEERS survey data

Table 3 shows that women were more often employed in the public sector than men in all the countries surveyed. This held true for all graduate employment, irrespective of the size of the public sector. However, there were great differences by gender. These were much smaller in Southern European countries such as Italy and Spain, where the public sector is rather small, than in the Nordic countries, which have a large public sector.

Table 4 shows that the strong representation of women in the public sector and the strong representation of men in the private sector hold true for graduates in almost all groups of field of study. Men and women were only equally distributed in these two sectors amongst arts (humanities and education) graduates.

Table 4. Public and Private Employment, by Field of Study and Gender (percentage of employed graduates)

	Field of study								Total
	Edu.	Hum.	Soc.	Law	Nat.	Math.	Eng.	Med.	
Public sector									
Male	63	46	24	31	39	24	16	63	29
Female	71	45	35	37	44	34	29	71	47
Total	69	45	30	34	41	27	19	68	38
Private sector									
Male	17	33	61	42	48	69	72	15	56
Female	13	35	46	39	43	60	56	14	36
Total	14	35	53	41	46	66	69	14	46

Question D5: Please state the kind of your current employer/institution.

Source: CHEERS survey data

6. OCCUPATIONAL GROUP

By using the most common categories of occupational groups (ISCO88), we can examine how far women succeed in finding employment in occupational groups that are usually considered as appropriate for higher education graduates. As can be seen in Table 5, amongst the European graduates employed about four years after graduation,

- somewhat fewer women (68%) than men (78%) were managers or professionals, i.e. worked in occupations generally seen as appropriate for graduates;
- in contrast, somewhat more women (22%) than men (15%) were technicians or in associate professional positions, i.e. in occupations sometimes seen as being on the borderline of being "appropriate" or "inappropriate";
- finally, about the same proportion of women and men (11% and 12%) worked as clerks, workers or in other positions.

Table 5. Occupation Groups, by Gender (percentage of employed graduates)*

	Male	Female	Total
Managers	10	10	10
Professionals	63	57	60
Technicians	15	22	18
Clerks and other	12	11	12
Total	100	100	100
Count	14325	12832	27157

Question C10: Please inform us about your current major activity (e.g.: job title and position).
* Managers: Legislators, senior officials and managers. Technicians: technicians and associate professionals. Others: clerks, workers and others.

Source: CHEERS survey data

Overall, women were in somewhat lower-ranking positions across all the fields of study. Those who graduated in medicine were clearly less often in professional positions than men; this was certainly because more women chose shorter medical study programmes (such as nursing and laboratory programmes), whereas men chose medicine to become medical doctors. Women who graduated in engineering, natural sciences and arts were slightly less often represented than their male counterparts in the managerial and professional ranks. In contrast, women who graduated in business and law were marginally more often in managerial and professional positions and those who qualified in social sciences were far more often in these positions than men (see Table 6).

Table 6. Occupational Groups, by Gender and Field of Study (percentage of employed graduates)

		Field of study								Total
		Edu.	Hum.	Soc.	Law	Nat.	Math.	Eng.	Med.	
Managers										
	Male	8	9	16	8	5	6	10	2	10
	Female	12	9	15	6	5	5	5	2	10
Professionals										
	Male	73	59	45	66	75	76	71	78	63
	Female	63	54	49	70	70	75	68	53	57
Technicians										
	Male	15	15	16	10	14	15	15	18	15
	Female	20	16	22	12	18	15	21	43	22
Clerks and other										
	Male	4	17	23	17	6	3	4	2	12
	Female	5	22	15	11	8	5	6	2	11
Total		100	100	100	100	100	100	100	100	100
Count		2488	3251	7978	2030	1589	1144	5652	2584	26716

Source: CHEERS survey data

7. WORKING HOURS

Working hours were investigated in this study in two different ways: on the one hand, as weekly working hours, and on the other, in terms of full-time vs. part-time employment. Both aspects are considered here. This study confirmed that men worked more hours per week than women. 16 per cent of the women employed about four years after graduation as compared to 6 per cent of the men worked part-time. And women spent on average 40 hours per week on paid work, as compared to 46 hours for men.

These gender differences can be observed in all occupational groups. Total working hours (regardless of sex) went from 40 hours in France to 47 hours in Austria. Table 7 also shows that women spend between three and seven hours less for paid work in the various countries than men. Differences between men and women, as far as part-time employment is concerned, were more striking, as Table 8 suggests. They were very great in the Netherlands (27% vs. 8%), Norway (21% vs. 4%) and Germany (25% vs. 8%), whereas they were marginal in Finland and the Czech Republic.

Table 7. Weekly Working Hours in Paid Work, by Country and Gender (arithmetic mean; employed graduates)

	Country											Total
	IT	ES	FR	AT	DE	NL	UK	FI	SE	NO	CZ	
Male	45.0	44.5	41.8	49.9	47.6	44.6	46.1	46.5	47.9	44.7	48.9	46.3
Female	37.7	40.5	37.7	43.7	41.4	38.8	43.4	42.0	43.6	38.4	44.3	40.9
Total	41.4	42.5	39.7	47.3	45.3	41.7	44.6	44.2	45.6	41.4	47.1	43.7

Question D7: How many hours per week do you work on average? Multiple reply possible.

Table 8. Full-Time Employment, by Country and Gender (percentage of employed graduates)

	Country											Total
	IT	ES	FR	AT	DE	NL	UK	FI	SE	NO	CZ	
Male	87	88	96	92	92	94	96	97	98	95	97	94
Female	74	77	88	80	75	73	91	95	90	78	95	83
Total	81	82	92	87	85	84	93	96	94	86	96	89

Question C10: Please inform us about your current major activity (c: full-time or part-time)?
Source: CHEERS survey data

The total working hours in the household were generally much longer for women than for men. While men on average spent six hours more on paid work than women (46 as compared to 41), as can be seen in Table 7, women (including the unemployed), worked six hours more in the household (14 as compared to 8), as can be seen in Table 9.

Table 9 contains further information about the working hours of men and women when children are taken into account. When it comes to working in the household, the impact of children becomes more conspicuous than in paid work.

The working hours of men represented on average 46 hours per week, regardless of whether they had children or not. This was not the case for women, who reduced their paid work by seven hours when they had children. Thus, women with children worked 36 hours a week on average, as compared to 43 hours for childless women (not shown in table). On the other hand, women with children (including those who were not employed) spent on average 28 hours per week in the household as compared to 8 per cent for women without children. Men spent the same number of hours on paid work regardless of children, as already mentioned. As expected, men with children also spent more time in the household than childless men, but this additional time (12 hours as compared to 7 hours) was much less than in the case of women.

Table 9. Weekly Working Hours in the Household, by Gender, Children in the Household and Country (arithmetic mean)

		Country								Total
		IT	ES	FR	AT	DE	NL	SE	NO	
Male		9	8	8	10	8	6	7	9	8
Female		17	13	10	24	15	9	11	17	14
Total		14	11	9	17	11	8	9	14	11
Men										
	With children	22	13	11	13	12	9	9	14	12
	Without children	7	7	8	7	7	6	6	6	7
	Difference	+15	+6	+3	+6	+5	+3	+3	+8	+5
Women										
	With children	48	28	24	42	39	19	15	26	27
	Without children	10	11	8	9	8	7	8	7	8
	Difference	+38	+17	+16	+33	+31	+12	+7	+19	+20

Question 18: How many hours per week do you (and eventually your partner) work in your household (cleaning, cooking, child care, etc.?)

Source: CHEERS survey data

8. INCOME

In order not to be distracted by different levels of income in the various countries, we present the relative income differences by gender. Table 10 shows the relative income advantage of men over women, both for all gainfully active persons and for those on full-time paid work.

Table 10. Gender-Ratio of Income, by Country (women = 100; employed graduates)

	Country											Total
	IT	ES	FR	AT	DE	NL	UK	FI	SE	NO	CZ	
Total	+19	+33	+26	+28	+33	+33	+26	+28	+42	+35	+49	+28
Only full-time	+16	+34	+22	+20	+23	+23	+23	+26	+40	+28	+42	+24

Source: CHEERS survey data

Professionally active men earned 28 per cent more on average than women (gross income, including eventually additional jobs). The income advantage was 24 per cent amongst those employed full-time. The Czech Republic and Sweden were the countries which had by far the largest income differences between men and women, with full-time employed men having respectively a 42 per cent and a 40 per cent higher income than women. Italy had the smallest gender difference, with men having a 16 per cent higher income than women.

Income differences according to gender varied by occupational group, as can be seen in Table 11. Among those, rather few, graduates who ended up in occupational groups such as clerks', workers' and other groups usually considered as inappropriate, the income advantage of men over women was much higher than in the managerial and professional or in associate professional ranks.

Table 11. Gender-Ratio of Income by Occupational Group (women = 100, all European graduates employed some four years after graduation)*

	Managers	Professionals	Technicians	Other	Total
Total	+25	+26	+18	+40	+26
Full-time	+19	+22	+16	+33	+22

Managers: Legislators, senior officials and managers. Technicians: technicians and associate professionals. Other: clerks, craft and related workers, service, shop and market sales workers, skilled and manual workers.

Source: CHEERS survey data

9. FIELD OF STUDY AND EMPLOYMENT

As shown above, some fields of study are male-dominated (engineering and mathematics), some are balanced (social sciences and natural science) and some are female-dominated (humanities, education and health fields). The question, to what extent the choice of fields of study pre-determines career differences according to gender, will be addressed with respect to these three types of fields of study.

Table 12 shows the effect of field choice in respect to five aspects of employment. The choice of field of study has a major impact on the type of employer. The majority of both men and women graduating from female-dominated fields obtained employment in the public sectors as compared to less than one third of those in gender-balanced fields and less than a quarter in the male-dominated fields. Within these three types of fields, men were more likely to work in the private sector than women, but this effect was smaller than that of field differences.

The choice of fields had little impact as regards occupational group. Women consistently took on associate professional positions more frequently. However, men ended up more frequently in other positions, usually considered as inappropriate.

Less frequent full-time employment of women can be explained to a large degree by the choice of female-dominated fields of study, where part-time employment was more likely than amongst graduates from male-dominated and gender-balanced fields. But in all the types of fields, women worked part-time more often than men.

The number of working hours was not determined by the choice of field of study. Within the three types of fields, the average working hours for women were similar.

The income advantage of men is explained to some degree by the more frequent choice of fields which are male-dominated or gender-balanced, but gender differences in income were higher within all three types than between the types of field groups.

Table 12. Employment Situation in Various Groups of Fields of Study, by Gender and Family Status of Women (percentage/means; employed graduates)

	Male-dominated Mathematics, Engineering		Balanced Social Sciences		Female-dominated Education, Humanities, Med.		Total
	Male	Female	Male	Female	Male	Female	
Kind of current employer/institution							
Public employer	17	30	28	37	57	62	38
Private employer	72	57	56	45	23	21	46
Occupation							
Manager	9	5	13	12	7	8	10
Professionals	72	70	53	55	69	56	60
Technicians	15	19	15	20	16	25	18
Clerks and other	4	6	20	13	8	10	10
Full-time or part-time							
Full-time	97	91	94	87	87	77	89
Part-time	3	9	6	13	13	23	11
Working hours	45	41	45	41	45	38	42
Income (1,000 EURO)							
Total gross income	31.1	25.6	29.1	23.4	25.6	21.9	26.2
Gross income of those employed full-time	32.0	27.0	30.6	24.9	27.6	23.7	27.9

Source: CHEERS survey data

The choice of female-dominated fields of study pre-determined to some extent the less advantageous employment of women, but it was not the dominant factor across various dimensions of employment. The frequent choice of female-dominated subjects explained the more frequent employment of women in the public sector, and it had a strong impact on the likelihood of women being frequently employed part-time. In contrast, the choice of field of study explained only to a limited extent the income differentials and to a marginal extent or not at all the access to professional and managerial ranks and the number of working hours. As regards these latter aspects, other factors clearly played a stronger role in determining inequality of employment by gender.

10. CHILD REARING AND EMPLOYMENT

Table 13 helps us to examine the degree to which women's family status is related to the gap between the employment situation of men and women. We took into account whether women had a partner, whether there were children in the household, and the age of the children.

Table 13. Employment Situation, by Gender and Family (percentage/means; employed graduates)

	Men Total	Women Total	Woman No partner	Woman + partner	Woman + old child	Woman + young child
Kind of current employer/institution						
Public employer	29	47	44	40	63	62
Private employer	56	36	39	41	26	22
Occupation						
Manager	11	10	10	11	9	6
Professionals	67	58	57	61	48	58
Technicians	17	24	23	20	38	32
Clerks and other	5	8	10	8	6	5
Full-time or part-time						
Full-time	94	83	87	86	84	70
Part-time	6	17	13	14	16	30
Working hours (mean)	45	40	40	41	41	35
Income (1,000 EURO)						
Total gross income	29.3	23.0	22.1	23.1	24.7	22.6
Gross income of full-time employed (mean)	30.7	24.8	23.8	24.8	26.1	25.1

Old child = over 6 years old; young child = youngest child is under seven years old.

Source: CHEERS survey data

Table 13 suggests that women who did not have a partner did not differ substantially in their employment situation from those who did or who had no children in their household. The cohabitation status as such was not very important for the employment status.

Second, there were clearly advantages in the employment situation of men compared to that of women without any children in the household. This held true for the aspects of employment surveyed.

As regards the majority of employment aspects examined, there was a consistent gap between men and women. Moreover, there was a gap between women with children and childless women. Women with children were less often in managerial and professional ranks, less frequently in the private sector, more often employed part-time and worked fewer hours per week than women without children. In comparison to the previous section, we can state that the childrearing responsibilities of female graduates had a stronger negative impact on their career than their frequent choice of female-dominated fields of study.

Two additional findings deserve attention. First, women with children were strongly represented in the public sector. We cannot disentangle the extent to which this reflects a choice of the public sector in order to find employment that allowed for child rearing. It may also be the case that the conditions in the public sectors encourage employed women to opt for having a child, or that women in other sectors may give up employment, rather than staying on part-time, in order to take care of their children.

Second, in contrast to the previous findings, we noted that women with children had a higher income than women without children. This could be explained by the higher average age of women with children and wage components related to age, years of service and experience, as well as by income supplements for women who had child responsibilities.

A more detailed analysis shows that men with children had a much higher income advantage over men without children than women with children in comparison to women without children (see Table 14). In assuming the same factors for the higher income of men with children that were mentioned in the previous paragraph, we can infer that women with children are in reality on a lower pay level (without those supplements) on average than women without children.

Table 14 makes us aware, however, that these findings based on the analysis of the responses of all European graduates do not apply for all individual countries. While the benefits of having children were huge for men in the Netherlands and France, the effects were the opposite in Sweden and Norway, where children had a negative impact on their wages. As regards women, the pattern is even more complicated. Women with children had a higher income than those without children in Italy, Spain and France, but a lower income in various others, notably the Nordic countries.

Table 14. Income Ratio of Graduates Having or Not Having Children, by Country and Gender (100 = persons without children; employed graduates)

	Country											Total
	IT	ES	FR	AT	DE	NL	UK	FI	SE	NO	CZ	
Men												
Total	+13	+9	+20	+12	+8	+29	+5	+6	–4	–4	+4	+26
Full-time	+8	+5	+11	+8	+5	+34	+6	+6	–5	–3	+8	+10
Women												
Total	+21	+8	+1	–25	–23	–23	–11	–6	–10	–10	–7	100
Full-time	+2	+9	+3	–3	–5	–9	–3	–5	–7	–4	–6	+4

Source: CHEERS survey data

11. CONCLUSION

Generally, the background of men and women was rather similar when they enrolled in higher education institutions. In some respects, women did have certain advantages over men before enrolling in higher education. They came more often from academic secondary education, they rated their grades slightly higher, and they were more internationally mobile, for educational as well as for employment reasons.

However, about four years after graduation, i.e. at the time of the survey, great differences appeared in favour of men. The most conspicuous was the gendered choice of educational field. The general picture is that women dominated in the humanities and education as well as in medicine and health studies, whereas men dominated in engineering and to a certain extent in mathematics as well.

Women were consistently more responsible for child rearing and family issues than men. Their working hours were shorter, both in terms of full-time vs. part-time employment and in terms of weekly working hours. Moreover, the impact of children was considerably stronger on women's work patterns than on men's. Men's weekly working hours were 46 hours, regardless of children, whereas those of women depended on whether they had children. Working hours in the household were considerably longer for women, and the impact of children was much greater on women than on men. Men's income was substantially higher, generally 22-24 per cent higher, when only full-time employment is considered. This difference was much greater when all employed persons were taken into account.

The cross-country comparison presented in this chapter shows that the countries can be roughly divided into three classes, i.e. Northern, Mid and Southern European countries. The findings suggest that the gender differences are a complex issue, confounded by many intervening factors. A striking observation is that despite women's effort to increase their human capital in terms of higher education, traditional patterns are constantly reproduced. That holds true for the horizontal segregation in the labour market, and to some extent for the vertical segregation as well.

Another interesting trend is that of decreasing fertility, which would reasonably lead to more similarities between younger men and women. The chapter shows, however, that traditional patterns in family issues persisted, even in Southern Europe where fertility rates are the lowest. At the same time, cross-country comparison reveals intricate and interesting findings on the impact of children. In contrast to previous findings, the CHEERS study indicates that women with children have a higher income than those without children in several countries, notably in Southern Europe (Italy, Spain and France).

Still another finding of the CHEERS study, which conflicts with existing research, is that not all men benefit from having children when it comes to wages. The benefits are huge for men in the Netherlands and France, but the effects are the opposite in some of the Nordic countries (Sweden and Norway), where children have a negative impact on men's wages.

The results of the CHEERS study could be examined further. One could take into consideration factors such as employment situation, rates of female employment, differences in welfare state systems, family systems, labour market regulatory systems and equal opportunities policies.

12. REFERENCES

Anker, R. (1998). *Gender and Jobs. Sex Segregation of Occupations in the World.* Geneva: ILO.

Becker, G. S. (1964). *Human Capital.* New York: Columbia University Press.

Carrier, S. (1995). "Notes and Issues: Family Status and Career Situation for Professional Women", *Work, Employment and Society,* 9(2), 343-58.

Castles, F.G. and Mitchell, D. (1993). "Worlds of Welfare and Families of Nations." In Castles, F.G. (ed.) *Families of Nations: Patterns of Public Policy in Western Democracies.* Aldershot: Dartmouth Publishing Company.

Castells, M. (1997). *The Power of Identity.* Malden, Mass.: Blackwell.

Esping-Andersen, G. (ed) (1996). *Welfare States in Transition: National Adaptations in Global Economies.* London: Sage.

Löfström, Å. (1993). "Kvinnor föder barn och tror på rättvisa löner. Optimalt för männen men kvinnorna då?", Kvinnolönas mysterier – myter og fakta om lönnsdannelsen. Nord 1993:16.

Rubery, J. and Fagan, C. (1995). "Gender Segregation in Societal Context." *Work, Employment and Society,* 9(2), 213-40.

Rubery, J., Smith, M. and Fagan, C. (1999). *Women's Employment in Europe.* Trends and Prospects. Routledge.

ROBERTO MOSCATI AND MICHELE ROSTAN[1]

REGIONAL WEALTH, EMPLOYMENT AND MOBILITY

1. INTRODUCTION – THE REGIONAL ECONOMIC CONTEXT

Countries may differ substantially in their regional economic and social disparities. In some countries, for example the Netherlands, a view prevails that living in a certain region is not very important for economic wealth and economic, social and cultural life, whilst in others, for example Italy, it is widely believed that living in a certain region greatly affects economic and social opportunities. The relevance of economic territorial differentiation is deeply rooted in both Italian history and socio-economic analysis (Bagnasco 1977, Viesti 2003), but the importance of the regional dimension in economic development is also widely recognised at the European level (Bagnasco and Sabel 1994, Crouch, Le Galès, Trigilia and Voelzknow 2001, Pyke and Sengenberger 1992, Sabel 1988) and in the global economy (Saxenian 1994, Storper 1997, Veltz 2002). Graduates from higher education institutions tend to be relatively privileged, but available information suggests that regional disparities can have a strong impact on the relatively privileged occupations as well. Since the labour market of a developing region cannot provide sufficient employment opportunities at all levels, the young people who live there are incited to attend higher education, hoping to find privileged professions and/or at least to postpone the risk of unemployment (Caciagli 2003, Keeble and Wilkinson 1999, La Spina 2003). Therefore, we shall examine whether regional differences in the 12 countries (11 European countries and Japan) surveyed in the CHEERS study affect graduates' employment and work. Hence, the graduates' transition from higher education as well as their employment status and the employment conditions about four years after graduation will be taken into consideration.

If the place of residence and the place of work have a major impact on career, regional mobility is an obvious way out. Therefore, a question will also be raised on how regional mobility within a country affects the transition to employment, employment status and employment conditions. In a highly differentiated country such as Italy, several analyses of the graduate labour market suggest that there is a tendency amongst students living in developing regions to try to enrol in universities that are in more wealthy areas both because the academic credentials obtained there are supposed to be more valuable and because there are better possibilities of entering a more promising labour market (Micali 1995, Moscati 1983, Reale 2002, Shavit and Westerbeek 1997, Treiman and Yip 1989).

In most countries, the graduates who were surveyed in this study were asked to provide information on both their place of study (the exact location of the institution

[1] Although this chapter is the result of a joint effort, sections 1, 3, 5 were written by R. Moscati, and sections 2, 4, 6, 7 were written by M. Rostan.

U. Teichler (ed.), Careers of University Graduates, 195–210

from which they graduated) and on their place of residence and work about four years after graduation, i.e. when the survey was conducted.

The sample was selected amongst all the graduates of the academic year 1994/95 in the twelve countries. Hence, it ensured a wide spread of fields of study, gender and region. But in a strict sense, sampling was not undertaken to ensure representativeness according to the various types of regions addressed in this chapter. This notwithstanding, the graduates who were surveyed came from such a broad range of regions that the data on differences of employment by region and on regional mobility that were subsequently analysed were close to a stratified sampling targeted according to region (in the case of Italy, the national sample was classified according to gender, field of study and region of study).

In establishing a definition of regions, we took the dominant classification in the European Union, the current Eurostat NUTS classification (NUTS2). For those regions where Eurostat data were not available, national classifications of territorial units were used (e.g. in Japan, the 47 provinces). The number of regions thus established ranged between 6 in Finland and 47 in Japan.

In order to measure the impact of regional economic conditions, we classified the regions on the basis of GDP per capita (income per inhabitant in Japan) according to four categories:

- economically very strong regions with a GDP per capita that was higher than one standard deviation above the national mean of GDP per inhabitant;
- economically strong regions with a GDP per capita that was between the national average and one standard deviation above;
- economically weak regions with a GDP per capita that was between the national average and one standard deviation below;
- economically very weak regions with a GDP per capita that was smaller than one standard deviation below the national average.

This classification thus used national standards. Obviously, an economic weak region of one country could be considered strong in another. In our study, however, we took for granted that the labour market continued to be a national labour market for most graduates and asked how far graduate employment was affected by the relative economic strength of the region within their country. Table 1 shows the distribution of regions in each country according to the four categories of regional economic strength.

Among Nordic countries, Norway and Sweden had only one very strong region each, coinciding with the region of the national capital, some weak regions with only one or no strong regions in between, and they did not have any very weak region. The structure of economic regional differences in Finland was fairly similar to those of Norway and Sweden. Hence, we called this pattern the "Nordic Model".

Austria and France showed a regional pattern that was very similar to the Nordic model: there was only one very strong region coinciding with the area of the national capital, some weak regions entwined with some strong regions and only one very weak region. Mindful of history, we called this the "Continental Centralised Model".

The United Kingdom and the Netherlands had more than one very strong region, some strong regions, some weaker ones and only one very weak region. We referred to them as the "Balanced Model", stressing, though, that half or more of their regions were economically weak.

In Germany and Japan, more than 7 out of 10 regions belonged to the middle categories – indicating relatively small differences by region – but both countries had several very weak regions. We called them "Moderate Regional Differentiation Model".

Table 1. Economic Strength of Regions, by Country (numbers of regions)

	Economic strength of regions				Strongest regions
	Very strong	Strong	Weak	Very weak	
Norway	1	1	5	0	Oslo/Akershus
Sweden	1	0	7	0	Stockholm
Austria	1	3	4	1	Wien
France	1	4	16	1	Île de France
Finland	2	0	3	1	Uusimaa (suuralue); Åland
Netherlands	3	2	6	1	Groningen; Noord-Holland; Utrecht
United Kingdom	3	12	21	1	Inner London; North Eastern Scotland; Berkshire, Bucks and Oxfordshire
Spain	4	3	8	3	Comunidad de Madrid; Cataluña; Comunidad Foral de Navarra; Baleares
Italy	4	7	3	6	Emilia-Romagna; Lombardia; Valle d'Aosta; Trentino-Alto Adige
Germany	5	16	11	7	Hamburg; Darmstadt; Oberbayern; Bremen; Stuttgart
Japan	5	17	19	6	Tokyo; Aichi; Shiga; Saitama; Kanagawa

Economic strength: GDP per capita (income per inh. for Japan); Region: NUTS 2 classification or national administrative units; GDP data (income for Japan) refers to 1996 (1995 for Norway); No data are available for the Czech Republic.

Sources: Eurostat New Cronos Update 6/99, Databank Eurostat; Statistics Norway 2000; Japan Almanac 2000, Asahi Shinbun

In Italy and Spain, the economic differentiation seemed to be sharper. These countries both had several very strong and several very weak regions. We referred to them as displaying a "Strong Regional Differentiation Model".

The analysis of the relationships between regional economic conditions and graduate employment was based on 9 of the 12 countries surveyed (data were missing for the regional structure of the Czech Republic, and graduates from Spain and Sweden were not asked about the region of residence and employment).

2. REGIONAL ECONOMIC CONDITIONS AND EMPLOYMENT STATUS

The relationship between the economic strength of a region and the employment status of graduates about four years after graduation was statistically significant in five countries: France, the United Kingdom, Italy, Germany and Japan (Table 2). In all these countries regional wealth had an impact on whether graduates were employed, were unemployed and sought employment, or whether they were primarily engaged in other activities (further study, professional training, family care etc.).

Table 2. Impact of Regional Economic Strength on Graduates' Transition to Employment and Employment Situation About Four Years After Graduation, by Country (significant differences)

	Employment status*	Full-time activity	Permanent contract	Smooth transition**
Nordic				
Norway	no	yes	no	yes
Finland	no	no	yes	no
Sweden	m	m	m	m
Continental centralised				
Austria	no	no	no	no
France	yes	yes	yes	no
Balanced				
Netherlands	m	no	no	no
United Kingdom	yes	yes	no	yes
Strong regional differentiation				
Italy	yes	yes	yes	yes
Spain	m	m	m	m
Moderate regional differentiation				
Germany	yes	yes	yes	no
Japan	yes	no	yes	yes
Total				
Significant differences	5	5	5	4
No significant differences	3	4	4	5
Missing data	3	2	2	2

* Employed, unemployed and other (education and training, household, other) activities.
** Short duration of job search after graduation (less than four months).
m = missing data

Source: CHEERS survey data

As can be seen in Table 3, there were differences among those countries where regional wealth had a significant impact on graduates' employment status. In most countries, the proportion of graduates who were employed varied by only a few per cent according to regional categories. In contrast, in France, graduates living in economically weak or very weak regions were 8 per cent less employed than those living in strong and very strong regions. In Italy, those living in economically weak and very weak regions had an even slightly lower level of employment than those living in economically strong regions.

We noted more or less the same pattern with respect to unemployment. As can be seen in Table 4, unemployment ratios (percentage of all graduates, not unemployment rates of the labour force) varied according to regional category by about 1 per cent in Germany and the United Kingdom and by about 5 per cent in Italy, with France and Japan in between. Differences seemed to be greatest in Germany and Italy: the share of unemployed graduates in weak or very weak regions was seven times higher than in very strong regions where the percentage of unemployed graduates was very close to the very low levels in the countries with low graduate unemployment in general.

Table 3. Employed Graduates Four Years After Graduation, by Economic Strength of Region of Residence and by Country (percentage of respondents)*

		Economic strength of region of residence		
		Very strong	Strong	Weak/very weak
Nordic	Norway	97.1	97.0	95.6
	Finland	97.9	–	98.3
	Sweden	m	m	m
Continental centralised	Austria	98.8	98.1	98.5
	France	86.1	87.9	78.1
Balanced	Netherlands	m	m	m
	United Kingdom	98.6	97.0	94.1
Strong regional differentiation	Italy	95.4	92.4	83.2
	Spain	m	m	m
Moderate regional differentiation	Germany	98.4	95.9	95.0
	Japan	91.8	90.1	87.6

* Employment incl. self-employment; not only the major activity is taken into account, e.g. if a graduate is engaged in further study and is also employed he was counted here as "employed".
m = missing data

Source CHEERS survey data

Table 4. Unemployed Graduates Four Years After Graduation, by Economic Strength of Region of Residence and by Country (percentage of respondents)

		Economic strength of region of residence		
		Very strong	Strong	Weak/very weak
Nordic	Norway	0.5	0.7	0.7
	Finland	0.2	–	0.2
	Sweden	m	m	m
Continental centralised	Austria	0.3	0.4	0.3
	France	5.2	5.1	8.5
Balanced	Netherlands	m	m	m
	United Kingdom	0.4	0.8	1.9
Strong regional differentiation	Italy	0.8	2.0	5.7
	Spain	m	m	m
Moderate regional differentiation	Germany	0.2	1.0	1.5
	Japan	1.7	3.2	5.2

m = missing data

Source: CHEERS survey data

Finally, substantially more Italian and French graduates of the poor and very poor regions than those of the relatively rich regions were primarily engaged in other activities (see Table 5). Many seemed to opt for advanced academic education and further professional training in order to enhance their employment opportunities.

Table 5. Graduates Engaged in Other Activities Four Years After Graduation, by Economic Strength of Region of Residence and by Country (percentage of respondents)

		Economic strength of region of residence		
		Very strong	Strong	Weak/very weak
Nordic	Norway	2.4	2.3	3.7
	Finland	2.0	–	1.5
	Sweden	m	m	m
Continental centralised	Austria	1.0	1.5	1.2
	France	8.7	7.0	13.5
Balanced	Netherlands	m	m	m
	United Kingdom	1.0	2.2	4.0
Strong regional differentiation	Italy	3.8	5.6	11.1
	Spain	m	m	m
Moderate regional differentiation	Germany	1.4	3.1	3.4
	Japan	6.4	6.6	7.2

m = missing data

Source: CHEERS survey data

It should be noted that we included not only those who were employed, but also those who, although they declared they were unemployed or outside the labour force, offered information in other parts of the questionnaire on their employment and work conditions at the time of the survey. We assumed that they were professionally active, even if they were not formally registered as such. Thus, the tables above show fewer graduates who were unemployed or outside the labour force than the respective tables in other chapters of this volume.

3. REGIONAL ECONOMIC CONDITIONS, TRANSITION FROM STUDY TO WORK AND EMPLOYMENT CONDITIONS

In looking at the employment situation beyond the most basic information, i.e. whether graduates were employed, unemployed or outside the labour force, we asked, first, how the process of the transition from study to work developed. By using a short length of search period after graduation (less than four months) as an indicator of smooth transition, we could show that the economic wealth of a region contributed only significantly to smooth transition in four of the countries for which information was available, namely Italy, the United Kingdom, Japan and Norway. In the first three countries we noted that the transition was protracted in economically weak and very weak regions, whilst the opposite held true in the last country (see Table 6).

Table 6. Smooth Transition, by Economic Strength of Region of Employment and by Country (percentage of employed graduates)*

		Economic strength of region of employment		
		Very strong	Strong	Weak/very weak
Nordic	Norway	82.5	81.9	87.8
	Finland	78.2	–	76.1
	Sweden	m	m	m
Continental centralised	Austria	67.3	65.9	65.5
	France	55.5	52.3	48.7
Balanced	Netherlands	77.6	77.2	74.8
	United Kingdom	83.5	74.5	71.7
Strong regional differentiation	Italy	55.4	47.8	35.2
	Spain	m	m	m
Moderate regional differentiation	Germany	73.4	75.1	71.9
	Japan	93.0	92.3	86.6

* Short duration of job search after graduation (less than four months after graduation).
m = missing data

Source: CHEERS survey data

A higher level of economic development seemed to affect more strongly not only graduates' likelihood of being employed at all, but also of being employed full-time than a rapid transition to the world of work. As Table 7 shows, there was a significant link in Norway, France, the United Kingdom, Italy and Germany: in these countries part-time employment was relatively frequent in the economically weak and very weak regions.

Table 7. Full-time Employed Graduates Four Years After Graduation, by Economic Strength of Region of Employment and by Country (percentage of employed graduates)

		Economic strength of region of employment		
		Very strong	Strong	Weak/very weak
Nordic	Norway	92.4	80.4	82.5
	Finland	95.6	–	95.7
	Sweden	m	m	m
Continental centralised	Austria	86.1	85.1	88.0
	France	94.7	95.8	88.7
Balanced	Netherlands	84.0	84.9	81.0
	United Kingdom	96.8	92.9	91.8
Strong regional differentiation	Italy	86.6	84.8	68.5
	Spain	m	m	m
Moderate regional differentiation	Germany	88.4	85.7	80.9
	Japan	97.3	96.0	96.6

m = missing data

Source: CHEERS survey data

As regards graduates' likelihood of having a permanent contract, regional economic differences mattered in five of those nine countries for which information was available. As Table 8 shows, graduates obtained a permanent contract more frequently in strong regions in Finland, France, Italy, Germany, and Japan, whilst there were no differences in the other four countries.

Table 8. Graduates with a Permanent Contract Four Years After Graduation, by Economic Strength of Region of Employment and by Country (percentage of employed graduates)

		Economic strength of region of employment		
		Very strong	Strong	Weak/very weak
Nordic	Norway	81.9	87.4	82.4
	Finland	70.2	–	60.9
	Sweden	m	m	m
Continental centralised	Austria	72.9	70.0	68.5
	France	85.8	84.9	76.6
Balanced	Netherlands	77.1	80.6	80.0
	United Kingdom	85.1	83.2	82.0
Strong regional differentiation	Italy	75.5	74.2	55.3
	Spain	m	m	m
Moderate regional differentiation	Germany	85.4	75.4	72.5
	Japan	94.8	91.0	90.2

m = missing data

Source: CHEERS survey data

4. GEOGRAPHICAL MOBILITY

The CHEERS graduate survey allowed us to analyse geographical mobility from the region where students studied and were awarded the degree to the region where they lived and were employed about four years after graduation. We examined how far the frequency of mobility varied according to country, field of study and gender, as well as the direction of mobility, as far as the economic strength of the region was concerned.

The available data did not include the analysis of additional incidences of regional mobility. We could not analyse mobility prior to graduation (e.g. choice of a higher education institution away from home or mobility during the course of study). In addition, we decided to forego the analysis of some modes of mobility which could have been analysed on the basis of the available data. First, we confined the analysis to mobility within the respective country, thereby excluding international mobility, which is treated in another chapter of this volume. Second, we did not analyse horizontal geographic mobility (according to the distance between the place of study and the place of residence and study about four years after graduation), but focused rather on non-mobility versus mobility and on the vertical mobility of those who were mobile, e.g. mobility from an economically poor to an economically rich region.

These measures of the place of study, as well as the place of residence and work about four years after graduation provided the opportunity of measuring:

- "*residence mobility*" (graduates who lived in a region that was not the one in which they graduated about four years after graduation) and

– "*employment mobility*" (employed graduates who were working in a region that was not the one where they graduated about four years after graduation).

58.6 per cent of the graduates kept their residence in the region where they had studied and 55.9 per cent worked in the region where they had studied about four years after graduation. By merging the information on both residence and employment mobility, it was possible to show (see Table 9) that 53.7 per cent, i.e. slightly more than half the graduates, were not mobile in any of the two dimensions and 36.6 per cent were both living and working in another region. The remaining 10 per cent worked in a different region from the one in which they lived. Hence, some had chosen to continue to live or to work in the region of their study.

Table 9. Typology of Regional Mobility Four Years After Graduation (percentage)

		Per cent
Non mobile: Living and working in the region of study		53.7
Mobile		46.3
From which		
Residence mobility while working in the region of study	2.6	
Residence and employment mobility to the same region	36.6	
Residence and employment mobility to different regions	3.5	
Employment mobility while living in the region of study	3.6	
Total		100.0
Count		(20,682)

Mobility: Graduates, who are employed four years after graduation in a region (NUTS 2) that is different from their study region or are living in a different region; internationally mobile graduates are not included.

Source: CHEERS survey data

5. PATTERNS OF GEOGRAPHICAL MOBILITY

The quota of regional employment mobility varied far more strongly according to country than according to field of study across countries. As Table 10 shows, about two-thirds of British graduates were employed in a region that was different from that of their studies because many had studied in a region that was not their place of residence prior to their studies; a substantial part of the regional employment mobility could be a return to the home region after graduation for employment purposes. But in several other countries, approximately half the graduates were also mobile after graduation for employment purposes. This was the case in Japan (54.2%), Germany (51.8%) and the Netherlands (49.7%). In contrast, the percentage of graduates who were regionally mobile for employment purposes in their early career was far below average in two countries. In Austria, only 33.0 per cent were employed in another region four years after graduation, and in Italy regional mobility of graduates in the early career was marginal (only 13.0%). The low regional mobility in Italy is striking because one would have expected the incentive for regional employment mobility to be very high as a consequence of great economic disparities between the regions.

Table 10. Regional Mobility Four Years After Graduation, by Country (percentage of employed graduates)*

	Country											Total
	IT	ES	FR	AT	DE	NL	UK	FI	SE	NO	JP	
Mobile	13.0	m	38.1	33.0	51.8	49.7	65.3	38.5	m	43.2	54.2	44.1
Non mobile	87.0	m	61.9	67.0	48.2	50.3	34.7	61.5	m	56.8	45.8	55.9
Total	100.0	m	100.0	100.0	100.0	100.0	100.0	100.0	m	100.0	100.0	100.0
Count	2399	m	2224	1849	3067	2646	2602	2292	m	3109	2977	23164

* Graduates who are employed four years after graduation in a region that is different from their study region; internationally mobile graduates are not included.
m = missing data
Source: CHEERS survey data

As could be expected, women were less mobile than men: 38.2 per cent of women changed their region of residence, as compared to 44.6 per cent of men, and 40.9 per cent of women were professionally mobile, while 47.0 per cent of men changed region for employment purposes. Altogether, 57.8 per cent of the women surveyed who were employed about four years after graduation and had not been internationally mobile during this period worked and lived in the region where they studied and graduated. The respective quota for men was 50.1 per cent.

This pattern, however, did not apply to all countries. Women were significantly less regionally mobile for employment purposes than men in only five of the countries for which information was available. We noted the greatest difference in Norway, followed by Japan and France, and the smallest significant difference in the United Kingdom and Germany (see Table 11). There were no significant differences in this respect in Austria, the Netherlands, Finland and Italy.

Table 11. Percentage of Regionally Mobile Graduates Four Years After Graduation, by Gender and Country*

	Country											Total
	IT	ES	FR	AT	DE	NL	UK	FI	SE	NO	JP	
Male	14.3	m	42.5	32.5	53.7	50.2	68.4	37.8	m	53.5	57.5	47.0
Female	11.8	m	33.7	33.7	48.9	49.1	63.2	39.0	m	36.0	46.4	40.9
Count	2399	m	2224	1849	3067	2624	2602	2292	m	3109	2977	23142

* Graduates, who are employed four years after graduation in a region that is different from their study region; internationally mobile graduates are not included.
m = missing data
Source: CHEERS survey data

Across countries, graduates in law changed region (38.2%) for employment purposes the least (see Table 12), followed by graduates in health (40.2%), arts and humanities (41.7%), and social sciences (41.8%). On the other hand, regional employment mobility was above average amongst graduates in engineering (52.0%) and business administration (45.2%). Many factors could contribute to these differences: in some fields, personal links could retain graduates in the region. Regional mobility was more likely in private sector than in public sector employment. If certain fields of study were provided by only a few higher education institutions, above-average regional mobility of graduates was a matter of fact. Finally, low quotas of regional mobility, as noted above, were more likely in women-dominated fields of study.

Table 12. Regional Mobility of Graduates Four Years After Graduation by Field of Study (percentage of employed graduates)*

	Field of study							Total
	Hum.	Soc.	Bus.	Law	Nat.	Eng.	Med.	
Mobil	41.7	41.8	45.2	38.2	44.2	52.0	40.2	44.1
Non mobile	58.3	58.2	54.8	61.8	55.8	48.0	59.8	55.9
Total	100.0	100.0	100.0	100.0	100.0	100.0	100.0	100.0
Count	5040	2643	3645	1827	2546	4561	2801	23064

* Graduates, who are employed four years after graduation in a region that is different from their study region; internationally mobile graduates are not included.

Source: CHEERS survey data

Differences in regional mobility by field of study were statistically significant in all countries except Italy, although they seemed to be less pronounced in Finland, the Netherlands and Germany. As could be expected, in the great majority of countries, the various occupations and economic sectors opened up different opportunities and attractions for regional mobility.

Graduates in engineering and business administration were amongst the most mobile in most countries. With respect to other fields, we noted a striking diversity between countries. For example, regional mobility was relatively high, compared to the average by field and country, amongst social sciences and law graduates in the Netherlands and in Germany, amongst natural sciences graduates in Japan, and finally amongst graduates in health studies in Austria (see Table 13).

Table 13. Regional Mobility of Graduates Four Years After Graduation, by Field of Study and Country (percentage of mobile employed graduates)*

	Field of study							Total
	Hum.	Soc.	Bus.	Law	Nat.	Eng.	Med.	
Italy	11.3	17.3	13.3	11.3	13.6	12.6	13.7	13.0
Spain	m	m	m	m	m	m	m	m
France	26.1	27.0	51.3	30.8	45.9	63.7	17.0	38.3
Austria	34.8	27.9	27.4	26.8	16.7	37.7	53.0	33.0
Germany	46.1	58.2	53.6	64.1	44.6	54.0	51.6	51.9
Netherlands	46.7	58.5	47.7	56.0	57.7	49.1	47.1	49.6
United Kingdom	66.2	61.3	66.9	67.2	65.1	73.2	53.0	65.3
Finland	41.0	40.1	46.0	34.2	34.0	32.6	38.1	38.5
Sweden	m	m	m	m	m	m	m	m
Norway	31.7	38.4	70.3	42.9	35.7	67.3	31.4	43.2
Japan	47.2	51.2	42.8	47.2	72.9	69.4	60.0	54.2
Count	5040	2643	3645	1827	2546	4561	2801	23064

* Graduates, who are employed four years after graduation in a region that is different from their study region; internationally mobile graduates are not included.m = missing data

Source: CHEERS survey data

6. REGIONAL ECONOMIC CONDITIONS AND GEOGRAPHICAL MOBILITY

As the analysis at the beginning of this chapter has shown, the employment status and the employment conditions differed by economic strength of regions consistently according to all measures used in Italy and according to the majority of measures in France, Germany, the United Kingdom and Japan. We therefore confined the analysis of regional mobility according to the regional economic strength to these five countries.

In analysing this relationship, we were primarily interested in "vertical" geographical mobility, i.e. mobility between regions of different economic strength. Four types of behaviour could be established:

- staying in economically strong regions,
- staying in economically weak regions,
- mobility from economically strong to economically weak regions, and
- mobility from economically weak to economically strong regions.

Table 14 shows how the proportion of graduates employed about four years after graduation varied according to vertical geographic mobility. We noted great differences in Italy and in France. In contrast, both in the United Kingdom and Japan we only observed marginal differences, whilst these were irrelevant in Germany.

Table 14. Percentage of Employed Graduates in Selected Countries, by Regional Mobility Behaviours*

	Mobility from study to residence			
	Staying in strong region	Staying in weak region	Moving to weak region	Moving to strong region
Italy	93.7	83.6	75.5	85.7
France	84.0	78.1	79.1	92.3
Germany	96.5	95.3	94.9	97.1
United Kingdom	96.3	93.5	95.3	99.1
Japan	91.4	87.4	88.8	89.1

* Employment incl. self-employment; not only is the major activity taken into account, e.g. if a graduate is engaged in further study and is also employed he was counted here as "employed"; without internationally mobile graduates.

Source: CHEERS survey data

In Italy, as could have been expected, staying in a strong region was linked to the highest employment quota (93.7%); the employment quota of those staying in an economically weak area (83.6%) was 10 per cent lower. Graduates moving from economically weak to strong areas increased their likelihood of being employed by 2 per cent (to 85.7%) compared to those staying in the weak region, but they were still employed to a much lesser extent than those who stayed in a strong region. Finally, the percentage of employed graduates who moved from strong to weak regions was the lowest (75.5%); other motives than those related to career prospects obviously played a strong role in this downward geographical mobility: returning to the home of the family, etc.

In France, the pattern was very different from that in Italy. Graduates staying in strong regions in France were also more likely to be employed about four years after graduation (84.0%) than those who stayed in economically weak regions (78.1%), but this difference was much smaller (6%) than in Italy. Moreover, it seemed to pay most for graduates in France to move from economically weak to strong regions (92.3% employment quota). Finally, those who graduated in strong regions in France and moved to economically weak regions were employed as often (79.1%) as those who stayed in a weak region about four years after graduation.

These findings suggest that mobility from an economically weak to a strong area in these two countries was associated with a greater probability of being employed. Surprisingly, this gain was weaker in the country where regional disparities were the greatest. Second, the data showed that, for most graduates, moving from an economically strong to a weak region was linked in most countries with employment opportunities in the latter region. Italy was an exception in this respect: downward geographical mobility after graduation, caused by family ties in many cases, was often accepted, even if there were few promising employment prospects.

7. CONCLUSION

In analysing how far the economic strength or weakness of a region determined the employment opportunities of graduates we noted that being employed, being employed full-time or being on a permanent contract differed substantially in the majority of the countries for which information was available, whilst having a smooth transition from study to work differed in only a minority of those countries. Only in Italy was living and working in an economically weak region linked with a highly disadvantaged employment situation in all those respects. There were similar differences, although on a smaller scale, according to most dimensions in France, the United Kingdom, Germany, and Japan. In the remaining countries, we observed more part-time employment in weak economic areas in Norway, where, surprisingly, graduates were more likely to experience a smooth transition in weak or very weak regions, and more temporary-contract employment in weak economic areas in Finland. Thus, it was possible to conclude that, in the majority of the countries for which information was available, regional economic differences did have an impact on both the likelihood of getting a job and on its quality of (in the United Kingdom only as far as part-time jobs were concerned and in Finland only as far as temporary jobs were concerned), whilst they affected the functioning of the graduate labour market in only a minority of countries.

The most striking regional differences of employment opportunities were found in a country where we noted a strong regional differentiation of wealth: in Italy. The second greatest differences were observed in France, which is characterised, as various other countries included in the CHEERS survey, by an economically very strong national centre, in Germany and Japan, which are characterised by moderate regional differentiation of economic strength, and finally in a balanced country but with a high proportion of weak regions, the United Kingdom. The countries with marginal or no differences of employment according to region either had an economically strong national centre or were relatively balanced. The findings, thus, suggest a link between the likelihood of being employed, transferring smoothly to employment and having favourable employment conditions and the national pattern of economic differentiation by region, though this link may not always be consistent.

Within about four years after graduation, almost half the graduates had moved from the region where they had studied and graduated. Mobility after graduation for the purpose of employment was most frequent amongst graduates from the United Kingdom, i.e. the country where the highest proportion of students studied away from their region of residence prior to study. It was also relatively frequent in Japan, Germany and the Netherlands. However, it was low in Austria and extremely low in Italy. In five countries of the nine for which information was available, women were significantly less regionally mobile for employment purposes than men. In almost all the countries, mobility varied significantly by field of study. Graduates in engineering tended to be very mobile, while the mobility quotas of graduates from other fields varied substantially by country.

In countries where employment opportunities differed greatly according to the economic strength of a region, upward geographic mobility was a way out: a move from an economically weak to a strong region was associated with a high probability of being employed. Mobility from an economically strong to an economically weak region also seemed to be associated with employment opportunities in most countries, although not in Italy where many graduates seemed to return to their region of origin, even if the employment prospects were bleak.

The findings on domestic mobility suggest, finally, that a national labour market for graduates functioned more or less well in some countries such as the United Kingdom, the Netherlands, Germany and Japan, whilst this was not the case in Italy where regional differences were most relevant.

8. REFERENCES

Bagnasco, A. (1977). Le tre Italie. Bologna: Il Mulino.

Bagnasco, A. and Sabel, C. (eds.) (1994). *PME et développement économique en Europe*. Paris: La Découverte.

Caciagli, M. (2003). *Regioni d'Europa. Devoluzioni, regionalismi, integrazione europea.* Bologna: Il Mulino.

Crouch, C. et al. (2001). *Local Production Systems in Europe: Rise or Demise?*. Oxford: Oxford University Press.

Keeble, D. and Wilkinson, F. (1999). "Collective Learning and Knowledge Development in the Evolution of Regional Clusters of High technology SMSs in Europe". *Regional Studies*, 33(4), 295-303.

La Spina, A. (2003). *La politica per il Mezzogiorno*. Bologna: Il Mulino.

Micali, A. (a cura di) (1995). *Sistema educativo e mercato del lavoro nel contesto internazionale*. Roma: ISTAT.

Moscati, R. (1983). *Università, fine o trasformazione del mito?*. Bologna: Il Mulino.

Pyke, F. and Sengenberger, W. (eds.) (1992). *Industrial Districts and Local Economic Development*. Genève: ILO.

Reale, E. (1992). *Il sistema universitario del Mezzogiorno*. Milano: Angeli.

Sabel, C. (1988). "Flexible Specialisation and the Re-Emergence of Regional Economies". In Hirst, P. and Zeitlin, J. (eds.). *Reversing Industrial Decline*. Oxford: Berg, pp.17-70.

Saxenian, A. (1994). *Regional Advantage: Culture and Competition in Silicon Valley and Route 128*. Cambridge (Mass.): Harvard University Press.

Shavit,Y., and Westerbeek, K. (1997). "Istruzione e stratificazione in Italia: riforme, espansione e uguaglianza delle opportunità". *Polis* 11(1), 91-109.

Storper, M. (1997). *The Regional World. Territorial Development in Global Economy*. New York: The Guilford Press.

Treiman, D. and Yip, K. (1989). "Educational and Occupational Attainment in 21 Countries". In Kohn, M. (ed.), *Cross-National Research in Sociology*. Newbury Park: Sage.

Veltz, P. (2002). *Des Lieux et des liens. Politiques du territoire à l'heure de la mondialisation.* La Tour d'Aigues: Editions de l'aube.

Viesti, G. (2003). Abolire il Mezzogiorno. Roma-Bari: Laterza.

VOLKER JAHR AND ULRICH TEICHLER

GRADUATES' INTERNATIONAL EXPERIENCE AND MOBILITY

1. INTRODUCTION

International mobility has been a frequent phenomenon amongst unskilled and skilled labour in the past. It was less frequent amongst highly-skilled professionals. As far as student and professional mobility was concerned, it was predominantly vertical or, more specifically, upward, i.e. from the poorer to the richer countries, or from places with a lower quality of learning and work to more demanding places. In the 1980s and 1990s, horizontal educational and professional mobility became more widespread between countries with similar qualities of education systems and with a similar level of economic development (Blumenthal et al. 1996; Teichler 1999).

In the late 1990s, the percentage of foreign persons amongst the highly qualified was about 4 per cent and available statistics allow us to estimate that about 3 per cent of highly qualified persons with EU citizenship or from other Western European countries were employed abroad (Jahr and Teichler 2001). This could still be considered as small, but, the opinion spread amongst students that study and a career abroad could be a possible and regular option and possibly an attractive one.

For many years, the European policy was viewed as one of the strongest factors in stimulating horizontal educational and professional mobility. Enriched learning through temporary study abroad, the freedom of working in any country of the European Union, and the promotion of the idea of a European citizenship were at the heart of European policies. In fact, the ERASMUS programme is generally considered as one of the most successful European activities in all sectors (European Commission 1994; Teichler 1996).

In recent years, the public debate in industrial societies has paid more attention to the "globalisation" phenomenon, i.e. trends towards a single world economy and society whereby nations, governments and boundaries lose importance. This seems to create pressure for convergence of national structures, world-wide competition, world-wide information gathering, co-operation with all parts of the world, as well as greater professional mobility, either through work with foreign employers, by being sent abroad by home companies or through work in global companies where these definitions and delineations gradually lose their relevance (Van der Wende 2001).

In the CHEERS study on higher education and graduate employment in 12 countries, attention was paid to international mobility prior to study, during the study period and upon employment. In addition, changes of citizenship were addressed, and different types of international experiences were taken into consideration. The CHEERS study is certainly the most comprehensive study ever undertaken on the links between pre-study mobility, mobility during the course of study and professional mobility.

U. Teichler (ed.), Careers of University Graduates, 211–224

One should bear in mind, though, that it cannot provide a full picture of the international experiences and mobility of graduates. A comparison of the survey findings and available statistics suggests that mobile graduates are under-represented in the survey. Obviously, their mobility made it more difficult to trace them.

The subsequent analysis addresses only graduates who were citizens of the country where they graduated at their time of graduation (in the case of Japan where this information is not available, the study includes only Japanese citizens at the time of birth). This approach was adopted, because otherwise, for example, an Italian graduating in the United Kingdom and then employed in Italy, i.e. an Italian "returner", would be considered a British graduate working in Italy, i.e. a British mobile graduate.

2. THE METHODOLOGICAL APPROACH

Available information in the CHEERS study regarding the extent of international experience and mobility of the respondents can be divided according to three life stages: prior to study, during the study period, and after graduation.

As regards the period prior to study, information is available, first, on the citizenship at birth. We define as foreigners those graduates who at the time of birth were not citizens of the country in which they graduated. Additional information is provided on experience abroad prior to enrolment: we define those who have spent at least four months abroad for educational or work purposes as having gained experience abroad. Finally, we identify those who completed secondary education abroad (in a country other than that where they were awarded their higher education degree).

In combining the dichotomic groupings according to these three dimensions, we were able to create eight types of international mobility and cooperation. As some of the possible combinations are less relevant and less frequent, we created four types of (non-) mobility up to enrolment: persons (a) with foreign citizenship at birth and with schooling in the country of former citizenship, (b) with foreign citizenship at birth and with schooling in the country of graduation, (c) with educational or work experience abroad, and (d) without educational or work experience abroad.

With respect to the study period, the graduates were asked to provide information on their number of stays abroad and the purposes of these during their course of study. We created a typology which only refers to the two major purposes of stay: (a) study abroad, (b) study and internship abroad, (c) internship abroad, (d) other activities abroad, and (e) neither study nor work experience abroad during the course of study.

The key variables for international experience after graduation refer only to work experience and therefore include persons in employment (or self-employed). Information is available on current and prior location of work (any time between graduation and the time the survey was conducted). In addition, respondents were asked whether they were employed abroad (i.e. by a foreign employer) or commissioned abroad by their home country (i.e. country of graduation) employer, but some graduates did not respond to the additional question.

Therefore, seven categories were established regarding employment abroad after graduation: (a) currently employed abroad, (b) currently commissioned abroad, (c) currently working abroad (residual, i.e. no information regarding a. and b.), (d) previously employed abroad, (e) occasionally commissioned abroad, (f) previously working abroad (residual and other), and (g) non-mobile.

In addition, international experience was analysed across various life stages. In order to keep the number of categories in bound, we merged the first three categories of mobility after graduation and "currently professionally mobile", and also experience and mobility prior or during the period of study and "prior experience abroad" and "no prior experience abroad".

The categories thus established are: (a) prior mobility and currently professionally mobile, (b) no prior mobility and currently professionally mobile, (c) prior mobility and previously professionally mobile, (d) no prior mobility and previously professionally mobile, (e) prior mobility and occasionally being commissioned abroad, (f) no prior mobility and occasionally being commissioned abroad, (g) prior mobility and not professionally mobile, and (h) no prior mobility and not professionally mobile.

The model of analysis described above could not be applied to all countries. The Czech Republic was not included because key information on international mobility was lacking in the questionnaire. Norway could not be included in parts of the analyses, because no information was gathered on international experience prior to study.

There are two minor distortions in this strategy. First, unfortunately, we had to drop the "Bildungsinländer" (e.g. the Turkish people born and educated in Germany, but not having German citizenship), and second, we also treated as citizens of the country of graduation the small number of persons who changed their citizenship during the first four years after graduation (because the respondents were not asked to state their citizenship at the time of the survey). It should be noted that the professionally mobile graduates could be under-represented in the sample because we were unable to trace them with a questionnaire survey that relied on prior addresses (home addresses, addresses made available by the higher education institution, etc.). We treat the data as minimum data rather than as representative data.

3. OVERALL MOBILITY

The extent of educational and professional mobility of home country graduates can be described best according to the following categories:

- those who were foreigners according to their citizenship at the time of birth,
- those who had completed secondary education abroad (i.e. not in the country of graduation),
- those who found first employment after graduation in a country that was not that of graduation,
- those who were professionally active abroad, and
- those who resided abroad about four years after graduation.

About 2 per cent of the graduates who responded *were not citizens* of the country where they had graduated. As Table 1 shows, the number of "foreign graduates" was by far the highest in the United Kingdom. As already stated, foreign graduates were be included in most of the subsequent analysis.

About 2 per cent of the European respondents who graduated in their home country had another citizenship at the time of birth. This proportion was by far the highest in Sweden (5.0%), as line b of Table 1 shows as well.

Table 1. Foreign Citizenship, Employment and Living Abroad, by Country (percentage)*

	Country										Total
	IT	ES	FR	AT	DE	NL	UK	FI	SE	NO	
a) Foreign graduates	.6	1.2	5.0	3.3	3.2	2.2	9.2	.5	7.5	3.3	3.6
b) Foreign citizenship at birth	.6	1.2	2.9	1.8	2.0	1.6	2.7	.2	5.0	1.8	2.0
c) Secondary education not in country of graduation	.5	.6	2.2	.8	.5	1.0	2.4	.6	2.0	1.2	1.2
d) First employment after graduation abroad	1.9	2.4	5.3	3.9	2.4	3.0	4.8	2.4	3.7	1.1	3.0
e) Employment abroad four years after graduation	1.1	1.3	4.1	5.4	2.2	1.9	3.4	4.1	4.5	0.4	2.7
f) Living abroad four years after graduation	0.9	1.1	3.9	6.0	2.3	–	4.2	4.4	4.2	0.7	2.9

Question I3: Please, provide some information about your citizenship and your country of schooling, study and work.

* a) percentage of all graduates; b) to f) percentage of home country graduates only.

Source: CHEERS survey data

1.2 per cent of the graduates who graduated in their home country obtained their secondary education qualification in a foreign country. This was most frequently true for French, British and Swedish respondents (about 2% each), as can be seen in line c of Table 1.

After graduation, 3.0 per cent of the graduates who had graduated in their home country found their first employment abroad. As line d of Table 1 shows, this was most frequent amongst French (5.3%) and British graduates (4.8%).

Also, 2.7 per cent of the European graduates surveyed who had graduated in their home country were employed abroad at the time of the survey, i.e. about four years after graduation. This ratio was higher than 4 per cent amongst Austrian, French, Swedish and British graduates (see line d in Table 1).

Finally, 2.9 per cent of the respondents who had graduated in their home country lived abroad at the time of the survey (see line e of Table 1). As one might expect, these data are similar to those employed abroad.

The available data suggest that a high degree of international mobility and experience can be found amongst British, French and Swedish graduates. We note there the highest quota amongst those holding foreign citizenship, having completed secondary education in another country, as well as amongst those who currently work abroad, who had their first employment in another country or reside abroad. Only with respect to current professional activity, an equally high proportion can be found amongst those who graduated in Austria. International mobility and experience were least common amongst those who graduated in Japan, Italy, and Norway.

Although there are limitations because of the small number of cases in some cells, the data allow us to make some statements concerning the countries the European graduates chose most frequently to work (see Table 2).

Table 2. Countries of Employment Abroad, by Country of Graduation (per cent; multiple responses; only home graduates)*

	Home country									Total
Host country	IT	FR	AT	DE	NL	UK	FI	SE	NO	
Italy		5	7	4	/	4	2	3	/	3
Spain	4	8	2	5	4	10	1	2	5	5
France	16		9	10	5	11	6	4	7	7
Austria	/	/		5	4	2	2	2	2	2
Germany	14	16	33		41	11	17	13	8	15
Netherlands	4	3	3	3		4	4	2	/	3
United Kingdom	27	29	10	18	12		14	13	20	16
Finland	/	/	/	/	/	/		2	3	1
Sweden	/	/	/	2	/	/	17		16	5
Norway	/	/	/	2	/	/	4	11		3
Czech Republic	/	/	2	2	/	2	/	/	/	1
Japan	/	/	/	2	/	4	/	3	3	2
USA	16	13	10	22	14	16	11	19	19	16
Other countries	39	58	47	57	51	67	54	51	49	53
Total %	123	135	127	133	139	134	134	127	135	131
Count	249	324	307	346	118	304	392	425	253	2725

Question D 16: If you have worked abroad: In which country(ies) and how many months (each)?
/ Cells with count < 5.
* Graduates having been employed or sent abroad by employer at some point about four years after graduation.

Source: CHEERS survey data

The United Kingdom and Germany were the most common European countries of employment for the European graduates, and the United States were also chosen as frequently. The United Kingdom was the favourite country for graduates from Italy and France, and Germany for those from Austria and the Netherlands. The United States were chosen most often, compared to the other countries of graduation and other countries of employment by graduates from Germany.

4. INTERNATIONAL EXPERIENCE AND MOBILITY PRIOR TO AND DURING THE PERIOD OF STUDY

Two percent of the home graduate respondents, as already stated, were foreigners at birth in the country where they graduated. Five sixth, however, completed secondary education in the country of graduation.

About 6 per cent of the home country graduates had a home country citizenship at birth, but had learning or work experience abroad prior to enrolment. As Table 3 shows, educational or work experience abroad prior to enrolment was by far the most frequent amongst Swedish graduates (22.8%), followed by Finnish graduates (10.1%). In contrast, only about 1 per cent or less of French, Italian, and Spanish graduates had this kind of experience at this stage.

Table 3. Experiences Abroad Before the Course of Study, by Country (per cent; home graduates only)

Mobility before course of study	Country IT	ES	FR	AT	DE	NL	UK	FI	SE	Total
Experiences abroad	1.4	.0	1.3	4.3	3.4	5.2	5.8	10.1	22.8	5.7
Foreigner	.6	1.1	2.5	1.7	2.0	1.6	2.7	.2	4.9	1.9
No experiences abroad	98.0	98.8	96.2	93.9	94.6	93.2	91.5	89.7	72.3	92.4
Total	100,0	100,0	100,0	100,0	100,0	100,0	100,0	100,0	100,0	100,0
Count	3096	2887	2845	2180	3393	3027	3051	2612	2496	25586

Question A6: Prior to your first enrolment in higher education, had you been employed abroad or had you received any education/training/apprenticeship abroad?

Source: CHEERS survey data

Educational or work experience abroad prior to enrolment was more frequent amongst women than amongst men. While the percentage of foreigners at birth did not vary by gender, 7.8 per cent of the women (not changing citizenship) as compared 3.4 per cent of men had international experience at this stage of life.

Graduates in medical sciences (6.1%), education, humanities (7.2 each) and social sciences (7.1%) had early international experiences most frequently. It was rarer amongst graduates in law (4.6%), engineering (3.8%), natural sciences (3.5%) and mathematics (2.3%).

17.6 per cent of the respondents had international experiences during their course of study. Among them:

- 11.1 per cent reported only study abroad,
- 4.4 per cent study and internship,
- 1.7 per cent only internships, and
- 0.4 per cent other experiences.

Mobility during the period of study was highest amongst Dutch graduates (29%), followed by those graduating in Sweden, Finland and Austria (20%-22%), as can be seen in Table 4. It was lowest amongst Japanese (10%) and Spanish graduates (12%).

Table 4. Experiences Abroad During the Course of Study, by Country (per cent; home graduates only)

Mobility during course of study	Country										Total
	IT	ES	FR	AT	DE	NL	UK	FI	SE	NO	
Yes	18.8	12.0	13.5	19.6	13.6	29.1	15.1	20.5	22.1	13.5	17.6
No	81.2	88.0	86.5	80.4	86.4	70.9	84.9	79.5	77.9	86.5	82.4
Total	100.0	100.0	100.0	100.0	100.0	100.0	100.0	100.0	100.0	100.0	100.0
Count	2802	2892	2728	1933	3204	2970	2717	2359	2284	3105	26993

Question B2: Did you spend any time abroad during your period of study (in order to work or to study)?
Source: CHEERS survey data

Women were slightly more mobile during the course of study than men. 18.6 per cent as compared to 15.5 per cent of men who studied abroad had internship or undertook other kinds of study-related activities.

There were substantial differences according to fields of study: graduates in the humanities (30%) were more mobile during the course of study than those in other fields. Those in social sciences (19%), engineering (17%), law (16%) and natural sciences (14%) were close to the average in this respect, while graduates in education and mathematics (9-10%) went least abroad for purposes of study during their course of study.

There were differences concerning the extent of mobility between the countries in several fields of study. While, for example, the students who were most mobile in the natural science and engineering fields came from the Netherlands, their counterparts in the humanities and social sciences came from Norway and Sweden.

5. WORK AND RESIDENCE ABROAD AFTER GRADUATION

About four years after graduation 3 per cent of those who graduated in their home country were working abroad (i.e. not in the country where they graduated). They are defined in the subsequent analysis as "currently working abroad". In addition, 17 per cent had been working abroad for some period between graduation and the time the survey was conducted. Amongst those, a temporary period commissioned abroad (11%) was more frequent than employment abroad, i.e. by a foreign employer (5%); no information was available for 1 per cent of respondents.

The proportion of some 20 per cent having worked abroad is impressive at first glance. One should be aware of the fact, however, that all in all, only one quarter of the professionally mobile graduates spent more than six months abroad. This holds true for almost two-thirds of those working abroad about four years after graduation, about one quarter of those employed abroad earlier and only for 3 per cent of those occasionally commissioned abroad.

Working abroad about four years after graduation was most frequent amongst Austrian, Swedish, Finnish, and French graduates (4%-5%), as can be seen in line 1 of Table 5. Being occasionally commissioned abroad, however, was most frequent amongst Dutch graduates. 56 per cent were working abroad after graduation, mostly for a short period.

Professional mobility after graduation was by far the least common amongst Japanese graduates (3%). In Europe, as can be seen in the sum of lines a, b and c of Table 5, it was the least common amongst German, Norwegian and Spanish graduates (about 12% each). In order to explain these findings, we must take into consideration, as was shown in the chapter by José García-Montalvo, José-Ginés Mora and Adela Garcia-Aracil, that the graduates from Germany and Norway had the highest average incomes, which could limit the incentive for working abroad.

Table 5. Experiences Abroad After Graduation, by Country (per cent; home graduates only)

Mobility after graduation	Country										Total
	IT	ES	FR	AT	DE	NL	UK	FI	SE	NO	
a) Currently working abroad	1.2	1.3	4.0	5.1	2.2	1.8	3.3	4.0	4.4	.4	2.7
b) Previously employed abroad	2.7	2.8	6.0	4.3	2.8	9.6	11.2	3.3	6.4	2.1	5.2
c) Occasionally commissioned abroad	9.2	7.7	17.4	8.4	6.6	20.3	10.5	11.0	7.0	8.7	10.7
d) Non-mobile	86.9	88.1	72.5	82.2	88.4	68.2	75.0	81.7	82.2	88.8	81.5
Total	100.0	100.0	100.0	100.0	100.0	100.0	100.0	100.0	100.0	100.0	100.0
Count	2813	2333	2504	2194	3303	2952	2978	2606	2524	3126	27334

Question I3: Please, provide some information about your citizenship and your country of schooling, study and work. Question D15: Have you, since graduation (multiple reply possible) … a) had regular employment abroad since graduation b) been sent abroad by your employer on work assignments

Source: CHEERS survey data

While men were less mobile than women prior and during the course of study, they were more often professionally mobile after graduation than women:

- About four years after graduation, 3.0 per cent of men as compared to 2.4 per cent of women worked abroad,
- prior to that time, 5.7 per cent of men as compared to 4.6 per cent of women were abroad, and
- men were far more frequently commissioned abroad occasionally than women (14.2% as compared to 7.5%).

As regards differences according to fields of study, we observe that the greatest professional mobility occurs amongst the graduates in natural science and engineering fields, which contrasts with the former observation on prior mobility. Least professionally mobile were graduates in medical sciences, law and education. Across almost all fields, Dutch graduates were the most mobile professionally, whilst

Japanese were the least mobile. Within Europe, German graduates in engineering, Swedish graduates in natural sciences, Italian graduates in mathematics and Spanish graduates in social sciences, humanities and law were the least mobile.

The information provided above referred to "home graduates", i.e. those graduating in the country of their citizenship. The study also shows that the graduates of these 12 countries who were foreigners at the time of graduation were often more mobile than the home country graduates. Amongst the foreign graduates (who did not get their secondary education in the country of graduation), only 42 per cent worked in the country of graduation four years later. 47 per cent returned to their home country, and 11 per cent worked in a country that was not their home country and their country of graduation.

6. INTERNATIONAL EXPERIENCES OVER VARIOUS LIFE STAGES

Of all the graduates who had been awarded their degree in their home country,

- about 9 per cent were internationally mobile both before graduation (prior to study and/or during the study period) and in some way after graduation – of these, 1.7 per cent were professionally mobile about four years after education, 2.7 per cent were previously mobile professionally and 4.2 per cent were occasionally commissioned abroad,
- 11 per cent were professionally mobile in some way after graduation without any substantial mobility before – of whom 1.3 per cent were professionally mobile about four years after graduation, and
- 13 per cent were not internationally mobile after graduation, although they had been mobile before graduation.
- 67 per cent neither went abroad for a considerable period before graduation nor were working abroad after graduation.

Altogether, the data suggest that those who were internationally experienced and mobile in one stage of their life were likely to be about twice as often mobile at another stage or more than their non-mobile counterparts of the respective stage. For example, those who were mobile before the period of study were 2.2 times as often mobile during the course of study as those who were not mobile before the period of study (36.7% as compared to 16.3%). Also those who were mobile before the period of study were more likely to be mobile after graduation than those who were not mobile before their studies (see Table 6). Finally, those who were mobile during their period of study were 2.7 times as often professionally mobile internationally as those who had not been mobile during their period of study.

Prior international experience lead least often to international professional mobility amongst Japanese and German graduates: only 10 per cent respectively 27 per cent of those who were mobile prior to graduation were also mobile after graduation. The highest quota in this respect, in contrast, could be observed amongst Dutch (58%) and French graduates (55%).

This does not mean, however, that those who had not been abroad during their course of study did not consider working abroad. 38 per cent of those who were not mobile during their course of study reported that they had considered working abroad (as compared to 67% of those who studied abroad). Only 9 per cent of those who were not mobile during their course of study actually sought employment abroad (as compared to 26 per cent of those who were mobile during their course of study), and only 4 per cent had regular employment abroad (as compared to 17% of those who were mobile during their course of study).

Table 6. Links between Mobility Prior to Study, During the Period of Study and After Graduation (per cent; home graduates only)

Mobility after graduation	Experiences abroad prior to study Mobile	Non-mobile	Foreigner	Experiences abroad during study Mobile	Non-mobile
a) Currently working abroad	6.5	2.7	3.6	7.3	1.5
b) Previously employed abroad	11.1	5.2	6.7	12.2	3.2
c) Occasionally commissioned abroad	9.7	10.9	14.0	18.4	8.6
d) Non-mobile	72.7	81.2	75.7	62.1	86.7
Total	100.0	100.0	100.0	100.0	100.0
Count	1419	21983	442	4525	20671

Source: CHEERS survey data

7. DIFFERENCES IN COMPETENCES, EMPLOYMENT AND WORK BETWEEN THE MOBILE AND NON-MOBILE GRADUATES

Graduates whose parents are higher education-trained are about one and a half times as likely to be internationally mobile after graduation as those whose parents had compulsory education. As parental background is generally viewed to be linked to the "cultural capital" of graduates, this could be seen as an indicator for an advantageous profile of competences.

Internationally non-mobile persons more often lived with their parents during their course of study. Those who were mobile after graduation had partners as often as non-mobile persons, but less often had children.

Respondents who were internationally mobile during their course of study do not differ from the non-mobile ones with respect to their study behaviour nor with respect to attitudes to their studies. Nor did they differ in the retrospective view of their studies. However, those who were mobile during their course of study rated their competences (including their international competences) at the time of graduation slightly more favourably than non-mobile persons. Table 7 shows the most visible differences.

This corresponds to the finding that internationally mobile graduates considered their work tasks as slightly more demanding than non-mobile graduates. Thus, the difference between perceived work requirements and actual competences is more or less equally perceived by internationally mobile and non-mobile graduates.

Table 7. Select Competences at Time of Graduation of Graduates Who Had Been Mobile as Compared to Those Who Had Not Been Mobile During their Course of Study (per cent**)*

Competences	Experiences abroad during study		Total
	Mobile	Non-mobile	
Foreign language proficiency	64	24	31
Analytical competences	68	59	61
Written communication skill	74	67	68
Broad general knowledge	66	60	61
Learning abilities	87	82	83
Working under pressure	60	55	56
Working independently	77	72	73
Initiative	58	53	53
Oral communication skill	62	57	58
Manual skills	32	37	36
Applying rules and regulations	31	36	35

Question E1: Please, state if you had the following competences at the time of graduation in 1994 or 1995 and to what extent they are required in your current work.
* 11 out of 36 items are selected where the difference is at least 5 per cent.
** 1 or 2 on a scale of answers from 1 = "To a very high extent" to 5 = "Not at all".

Source: CHEERS survey data

Respondents who were internationally mobile after graduation were more strongly represented amongst the graduates from long university courses than those from other higher education institutions or short university programmes. In all fields of study, they obtained slightly better marks (about 0.1% better on average) than their non-mobile fellow students and more often decided to add another study period after having completed their reference studies. Looking back, if they were free to choose again, internationally mobile graduates would be slightly more likely to study again and to choose the same course of study than non-mobile graduates.

Internationally mobile graduates less often sought part-time employment. They started their job search slightly later than non-mobile graduates, but their search period was slightly shorter. They were more successful in their search, by contacting employers and through contacts established during their course of study. Mobile graduates not only quoted international experience and foreign language proficiency more frequently than non-mobile graduates as important recruitment criteria, but also a broad range of other criteria.

Internationally mobile persons were more often employed full-time (93% as compared to 89% of the non-mobile ones). There were no differences as regards permanent jobs (about 75% for both groups). Mobile graduates were relatively often active in predominantly private economic sectors and less frequently than non-mobile graduates in predominantly public sectors (see Table 8).

Table 8. Economic Sector of Employment of Mobile and Non-Mobile Graduates About Four Years After Graduation (percentage of those employed about four years after graduation)

Economic sector	Kind of mobility Currently working abroad	Previously working abroad	Previously commissioned abroad	Mobile total	Non-mobile	Total
Production	36	33	43	39	24	26
Business	27	31	29	29	25	26
Public administration	4	5	5	5	9	8
Education	18	13	14	14	20	19
Health	10	11	4	6	17	15
Other	6	7	5	6	5	5
Total	100	100	100	100	100	100
Count	(600)	(1196)	(2631)	(4428)	(19944)	(24372)

Question D5: In which economic sector are you currently working?

Source: CHEERS survey data

Internationally mobile graduates reported a higher income than non-mobile graduates (about 18%), as is seen in Table 9. Those currently working abroad earned the highest wages.

Table 9. Annual Gross Income of Mobile and Non-Mobile Graduates About Four Years After Graduation (in thousand EUROs; means and percentage of full-time employed graduates about four years after graduation)

Annual gross income	Kind of mobility Currently working abroad	Previously working abroad	Previously commissioned abroad	Mobile total	Non-mobile	Total
1,000 to 10,000 Euros	3	4	2	3	4	4
11,000 to 20,000 Euros	14	16	13	14	19	18
21,000 to 30,000 Euros	22	35	34	33	40	38
31,000 to 40,000 Euros	22	24	26	25	23	23
41,000 to 50,000 Euros	17	12	14	14	9	10
51,000 to 60,000 Euros	9	3	6	6	3	3
61,000 Euros and more	14	5	5	6	2	3
Total	100	100	100	100	100	100
Count	535	981	2279	3795	15230	19026
Arithm. mean	40.7	32.9	33.8	34.6	28.9	30.0
Median	35.0	29.0	31.0	31.0	27.0	28.0

Question D11: What is your approximate annual gross income? (thousand EUROs).

Source: CHEERS survey data

Internationally mobile graduates considered their position more often as adequate, perceived closer ties between study and work tasks, and were more satisfied with their job than non-mobile graduates. Non-mobile students considered more often the field of study as the only possible or by far best field, whereas the internationally mobile graduates thought more often that other fields were as suitable.

8. INTERNATIONAL WORK TASKS AND COMPETENCES

It is generally assumed that international dimensions of jobs tasks grow with internationalisation and globalisation. This does not only hold true for those who are internationally mobile, but also for those who are not internationally mobile in the course of their career. Non-mobile graduates stated that they spent on average 7 per cent of their working time in an international context. Even though this figure is much lower than for graduates working abroad about four years after graduation (over 50%) and for graduates who previously worked abroad or were occasionally sent abroad by their employers (about 25%), it is worth noting.

Moreover, of the non-mobile graduates

- 21 per cent considered professional knowledge of other countries,
- 32 per cent stated frequent communication with partners and clients in a foreign language,
- 33 per cent considered knowledge and understanding of international differences in culture and society, and
- 40 per cent saw working with people from different cultural backgrounds

as important for their work about four years after graduation (see Table 10).

Table 10. Importance of Competences for Graduates' Work about Four Years After Graduation (per cent; employed graduates about four years after graduation)*

	Kind of mobility					Total
	Currently working abroad	Previously working abroad	Previously commissioned abroad	Mobile total	Non-mobile	
a) Professional knowledge of other countries (e.g. economic, sociological, legal knowledge)	58	39	37	40	19	23
b) Knowledge/understanding of international differences in culture and society, modes of behaviour, life styles, etc.	71	52	47	52	34	37
c) Working with people from different cultural backgrounds	82	64	64	66	43	48
d) Communicating in foreign languages	85	57	67	67	32	39

Question E3: How important do you consider the following competences in your current work?
* 1 and 2 on a scale of answers from 1 = "To a very high extent" to 5 = "Not at all".

Source: CHEERS survey data

Again, those who were mobile after graduation considered their jobs tasks as more visibly international in those respects than those who were not mobile. Yet preparation for international work assignment was also quite important for those who were not working abroad.

9. CONCLUSION

With internationalisation and globalisation, the proportion of highly qualified foreigners has reached the same level among the respective section of the labour force in Europe as the proportion of unskilled and skilled foreign workers. The CHEERS study shows that, in addition, a substantially a higher proportion of graduates work abroad for a short period after graduation or is commissioned abroad occasionally by their employers.

Working abroad is more frequent among persons with prior international experiences. Actually, life and learning prior to the course of study doubles the likelihood of studying abroad, and studying abroad more than doubles the likelihood of working abroad after graduation.

Graduates working abroad tend to be slightly more highly qualified than other graduates in various respects. Their employment and work situation is also slightly more favourable and that of non-mobile graduates.

The trend towards internationalisation and globalisation is not confined to increasing mobility. Rather, the job tasks of a substantial proportion of non-mobile graduates are visibly international in various respects. For example, many of them have to apply foreign languages, to communicate frequently with foreigners, to have knowledge on other countries in their areas of expertise and to understand culture and society of persons their have to deal with on their job.

10. REFERENCES

Blumenthal, P. et al. (eds) (1996). *Academic Mobility in a Changing World.* London and Bristol, PA: Jessica Kingsley Publishers.

European Commission (1994). *Cooperation in Education in the European Union 1976-1994.* Luxembourg: Office for Official Publications of the European Communities. 1994.

Jahr, V. and Teichler, U. (2001). "Mobility During the Course of Study and After Graduation." *European Journal of Education* 36(4), 443-58.

Teichler, U. (1996). "Student Mobility in the Framework of ERASMUS: Findings of an Evaluation Study," *European Journal of Education* 31(2), 153-79.

Teichler, U. (1999). "Internationalisation as a Challenge for Higher Education in Europe." *Tertiary Education and Management*. 5(1), 5-23.

Wende, M.C. van der (2001). "Internationalisation Policies: About New Trends and Contrasting Paradigms." *Higher Education Policy* 14(3), 249-59.

EGBERT DE WEERT

GRADUATE EMPLOYMENT IN EUROPE: THE EMPLOYERS' PERSPECTIVE

1. INTRODUCTION

In the framework of the CHEERS project, the graduate survey is supplemented by in-depth interviews of employers in order to gather evidence on their experiences with graduates and on how they perceive higher education institutions, their courses and their graduates. Issues addressed in the graduate survey are taken up in open interviews where employers express their views on the links between higher education and the world of work. They express the views on the demand-side of the labour market and contextualise analyses of the graduate surveys by studying the different higher education systems and the differences in the characteristics of occupations and firms.

The following themes will be discussed in this chapter:

- demand for graduates and recruitment strategies,
- match between educational qualifications and job requirements,
- key skills and competences required on the job,
- general views on the relationships between higher education and work.

Before presenting the results, we will describe the general design and methodology of the study. Both the choice of employers and further details concerning the interviews carried out will be discussed.

2. THE DESIGN AND METHODOLOGY OF THE EMPLOYERS' STUDY

Although studies of surveys of employers are less widespread than those of graduates, some national studies were illustrative for the design and methodology of this part of the CHEERS project. The large-scale research carried out in the United Kingdom by Roizen and Jepson (1985) on employer expectations concerning higher education has become a classic in its field. The interviews in companies and their personnel services constituted an important component of the German research project on qualification and future employment needs (cf. Baldauf and Teichler 1995). Similarly, Webbink and Paape (1997) also used interviews in their study on the recruitment policies of Dutch companies. These studies deal with questions that must be addressed in a large international project: should the interviews be carried out on the basis of a standardised questionnaire or be kept as open as possible? Which persons in companies should be selected as representing the views of "employers"? Which employment sectors should be included and how many interviews should be carried out? What are the major issues and questions and how should they be phrased?

U. Teichler (ed.), Careers of University Graduates, 225–246

It was agreed by the research team that a semi-structured interview with a clear core of structured and standardised questions would be the most appropriate procedure. If we left the personal interviews completely open, we would get divergent answers which only partly reflected national styles with no clear focus. Some frame of reference was needed, both between the interviews within the individual countries and between countries in order to obtain comparable views. Therefore, a checklist was developed and open and closed questions were formulated. They would function as a common framework for the interviews in all the countries. At the same time, it was stressed in the guidelines that the structured questions should not interrupt the flow of conversation and that the interviews should allow interviewees to express their own viewpoints and refer to their specific contexts.

In devising the interview checklist and the closed questions, we created as many links as possible with the questionnaire of the graduate survey and its first results. The checklist and the closed questions were grouped around the following major topics:

(a) *Demand for graduates*: what was the demand of the company for those with higher education qualifications? Also, interviewees were asked to provide further data such as the number of employees with a higher education degree, the number of recent graduates, and the change over time in the share of graduate intake compared to that of persons with lower educational qualifications.

(b) *Recruitment strategies*: what were the employers' recruitment channels and strategies to deal with the information problem in recruiting people: for example, a trial period, tests and assessments, or educational level? What were the main criteria in the recruitment process, and what weight was given to a degree and the type of institution?

(c) *Match between competences acquired and job requirements*: to what extent were specific skills or a broad frame of competences expected, and to what extent was a certain degree considered indispensable or a range of degree levels seen as acceptable? Responses could help to understand whether a match was perceived, if a certain type and level of qualification were provided, or whether there was room for substitution among graduates with different fields of study at the same educational level (horizontal substitution) and among persons with different levels of qualification (vertical substitution).

(d) *Key skills and competences*: what were the relationships between graduates' acquired knowledge and skills and those required on the job? This included policies to develop competences through additional training.

(e) *Work organisation and (expected) developments*: how was graduates' work structured? What developments were expected which may have implications for job requirements?

(f) *Perspectives on higher education*: what measures did the interviewees recommend to bridge the gaps between education and work? Which policies were seen as useful or desirable regarding the transition from higher education to work? What were the changing challenges in the world of work for higher education?

As already stated above, certain questions were considered essential in all countries. National teams were free to select among the other questions and to add others in line with country-specific areas of interest.

A match between the graduates surveyed and their employers was not sought in selecting the employers. Apart from the practical problem in most countries of delineating the name of the employment organisation, there was no advantage in addressing the employers of graduates in our study, because we did not intend to ask them particular questions about the graduates surveyed.

In each country, employers were selected from the following sectors:

- Production or R&D companies in the sphere of new technologies (electronics/IT),
- Companies in the areas of commercial and business services (banking, insurance, consulting branches, communications),
- Small and medium size companies of the same branches, and
- Organisations in the public sector.

In addition, national teams could make further selections according to their preferences.

As the number of interviews in each country had to be limited, there is no claim of representative distribution. The basic aim was to provide an impression of the views of a number of employers from various sectors on current issues regarding graduate employment and work.

A decision had to be made regarding the target group within companies. Top managers could be considered the most suitable because they had the strongest impact on the decisions made in the companies. However, studies based on interviews with high-level managers yielded rather general statements on human resources. As this study aimed to gather in-depth information on the relationships between higher education and employment, we chose personnel officers who were involved in the recruitment process, were experienced in selecting graduates, and could assess their qualities. In some cases, employers' representatives and direct supervisors were also interviewed.

Altogether, 154 interviews were undertaken in nine countries included in the CHEERS project. This means that over 17 interviews were carried out on average in each country. The Czech Republic, Sweden and Japan were not able to participate in this part of the CHEERS project.[1] Table 1 gives an overview of these interviews according to economic sector and size of the company.

[1] At a later stage, the Japanese team developed this qualitative study by focusing on the recruitment policies of Japanese firms based in Japan compared with Japanese firms or branches in some European countries, as well as European firms based in Europe and Japan respectively.

Table 1. Interviews by Economic Sector and Size of the Company (numbers)

	Large	SME	Total
Electronics	20	17	37
IT	15	16	31
Commercial services	21	18	39
Public sector*	20	4	24
Other	13	10	23
Total	89	65	154

* Companies (owned directly or indirectly by the state or by municipalities) in the process of becoming private due to privatisation are counted here as belonging to the public sector.

Source: CHEERS survey data

National employers' associations were helpful in tracing the targeted persons in the organisation and motivating them to participate. Most of the persons who were contacted were very cooperative and showed great interest in our research project.

The following is a summary of the main findings of the interview transcripts, most of which had to be translated into English. This chapter discusses the themes in broad terms. Therefore, we often quoted the employers extensively. The terms employer, firm, company, organisation are used interchangeably to denote the employing organisation.

3. DEMAND FOR GRADUATES AND RECRUITMENT STRATEGIES

Employment organisations varied in the way they organised their graduate recruitment. Some left it to the central office, whilst others decentralised it: various small units of the company were responsible for recruitment. Others maintained centralised recruitment and adopted a company culture.

Recruitment strategies and selection procedures can be conceived as the organisational expressions of the employers' views on graduates. The procedures and decisions taken indicate the way in which they cope with the information problem in recruiting graduates, for example through a trial period, by using tests and assessments, or in considering the degree level or other information as criteria of competences required on the job.

In order to understand this process we asked about recruitment channels, about the way applicants were screened for jobs and what factors played a role in selecting a candidate. What weight was placed on a degree from a particular institution or from different types of institutions and on other criteria? Did employers currently consider the supply of graduates as shortage or oversupply, and how did they vary their strategies according to these considerations?

3.1. Recruitment Channels

There was a large variety of recruitment channels to find job-seeking graduates. Most organisations recruited predominantly through newspaper advertisements, both locally and nationally, although national newspapers were becoming less attractive because of the high costs involved compared to the outcomes.

Other important channels were unsolicited or spontaneous applications and personal contacts. In some countries, unsolicited applications were the most common way of recruiting personnel. Commercial employment agencies and career services provided by higher education institutions were also frequently mentioned, but some employers stated that the commercial employment agencies were not interesting partners because of the high costs they charged. Personal contacts included both individual and structured contacts between the company and the higher education departments, their staff and their students. Lectures presented by employees from companies as in-house workshops for students were also considered a way of increasing students' interest in the company. Employers said that work placements, internships or apprenticeships were particularly important in attracting interesting candidates, and a substantial proportion of recruitment decisions resulted from these activities. Job centres and advertisements by graduates themselves were hardly used or not used at all because they were not considered very effective.

Furthermore, the internet was becoming an important recruitment tool, and it was expected to increase dramatically in the future. Several companies wanted to recruit most of their new staff via the internet rather than via agencies or otherwise. One firm stated that all graduate applicants had to apply on-line, not purely for convenience's sake, but because "the sort of people we're looking for will search via internet".

In addition to these channels, employers in some countries used active recruitment strategies and focused on particular target groups. Some visited higher education institutions, some organised career fairs which were held either nationally or on campus. "Company-days" organised by student organisations were seen by many employers as an opportunity to get in touch with individual students and to increase their interest by informing them about the career possibilities in their company. Some companies instigated a programme where they visited universities or particular departments or invited students to visit their company during "open days". Some companies even reported that they had invested in recruitment vehicles which were equipped with mobile presentation units.

All these activities show that recruitment is a very multi-faceted phenomenon which changes continuously. Many companies have improved their website to make it more accessible for possible future employees and to position the company on the labour market. Recruitment centres and academic liaison teams have been extended and have often adopted a more targeted approach to particular higher education institutions or particular regions. Recruitment units collaborated closely with human resources (HR) consultants and line-management.

3.2. Distinctions between Institutions and Degree Levels

From a sociological point of view, recruitment strategies focused on the extent to which the type of institution was used as a screening instrument in the selection process of highly qualified people. There seemed to be a large country and field difference in the importance given to the institution where the graduate studied. These institutional effects were greater in systems with a large diversity of institutions and where the reputation of the institution attended mattered (cf. Murdoch 2002; Brennan 2002).

In the interviews we were interested in whether employers considered graduates from particular types of institutions or degree levels as distinct pools of candidates or considered the higher education system as more or less unified in their recruitment procedures and criteria.

In countries with a pronounced differentiated structure – Germany, France and the Netherlands – employers generally placed emphasis on this distinction and tuned their recruitment strategies accordingly. They had explicit views on the major distinctions between graduates from the different institutions and reserved different positions for these graduates. The salaries differed accordingly. Some employers had established separate recruitment units for university and non-university graduates. Many stressed that the two types of graduates complemented each other quite well. Hence, university graduates were more involved in developmental work and non-university graduates did more practically-oriented work. The differences, however, could diminish in the course of career, depending on the individual career development.

Some IT-companies and commercial services such as banking and insurance companies, however, did not place emphasis on the type of higher education and recruited graduates from different types of institution for the same kind of jobs. But they often maintained salary differences according to educational level. Hence, university graduates were better paid than graduates from non-university institutions.

In countries with a newly emerging binary structure – Austria, Finland and Norway – employers mainly focused on university graduates, but were increasingly discovering the non-university sector. Obviously, they made a clear distinction between university graduates and graduates from the new higher vocational institutions: *Fachhochschulen* in Austria, AMKs in Finland, and State Colleges in Norway.

In countries with a dominant unified system, such as Italy and Spain, employers made hardly any distinction between graduates from different universities. Some Italian employers, mainly in the technical sector, said that they considered graduates from polytechnic institutes as being on an equal level as university graduates and recruited them interchangeably for the same positions.

The UK was a special case and is worth discussing in more detail. Most employers we spoke to make a distinction between institutions and target institutions. They targeted primarily graduates from old universities, red-brick universities and possibly universities of the 1960s, because they expected a higher level of competence from graduates from these universities. Many employers kept lists of what they considered to be good universities, or looked at where applicants' university was placed in the "league tables". There were various reasons for this preference for the top and medium-level universities: historical, because it was believed that graduates from these institutions would culturally fit the company, respond to the kind of academic profile needed or have been successful in the past. Employers also relied on casuistic analysis of where their best candidates came from.

The fact that many employers in the UK maintained their traditional sifting mechanisms in their marketing, however, does not mean that graduates from the new universities were ruled out. Most employers stressed that they would accept applications from any institution and would process them by taking individual merits into consideration. Any applicant from these institutions would get exactly the same treatment as everyone else coming through the recruitment process.

A few UK employers – especially in the sphere of commercial services – indicated that their target area had broadened in the last few years. Some stated that where recruitment used to focus on class of degree and Oxbridge, the recruitment pool was now widened to include specific courses in the new universities. A recruiter from a bank expressed this change as follows:

> "I suppose, although this is changing, that there is the idea that the top flight universities provide better candidates. I would actually challenge that in that the types of skills that we need are not necessarily highly academic. We are looking for rounded individuals. We have tended to get some really good candidates from the new universities".

3.3. *Value of a Degree*

Several factors played a role in the graduate selection process. The question we asked was "what is exactly the value of a particular degree?" It seems that employers attributed different characteristics to degrees. In some countries, they were primarily considered a guarantee of knowledge and skills. In that sense, degrees provided information about what candidates had learned. Several employers had a very clear conception of what the content of a particular degree involved, especially regarding the hard sciences. This characteristic applied both to university and to the well-established non-university sector (such as the *HBOs* in the Netherlands and *Fachhochschulen* in Germany and Austria) although employers sometimes had information problems because of the increasing number of courses and the differentiation between courses.

Another characteristic of a degree was that it showed that graduates were able to absorb and retain knowledge and take on the tasks that employers wanted them to do, as well as per severance, the ability to concentrate for an extended period to finish something and to organise their day. Graduates were supposed to have a sum of general intelligence as well as a certain level of maturity. Employers considered a degree as "a demonstration of application and discipline and having reached a certain standard of verbal and written reasoning. It is evidence of hard work and commitment and we take it as a sort of a base level of potential that people have".

The value of certain degrees was regularly mentioned. For example, a degree in maths or physics or computer science proved an ability to look at complex issues in the way that was required. In this sense, it was a useful system of pre-selection of good potential recruits.

These two characteristics were observed in most European countries, although the emphasis placed on the former (degree as a guarantee of knowledge and skills) was stronger in continental Europe and the latter (degree as demonstration of abilities) was more frequent in the British tradition. Another characteristic, however, was increasingly becoming more relevant in most countries, namely its indication of further training capabilities and development potentials. This aspect was mentioned very often and was closely connected with the efforts that many employers put into the further development of competences of graduates once they were recruited (this will be discussed below).

For most employers, a degree was a prerequisite for the respective job. Someone termed it a "qualifier": you simply need to have it, but it is not a guarantee of competences. Although some employers did not necessarily need a graduate, like in some branches of the IT-services, they saw the degree as a necessity because clients expected them to have graduates. Clients normally wished to see staff CVs and looked for IT-experts who held a degree.

3.4. *Criteria used in the Recruitment Process*

However, having a degree did not automatically qualify someone for a job. In the words of an employer: "the degree is the ticket for entry, it doesn't get you through the race". Therefore, we asked about the important criteria in selecting candidates and about the instruments of assessment.

The initial screening of the applications was usually based on the graduates' field of study, the courses and other activities. Employers tended to differ in the importance they gave to grades. In some countries, it was an important part of the screening process, whereas in others, employers did not consider them as important or did not even look at them.

Interviewees regularly stressed that they put a strong emphasis on a combination of personal qualities and technical capabilities. Personal qualities encompassed characteristics such as reliability, sensibility, personal attitudes, an aptitude to learn, and the ability to work in a team and to fit in the culture of the company. Thus, they took into consideration the candidates' extra curricular activities, e.g. being an active member in a student association, work experience during the holidays not just to earn money and international experience. Employers assessed these qualities individually.

Employers were interested in students' attitudes and motives. Particularly in electronics and IT companies, they sought those who had a real interest in the subject and were unlikely to drop out. Some employers were horrified by the growing practice of some recent graduates of sending a standard application by e-mail to many companies and listing all the companies in the greetings.

In order to assess these qualities and skills, some employers used psychometric tests, capacity tests, aptitude tests, and role-playing. The test scores tended to carry substantial weight because they were believed to ascertain that candidates had strengths which enabled them to work as good team players or show evidence of an ability to learn. Some employers called in selection centres where candidates had to do a number of exercises, as well as group exercises in order to be assessed on group work and leadership potential. Additionally, interview cycles with professional recruiters and line-managers were held, usually in different rounds. In some cases, recruiters and development managers were experienced in conducting competence-based interviews to establish candidates' behavioural, interpersonal and technical capabilities.

Although employers could face difficulties in recruiting graduates with certain skills, none argued that recruitment standards had been watered down as the consequence of shortage of supply. The shortages did not make it easy to be employed, for example by an IT company. On the contrary, IT companies remained selective and sought candidates with sufficient IT affinity and who were excellent as far as their motivation, interpersonal skills and career focus were concerned.

It should be added that large companies were in a better position to recruit sufficient numbers of graduates than medium-sized and small companies. Some small and medium-sized companies stated that they suffered mostly from a skills shortage because they did not have the resources to spend on the recruitment process.

Finally, a word should be said about regional and international recruitment. Some employers had difficulty in attracting highly qualified graduates to their region. A particular region may not be that charming, and some candidates were not ready to travel. This regional factor was very important in Spain and Italy, but also in the Netherlands, where HBO graduates seemed to prefer to work in their home region. As a consequence, some employers tended to seek graduates from their region rather than from the national or international market.

There was some international recruitment, for example foreign people who studied in the country under consideration. Also, recruitment of graduates from neighbouring countries was customary in some countries, e.g., Scandinavian countries. A few employers said that they recruited from Asia and Eastern European countries. As a rule, however, they were not very active on the international labour market. In response to a question about reasons, employers stated that it was time-consuming and costly to invite people from abroad for an interview and stressed the language requirements and the complicated formal procedures. Furthermore, they feared problems in evaluating foreign credentials. Although many employers emphasised that their companies operated increasingly across national boundaries, this had not yet been reflected in international recruitment practices.

4. MATCH BETWEEN EDUCATIONAL QUALIFICATIONS AND JOB REQUIREMENTS

In this section, we ask about the links between field of study and occupational category and the preferences for specialist or generalist competences. Moreover, we ask about the match between education and job requirements and about the frequency of substitution according to field of study at the same educational level (horizontal substitution) and according to educational level (vertical substitution). In this context we were also interested in employers' views on the correspondence between graduates' jobs and their level of educational attainment.

4.1. The Subject Balance: Specialists or Generalists?

Whether employers prefer to take on those with specialist or generalist education is a question that cannot be answered very straightforwardly, as most employers hired both categories. Broadly speaking, most employers made a distinction between different levels and different subject areas and sought a clear match between field of study and particular jobs. But countries may differ in the extent to which the labour market is regulated by specialist educational qualifications. As an earlier British-German study pointed out, German higher education is providing the foundation for professional specialists, whereas in British higher education emphasis is laid on a broad education of the mind (Brennan et al. 1996).

In the interviews, it turned out that employers in some countries attached great value to particular fields of study and were fairly up-to date with the teaching and the content of the curricula and the target of these degree programmes. Examples were found in several countries in continental Europe. British employers, however, tended to take a more generalist approach. A science-based degree or good levels in maths and English were mentioned as dominant features. They put more emphasis on the potential for subsequent training. In the words of one employer:

"Any subject will do for all the jobs. It is just that people with certain degrees tend to have more aptitude for the jobs we have. Some of our best analysts might be English or history students. We give them loads of training when they join".

This quotation, however, should not be generalised to all the employers in our study, as we also spoke with British employers who looked for specific subjects.

In addition to possible national differences, the responses could be grouped in types of employers: those who matched education and job requirements along the "very specific" continuum and those who adopted a more general approach. One group of employers we interviewed had highly specific manpower requirements and focused almost entirely on specific fields and areas. They took on graduates in any appropriate field from any institution in which the course was offered. They included the electronics and manufacturing firms that strongly focused on engineering subjects. Employers looked at the study fields in which graduates specialised.

A second group drew from a rather broad spectrum of courses and invited anybody with the required educational level to apply. Many employers were in commercial and business services, as well as in some institutions in the public domain, where a more generalist approach was chosen.

One example was a management consultancy company who liked to have engineers, not because of the content of their studies, but because of their analytical skills. These employers valued general qualifications as a basis on which special skills could be developed through on-the-job learning. Employers in this group often pointed to the fact that graduates with certain degrees tended to have better aptitudes for the job, e.g. graduates from business studies because they felt more attracted than others to work in a bank. These employers took the view that there was a link between students' preferences for particular fields of study and certain personality types, a link which may affect their selection process.

A third group of employers also addressed a wide spectrum of fields of study, but they were more selective and look for particular knowledge and degrees. In the IT branch this was becoming the general approach. The software branches increasingly required "product-knowledge" and favoured a degree in which this subject had been covered. In the words of an employer: "in the past the biggest bottleneck was that graduates were well educated, their conceptual level was adequate but they were not employable, because they didn't know an electronic environment". In other words, graduates in this sector needed to have product-knowledge, software-testing abilities, and programming language. As another employer put it: "some divisions will not accept graduates who have not got C++ programming skills".

In other words, in the IT branch, we saw a preference for more specialist areas, although this was not necessarily connected with a specific course. Different disciplines could be interchangeable. For example, when graduates were recruited to be programmers, graduates from IT or from a related discipline such as mathematics or physics were sought. The same could also be said of jobs in R&D where substitution of different disciplinary backgrounds was becoming more common.

4.2. Appropriateness of Degree Level

In order to have an opinion on the phenomenon of over-education and over-qualification, we asked the graduates whether their employment and work corresponded to their level of education. In the employers' interviews we presented some of the results and asked them whether graduates had been appointed for jobs that were previously occupied by those with lower educational levels.

Almost all the employers we spoke to said that this did not exist in their organisation and that the graduates' work corresponded to their level of education. There were a few exceptions where some employers stated that they had sometimes recruited graduates for jobs below their level or had kept them too long in low-level jobs. But these employers said they were now keen to achieve a match. They argued that graduates who were worked below their level would become dissatisfied, lack motivation and tend to leave. The unfairness of paying a graduate more for the same job than somebody else was also mentioned. Some other employers pointed to an opposite direction: sometimes lower-level persons were employed in positions that were previously held by higher education graduates because of skills shortages and received further training on the job.

Several employers drew attention to the fact that there had been changes in their organisation. The number of higher education graduates had increased in relation to those with lower educational qualifications. The outsourcing of activities, particularly those that did not belong to the core business of the company or exporting work to cheap labour countries were also mentioned.

According to most employers, there were fewer low-skilled jobs on the shop floor because of technological developments in IT. IT left more time for work which required thought. As an employer in production/developing firm said:

> "We are tending to focus on recruiting higher skilled and more experienced people who tend to be graduates rather than taking in younger less qualified people who used to do computer-aided drafting and repetitive calculations".

Several employers argued that an increasing number of graduates had to be employed because technological and economic changes made it imperative to raise skill levels in the workforce. Consequently, the job content had changed over time, requiring higher levels of education. For example, project planning and project management had changed considerably with automation. Specifically, employers could substitute computers for low-skill work and at the same time increase their demand for workers with high cognitive and social skills.

Several employers pointed to the fact that graduates would be better at writing reports, expected to develop the ability to meet with customers and be sufficiently knowledgeable about how the organisation operated to help solve customer problems. Graduates brought additional skills and knowledge to the job and were assumed to be able to design systems to improve the quality of their work.

Higher education degrees were also increasingly in demand in non-technological areas. In several countries, respondents from banking and insurance companies pointed out that customers' consultation encompassed the whole environment of the customer, the personal situation, and risk estimation which had to be taken into account before setting up the financial scheme.

Employers also often pointed out that they appreciated graduates' flexibility. Their highly abstract learning experience enabled them to deal with unstructured (not-routine) work processes and to switch more easily to some adjacent field. Their ability to develop the company's activities was also considered important.

5. KEY SKILLS AND COMPETENCES REQUIRED ON THE JOB

5.1. Acquired and Required Knowledge and Skills

Several recent studies in European countries stressed the increasing importance of general knowledge, interactive and personal skills and generic competences as compared to specific disciplinary knowledge and expertise (see The British research by Harvey 2000; the overviews on France by Paul and Murdoch 2000; on Germany by Schomburg 2000; on Spain by Mora et al. 2000; on the Netherlands by Allen et al. 2000). In order to have a better understanding of this shift in emphasis, the interviews focused on the knowledge and skills employers considered important for the work in their organisation and the extent to which, in their view, graduates were trained to master their tasks. We used a list of skills that had already been used in the graduate questionnaire (question E1) as a starting point in order to compare the outcomes of the employers' interviews with the results of the graduate survey.

As far as the knowledge-component was concerned, almost all the employers considered field-specific theoretical knowledge and the knowledge of practical methods as quite important. They attributed more weight to these dimensions of knowledge than to cross-disciplinary thinking/knowledge. Employers quoted several other skills and competences as necessary on the job.

If we take all interviewees in all the countries, it seemed that they found that the strongest discrepancies between required skills and the degree to which graduates mastered them concerned the following skills (in order of discrepancies):

– Ability to work in a team,
– Problem-solving ability,

- Planning, co-ordination,
- Communication skills,
- Taking responsibilities, decisions,
- Field-specific knowledge of practical methods,
- Field-specific theoretical knowledge.

The skills with the greatest discrepancies were non-cognitive in nature and not related to knowledge of a particular subject. The top five types of skills belonged to this category. Although some country-specific differences could be noted, employers of the various countries showed remarkable consensus, especially regarding the ability to work in a team. A representative of a large banking company put this general impression as follows:

"We have been a little frustrated in some aspects, particularly with people who are coming straight from university. We have had some problems to do with just getting used to being at work. Some problems with team work which is really important to us. Pursuing a degree is quite an individual matter whereas our work is far more team-based and not based on individual glory".

Other employers expressed themselves in a similar way. In countries where more emphasis was being put on personal skills, employers maintained that they were not what they should be. Graduates should be able to work in a team and share information. Some employers attributed this mismatch to an overemphasis on subject specialisation. Those who were highly specialised seemed to be unable to communicate their ideas at a more general level, making them less successful in their work.

A discussion point remained whether employers would favour more emphasis on cross-disciplinary knowledge. It was quite clear that multidisciplinary teams were becoming increasingly the norm. Many employers, however, stressed that it was basically a question of personal skills, of being able to communicate with people with other disciplinary backgrounds and other frames of references. These employers believed that oral and written communication skills were not what they should be. The ability to write comprehensible reports could also be a problem.

Employers also noted shortcomings regarding graduates' problem-solving abilities, managerial and executive abilities, and entrepreneurial awareness. This observation was mostly heard in countries where the university was the prevailing type of institution (Spain, Italy and Austria). The strong bias towards theoretical issues and no interest in problem-based approaches in the learning process were mentioned (see below).

With regard to cognitive aspects such as field-specific knowledge, the discrepancies seemed to be most frequent in particular fields of study. The lack of programming skills in IT-courses has already been mentioned. Not involving students in design work in engineering courses was another complaint. But, generally speaking, there did not seem to be any systematic discrepancy.

Other skills and competences were considered important, but most employers thought that graduates mastered them sufficiently. Examples included computer skills (graduates very often mastered them better than was required), broad general knowledge, foreign languages and learning abilities. Concerning the latter, employers from different sectors stated that many of the lacking skills could be rectified through professional practice. "All the things they may lack are usually trainable" was a statement that was often heard. Graduates were not expected to master these skills when they started work.

Some employers said that certain skills could not be learned in the classroom but only in a practical context. They stressed that their recruitment process was quite rigorous, since they selected their candidates according to personal skills, with the potentiality to develop, to think problems through, to be able to look beyond the existing frames, to engage with others, and to plan. These employers were rather sceptical about the possibility and the effectiveness of learning management skills in higher education courses. These skills should be acquired on the job. Graduates were never recruited for a management position in technically-oriented companies. Positions such as project leaders were always obtained after having been in a specialist technical post.[2]

5.2. *Use of Knowledge and Skills*

With reference to the questions in the graduate survey on the extent to which graduates felt that they used the knowledge and skills they acquired in the course of study, we asked employers about their view on these empirical findings. Several argued that non-utilisation or under-utilisation did not apply to most of the graduates' jobs and that skills were used in their company. It also depended on whether it concerned specific specialist (for example R&D-oriented functions) or more generalist types of functions.

Other employers, however, were not surprised by the outcomes of the graduate survey. Some employers were even surprised that the percentages were so low. These employers associated this with the graduate's expectations of the transition from education to work. Employers felt that most graduates thought they knew everything and that they expected to be employed in their field immediately. An employer in IT-network management expressed this as follows:

> "All of a sudden they are put into a role where in most organisations they are not given a huge amount of responsibility. And it takes a bit of adjustment to get into the role… A lot of graduates probably feel quite disheartened in their first job… it takes a while to appreciate that 'okay I've got a good degree but now is when I really learn'..."

---

[2] This phrasing of different types of competences reflects the distinction Barnett makes between general intellectual and general personal competences on the one hand and vocationally specific competences on the other (Barnett 1994). Employers tended to attribute less relevance to the latter type, such as management skills.

Several employers found that many graduates lacked realism about their capabilities. Perhaps a labour market situation with excessive shortages in many employment sectors reinforced the impression that all companies were waiting for them and that they could make their demands. "They (...graduates) expect a huge career progress straight away".

The reasons why employers did not comply with these demands must be considered in the context of personnel policies. According to employers, graduates had to accept the fact that careers normally started with more simple tasks, as it took time to adapt from an academic to a work-based environment. During this period they had to become familiar with the work organisation and learn about the culture of the organisation.

Some employers purposefully began by putting graduates in basic positions. One example was an IT company where graduates in their first period were mainly charged with operational tasks, e.g. working at a service desk. This type of work was perceived as inferior, but the company considered that it was an important learning process during which graduates could acquire practical experience as a basis for further professional development. But graduates could put their "mark" on the job. At the same time, it was emphasised that it was part of human resource management (HRM) in which elements such as competence development, employability and further training were becoming increasingly important.

5.3. Policies to Further Develop Competencies

Almost all the employers we spoke to stressed the importance of policies to update and develop their employees' competences. They took training very seriously because they considered it to be part of the recruitment strategy to attract good people, to invest in them, and to keep them motivated. Employers put great efforts in further training possibilities and several percentages of the salary costs reserved for further education and training were quoted. Many graduates started their career as trainees in a training programme in which all recent graduates were exposed to a number of common elements (a foundation programme) and a number of elements were tuned to particular functions. In addition, employees could follow courses which were pertinent to their roles and were prescribed by their unit or department. Several companies had learning centres and networks where people could update their skills (in-company training or at the company's "academy"), and organised in-house seminars on a regular basis. Others sent their employees to formal external courses.

The range of courses could be very broad, from very subject-specific courses to courses which focused on the development of interpersonal skills. On-the-job training was also mentioned frequently as part of competence development, as well as job rotation schemes, where graduates were involved in various projects, thus acquiring different experiences. Many employers, both in the public and the private sector, stressed that there was a huge learning curve in the first few years after graduation.

Most of these training activities were tailor-made and concerned organisation-specific knowledge and skills. There was a growing trend to think in terms of job roles belonging to larger job families along with a set of competences. This contributed to a better monitoring of competence development. Besides this specific training, people were also encouraged to study for further professional qualifications. Financial support was provided on a regular basis, and was sometimes shared between employer and employee.

The appraisal process in which the line manager and the graduates considered achievements and difficulties once or twice a year served to determine whether additional training was required. They then looked forward and the graduates were asked what they wanted to achieve in the coming year and what their training needs were. Sometimes further training was mandatory, and sometimes it was voluntary, but in both cases it had a clear organisational focus in order to make better use of human resources.

Most employers agreed that it was the responsibility of each individual employee to determine their training needs. Graduates themselves were supposed to take the initiative, mostly on the basis of a personal document in which they described their work problems and their personal development plans. They were, as one employer put it, "managers of their own career" and were supposed to invest in their own competence development.

The investments in further training differed between employment sectors. In the large companies in the private sector they were increasingly common practice. In the public sector, employers in some countries tended to be sceptical about the employees' handling of career planning and further training programmes.

Compared to the large companies, the SMEs were at a disadvantage. Not only did large companies have more training facilities in-house, but the budgets spent on training were usually higher. Some SMEs spent relatively more resources to train people, but it made them vulnerable because other companies may poach their workers. Large companies could bear those risks because they could counterbalance them more easily. "If you are a small company and six decide to go, you are paralysed". On the other hand, SMEs considered it increasingly important to offer training opportunities for their personnel, not only because of the importance for the work itself, but also to be an attractive employer for higher education graduates in terms of recruitment and retention.

6. PERSPECTIVES ON HIGHER EDUCATION AND WORK

In the final section of the interviews employers were asked about their view on the higher education system in the respective countries and on current developments. We asked them about initiatives to bridge the gap between education and work, the desirability of more diversity of course programmes such as short versus long cycles, more applied courses, more or less research training or more interdisciplinary studies. The issue of international homogeneity versus diversity was also touched upon.

6.1. Work placements

Most employers quoted various forms of degree-related work placements as the most important factor in facilitating the transition from higher education to work. Experiences with practical training periods, which in some countries were mandatory for students and in others optional, were generally very positive. Particularly Work placements were greatly appreciated in the applied sector of higher education. They helped students to make career decisions and to understand how the organisation was structured and how it operated. Moreover, they developed students' maturity and confidence when they entered the workplace on a permanent basis. In countries where placements were not compulsory, employers stated that those who had done them behaved differently and were much more successful in the recruitment process than those who had not.

In a similar vein, employers evaluated positively the new forms of apprenticeships that were being introduced in some European countries. For example, dual education as it was emerging in Dutch *HBOs* and which was similar to the German system where students alternate courses and work was considered a valuable initiative and the experiences so far had been positive. Many employers were willing to participate in these innovations. The benefits of British sandwich courses were also mentioned. Students got experience throughout their course and their training was subsidised. Some employers would prefer that an extra year that included apprenticeship should be added to in full-time degree courses. Work experience broadened students' minds and gave them an opportunity to do something independently. One employer carried things to the extreme by stating that:

> "we would love a specific degree just for us. One year at the university and then one year in a placement and then year back in university and then back in work again and then got the diploma at the end. So tailor-made graduates used to the work culture of the organisations, the projects, and with the technical knowledge. But this restricts the individual's choice".

Another reason why employers were positive about apprenticeships was that they considered these as a way of attracting young people. Employers could observe whether students were good or not. They tried to keep good apprentices and offer students permanent employment after graduation. Hence, the provision of apprenticeships and other forms of work placements (including summer holiday jobs) was becoming part of companies' recruitment strategy.

6.2. Partnerships

Other ways of facilitating the transition from education to work were mentioned. Employers were generally in favour of greater exchanges between higher education institutions and employment organisations. Some employers, particularly in the new economy sector, would like to see closer contacts with higher education institutions. Some stated that there were already quite strong links with particular universities. But there was a lot of scope. Employers we spoke to did not wish to end up with courses like the IBM IT course at some American universities. They did not see such a one-sided instrumentalist approach as a good answer. Rather, they saw interaction as a way of narrowing the gap between graduates' competences and the requirements of working life. Partnerships could focus on defining required competences and the way these could be translated into curricular development. But employers did not want to go so far as to "cement" students' careers before they had had a chance to start these. Some breadth was necessary so that people could enter a range of jobs.

Involvement in quality assurance systems and accreditation were also mentioned several times as useful for tuning.

6.3. *Problem-based Learning*

There seemed to be a consensus among employers from different countries regarding the importance of more practical and problem-based learning in higher education. University education was often considered too theoretical and employers complained about the lack of practical orientation. They believed that theory and practice should be more closely connected – in German "*verknüpft*" – in order to make university courses more useful for the world of work. It was interesting to note that the criticism of university education was stronger in countries where the non-university higher education sector was less established. For example, employers in Spain, Austria, Norway, Italy and Finland frequently referred to the rigidities of the university system, the traditional teaching methods and the over-emphasis on traditional academic learning. Also, the authoritarian attitude of some university professors constituted a barrier for further collaboration.

Interviewees regularly referred to project-based learning as a way of overcoming these difficulties. This included problem-based learning as practised at some universities or departments, or project work as opposed to traditional classroom teaching. The advantages were obvious to employers, and they spoke positively about those institutions where this was practised. Students learned to develop mentally their way through a potential problem, to anticipate problems and to plan their own project. For employers, the effects of these teaching methods were important in term of interpersonal and problem-solving skills. Moreover, these methods "contribute to a degree of lateral thinking ability which graduates need".

Engineering courses that included some elements of design, e.g. courses in design and information sciences, were also considered valuable.

6.4. *Differentiation of Institutions and Courses*

Employers attached great value to institutional differentiation, particularly with regard to the non-university professional higher education sector. This was confirmed in countries with a firm binary structure – Germany and the Netherlands. There were exceptions in certain sectors where this distinction was considered less important.

In the same way, employers in other countries increasingly appreciated the new types of non-university institutions. A few statements illustrated this.

"...Engineers educated at State Colleges are more capable than we initially thought" ...

"... they have more practical programming skills than university graduates"... (Norway);

"...the new AMK's have been more flexible and sensitive to employers' needs than universities... talking about programming languages they (universities) prefer those which are not so usable in working life ... The AMK's have based their studies in the right languages..."(Finland);

"... we are quite satisfied with the quality of training of the Fachhochschulen "...we will recruit more people from Fachhochschulen than university graduates in the near future... "Fachhochschulen react more flexible to innovations than the university as long as there is this non-flexible system of professors who simply give their lectures and not much more..." (Austria);

"... Italian universities are good universities, but they don't train people to work...Universities don't supply what we need"... "there are very few possibilities to employ immediately fresh graduates in our job" ... "short-cycles are welcome, because an intermediate level between university graduate and secondary school degree owner should be useful on many positions..."(Italy).

Employers in these and other countries would like to see the extension of practical courses outside the university system. The value attached to a differentiated institutional structure in Germany, the Netherlands and France has already been mentioned. In the UK, where the binary system was abolished in 1992, some employers expressed mixed feelings move. A few statements from different British employers illustrate these:

"...the re-titling of polytechnics to universities was wrong". (...) "I think roles are distinct: polytechnics were very much more about applied learning, and universities about broader, academic, theoretical – not that you cannot have both types of learning on the same institution". "The course content of the old polytechnics seemed to be very geared to practical aspects, rather than theory". "I don't understand why good polytechnics are now bad universities..."

Apart from the pros and cons of binary structures, employers in some countries took the view that national systems lacked the courage to differentiate. Illustrations of employers' views could be quoted: the establishment of centres of excellence for the high-flyers, short versus long educational cycles, more or less research training, disciplinary or inter- and multidisciplinary studies, etc. In some countries, employers were more pronounced on these matters, whilst in others they thought that there were already too many different qualifications. They considered their national higher education system very versatile and a further extension of degree qualifications would not contribute much.

Rather, employers would like to have more information about what a specific degree course from a specific university would actually "produce" and how this would relate to degrees from elsewhere. In this context, several employers referred to the emerging bachelor-master structure in Europe. They did not seem to have very strong opinions on this, although they generally favoured greater international homogeneity of higher education courses. But they warned that this should not lead to very broad courses as a first degree.

The length of the degree remained a debatable issue. Some interviewees could see some value in two-year foundation degrees, whereas for others these were confusing for students and employers. In other countries where university courses were relatively long, some employers advocated shorter studies so that graduates could enter professional life at an earlier age, followed by further training courses. These employers considered shorter study cycles with less emphasis on research education as beneficial and more efficient. On the other hand, some British employers referred to the benefits of the German and French graduates because they had had more training. But, generally speaking, it was impossible to draw final conclusions on the most desirable study duration on the basis of our research material. Perhaps the employers could agree with the way an employer of an engineering company put it: "You can teach lots of things to someone, but how much do they need? I don't think there is a problem per se with the length of degrees. You have to give people time to develop themselves".

7. CONCLUSION

The interview study provided substantial information on employers' views on the transition from higher education to work, the required qualifications and the actual competences and the higher education system. Although it was difficult to draw general conclusions, a few points emerged.

Employers had developed their recruitment activities and considered it very important to attract highly qualified graduates. In some countries, they were more selective than in others where the general thrust was on the standard quality of higher education. Even where employers experienced on the one hand a shortage and on the other a high supply of graduates on the labour market, they did not reduce their requirements in selecting graduates who fitted the existing criteria to a lesser degree.

Employers considered a higher education degree as a pre-requisite for an increasing number of jobs in their organisation. This was mainly due to technological developments and developments in the work organisation. These required interpersonal abilities and the ability to work in project teams where graduates had to communicate with people from different educational backgrounds. Greater competition on the basis of capital and on-time delivery and a strong focus on customers were important developments in the work organisation.

Employers did not expect higher education to turn out a finished product. Further professional development was needed, and employers put much effort in providing additional training. In some countries, the national higher education system was criticised for a lack of institutional differentiation. The non-university higher education institutions were a valuable element and in those countries where this sector was emerging, the expectations to date were positive.

Employers realised that work organisation was changing continuously and that it was impossible for higher education to react constantly to these changing requirements. Hence, employers attributed more weight to learning abilities rather than to seeking for an employee with a perfect match. Graduation was just one step after which much learning and development were needed. This was a clear trend in the European graduate labour market.

8. REFERENCES

Allen, J., Boezerooy, P., de Weert, E. and van der Velden, R. (2000), Higher Education and Graduate Employment in the Netherlands. *European Journal of Education*, 35(2), 211-20.

Baldauf, B. and Teichler, U. (1995), *Berufseinstieg von Hochschulabsolventen und – absolventinnen. Strukturdaten zu Beschäftigung und Bedarf. Betriebsbefragung*. Kassel: Wissenschaftliches Zentrum für Berufs- und Hochschulforschung der Universität Gesamthochschule Kassel.

Barnett, R. (1994), *The Limits of Competence. Knowledge, Higher Education and Society*. London: Open University Press.

Brennan, J., Lyon, S., Schomburg, H. and Teichler, U. (1996), "Employment and Work of British and German Graduates." In Brennan, J., Kogan, M. and Teichler, U. (eds.), *Higher Education and Work*. London: Jessica Kingsley, pp. 47-99.

Brennan, J. (2002), "Transforming or Reproduction? Contradictions in the social role of the contemporary university." In Enders, J. and Fulton, O. (eds.) *Higher Education in a Globalising World*. Dordrecht: Kluwer Academic Publishers, pp. 73-87.

Harvey, L. (2000), "New Realities: The Relationship between Higher Education and Employment." *Tertiary Education and Management*, 6, 3-17.

Mora, J.G., Garcia-Montalvo, J. and Garcia-Aracil, A. (2000), Higher Education and Graduate Employment in Spain. *European Journal of Education*, 35(2), 229-39.

Murdoch. J. (2002), *The Effect of the Reputation and the Teaching Quality of Higher Education Departments on Graduate Employment – A comparison across seven European countries and Japan*. Dijon: University of Bourgogne (Thesis).

Paul, J.J. and Murdoch, J. (2000), "Higher Education and Graduate Employment in France." *European Journal of Education*, 35(2), 179-87.

Roizen, J. and Jepson, M. (1985), *Degrees for Jobs. Employer Expectations of Higher Education*. Buckingham: Society for Research into Higher Education & NFER-Nelson.

Schomburg, H. (2000), "Higher Education and Graduate Employment in Germany." *European Journal of Education*, 35(2), 189-200.

Webbink, D. and Paape, A. (1997), *De Dynamische Relatie tussen Hoger Onderwijs en Arbeidsmarkt*. (the dynamic relationship between higher education and labour market) Den Haag: Ministerie van Onderwijs, Cultuur en Wetenschappen.

HARALD SCHOMBURG

WORK ORIENTATION AND JOB SATISFACTION

1. INTRODUCTION

Subjective orientation or motivation can be viewed in the framework of a study on employment and work from different perspectives. First, job motivation can be seen, as many psychologists do, as a person's relatively stable attribute, as his or her identity. In this case, motivation can be taken into consideration as an independent variable which explains strategic options with respect to employment and work. In a somewhat different approach, often chosen by educational psychologists or sociologists, job motivation can be considered as emerging and changing in the course of pre-career education. In this case, it would be interesting to examine how it reflects experiences and the context during the course of study, but, again, one could ask how job motivation shapes strategic options with respect to employment and work. Third, the focus of analysis could be the changes in job motivation as a response to career experiences. In this case, it would be seen as adaptations to external circumstances, as consequences of the inclination to avoid cognitive dissonances between the environment and individual desires. The research literature provides selective evidence for all the various approaches. Mortimer and Lorence (1979), for example, reported a rather high individual stability of work orientations amongst graduates in the U.S. over a period of ten years after graduation. Schomburg and Teichler (1998) showed in a longitudinal study of German graduates over a period of ten years that graduates adapted their motives to external conditions, showed stable job motivations no matter how much they corresponded to their work situation, and actively changed their work situation to correspond to their motivations.

The CHEERS study did not address orientations and motivation in such detail that the strengths of the various approaches could be tested. But it provided information about the graduates' life goals, their work orientations and their job satisfaction about four years after graduation, and we were in a position to analyse how far work orientations and job satisfaction were linked to their professional situation.

2. LIFE GOALS

At the top of the life goals of graduates about four years after graduation were those which could be linked to the concept of post-materialistic orientation (Inglehart 1977): personal development was rated by about 90 per cent of the graduates in all countries as "important" or "very important" (see Table 1). Hence, the differences between countries were remarkably low. "Work" (77%) and "family" (75%), i.e. goals which do not fit clearly in the concept of materialism versus post-materialism, were quoted as important by three-quarters of the graduates. "Varied social life" (65%) and "making money" (64%) were quoted by two thirds, whereas "academic

U. Teichler (ed.), Careers of University Graduates, 247–264

inquiry" (56%) and "social prestige" (37%) were less frequently emphasised. We found the greatest differences between countries with respect to "academic inquiry": high ratings by the graduates from Italy and Spain and very low ratings by the graduates from Austria and Germany.

Table 1. Importance of Life Goals Four Years After Graduation, by Country (per cent)*

	Country								
	IT	ES	FR	AT	DE	NL	UK	SE	EUR
Personal development	93	90	89	95	91	93	89	95	92
Work	80	84	68	79	76	78	72	83	77
Home/family	82	74	74	73	68	77	72	84	75
Varied social life	59	53	73	66	63	77	55	75	65
Making money	45	68	60	70	71	60	64	71	64
Academic inquiry	87	87	72	29	19	70	48	35	56
Social prestige	35	33	27	49	43	34	35	38	37
Count	3054	2984	2991	2277	3460	3042	3385	2587	23781

Question G2: Please indicate the importance you gave to each of the following life goals – in the past and now.
* Responses 1 and 2 on a scale of answers from 1 = "Very important", to 5 = "Not at all important".
Source: CHEERS survey data

The high number of graduates stating various of these goals as important in their life suggests that a clear distinction between materialistic and post-materialistic orientation cannot be made. Rather, for most graduates, materialistic and post-materialistic orientation were linked. 39 per cent indicated the four goals "home/ family", "making money", "work" and "personal development" as important and for another 36 per cent, three of these goals were important.

The two goals "making money" and "personal development" were important for most graduates (59%). The combination of "making money" and "family" held true for 49 per cent (see Table 2), whilst only 14 per cent preferred solely "making money" and 26 per cent solely "home/family". Only a small minority considered neither family nor making money as important life goals.

This pattern held true for most of the countries, with three exceptions. First, Italian graduates preferred more frequently "home/family" (44%) and less often "making money" (7%). In Sweden, a high proportion of graduates put emphasis on both. Family orientation was least frequent and materialistic orientation (making money) was the most frequent (21%) amongst German graduates.

Table 2. Importance of the Life Goals "Family" and "Making Money" Four Years After Graduation, by Country (per cent)*

	Country								Total
Life Goals	IT	ES	FR	AT	DE	NL	UK	SE	
Family and money	38	53	46	53	51	47	48	62	49
Only money	7	15	14	17	21	13	16	10	14
Only family	44	20	27	20	17	30	23	22	26
Neither family nor money	11	12	12	9	11	10	12	6	11
Total	100	100	100	100	100	100	100	100	100

Question G2: Please indicate the importance you gave to each of the following life goals – in the past and now.
* Responses 1 and 2 on a scale of answers from 1 = "Very important", to 5 = "Not at all important".
Source: CHEERS survey data

Table 3. Importance of the Life Goals "Family" and "Making Money" Four Years After Graduation, by Country and Gender (per cent)*

		Country								Total
Life Goals		IT	ES	FR	AT	DE	NL	UK	SE	
Family and money	M	41	50	44	54	50	48	45	60	49
	F	37	56	48	52	51	45	50	63	50
Only money	M	9	16	16	17	22	15	21	14	17
	F	5	14	12	18	19	10	13	7	12
Only family	M	37	19	25	19	15	25	20	19	22
	F	50	21	29	21	20	35	26	25	29
Neither family nor money	M	13	15	14	9	12	11	14	7	12
	F	8	9	11	9	10	10	11	5	9
Total		100	100	100	100	100	100	100	100	100

Question G2: Please indicate the importance you gave to each of the following life goals – in the past and now.
* Responses 1 and 2 on a scale of answers from 1 = "Very important", to 5 = "Not at all important".
M = Male; F = Female
Source: CHEERS survey data

Table 3 shows that the combination of the goals "home/family" and "making money" differed somewhat by gender. The most striking differences were found in Italy where 50 per cent of the women only mentioned "home/family", compared to 37 per cent of the men. There was a similar difference in the Netherlands (35% as compared to 25%).

Altogether, some 50 per cent of all graduates stated that both "home/family" and "making money" were important for them. Obviously, "home/family" was not seen as an important life sphere for female graduates only.

Table 4. Importance of Life Goals at the Time of Graduation, by Country (per cent)*

	Country								
	IT	ES	FR	AT	DE	NL	UK	SE	EUR
Personal development	86	83	78	84	80	86	78	87	83
Work	70	77	56	68	65	75	60	82	69
Varied social life	53	46	62	71	64	74	57	77	62
Academic inquiry	84	81	68	37	27	65	49	39	57
Home/family	66	57	46	42	36	52	50	50	50
Making money	33	57	46	53	56	53	52	52	50
Social prestige	30	36	29	47	37	37	32	37	35
Count	3067	3011	3007	2282	3473	3062	3413	2611	23926

Question G2: Please indicate the importance you gave to each of the following life goals – in the past and now.
* Responses 1 and 2 on a scale of answers from 1 = "Very important", to 5 = "Not at all important".
Source: CHEERS survey data

The graduates were also asked to indicate retrospectively the importance of the life goals *at the time of graduation* (see Table 4). Here we found that the importance of various goals grew over time: home/family (+25%), making money (+14%), personal development (+9%), and work (+8%).

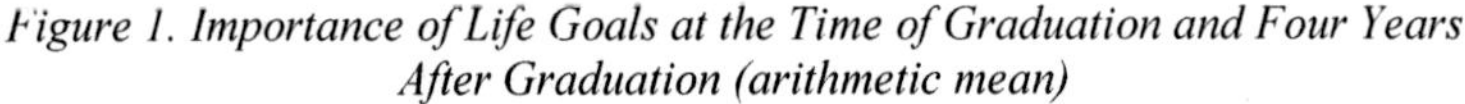

Figure 1. Importance of Life Goals at the Time of Graduation and Four Years After Graduation (arithmetic mean)

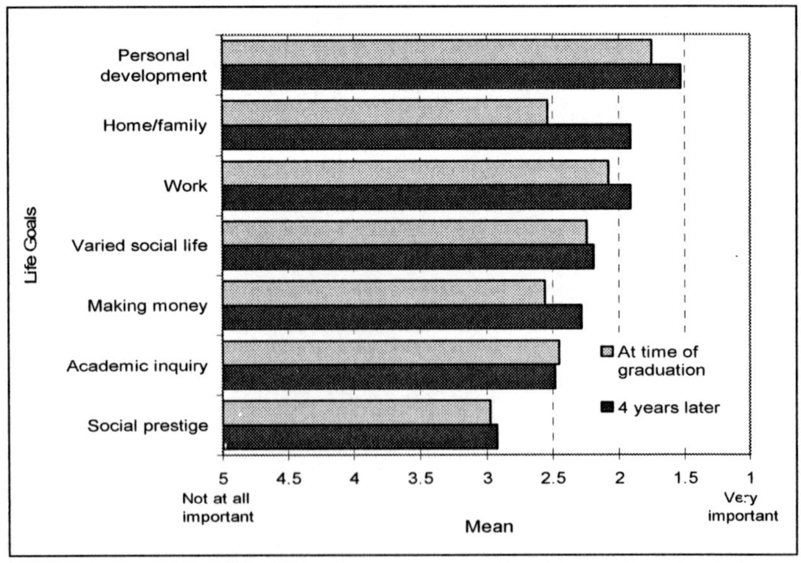

Question G2: Please indicate the importance you gave to each of the following life goals – in the past and now. Scale of answers from 1 = "Very important" to 5 = "Not at all important".
Source: CHEERS survey data

Obviously, the graduates believed that the first years in professional life were a period during which they changed their life goals considerably: they became not only more family-oriented, but also more money-oriented and put more emphasis on work and personal development. In contrast, their goals did not generally change with respect to social prestige, varied social life and academic research (see Figure 1).

3. WORK ORIENTATION

The graduates were asked to rate the importance of characteristics of an occupation on a list of 19 items. Prior research which is reflected in the formulations of the items (Luthans 1992) often made a very simple distinction between *extrinsic* and *intrinsic* work orientations, whereby intrinsic aspects were viewed as related to the content and extrinsic aspects as related to the results and the conditions of work. In formulating the questionnaire we considered that this distinction was useful, but we took into consideration additional sub-dimensions.

Figure 2. Work Orientation of Graduates (arithmetic mean; 12 countries)

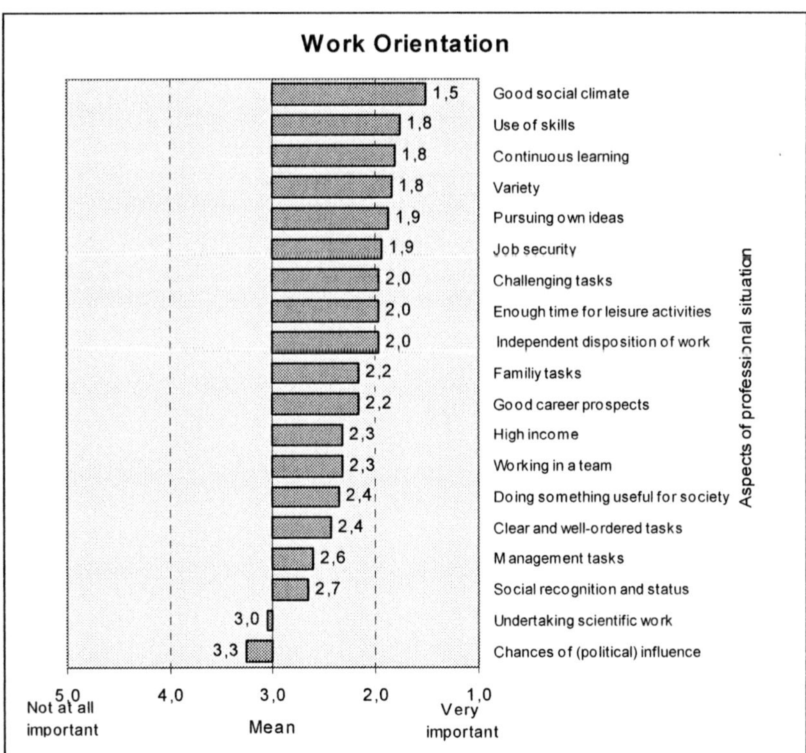

Question G3: How important are the following characteristics of an occupation for you personally? Scale of answers from 1 = "Very important" to 5 = "Not at all important".

Source: CHEERS survey data

As Figure 2 and Table 5 show, a good social climate (91%), and the possibilities of using acquired knowledge and skills (84%) seemed to be important for nearly everyone. Variety, the opportunity of pursuing one's ideas, the opportunity for continuous learning, challenging tasks and independent work were also important for more than three quarters of the graduates.

These findings indicate a high relevance of intrinsic work aspects amongst professionals. However, some extrinsic aspects were also frequently rated as important: job security (74%), enough time for leisure activities (74%), good career prospects (67%), good opportunities for combining employment and family tasks (67%) and a high income (61%).

Of all the 19 aspects stated, only a relatively small number of graduates considered the opportunity of undertaking scientific/scholarly work (37%) and chances of (political) influence (29%) as important.

There were remarkable differences between the countries regarding the political motive ("chances of political influence"), whilst professional autonomy ("opportunity of pursuing one's ideas") varied only slightly by country (see Table 5). Some other findings are worth noting: Good career prospects were important for 87 per cent of the graduates from Spain, but only for 54 per cent of those from Japan and 56 per cent for those from Germany and Norway. Challenging tasks were important for 90 per cent of the graduates from Norway, but only for 49 per cent of those from France.

With respect to most other aspects, the answers were very similar across countries. Surprisingly, however,, graduates from both Japanese and European higher education institutions stressed communicational and professional values and, surprisingly, only 54 per cent of the Japanese graduates stated "good career prospects" as important or very important, compared to 69 per cent of the European graduates.

As expected, the different aspects of work orientations were closely related. With the help of main component analysis, undertaken separately by country, and by selecting different variables, it became evident that the dualistic model of intrinsic versus extrinsic orientations was not appropriate.

Table 6 presents the findings of a factor analysis where 15 variables of work orientation were taken into consideration for all 12 countries together. Five dimensions emerged:

- autonomy ("independent work", etc),
- status ("high income", etc.),
- routine ("clear and well-ordered tasks", etc.),
- communication ("possibility of working in a team", etc), and
- leisure ("enough time for leisure activities", etc).

Most of these could be linked to only a single factor: only two items were related to two factors. "Variety" seemed to be related to the autonomy and communication factors and, "possibilities of using acquired knowledge and skills" was related to the autonomy and routine factors.

Table 5. Work Orientations, by Country (per cent)*

	Country													Total**
	IT	ES	FR	AT	DE	NL	UK	FI	SE	NO	CZ	EUR	JP	
Good social climate	89	96	94	94	93	97	79	92	97	95	81	91	90	91
Possibilities of using acquired knowledge and skills	82	91	77	80	70	82	89	96	91	96	78	85	84	84
Opportunity of pursuing one's ideas	83	82	82	85	79	90	71	83	87	76	79	81	78	81
Variety	70	69	73	81	81	90	83	86	87	89	82	81	84	81
Opportunities for continuous learning	90	93	68	89	82	87	62	92	94	92	63	82	68	81
Challenging tasks	82	74	49	83	78	89	79	87	86	90	61	78	64	77
Largely independent work	80	66	85	87	85	62	51	88	85	86	65	76	70	75
Job security	69	92	71	68	78	65	77	78	68	79	79	75	71	75
Enough time for leisure activities	68	84	73	70	68	81	76	78	73	79	55	73	83	74
Good career prospects	72	87	69	63	56	69	82	58	64	56	81	69	54	67
Good chances of combining employment with family tasks	78	78	85	58	55	62	56	51	84	77	50	67	60	66
High income	57	69	54	58	55	50	59	74	67	66	68	61	60	61
Possibility of working in a team	53	68	63	73	73	71	62	47	67	71	46	63	43	61
Chance of doing something useful for society	69	78	67	53	43	62	55	43	47	60	58	58	67	59
Clear and well-ordered tasks	63	78	70	50	42	44	49	60	29	58	66	56	60	56
Co-ordinating and management tasks	56	49	38	58	55	51	52	41	48	48	55	50	27	48
Social recognition and status	44	44	46	51	44	39	41	52	65	46	60	48	38	47
Opportunity of undertaking scientific/scholarly work	40	54	38	33	24	37	30	29	32	55	18	36	46	37
Chances of (political) influence	52	35	25	19	17	27	15	18	92	24	6	29	32	30

Question G3: How important are the following characteristics of an occupation for you personally?
*Responses 1 and 2 on a scale of answers from 1 = "Very important", to 5 = "Not at all important".
** Count by Country: IT (3043); ES (3002); FR (2992); AT (2285); DE (3460); NL (3008); UK (3373); FI (2647); SE (2594); NO (3246); CZ (2993); EUR (32644); JP (3384); Total (32541).

Source: CHEERS survey data

Table 6. Dimensions of Work Orientations of Graduates from 12 Countries (main components; factor loadings; varimax rotation)

	Dimensions of work orientations				
	Autonomy	Status	Routine	Commun-ication	Leisure
Independent work	.72				
Opportunity of pursuing one's ideas	.66				
Challenging tasks	.61				
Opportunity for continuous learning	.55				
Variety	.45			.42	
High income		.81			
Good career prospects		.71			
Social recognition and status		.66			
Clear and well-ordered tasks			.75		
Job security			.60		
Possibilities of using acquired knowledge and skills	.48		.57		
Possibility of working in a team				.74	
Chance of doing something useful for society				.59	
Enough time for leisure activities					.80
Good chances of combining employment					.70

Only rotated factor weighing above 0.4 are presented in the table

Source: CHEERS survey data

4. TYPOLOGY OF WORK ORIENTATIONS

A cluster analysis was conducted (procedure: K-means) on the basis of the established five dimensions (factor score variables) in order to obtain a typology of work orientations. Six clusters are presented in Figure 3 and Table 7.

(1) 12 per cent of the graduates could be called *traditional professionals* or task-oriented professionals. They appreciated a high degree of work autonomy, they liked to focus on complex and difficult tasks and to have the opportunity of making use of the knowledge they acquired. Status attributes were also important, whilst leisure time and home and family were not held in high regard.

Traditional professionals were exceptionally frequent amongst the graduates from Finnish institutions and exceptionally rare amongst those from Dutch institutions. This type of work orientation was more common amongst graduates in the humanities and law than amongst those from other fields of study. Men were slightly more often traditional professionals than women.

Figure 3. Typology of Work Orientations of Graduates from 12 Countries (per cent)

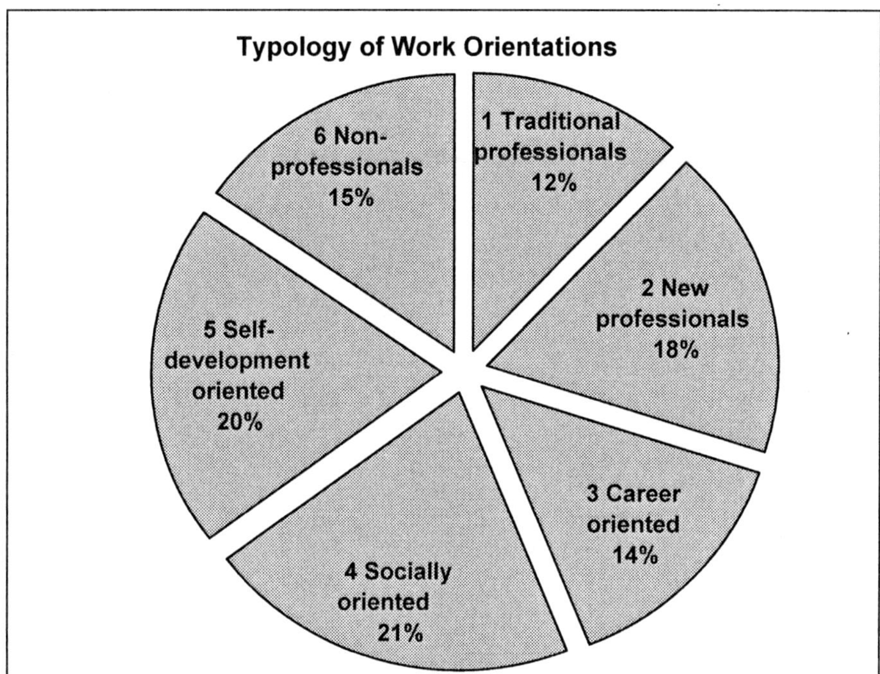

Question G3: How important are the following characteristics of an occupation for you personally? Scale of answers from 1 = "Very important" to 5 = "Not at all important". The typology is based on a cluster analysis with five factor score variables of work orientations.

Source: CHEERS survey data

(2) A somewhat larger proportion of graduates, i.e. 18 per cent, could be called *new professionals*. They resembled old professionals as far as work-related orientations were concerned, but they put little emphasis on status dimensions. Moreover, they appreciated good opportunities of combining work and family life and they also wanted to have enough time for leisure activities.

This second type varied substantially by country. It was most frequent in Norway (27%) and least frequent in the Czech Republic. It was more common amongst women (22%) than men (12%), and it could be observed more frequently amongst graduates who were employed in the public sector (23%) than amongst those in the private sector (12%).

Table 7. Selected Work Orientations of Graduates, by Typology of Work Orientations (arithmetic means)

	Typology of work orientations						Total
	Traditional professionals	New professionals	Career orientation	Socially oriented	Self-development	Non-professionals	
	1	2	3	4	5	6	
Possibilities of using acquired knowledge and skills	1.4	1.5	2.5	1.5	1.7	2.3	1.8
Independent work	1.6	1.6	2.6	2.3	1.4	2.4	2.0
Opportunity of pursuing one's ideas	1.8	1.6	2.1	1.8	1.5	2.7	1.9
Good career prospects	2.2	2.8	1.9	1.8	1.6	2.8	2.2
Clear and well-ordered tasks	2.1	2.4	3.0	2.0	2.8	2.4	2.4
Job security	1.9	2.2	2.1	1.6	2.1	1.9	1.9
Possibility of working in a team	3.2	2.1	1.9	1.8	2.3	2.9	2.3
Chance of doing something useful for society	3.1	1.8	2.3	1.8	2.7	2.7	2.4
Enough time for leisure activities	2.6	1.7	1.7	2.3	1.7	1.9	2.0
Count	4177	6170	4651	7159	6913	5147	34217

Question G3: How important are the following characteristics of an occupation for you personally? Scale of answers from 1 = "Very important" to 5 = "Not at all important". The typology is based on a cluster analysis with five factor score variables of work orientations.

Source: CHEERS survey data

(3) 14 per cent of the respondents could be characterised as *career-oriented* graduates. Income and career opportunities were most strongly strived for, whilst work-related aspects, such as autonomy, using their knowledge or doing work related to science, were not seen as crucial.

Again, we noted striking differences by countries. Career orientation was frequent amongst graduates in the Netherlands (26%) and the United Kingdom (25%) and least common amongst those from Finland (4%), Norway (8%) and Italy (9%).

(4) A substantial share of graduates (21%) could be called *socially oriented.* They mostly appreciated team work and doing something useful for society. They enjoyed job security and well-ordered tasks. Like the first and second type, they also considered using their knowledge and being involved in scientific work as important.

Socially oriented graduates were most common in Spain (36%) and the Czech Republic (32%). In contrast, this orientation was least often observed amongst graduates in Sweden (10%), Finland and Japan (both 14%).

Figure 4. Typology of Work Orientations, by Country (per cent)

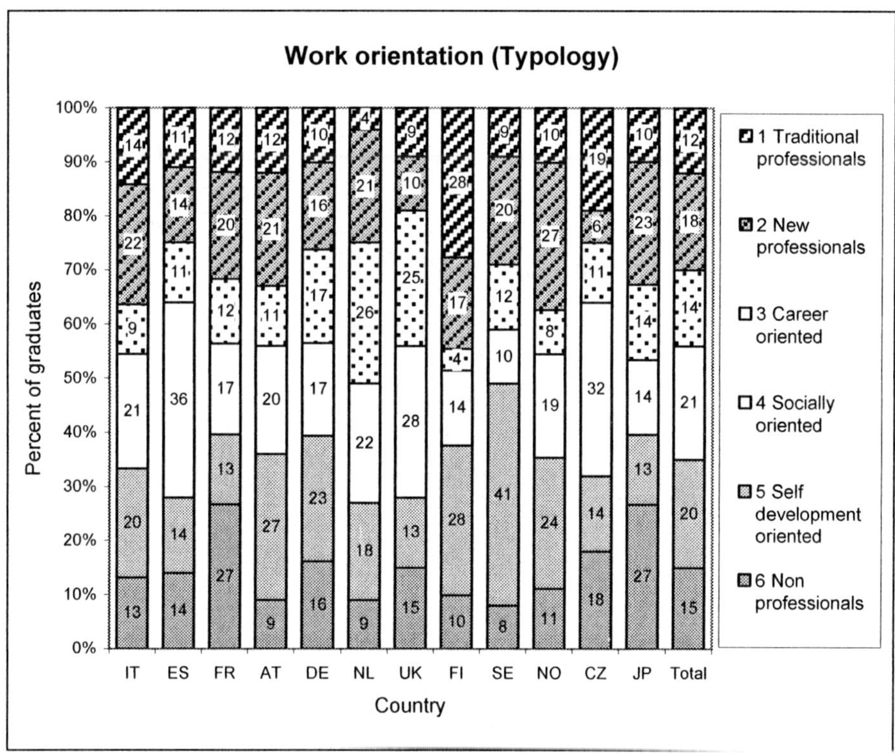

Question G3: How important are the following characteristics of an occupation for you personally? Scale of answers from 1 = "Very important" to 5 = "Not at all important". The typology is based on a cluster analysis with five factor score variables of work orientations.

Source: CHEERS survey data

(5) A fifth type, comprising 20 per cent of graduates, could be termed as *self-development-oriented.* On the one hand, these graduates were more strongly work-oriented and status-oriented than the traditional professionals and, on the other, they cared less about job security, the relevance of their work for society and for social communication than all the other graduates.

This emphasis on self-development was by far the most widespread amongst graduates in Sweden (41%) and Austria (27%). It was only slightly more common amongst men (22%) than women (19%) and it was somewhat more pronounced amongst those employed in the private sector (24%) than in the public sector (17%).

(6) Finally, 15 per cent of the graduates could be called *non-professionals*. They were neither ambitious as far as status and career were concerned nor were they very interested in matters of work assignment such as challenging work tasks. Last but not least, they neither emphasised the socio-communicative dimensions of work nor were they very interested in doing something useful for society.

The highest proportion of "non-professionals" was found amongst graduates in France and Japan (27% each). In contrast, less than 10 per cent of the graduates from Austria, the Netherlands and Sweden belonged to this type. As one might expect, this orientation was frequent amongst graduates in low positions, i.e. those working as clerks and skilled workers.

5. WORK ORIENTATION AND SITUATION

As already stated, the graduates were not only requested to state their motivations but also their actual situation. As one might expect, the work situation was seen by most graduates as not fully matching their ambitions. These ratings were on average 4 points lower on a five-point scale than those of their motivations. High ratings of the work situation were up to 29 per cent below high ratings of the work orientation, as can be seen in Table 8.

Graduates were very disappointed with their income and career opportunities and the lack of leisure time. On the other hand, their motives were fully met on average, as far as social status and recognition and the opportunity of working in a team were concerned. Italian, Spanish and French graduates perceived their motives as less frequently met by their situation.

Table 8. Comparison between Work Orientation and Work Situation (per cent)*

	Work orientation	Work situation	Difference (situation-motivation)
Good social climate	91	70	–21
Possibilities of using acquired knowledge and skills	84	66	–18
Challenging tasks	77	64	–13
Independent work	75	64	–11
Variety	81	62	–19
Job security	75	62	–13
Possibility of working in a team	61	61	0
Opportunity for continuous learning	81	58	–23
Opportunity of pursuing one's ideas	81	57	–24
Chance of doing something useful for society	59	46	–13
Enough time for leisure activities	74	45	–29
Good chances of combining employment with family tasks	66	43	–23
Social recognition and status	47	43	–4
Clear and well-ordered tasks	56	42	–14
Good career prospects	67	41	–26
Co-ordinating and management tasks	48	39	–9
High income	61	34	–27
Opportunity of undertaking scientific/scholarly work	37	23	–14
Chances of (political) influence	30	22	–8

Question G3: How important are the following characteristics of an occupation for you personally? How far do the following characteristics of an occupation apply to your current professional situation?
*Work orientation: Responses 1 and 2 on a scale of answers from 1 = "Very important", to 5 = "Not at all important".
*Work situation: Responses 1 and 2 on a scale of answers from 1 = "To a very high extent" to 5="Not at all".
Source: CHEERS survey data

The structure of the dimensions of the professional situation was very similar to that of the work motivation with respect to autonomy, status, leisure, and routine, as the results of a factor analysis show. But, additionally, using knowledge and relevance of work for society were also relevant dimensions.

6. TYPOLOGY OF WORK SITUATION

The seven dimensions of the work situation were used (as factor score variables) in a cluster analysis (K-means method in combination with Ward) in order to establish a typology of the professional situation. The eight types of work situation thus established resemble in some respects those of the work orientations, but the differences are worth noting.

(1) A *traditional professional situation* was reported by 10 per cent of the graduates. They had a high degree of autonomy, a high status, as well as managerial and coordinating work tasks. the job role was not viewed as strongly characterised by scientific work nor by relevance for society, and it did not seem to leave much time for leisure and family.

This work situation was over-represented amongst graduates in engineering and the social sciences. It was more frequent amongst men than women. It held true more frequently in the private sector than in the public sector. Differences by country are also worth noting: a traditional professional situation was most frequently reported by graduates in the Czech Republic (20%), Germany (19%), and Austria (18%).

(2) The proportion of graduates reporting a *new professional situation* was about twice as high (21%) as for those reporting a traditional professional situation. Their situation was similar to that of the first type as far as work assignment and status dimensions were concerned, but they reported that the job left much time for leisure and family.

Differences by country were most striking as far as this type was concerned: the new professional situation was by far the most frequent for graduates in Sweden (68%) and also clearly above average for those in the Netherlands.

(3) Some graduates defined their work situation as *highly regulated* (12%). They often had well-ordered work tasks, and a high level of job security. Like with the second type, work left a great deal of time for leisure activities, but work autonomy and status were low.

Differences by country were smaller than in the case of the first two types. Hence, graduates from Norway and Finland (16% each) experienced a highly regulated work situation most frequently. There were also few differences by field of study: graduates in law and medicine stated a highly regulated situation more frequently (16% each) than those from other fields.

Figure 5. Typology of Professional Situation (per cent)

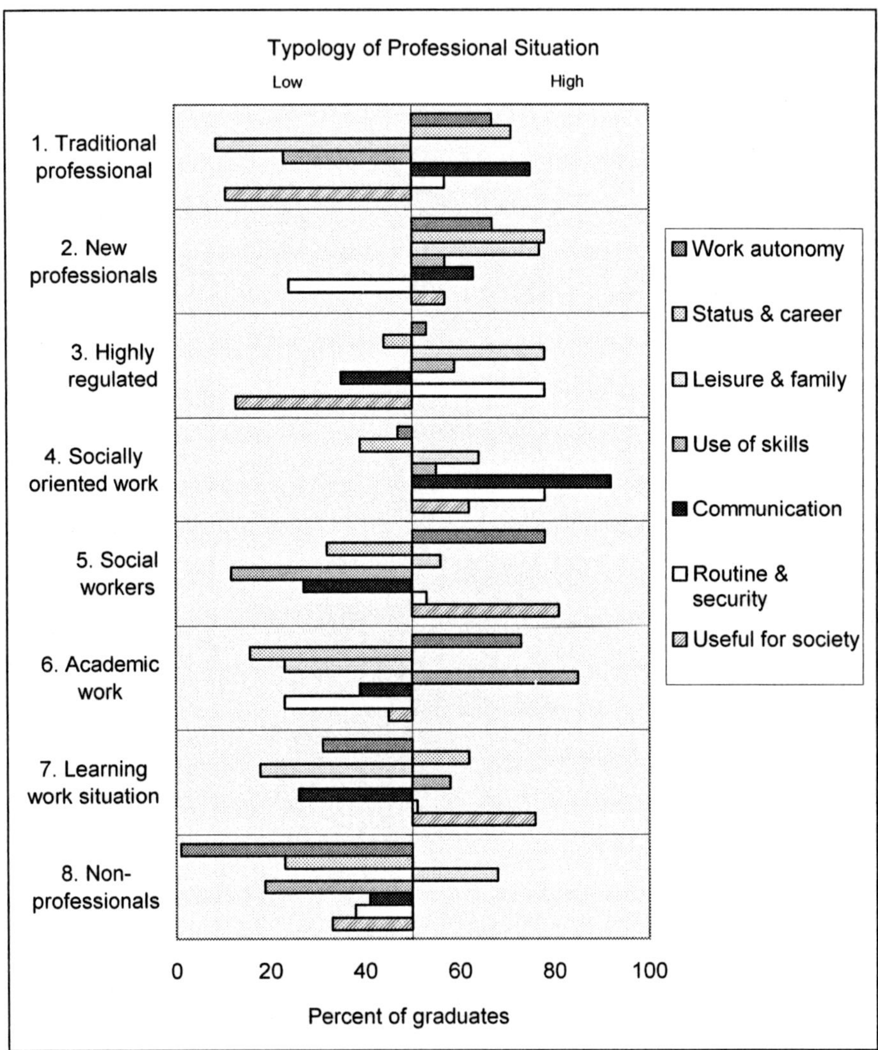

Factor score variables with a mean of 0 are dichotomised: High = Lo through 0.

Source: CHEERS survey data

(4) A *socially oriented work situation* was reported by 16 per cent of the graduates. Team work was usual for them, and they considered their work as relevant for society. They also frequently reported clear and well-ordered tasks, the opportunity of using their knowledge on the job, high job security and enough time for leisure activities.

This situation applied most frequently to women and was characteristic of the public sector of education. It was most frequently reported by graduates in teacher education and medical fields. As regards the country, graduates in Spain (28%) often defined their work situation as socially oriented.

(5) *Low-status social work assignment* was reported by 9 per cent of the graduates. They considered their work as relevant for society and as highly autonomous. In contrast to the fourth type discussed above, they defined their work situation as lacking a good social climate and team-work.

This type of work situation was most frequently reported by graduates from France. It was relatively frequent for graduates in humanities and education, and it often applied to graduates in the public sector and self-employed graduates.

(6) 8 per cent of the graduates were in an *academic work situation* about four years after graduation. This was often characterised, in addition to research work, by good opportunities to use their knowledge and great autonomy. In contrast, many graduates of this type had a temporary work contract, reported low job security and considered their status as low.

This type was most frequent amongst graduates in Finland. Graduates in natural sciences, humanities and medical fields reported an academic work situation more frequently than those from other fields of study.

(7) A *learning work situation* was characteristic for 18 per cent of the graduates about four years after graduation. As one might expect, autonomy was rated as low, but many of the graduates who were still in this initial phase of their career rated the social climate at the work place as good and characterised by team work. Moreover, many were convinced that their work was socially relevant.

This type of work situation was most frequently reported by graduates in Japan (39%) – a country where many graduates start off with modest work tasks and are gradually trained to take on higher responsibilities. It also holds true for a substantial proportion of medical graduates – a field that is notorious for long training periods after graduation.

(8) Finally, 8 per cent of the graduates were in a *non-professional situation* characterised by a low status, a low level of autonomy and hardly any opportunity to use their knowledge on the job. They reported having enough time for leisure activities. Graduates in Italy (14%), Japan and Spain (13 per cent each) were above average in a non-professional situation.

7. JOB SATISFACTION

The extent to which a person is satisfied with his or her job is a function of both the expectations and the actual work and employment situation. Therefore, the comparison undertaken above between the work orientations and the actual work situation lets us assume that the graduates are not satisfied with all aspects of their work situation.

Actually, about two thirds of the graduates surveyed stated that they were satisfied with their current work. The proportion of those who were satisfied varied substantially by country, as can be seen in Table 9. It ranged from about three quarters amongst the Norwegian (78%) and Finnish graduates (74%) to less than half of the Italian and Japanese graduates (48% each).

Table 9. Job Satisfaction, by Country (per cent and arithmetic mean)

	Country												Total
	IT	ES	FR	AT	DE	NL	UK	FI	SE	NO	CZ	EUR	JP	
1 Very satisfied	11	20	25	26	16	21	19	25	25	33	23	22	10	21
2	37	40	40	42	46	51	38	49	44	45	51	44	38	43
3	34	27	22	21	26	22	25	18	20	18	20	23	24	23
4	14	10	9	7	9	6	13	7	8	3	5	8	22	10
5 Very dissatisfied	4	3	4	3	3	1	6	1	2	1	1	3	6	3
Total*	100	100	100	100	100	100	100	100	100	100	100	100	100	100
Arithmetic mean	2,6	2,4	2,3	2,2	2,4	2,2	2,5	2,1	2,2	1,9	2,1	2,3	2,8	2,3

Question G1: Altogether, to what extent are you satisfied with your current work? Scale of answers from1 = "Very satisfied" to 5 = "Very dissatisfied".
* Count by Country: IT (2538); ES (2221); FR (2401); AT (2104); DE (3254); NL (2908); UK (3157); FI (2438); SE (2404); NO (3109); CZ (2630); EUR (29165); JP (3023); Total (32187).

Source: CHEERS survey data

By taking into account both the country and the field of study, we note that more than 80 per cent amongst graduates in mathematics and computer sciences in Austria and Finland (84% each), in law in the Czech Republic (82%) and Norway (81%) as well as in natural sciences in Norway (83%), humanities in the Czech Republic (82%) and education in Finland (81%) were satisfied. Altogether, the job satisfaction only varied moderately by field of study in the countries with a high degree of job satisfaction.

In contrast, we noted substantial differences by field of study in Japan and Italy. Lowest proportions were stated by Italian graduates in humanities (38%) and education (40%).

On average, across all countries women were as satisfied with their work situation as men. Differences were visible though if the country and the field of study were also taken into consideration. For example, women across all fields of study in Germany were less satisfied with their current work than men. In contrast, such a difference was applicable in Japan only in mathematics and computer science: men (72%) were clearly more satisfied with their current work situation than women (32%).

Table 10 shows the result of a multiple regression analysis aiming to explain the factors contributing to job satisfaction. Only 17 out of 36 variables analysed are presented which have standardised regression coefficients of at least +/–0.1 or are significant in at least three countries.

The following factors turned out to be irrelevant for job satisfaction: professional education or academic study subsequent to graduation, type of secondary education and type of higher education institution, most of the graduates' competences, regional mobility and international mobility, working time, the size of company as well as using one's knowledge on the job.

Table 10 suggests that work autonomy is the single most important factor for job satisfaction. Status and career is the second and use of knowledge on the job is the third most important factor. In some countries, time for leisure activities and family plays a role as well – dimensions which were often viewed as having gained importance for graduates in recent years. Thereby, both the respective work orientation and the actual work situation come into play.

Table 10. Causes of Job Satisfaction, by Country (standardised regression coefficients)

	Country											
Independent variables	IT	ES	FR	AT	DE	NL	UK	FI	SE	NO	CZ	JP
A. Socio-biographical background												
Gender: Male							0.04		0.05			0.04
Age				0.05	0.06							0.05
Autonomy – work orientation	0.05	0.09	0.1	0.06		0.1	0.1		0.11	0.09	0.12	0.04
Status/career – work orientation	0.11	0.09	0.13	0.13	0.06	0.13	0.11	0.11	0.12	0.08	0.08	
Leisure/family – work orientation							0.05	0.08			0.06	0.05
B. Study												
Study duration			0.07				0.04			0.07		
Planning/organisation competences		0.06	0.06	0.06								
C. Transition												
Mostly regularly employed	0.05			0.1	0.05		0.05					
D. Employment												
Private sector		0.11	0.07						0.17	0.05	0.05	0.07
E. Personal situation												
Children	0.05					0.05			0.05			
F. Prof. Situation												
Income		0.07	0.09	0.08	0.16		0.10	0.09	0.10	0.07		
Time before first employment							0.04				–0.05	0.06
Position										0.06		
Use of skills	0.19	0.19	0.14	0.12	0.13	0.04	0.21	0.16	0.19	0.22	0.15	0.14
Work autonomy	0.32	0.26	0.38	0.31	0.29	0.42	0.31	0.29	0.24	0.38	0.34	0.32
Status/career	0.26	0.23	0.25	0.28	0.25	0.19	0.24	0.28	0.14	0.20	0.30	0.24
Time for leisure/family			0.08	0.08	0.10	0.06	0.11	0.08		0.10		0.13
Explained variance (percentage RSQ)	40	37	43	34	32	29	41	34	18	37	33	41

Source: CHEERS survey data

We noted a similar role of these factors across all countries. The idea of what makes a satisfying job seemed to be more or less the same across the countries surveyed. Hence, the factors turned out to be independent: for example, a high status was not automatically linked to autonomy, but graduates reporting a high autonomy, a high status or both tended to be satisfied with their current work.

8. REFERENCES

Baethge, M., Denkinger, J. and Kadritzke, U. (1995). *Das Führungskräftedilemma.* Frankfurt/ Main and New York: Campus.

Inglehart, R. (1977). *The Silent Revolution: Changing Values and Political Styles Among Western Publics.* Princeton: Princeton University Press.

Finch, M. D., Shanahan, M. J., Mortimer, J. T., and Ryu, S. (1991). Work Experience and Control Orientation in Adolescence. *American Sociological Review*, 56, 597-611.

Luthans, F. (1992). *Organisational Behaviour.* Sixth edition. McGraw/Hill.

Mortimer, J.T., Lorence, J. and Kumka, D. (1986). *Work, Family and Personality: Transition to Adulthood.* Norwood, N.J: Greenwood Publishing Corporation.

Mortimer, T. and Lorence, J. (1979). "Work Experience and Occupational Value Socialization: A Longitudinal Study." *American Journal of Sociology*, 84, 1361-85.

Schomburg, H. and Teichler, U. (1998). "Studium, Studienbedingungen und Berufserfolg." In Teichler, U., Daniel, H.-D. and Enders, J. (eds) *Brennpunkt Hochschule. Neuere Analysen zu Hochschule, Politik und Gesellschaft.* Frankfurt/M. and New York: Campus, 141-72.

Shanahan, M. J. et al. (1991). Adolescent Work Experience and Depressive Affect. *Social Psychology Quarterly*, 54, 299-317.

ULRICH TEICHLER

CONFIRMING CONVENTIONAL WISDOM AND CONTRIBUTING TO NEW INSIGHTS: THE RESULTS OF A COMPARATIVE STUDY ON GRADUATE EMPLOYMENT AND WORK

1. THE AIM OF A FINAL ANALYSIS

This comparative study on the employment and work of higher education graduates in 11 European countries and Japan turned out to be a gold mine to examine how far previous notions on these links could be confirmed across a large number of economically advanced countries, how they varied between the countries, or whether we should reconsider conventional wisdom. The CHEERS study benefited from three features of its design. First, the long questionnaire covered such a broad range of important dimensions that many interesting issues could be addressed in the analysis of the data. Second, a comparison across countries could make us more aware of whether certain features of graduate employment and work could be considered as more or less universal for mass higher education systems in economically advanced societies or whether we observed national specificities concerning, for example, the characteristics of higher education, professionalism, labour market and social conditions. Third, a team of several dozens of researchers from different disciplines and countries made us see the various ways of analysing and interpreting the links between higher education and the world of work.

Admittedly, this approach cannot claim to have only advantages over any prior research in the field. Although some 40,000 graduates were willing to respond to the long questionnaire and the overall return rate of about 40 per cent could be considered satisfactory, the research team still had to ask themselves whether shorter questionnaires were not more suitable to yield high return rates and representative findings. The finding of common elements and differences across countries, thought-provoking as this may be, caused great problems of analysis. Often, it proved impossible to provide sufficient evidence as to whether certain findings could be attributed predominantly to characteristics of the national higher education systems, discrepancies between demand and supply of graduates, imperfections of merito-cratic settings, national perceptions of desirable professional roles, etc. Last but not least, if a large number of researchers from different disciplinary backgrounds and countries analysed a common data set, they were likely to produce many interpretations which could not be synthesized coherently.

The aim of this chapter is to reconsider the analyses of the CHEERS study presented in this volume, as well as those published before. It is not a comprehensive summary. Rather, the aim is to underscore and illustrate major findings which could

U. Teichler (ed.), Careers of University Graduates, 265–276

be seen as confirming conventional wisdom and notably those which called for a change in established views and new interpretations.

2. HIGHER EDUCATION, THE LABOUR MARKET AND SUCCESSFUL CAREERS

2.1. *Three Major Issues*

As was pointed out in the introductory chapter of this study, many analyses of the relationships between higher education and the world of work focus primarily on the relationships between graduates' educational attainment and their professional success. In the framework of this thematic area, which is one priority area of the CHEERS study, one is led, therefore, to address three issues of the general debate about higher education and the labour market.

- First, does the expansion of higher education match the changes in graduate employment and work, or do we observe a substantial shortage or a substantial oversupply of graduates?
- Second, how can the links between higher education and the labour market be interpreted with respect to the educational and professional careers of individuals? Are the educational investments in time, efforts and possibly financial costs rewarded as a rule, and is there a clear meritocratic link between educational attainment and professional success?
- Third, what is the situation at the problematic bottom line of the links between higher education and graduate employment? How many graduates face serious employment problems? What is the nature of these problems?

Obviously, a study such as the CHEERS study, i.e. a survey of higher education graduates undertaken at a certain moment in time, cannot provide perfect answers to these questions. A comparison of the employment situation of persons with different levels of educational attainments is commendable, as is an analysis of changes over time. However, the CHEERS study provides relevant information in this framework; moreover, we can interpret the results of this study in the light of the findings of other studies.

2.2. *Expansion Beyond Demand or a Changing Demand?*

There are no indications in the CHEERS study that the expansion of higher education in the 12 countries surveyed clearly contradicted the development of employment and work opportunities for graduates. For example, 70 per cent of the graduates surveyed who had graduated in the mid-1990s were employed about four years after graduation as professionals, managers or in similar professions, i.e. in occupational categories that usually require a degree. A comparison with surveys undertaken in the 1970s and 1980s in various countries suggests that this proportion is more or less stable. Also, other findings of the CHEERS survey are in tune with the interpretation that graduates in most of the countries surveyed did not have fewer opportunities of working in typical graduate jobs. For example, it is worth noting in this context that only 12 per cent of the graduates surveyed considered that their occupational situation about four years after graduation did not correspond to their level of educational attainment.

There are indications in the CHEERS data, though, that the graduation rates greatly surpassed the respective increase of professional and managerial positions in certain countries. Most graduates in Norway and in Japan were employed in associate professions or other middle-level occupations, and the enrolment rates in these two countries were exceptionally high in comparison with other countries around 1990, i.e. at about the time when most of the graduates surveyed began their studies. However, the CHEERS study does not show a high correlation across countries between the graduation rate and the number of graduates obtaining employment in professional and managerial ranks.

One could argue, though, that the extent to which graduates are employed in these positions is no longer as pertinent as an indicator of a link between higher education and the world of work. As long as less than a quarter of the corresponding age group in a country had been awarded a degree, access to professional and managerial position could have been the bottom line of professional success after graduation. When higher education expansion reached a higher level, sometimes called – with an element of exaggeration – "universal higher education", and when graduation rates from degree programmes represented more than about one quarter of the age group, employment in middle-level positions was no longer the unfortunate fate of the minority of less successful graduates. Preparation for middle-level positions became a regular function of certain sectors of the higher education system.

2.3. *Towards Closer Links between Educational and Professional Success?*

By and large, the CHEERS survey confirms that learners' efforts and investments are rewarded when the first few years after graduation are analysed. As has already been pointed out, most graduates succeeded in finding employment in occupations and positions that are considered typical for graduates.

With the expansion of higher education, rewards for educational investments and the persistence of an educational meritocracy can no longer only be examined by comparing the career of persons with clearly distinct levels of educational attainment (for example higher education graduates and school leavers entering the labour market). Rather, one must analyse whether differences such as the type of higher education and programme, the reputation of the higher education institution or the grades obtained during the course of study and in examinations become increasingly important for graduates' subsequent employment.

It is often claimed that other types of higher education institutions and short university programmes challenge the established educational hierarchy through more targeted professional training. The CHEERS data suggest, however, that graduates from these programmes were more often than university graduates in positions which they did not consider as corresponding to their level of education. Former graduates saw short and vocational programmes as more clearly linked to job assignments, but they also considered many of their competences to be of a lower level than those of graduates enrolled in long university programmes.

The reputation of the university was seen to be very important for the subsequent employment of graduates in Japan. In European countries, however, many graduates did not consider this as crucial for their recruitment, and the proportion of those who found that the institution was crucial for their employment varied to a lesser extent by country than one would have expected according to conventional wisdom. Differences in reputation were most important for graduate employment in France and Norway, but not in the United Kingdom, as one would have expected.

On the other hand, it was widely assumed that more or less automatic career reward for educational achievement had been challenged in recent years and that the trust on the part of students and graduates had declined. Three interrelated findings of this study are interesting in this context. First, it was often claimed that widespread employment problems were more likely to reduce trust in the relevance of educational success for subsequent professional success than to stimulate students to strive even more strongly for educational success. Second, competences which were only shaped indirectly and to limited extent during the course of study, such as applying knowledge to professional assignment, socio-communicative competences, work styles and work-related values, became more important for future assignment. Third, the process of transition seemed to develop a dynamic of its own for job-seeking where relying on personal connections, establishing early contacts with employers, obtaining support from the higher education institution, investing substantial time in the search process, coaching for employment interviews, etc. were widely viewed as being almost as important as the acquisition of competences needed for the job.

The CHEERS study does not call into question the fact that many students are extremely concerned about their future employment. This is confirmed, for example, by the finding that about 40 per cent of the graduates saw their future employment and work in a more negative light than it actually was. Obviously, many students also sought to improve their employment opportunities by other means than academic success. Amongst the more than 40 per cent who spent a substantial amount of time on training and professional work before they enrolled in higher education and amongst the majority of students who spent a great deal of time on internships and gainful work, a substantial proportion considered this as a better investment of their time for enhancing their employment prospects than investing it in academic study. Last but not least, about 30 per cent of the graduates reported that personal connections, prior contacts with employers and help from their higher education institutions were the most important ways of finding their first job after graduation, i.e., ways where other criteria came into play.

These findings, however, do not suffice to draw the conclusion that the reward of high educational achievements is seriously challenged. Rather, the relationships between higher education and career can neither be interpreted as closely tied nor as marginal, and this can be interpreted as a moderate meritocracy.

2.4. The Frequency of Serious Employment Problems

Graduates' employment problems were an issue of concern in many countries of the CHEERS study. One must bear in mind, though, that there is no indisputable yardstick for establishing the number of graduates who faced serious employment problems. We could claim that it was high, if we look at graduate unemployment a few months after graduation or if we consider all graduates who are not in a professional or managerial occupation as inappropriately employed.

The authors of this publication, however, point out that these yardsticks could be too rigid. Not being employed during a period of job search and initial trial and error before the career being viewed as desirable may not be infrequent, but about four years after graduation only 4 per cent of graduates were unemployed, i.e. not employed and seeking employment. In addition, of those who found employment, only 15 per cent had been seeking their first job for more than six months after graduation. Moreover, approximately half of the some 30 per cent of professionally active graduates who were not employed in managerial and professional ranks noted close links between study and employment. Hence, the notion of "mismatch" would be an exaggeration.

Only 8 per cent of the graduates surveyed in the CHEERS study stated that their higher education studies were not at all related to their area of work about four years after graduation. 14 per cent considered their professional situation as rather inappropriate for a graduate, but a substantial proportion did not choose this option because of the labour market situation, but rather because they preferred living and working in certain localities or considered this work assignment as interesting or the conditions as desirable.

If we consider part-time employment and temporary contracts as indications of precarious employment, we could argue that precarious employment was quite frequent about four years after graduation. 11 per cent of those who were employed four years after graduation had part-time work, and 22 per cent had temporary contracts. The CHEERS study, however, shows that indefinite contracts were challenged as the normal pattern of employment in some European countries. In addition, temporary contracts were most widespread at early career stages in the academic profession and in some other public service professions, i.e. in professions which were quite popular amongst graduates. Last but not least, part-time employment was most frequently chosen about four years after graduation by women with children.

Pointing out that very few students graduating in the mid-1990s faced serious employment problems and hardly noted any link between study and work assignments does not mean that the gravity of problems should be played down with regard to those who were most seriously affected. But the CHEERS data clearly suggest that most of those who could consider themselves in a difficult employment situation about six months after graduation were likely to interpret these problems later as problems of transition. And by using a multitude of criteria of the links between study and employment, the CHEERS study clearly shows that employment outside the traditional professional areas of graduates is not an indication that study was irrelevant for employment and work.

2.5. *Common Issues and Country-Specific Conditions*

The relationships between higher education and graduate employment undoubtedly had common characteristics in most of the economically advanced countries during the 1990s. About two-thirds of the graduates or more were employed in professional and managerial occupations, and even more considered themselves to be in a position that was more or less commensurate with their level of educational attainment. Most of them experienced that successful study was likely to be rewarded in their career. Employment problems predominantly occurred in the process of transition from study to employment. The majority of graduates' career paths during the first years after graduation were predetermined by their first employment, even though changing employers was quite frequent.

Differences by country, however, were substantial. In Norway and Japan, graduate employment had already reached a new stage which could be called the upgrading of the middle-level professions. While the link between field of study and area of employment was quite close in many countries, great flexibility could be observed in this respect in the United Kingdom. Many graduates in the Nordic countries found employment in the public sector, where more graduates saw a closer link between knowledge and job assignment and were more satisfied, but where we noted less flexibility in also absorbing graduates in middle-level occupations. A high degree of job security remained widespread in the late 1990s, notably in Japan, while long-term contracts were challenged as normal in the Netherlands and Spain. Immediate transition from higher education to employment remained typical for graduates in Japan, while in some European countries a search and transition period of up to six months after graduation had become the dominant mode. Graduates from Japanese universities considered the reputation of the university as important for their career more often than their colleagues in Europe, and they considered direct help from the university as crucial in finding their first employment. Graduates in Italy, France and Spain did not only experience more protracted periods of transition but were more likely to face employment problems and find positions and work tasks that did not correspond to their level of education.

3. LEARNING, COMPETENCES AND WORK

3.1. *Major Issues beyond Graduate Employment*

Higher education institutions are responsible for knowledge generation, transmission and preservation. Students are taught and provided with various opportunities of enhancing their knowledge base on their own. The second major theme of research on the relationships between higher education and the world of work is that of the links between the acquisition of knowledge during the course of study and the utilisation of this knowledge on the job.

When the relationships between higher education and the labour market became a key issue of both higher education and labour market and social policies in the 1960s and 1970s, most analyses were based on quantitative-structural data, i.e. occupational categories, remuneration, fields of study, level of degrees and type of higher education institutions. Retrospectively, we tend to criticise this period of public debate and research for taking for granted that higher education was well tuned to the world of work if most engineering graduates were employed in the occupational category "engineers". Both debates and research noted a need to no longer take for granted that a close "match" between educational and employment categories was a good indicator of a good preparation for future professional assignments, since, on the one hand, an engineer could have been badly prepared for subsequent work by engineering programmes, and, on the other hand, those who were employed in an occupation that did not correspond to the field of study and did not require a degree could have many opportunities of using the knowledge they had acquired during their course of study on the job.

The links between curricula, teaching and learning and competences on the one hand and job tasks on the other became the second major area of research, not only because structural links between educational and employment categories were not sufficient to infer close links, but also because it was more likely that ideas for reforms of curricula, teaching and learning would be developed if systematic information was available. As was shown in the introductory chapter, five questions were seen as the most intriguing in this domain.

- First, do the study programmes and the knowledge acquired in these correspond to the job requirements?
- Second, how far are the relationships between higher education and the world of work flexible?
- Third, are there areas where the discrepancies between study and the immediate job requirements could be productive in challenging outmoded practices and contributing to innovation, upgrading occupations and societal change?
- Fourth, to what extent are competences required by systematic cognitive knowledge, and to what extent have students acquired abilities to transmit their knowledge to work tasks, conductive working styles and values, socio-communicative skills and similar competences?
- How does the growing need for lifelong learning affect the relationships between pre-career study and learning during the first years and the job assignment?

The CHEERS study elicited interesting findings in most of these aspects. However, its contribution is marginal as far as understanding the changing links between higher education and the world of work amidst a growing popularity of concepts of lifelong learning is concerned. During the first years after graduation, initial professional training as well as training and learning to adapt obviously played a more important role than continuing professional education if the occupational area and the field of study were not linked. The CHEERS study did not attempt to examine whether pre-career higher education programmes had changed in response to growing continuing professional education.

3.2. Links Between Study and Work Assignments: How Close, Flexible and Dynamic?

About four years after graduation approximately half the graduates surveyed reported that they made great use of the knowledge they acquired in their course of study, and only 21 per cent perceived little professional use of their knowledge. In the context of other responses with respect to their professional status and job satisfaction, we can draw the conclusion that many graduates considered it normal and satisfactory that study was somewhat useful for their professional work; a very close link and a very targeted preparation for the work assignments did not seem to be the common expectation.

Only 38 per cent of the graduates considered their field of study as the only one possible or by far the best for their area of work. 38 per cent also believed that other fields of study could also prepare for their area of work, and 11 per cent stated that the field of study was not important with respect to their work assignment. This flexible link was more often perceived than a "mismatch": Only 9 per cent perceived another field as more useful, and 8 per cent saw no use in having studied at all.

For the majority of graduates, great use of one's knowledge as well as challenging and demanding work tasks were related to the status and income categories they expected. The available data, however, suggest that at least one third of the graduates who were in a lower position than a graduate would expect as normal also stated that they made some use of the knowledge they had acquired during their course of study in the framework of their work assignments.

By and large, a closer link between study and job assignment was perceived by graduates working in the public sector. We noted that a greater number of graduates stated a clear link between study and work assignments in countries where a large number found work in the public sector, i.e. in the Nordic countries. This reflects in part the public control of professions for which a certain field of study is the required entry qualification, in part a general tendency of the public sector to foster a close link between curricula and work assignment, and in part lesser flexibility of the middle-level occupational areas with respect to upgrading.

The graduates' perceptions of links between study and work assignments differed greatly by country: A close link was reported by a large proportion of graduates in the Nordic countries, but only by a small number in France and Japan. For example, little utilisation of knowledge was stated by 12 per cent or even fewer of the graduates in Finland, Norway and Sweden, but by 36 per cent in France and 47 per cent in Japan. These differences cannot solely be explained by the expansion of higher education. Rather, as already discussed, different quotas of employment in the public sector and in the professions came into play. Moreover, the educational and professional traditions of specialisation in France could reinforce high expectations with respect to a close link, which, in turn, elicit a radical negation of such a link if it is only loose.

Questions in the CHEERS survey were not formulated in a way which would help to disentangle how far graduates acted in an innovative and critical way with respect to the prevailing job "requirements". However, most graduates (57%) stressed the fact that they had opportunities of pursuing their ideas and almost two-thirds (64%) stated that they could organise their work independently. Almost half (46%) believed that they could do something useful for society, but less than one quarter (22%) found many opportunities of exercising a political influence through their professional work.

The graduates' retrospective assessment of study cannot be perceived as overwhelming praise. More than 40 per cent found that practical emphasis was lacking. This did not mean, however, that those who had been enrolled in study programmes and other types of higher education institutions which advocated more targeted job preparation and a stronger practical orientation than universities and their long study programmes were better prepared for their future assignments. Many graduates from short study programmes and from other types of higher education institutions retrospectively appreciated these approaches, but, on average, they noted greater discrepancies between their competences upon graduation and the job requirement, and a higher proportion stated that their profession did not correspond to their level of educational attainment. On the other hand, we noted that graduates who had been enrolled in study programmes which lay great emphasis on the acquisition of practical experiences had, on average, a relatively high income about four years after graduation.

3.3. Competences beyond Systematic Cognitive Knowledge

On average, graduates considered both the field-related knowledge and the broad general knowledge which they had acquired during their course of study as corresponding to the requirements of their job. However, deficiencies were noted with respect to all the other areas of competences addressed in the CHEERS survey. According to a comparison between the competences at the time of graduation and the job requirements about four years after graduation, graduates saw a need to enhance their competences notably with respect to negotiation, planning, applying rule, decision-making, leadership, time-management and working under pressure. In addition, a need to enhance computer skills was also frequently noted.

An abundance of terms and concepts concerning the competences by systematic cognitive knowledge to be acquired by graduates is found in the public debate and prior research debates. The CHEERS questionnaire, reflecting this, was based on the assumption that abilities of transmitting knowledge to work tasks, working styles, socio-economic skills and motives and values that were conducive to work were the most widespread areas of competences under consideration, but it opted for the formulation of an even wider range of aspects in order to ensure conceptual reconsideration with the help of the findings of multi-variate analyses.

The authors of this volume presented three different ways of classifying competences and job requirements. They all found that socio-communicative competences were an important dimension in its own right. They also agreed that graduates perceived deficiencies in operative and organisational competences, whereby abilities of knowledge transfer, work styles and values were classified differently. Finally – although they used different terms – they seemed to agree that competences of reasoning, reflection, creativity were domains of their own which graduates wished to enhance.

In comparing the respondents' retrospective views on their study programmes and competences upon graduation we noted, not surprisingly, a greater visible impact of the programmes on systematic cognitive knowledge than on other competences. For example, those who noted great emphasis on the quality of teaching tended to rate their general knowledge highly, and those who noted an emphasis of their study programme on theories also considered themselves well qualified in theories and methods. This does not mean, however, that other dimensions were not related to study: the CHEERS study also shows that those who had experienced a strong practical emphasis of the study programme considered themselves relatively well prepared for leadership and management tasks, and those who had noted a strong emphasis on communication between teachers and students as well as between students, considered themselves able to adapt and communicate with other people.

4. THE PROFESSIONAL RELEVANCE OF VALUES AND ORIENTATIONS

The more intellectually demanding job roles are the less clearly they are determined by rules, instruments, work environments and social control. Rather, highly qualified workers are expected to handle indeterminate work tasks, to reflect on established professional practice and to seek innovative solutions, and they have many opportunities of interpreting their work tasks and choosing possible options. Therefore, graduates' values and orientations can play a crucial role in constantly redefining job "requirements" and in shaping professional work and its outcomes.

The high relevance of the graduates' values and orientation can be viewed as conventional wisdom. Debates and research on the "professions" and on "leadership" tended to address the relevance of intrinsic motivation, professional ethics and socio-political views held by graduates. This notwithstanding, a substantial proportion of well-known research projects on the relationships between higher education and the world of work neglected students' and graduates' values and orientations or took for granted that the norms of the *homo oeconomicus* and the status seeker prevailed, irrespective of what the graduates might say. The CHEERS study, in contrast, attempted to map the graduates' values and orientations and to measure the extent to which these explained their professional activities.

The findings suggest that values other than income, status and employment conditions prevailed. For example, graduates quoted personal development, work and home and family most frequently as central, while money, social prestige and varied social life were evoked more rarely. Job satisfaction was more closely associated with autonomous and challenging work and the opportunity of using competences than with income, position, job security, time for leisure and other dimensions of employment. Altogether, graduates considered themselves to be more strongly driven by intrinsic than by extrinsic motives.

A closer look reveals that the composition of values varied substantially. One out of seven graduates was predominantly status-oriented and income-oriented with little concern about the intrinsic dimensions. For more than a quarter of the graduates, intrinsic and extrinsic motives seemed to coincide: They either stated high or low ambitions in both respects. More than half, however, stressed their interest in the challenges of their work or their appreciation of self-development and perceived income, status and other employment conditions as being less important.

The CHEERS study suggests that values and orientations were most relevant for the graduates' professional activities. Not surprisingly, though, many graduates considered their work situation as not fully meeting their desires. Discrepancies between orientations and actual work situations seemed to occur almost as often with respect to status and income, opportunities of pursuing own ideas and using knowledge as with respect to opportunities of spending time on leisure and family. Some graduates accepted these discrepancies and adapted to them, while others tried to transform their work and employment conditions to meet their values and orientations.

There were differences in the values and orientations by country. For, example, a status orientation that was not strongly linked to professional intrinsic motives could be observed more frequently in the Netherlands and in the United Kingdom than in the other countries. Altogether, these differences were less striking than those of the employment conditions and work situations.

Finally, the relevance of values and norms affected career choices in various other respects. In some countries, affiliation with a region was held in such high esteem that some graduates forewent bright career opportunities in order to live a certain region. There were indications that international mobility was greatly appreciated by some graduates for many other reasons other than income, status and satisfactory employment conditions. Last but not least, child care continued to be a central issue for women; we noted a strong preference by women for employment in the public sector, especially in countries where political efforts were made to counterbalance their professional disadvantages.

5. CONCLUSION

The comparative study on graduate and employment presented in this publication provided such a wealth of information with respect to many dimensions that any effort to summarise the findings in just a few sentences is bound to be futile. Obviously, many of the findings confirmed conventional wisdom, whilst others were surprising and called for new interpretations. Many underscored basically common issues of economically advanced countries, whilst others revealed varieties across countries.

In looking back at this volume and at other publications addressing the results of the CHEERS study, we noted that social researchers were somewhat limited to contemporary interpretative frameworks. An internationally comparative survey of persons who began their course of study at higher education institutions in the 1990s, graduated in the mid-1990s and were surveyed at the end of the decade, is likely to paint a portrait of graduate employment and work of a certain period of time. The 1990s were a period of continuous growth of higher education and of a growing belief that societies were moving towards a "knowledge society". Employment problems grew in many economically advanced societies. Neo-liberal views spread with their gospel that a society was well served by stronger market regulations and incentive mechanisms. Finally, the idea that globalisation would challenge the distinctions between nation states gained momentum.

The results of the CHEERS study, however, could be seen as indicating less dramatic changes in the relationships between higher education and the world of work than the discussions about macro-tends of modern societies suggest. Upgrading of middle-level occupations towards typical areas of graduate employment had progressed substantially in only a minority of economically advanced countries. Graduates were exposed to serious employment problems to a lesser degree than the public debates suggest, and the graduates themselves anticipated this while they were still enrolled in study programmes. Intrinsic professional motives did not seem to weaken under conditions of a Zeitgeist in favour of the *homo oeconomicus* and status seeker. And national characteristics of study, graduate employment and work did not seem to give way rapidly to convergent pressures of globalisation.

Obviously, however, notions such as these can only be tested if studies such as the one presented in this volume are repeated. Future research will tell us whether notions such as knowledge society or globalisation will be appropriate in depicting changing relationships between higher education and graduate employment and work.

LIST OF CONTRIBUTORS

Jim Allen, Dr., Research Centre for Education and the Labour Market (ROA), Maastricht University, The Netherlands

Clara Åse Arnesen, Dr., Norwegian Institute for Studies in Research and Higher Education (NIFU), Oslo, Norway

Torgerdur Einarsdottir, Dr., Faculty of Social Science, University of Iceland, Reykjavík, Iceland

Adela Garcia-Aracil, Dr., Institute for Innovation and Knowledge Management, INGENIO (CSIC-UPV), Universidad Politecnica de Valencia, Spain

José García-Montalvo, Professor, Istituto Valenciano de Investigaciones Económicas (IVIE), Universitat Pompeu Fabra, Spain

Volker Jahr, Department of Civil Engineering, University of Kassel, Germany

Brenda Johnston, Dr., Centre for Higher Education Management and Policy at Southampton (CHEMPaS), University of Southampton, United Kingdom

Paul Kellermann, Professor Dr., Institute of Sociology, University of Klagenfurt, Austria

Osmo Kivinen, Professor Dr., Research Unit for the Sociology of Education (RUSE), University of Turku, Finland

Brenda Little, Dr., Centre for Higher Education Research and Information (CHERI), The Open University, London, United Kingdom

José-Ginés Mora, Professor Dr., Centro de Estudios en Gestion de la Educacion Superior (CEGES), Universidad Politecnica de Valencia, Spain

Roberto Moscati, Professor Dr., IARD Istituto di Ricerca, Milano, Italy

Jake Murdoch, Dr., Associate Professor, Département d'Administration et Fondements de l'Education,, Faculté des Sciences de l'Education, Université de Montreal, Canada

Jouni Nurmi, Dr., Research Unit for the Sociology of Education (RUSE), University of Turku, Finland

Jean-Jacques Paul, Professor Dr., Université de Bourgogne, Institut de Recherche sur l'Economie de l'Education (IREDU), Faculté des Sciences Mirande, France

Michele Rostan, Dipartimento di Studi Politici e Sociali, Università degli Studi di Pavia, Italy

Harald Schomburg, International Centre for Higher Education Research Kassel (INCHER-Kassel), University of Kassel, Germany

Trine Stavik, Norwegian Institute for Studies in Research and Higher Education (NIFU), Oslo, Norway

Ulrich Teichler, Professor Dr., International Centre for Higher Education Research Kassel (INCHER-Kassel), University of Kassel, Germany

Rolf van der Velden, Professor Dr., Research Centre for Education and the Labour Market (ROA), Maastricht University, The Netherlands

Egbert de Weert, Dr., Center for Higher Education Policy Studies (CHEPS), University of Twente, Enschede, The Netherlands

Gunhild Sagmeister, Dr., Institute of Sociology, University of Klagenfurt, Austria.

HIGHER EDUCATION DYNAMICS

1. J. Enders and O. Fulton (eds.): *Higher Education in a Globalising World.* 2002
ISBN Hb 1-4020-0863-5; Pb 1-4020-0864-3

2. A. Amaral, G.A. Jones and B. Karseth (eds.): *Governing Higher Education: National Perspectives on Institutional Governance.* 2002 ISBN 1-4020-1078-8

3. A. Amaral, V.L. Meek and I.M. Larsen (eds.): *The Higher Education Managerial Revolution?* 2003 ISBN Hb 1-4020-1575-5; Pb 1-4020-1586-0

4. C.W. Barrow, S. Didou-Aupetit and J. Mallea: *Globalisation, Trade Liberalisation, and Higher Education in North America.* 2003 ISBN 1-4020-1791-X

5. S. Schwarz and D.F. Westerheijden (eds.): *Accreditation and Evaluation in the European Higher Education Area.* 2004 ISBN 1-4020-2796-6

6. P. Teixeira, B. Jongbloed, D. Dill and A. Amaral (eds.): *Markets in Higher Education: Rhetoric or Reality?* 2004 ISBN 1-4020-2815-6

7. A Welch (ed.): *The Professoriate. Profile of a Profession.* 2005 ISBN 1-4020-3382-6

8. Å. Gornitzka, M. Kogan and A. Amaral (eds.): *Reform and Change in Higher Education. Implementation Policy Analysis.* 2005 ISBN 1-4020-3402-4

9. I. Bleiklie and M. Henkel (eds.): *Governing Knowledge.* A Study of Continuity and Change in Higher Education - A Festschrift in Honour of Maurice Kogan. 2005
ISBN 1-4020-3489-X

10. N. Cloete, P. Maassen, R. Fehnel, T. Moja, T. Gibbon and H. Perold (eds.): *Transformation in Higher Educatin.* Global Pressures and Local Realities. 2005
ISBN 1-4020-4005-9

11. M. Kogan, M. Henkel and S. Hanney: *Government and Research.* Thirty Years of Evolution. 2006 ISBN 1-4020-4444-5

12. V. Tomusk (ed.): *Creating the European Area of Higher Education.*Voices from the Periphery. 2006 ISBN 1-4020 4613 8

13. M. Kogan, M. Bauer, I. Bleiklie and M. Henkel (eds.): *Transforming Higher Education.* A Comparative Study. 2006 ISBN 1-4020-4656-1

14. P.N. Teixeira, D.B. Johnstone, M.J. Rosa and J.J. Vossensteijn (eds.): *Cost-sharing and Accessibility in Higher Education: A Fairer Deal?* 2006 ISBN 1-4020-4659-6

15. H. Schomburg and U. Teichler: *Higher Education and Graduate Employment in Europe.* Results from Graduates Surveys from Twelve Countries. 2006 ISBN 1-4020-5153-0

16. S. Parry: *Disciplines and Doctorates.* 2007 ISBN 1-4020-5311-8

17. U. Teichler (ed.): *Careers of University Graduates.* Views and Experience in Comparative Perspectives. 2007 ISBN 978-1-4020-5925-4

Printed in the United Kingdom
by Lightning Source UK Ltd.
120029UK00008B/115-126

9 781402 059254